UNIVERSITY LIBRARY DUNDEE

Date of Return

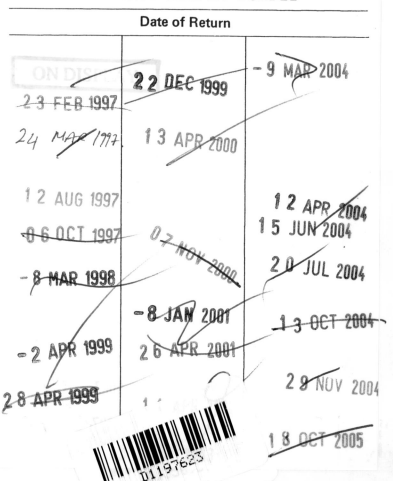

Reading Comprehension Difficulties

Processes and Intervention

Reading Comprehension Difficulties

Processes and Intervention

Edited by

Cesare Cornoldi
University of Padova

Jane Oakhill
University of Sussex

LEA LAWRENCE ERLBAUM ASSOCIATES, PUBLISHERS
1996   Mahwah, New Jersey

Copyright © 1996 by Lawrence Erlbaum Associates, Inc.
All rights reserved. No part of this book may be reproduced in
any form, by photostat, microfilm, retrieval system, or any other
means, without the prior written permission of the publisher.

Lawrence Erlbaum Associates, Inc., Publishers
10 Industrial Avenue
Mahwah, New Jersey 07430

Cover design by Gail Silverman

Library of Congress Cataloging-in-Publication Data

Reading comprehension difficulties : processes and intervention /
   edited by Cesare Cornoldi, Jane Oakhill.
         p.   cm.
   Chapters written by researchers based on presentations given at a
meeting sponsored by Bracco and Centro Diagnostico Italiano, held in
Milano on May 27–28, 1994.
   Includes bibliographical references and index.
   ISBN 0-8058-1845-6 (alk. paper)
   1. Reading disability—Congresses. 2. Reading comprehension—
Congresses. I. Cornoldi, Cesare. II. Oakhill, Jane.
LB1050.5.R363 1996
372.4′3—dc20   95-52843
                                                          CIP

Books published by Lawrence Erlbaum Associates are printed on acid-free paper,
and their bindings are chosen for strength and durability.

Printed in the United States of America
10 9 8 7 6 5 4 3 2 1

Acknowledgments

The origin of this book was in a Seminar that was sponsored by Bracco and its diagnostic center, Centro Diagnostico Italiano (CDI). A number of researchers were invited to present their research on reading comprehension and comprehension difficulties, and then to write a chapter based on their presentation. The meeting was held in Milano on May 27th and 28th, 1994, and was organized by the Psycho-Educational Service within the CDI Centre (Centro Psicopedagogico per lo Studio e la Prevenzione delle Difficolta' di Apprendimento). We are grateful to Bracco and CDI, who provided the financial support for the organization of the seminar, and to Drs. Vanna Baffi and Giancarlo Scotti, heads of the Psycho-Educational Service, who devoted their enthusiasm and energies to its success.

Contents

PART V

Introduction:
Reading Comprehension Difficulties

Every day, schools all over the world deal with the problem of recognizing the characteristics of children with learning disabilities and deciding how to help them. Some disorders are fairly easy to recognize (e.g., mental retardation), or very specific to single components of performance, and quite rare (e.g., developmental dyscalculia). The school, however, must consider much larger populations of children with learning difficulties, who cannot always be readily classified. These children present high-level learning difficulties that affect their performance in a variety of school tasks. A typical characteristic of such children is often their difficulty in understanding a written text. In many instances, despite good intellectual abilities, a superficial ability to cope with written texts and to use language appropriately, some children cannot find their way in the written texts they must read. They do not seem to grasp the most important elements, the connections between the different parts, or to be able to search out the pieces of information they are looking for. Sometimes these difficulties are not immediately detected by the teacher in the early school years. This may be because the most obvious early indicators of reading progress in the teacher's eyes do not involve comprehension of written texts, or maybe because the first texts a child encounters are quite simple and only reflect the difficulty level of the oral messages (sentences, short stories, etc.) with which the child is already familiar. However, as years go by and texts get more and more complex, comprehension difficulties will become increasingly apparent and increasingly detrimental to effective school learning.

Does a reading comprehension problem exist in schools?

Written text comprehension is one of the abilities that is most often evaluated in schools all over the world. And every day teachers deal with children who have not completely understood what they have read. It is difficult to doubt the existence and the importance of the problem. However, this problem is not always presented in terms of a specific "reading comprehension difficulty" or "disability." Comprehension difficulties are often an aspect of learning disabilities or of developmental cognitive difficulties more generally. In a sense, however, these problems can be related to written text comprehension, for example, language disorders (occasionally with specific mention of the receptive aspect) or a text decoding problem (e.g., developmental dyslexia). The scientific literature reflects this trend, because problems with decoding, dyslexia, and language disorders have attracted more interest from researchers than have specific comprehension problems, and have occupied more room in specialized journals. On the contrary, normal reading comprehension has been a favorite with researchers. Over the last 20 years, great efforts have been made to investigate the normal processes of text comprehension. On the other hand, scarce interest has been paid to subjects who have comprehension difficulties. This neglect really is a shame for several reasons but especially because we do not have enough direct information enabling us to understand and help children with these disabilities. Moreover, research does not take advantage of the precious information that can be gathered from these children in order to reach a better understanding of the nature of written text comprehension in the population more generally.

This book is an attempt to remedy this situation. Although the existence of a text comprehension problem cannot be denied, it is unlikely to be presented as such. We have already mentioned the fact that this problem is sometimes only identified in association with other problems, such as written text decoding, communication abilities, and spoken language. In other cases, because of its pervasiveness (inevitably a written text comprehension problem reflects on a very large variety of school difficulties), it is "covered" by a wider definition of school difficulties, such as a general learning disability, slow learning, study problems, and so on. It is apparent that students who find it difficult to fully understand what they read will no doubt have difficulties in studying, assimilating new information, and in many other situations (from problem solving to reasoning with linguistic contents) requiring text comprehension.

How important and widespread is the problem?

Therefore, there are many reasons for considering reading comprehension one of the main goals of learning and education. No matter how technology transforms social organization, a variety of texts will have to be processed by people, and reading comprehension will probably always be required. Even if we have available in the future instruments to transform written texts into oral ones, we will be able to avoid decoding but not comprehension problems. Even if multimedia communication drastically reduces the space of traditional written texts (books, newspapers, etc.), reading comprehension will be implicated in the processing of messages transmitted through other media. Comprehension of text files presented in a computer screen will involve some specific processes of interest, but also many other processes overlapping with those required by written texts. Today, good reading comprehension remains the most important key for school learning. In fact, every subject requires the processing of texts, their further elaboration and assimilation. The typical profile of a child with a reading comprehension problem (sometimes defined as a "poor comprehender") describes children who are slow in learning because they are not able to learn at the same rate as their classmates from lectures and textbooks. In general, teachers and administrators frequently rate the learning ability of their pupils, coming to the conclusion that many of them experience severe problems. If we were to use these assessments to estimate the proportion of pupils with a reading comprehension problem, we would arrive at the conclusion that the problem is very common and relevant in schools. However, this estimate would be inaccurate, because the relationship between a specific reading comprehension problem and school failure is not necessarily reciprocal. Children with a reading comprehension problem will probably fail in school, but pupils who fail in school do not necessarily have a reading comprehension problem. A correct estimate of the proportion of children with a specific reading comprehension problem requires the definition of unambiguous and operational criteria and procedures. This is a difficult task, as can be witnessed by the variety of procedures illustrated in the different chapters of this book, which come from different countries and research traditions. For example, Cornoldi, De Beni, and Pazzaglia present data obtained from a systematic testing of 1,285 boys and girls ages 11 to 13. In this group, 66 subjects (approximately 5% of the population) were classified as having a highly specific, mild or severe, reading comprehension problem. This research involved Italian subjects, and must be calibrated with reference to different procedures, populations, and languages. In fact, different standards of achievement in a reading comprehension competence have been described for random populations from different countries (e.g., Thorndike, 1973). One of the few existing cross-cultural comparisons has suggested that the proportion of children with a reading comprehension level well below their intelligence level is between 2% and 4.5% in the United States and from 3.65% to 8.5% in Italy, depending on the criterion adopted (Lindgren, Di Renzi, & Richman, 1985).

Is the problem specific?

How specific is a reading comprehension problem? The chapters included in this volume present a variety of positions in this respect, demonstrating the extent to which this question is debated. Researchers asserting that the problem is not specific can find relevant evidence supporting their position. The most compelling evidence comes from the observation that very often a reading comprehension difficulty is associated with one or more other characteristics, in particular: problems in decoding, problems in oral language, mental retardation, or, as already discussed, a general problem with learning and studying. The first chapter in this volume, by Gough and his colleagues, presents evidence in favor of a dissociation between decoding and comprehension, but tends to view as identical the comprehension processes involved in processing written and auditory texts, the only difference between the two tasks being the necessity for decoding in one and not the other. The multiplicative relationship between decoding and oral comprehension as an index of reading comprehension ability assumes that when either decoding or oral comprehension is equal to zero, reading comprehension is not possible. Further, if the decoding level is held constant, the only variable that predicts reading comprehension ability should be the ability to understand an oral text. This assumption finds confirmation in cases where the two aspects are related. However, there is also a large amount of evidence suggesting that children can have poor decoding abilities, but good comprehension abilities. This dissociation is complemented by the opposite dissociation showing that some children have good decoding abilities, but do not understand what they read, as happens in a dramatic way in cases of hyperlexia, which is often associated with autism (e.g., Healy, Aram, Horwitz, & Kessler, 1982). However, this dissociation can also be observed in larger groups of children (as documented by many chapters of this book). A distinction between decoding and comprehension can be made clearer when the procedures for measuring the two skills are made independent. For example, it has been suggested that slow, non-automatic, decoders may expend so much effort in decoding that they are no longer able to understand what they read (Perfetti, 1985). The role of single-word decoding as a contributor to reading comprehension ability can, however, be reduced by using reading comprehension tests which do not pose speed constraints. If decoding is equal to zero (as in the early phases of reading acquisition), then comprehension will also be equal to zero, but very soon in the school career of the child (in this book we have evidence in the Stothard and Hulme and in the Oakhill and Yuill chapters of early dissociations), the two aspects will start to be distinguishable. To what extent they can be really distinguished is a question that remains open and is debated in many ways in the book. Even more strict is the relationship connecting different aspects like oral comprehension, reading comprehension, and mental retardation. We think that these relationships are essentially unidirectional. First, a comprehension difficulty that extends to oral messages, which are traditionally more simple, will also affect reading comprehension. Secondly, more general intellectual abilities, involving reasoning, thinking, knowledge base, and so on will also dramatically affect reading comprehension (as generally happens in mental retardation). In fact, language disorders and low intelligence in children ages 3 to 6 are powerful predictors of later problems in reading comprehension (Tramontana, Hooper, & Selzer, 1988). Furthermore, mentally retarded children are often characterized by their reading comprehension problems. However, this evidence cannot be used to conclude that these relationships hold in both directions, that is, that children with a reading comprehension problem (a) are also mentally retarded, and (b) also present problems in oral comprehension. Case (a) is automatically rejected when the standard most common procedures for the identification of children with learning disabilities are adopted (see Hammill, 1990). In fact, these procedures include a child in the reading disabled group only when some exclusion criteria are absent: exclusion criteria are the presence of strong emotional problems, a relevant sociocultural disadvantage, and a low intelligence level. Case (b) appears more complicated, and we agree that oral and written comprehension have many processes in common. At the same time we think that they can be, at least partially, separated. For example, why do school professionals frequently report cases of a reading comprehension problem, but do not report the same for oral comprehension?

In order to explore the issue we could consider the differences in processes involved in the two tasks. Oral comprehension, because it uses the auditory channel, does not enable subjects to proceed at their own rate, to go back or to reconsider the text, poses even higher memory demands than reading comprehension. However, in its favor, oral communication is facilitated by a large variety of supporting elements, like context, non-verbal signals, prosody, and so on. These are characteristics that are not available during reading comprehension. Therefore, oral comprehension problems are much better disguised because there are many contextual cues to indicate what is being communicated. However, differences between the two aspects are more evident from an ecological perspective, that is, by considering the effective tasks where in everyday life (school included), oral and reading comprehension are involved. In fact, we can see that the comprehension requests are more severe when children must cope with written texts. The increase in complexity and difficulty of written texts presented to children between ages 6 to 14 is dramatic. This increase is almost certainly greater for written than for typical oral texts, unless written texts are presented in an oral version.

How can a reading comprehension difficulty be defined and identified?

The preceding discussion helps us to recognize different possible criteria for defining (and then for identifying) children with reading comprehension difficulties. Variations in criteria and procedures can explain differences in research outcomes and in proposals for treatment. A very simple criterion could be the following: children have a reading comprehension problem when their performance on a standardized reading comprehension test is below a predefined cut off (e.g., the 8th percentile). This criterion can be very useful in a school context. It is simple, not theory biased, immediately usable; it will certainly identify children needing help. The criterion can also be plausible from a theoretical point of view, if it is assumed that all different aspects of psychological functioning are highly interconnected and cannot be separated. However, from the viewpoint of intervention, the criterion assumes that all these children will need help. People with practical experience in the field will certainly reject this conclusion. For example, poor readers with an average or high IQ typically require different interventions than do mentally retarded children. As the reader will see from the chapters of this book, the aforementioned criterion can be substituted by a variety of others. Many researchers assume that children with a reading comprehension problem will have different characteristics depending on which, if any, other problems are associated with it. In particular, many chapters are focused on children who have reading comprehension difficulties but do not have many of the other problems often associated with such difficulties and, in particular, have average or even good levels of IQ and decoding. This approach has some commonalities with neuropsychological approaches based on the dissociation between different aspects of cognitive functioning (e.g., Shallice, 1988). This approach is also related to research and practice in the field of learning disabilities, which looks for discrepancies between general estimates of intelligence and specific achievement levels, and also looks for subtypes of reading disabilities (but IQ discrepant poor readers can be, in many ways, similar to non-discrepant ones; see Stanovich & Siegel, 1994). Researchers looking for groups of subjects of a specific type are forced to raise the inclusion criteria, in order to form groups including not only the most severe cases, but also mild and less characteristic cases.

However, these less stringent criteria are also able to offer important information, showing differences between the groups of poor comprehenders and the control groups (or subgroups representing another type of learning disability). This book offers a great deal of evidence in this respect. It is important to observe that although these chapters present procedures and observations coming from distant and heterogeneous laboratories, they nevertheless show important elements of convergence.

Has the "syndrome" a single pattern or can different subtypes be identified?

In this volume a series of chapters examines groups of children with a reading comprehension difficulty, showing that they typically have specific characteristics and deficits. These data are useful, not only because they provide a deeper understanding of this particular population of children, but also for identifying variables that are critically related to reading comprehension. However, these group data do not necessarily imply that all children with a reading comprehension difficulty present exactly the same profile and the same deficits. The presence of a perfectly homogeneous group should contrast both with common sense and evidence concerning other types of learning disability.

Variability within the reading comprehension disability group does not exclude the possibility of finding typical characteristics. With reference to this issue, Fletcher and Morris (1986, p. 60) observed, "Every child is like all other children, some other children, and no other children. The goal of classification research is to develop a set of objective criteria whereby subjects can be classified into homogeneous groups. It is important to recognize that classification hypotheses underlie even the simplest contrasting-groups study. Inherent in forming groups for any study is the assumption that the contrasted groups represent homogeneous entities that differ on the set of attributes used to define the groups. In the case of disabled learners, these attributes have been age levels, IQ and achievement scores, and other exclusionary criteria." The case of a reading comprehension difficulty meets these requirements, which are typical in the field of learning disabilities (when these are not restricted to the most severe, possibly organic cases). In fact, the difficulty is based on an inclusion criterion (low achievement level in reading comprehension) and on exclusion criteria (good achievement in other areas; no handicap or other emotional and sociocultural factors). This inclusion–exclusion approach has been fruitful in other areas, producing both research and organizational models, and has been the basis for the field of learning disabilities. However, this area is also open to criticism and needs further research.

One particular critical point concerns variability within types of learning difficulties. Variability has also been shown for types of learning disabilities that are highly specific, less frequent, and highly researched. For example, developmental dyslexia appears very heterogeneous. Some authors have proposed a distinction between subtypes, like surface dyslexia versus phonological dyslexia (Coltheart, Masterson, Byng, Prior, & Riddoch, 1983) or language-based versus visually based dyslexia (Bakker & Vinke, 1985). But other authors have found much more variability in the population of dyslexic children. Similarly, for developmental dyscalculia, different subtypes of deficit have been described (e.g., Geary, 1993). Given these premises, we should not be surprised that research concerning children with a specific reading comprehension difficulty will develop in similar directions; both finding overlapping characteristics, but also examining single cases looking for more-detailed specifications. In fact, in the case of a reading comprehension difficulty, the population of interest is larger, and the critical variable, reading comprehension, is more complex, than is the case with dyslexia or dyscalculia. If decoding and simple calculations can be more easily explained in terms of a limited number of encapsulated, independent, low control functions (Fodor, 1983), the same assumption appears more difficult for reading comprehension, because it probably involves a higher number of functions and a greater degree of central control.

What are the main characteristics associated with a reading comprehension difficulty?

The large range of positions presented in this book offers the possibility of recognizing a series of variables related to reading comprehension. Furthermore, it is possible to follow the debate concerning the effective role they have in comprehension. As already mentioned, the present book offers the possibility of reconsidering the debate concerning the relationship between decoding and comprehension. In this respect the books by Perfetti (1985), on one side, and Yuill and Oakhill (1991), on the other side, represent two substantially different positions that are now open to further challenge. Another aspect, which has been emphasized in the literature on reading comprehension, is metacognitive monitoring. In the past, many authors have argued that poor monitoring is related to reading comprehension problems. However, the generality of this position has been criticized (Cornoldi, 1991). The fact that poor comprehenders monitor texts less effectively is not in dispute. The main point of contention concerns the nature of the relation between comprehension and monitoring. Poor monitoring could, in fact, be a consequence of poor comprehension rather than a cause. This problem is also considered extensively, and from different perspectives, in this book (e.g., in the chapters by Ruffman; Ehrlich; Perfetti, Marron, & Foltz; and Cornoldi, De Beni, and Pazzaglia). Many chapters also illustrate the role of other variables, which growing evidence is showing to be related to reading comprehension. The emerging evidence concerning the extent and nature of the relation between working memory and reading is further examined here in a few chapters (in particular in that by Oakhill and Yuill). Other important variables are inferential ability (Oakhill and Yuill), knowledge (Perfetti et al.; Barnes and Dennis), syntactic competence, knowledge of the nature of the reading process, and vocabulary. In addition, substantially new lines of research are presented. For example, Cain examines the role of narrative competence in reading comprehension. Yuill shows how riddle comprehension ability is critically involved in reading comprehension. These findings on narrative skills and riddles might seem of only tangential relevance to the central problem, but we feel that this is not the case. For example, Yuill shows that a training program focused on riddle comprehension can have positive effects on a more general reading comprehension ability, and Cain emphasizes how the ability to produce coherent narratives may be related to, indeed may be an index of, the ability to appreciate cohesion in narrative comprehension.

When can other well-identified problems add to our understanding of reading comprehension difficulties?

When studying reading comprehension difficulties, an important related issue is whether such problems also arise in children with clearly defined disabilities, or brain pathology, and what such cases might tell us about reading comprehension problems in the population more generally. A well known example of this situation is found in deaf children, whose intellectual and general cognitive potential is well above their reading comprehension level. If we consider that deaf children do not have, in principle, any cognitive deficit, it may be surprising to find that they typically reach very low levels of reading comprehension skill. This finding raises interesting theoretical questions about the sources of comprehension problems, and the educational challenge of preventing them. These issues are considered in the overview by Marschark and Harris. Other cases of a more or less specific reading comprehension difficulty can be found within developmental neuropsychology. The contribution of neuropsychology to the comprehension of cognitive functioning is well known and in this volume is discussed by Barnes and Dennis. They present a specific group of young neuropsychological patients where it is sometimes possible to find a dissociation between particular reading comprehension skills and other cognitive functions. Early onset hydrocephalus children are characterized by an early disturbance of pressure in the brain, which arises from an imbalance in the production and absorption of cerebrospinal fluid. This leads to dilated ventricles and loss of brain volume, especially in the white matter. Children with this disturbance are apparently characterized by good verbal abilities and poor non-verbal abilities, as illustrated by a superiority of verbal IQ with respect to non-verbal IQ. Rather surprisingly, such children sometimes have specific comprehension difficulties. Barnes and Dennis present a case of a child who performs very well when the task is to infer words from context (as required by a closure test), but is otherwise poor on inferential abilities. This evidence is further supported by a group analysis showing that average intelligence hydrocephalic children have specific difficulties in using a knowledge base and in making a variety of inferences. The differences found between these children and other poor readers again suggest that specific subgroups can be found within a reading comprehension difficulty syndrome, and that these subgroups may require specific forms of educational intervention.

Which educational strategies are effective in preventing and treating reading comprehension difficulties?

We are convinced that remediational research focused only on techniques and their effects is shortsighted and will eventually fail. From our point of view, remediation research must be based on a theoretical hypothesis concerning the contribution of the manipulated variables to the ability that the training aims to improve. All of the chapters in this volume are based in this perspective, offering a variety of intervention suggestions that are theory driven. Readers may be surprised by the large variety of suggestions if they do not consider the complexity of the reading comprehension process, and the large number of variables involved. This high number of variables could lead to pessimistic predictions about the possibility of treating reading comprehension problems. This pessimistic attitude was perhaps reinforced in the past by the associated consideration of a reading comprehension difficulty and other related syndromes, like dyslexia, general learning disabilities, and, in particular, mental retardation.

The consideration of a specific reading comprehension difficulty as a distinct kind of learning difficulty has helped to show that this problem is surprisingly highly amenable to treatment. In a meta-analysis of the educational research, Mastropieri (personal communication, 1994) found that the effect size of programs devoted to ameliorating reading comprehension difficulties approaches one positive standard deviation. The methods and results presented in many chapters of this book show that highly specific techniques can also have significant effects on general reading comprehension ability. These effects have important theoretical implications, suggesting, for example, that variables associated with reading comprehension are not the simple consequence of the reading comprehension ability but may have a causal role in its development. However, in order to make progress in this area, we really need to have more information about which cognitive abilities and reading subskills are causally related to comprehension skill because, obviously, these would be the skills and abilities most worth training. For example, if the specific variable treated is able to explain only a small portion of the variance related to reading comprehension ability more generally, and if not all children with a reading comprehension difficulty have a substantial problem in that variable, why did the specific treatment have such general effects? From such results, models assuming either the interconnection of the different processes underlying reading comprehension or the manipulation of more variables than claimed by apparently specific treatments seem more adequate, but alternative hypotheses can also be considered.

Many of the intervention suggestions proposed in the book have another important advantage. In fact, in focusing on variables underlying or predicting a reading comprehension difficulty, they move the object of remediation from the reading process itself to tasks that do not necessarily depend on reading at all. This shift has an advantage for the treatment of poor readers who can prefer to be considered for other skills rather than for their deficit. The chapter by Stanovich, West, Cunningham, Cipielewski, and Siddiqui offers a wide perspective on how general literacy factors can predict success in reading comprehension and, conversely, how extensive reading for comprehension can predict success on a number of other skills. Other chapters focus on other relevant variables that could also be manipulated before children begin formal instruction in learning to read. For example, oral comprehension abilities can be enhanced or specifically treated in young children. Similarly some metacognitive competences concerning oral communication, comprehension of ambiguities, lexical knowledge, and so on could be the object of specific attention even in 4- and 5-year-old children, especially if low scores in predictors of success in reading comprehension identify them as subjects at risk.

What supplementary information can we get from an international perspective?

Psychology often runs the risk of being parochial. Cross-cultural effects are evident in the scientific psychological literature. However, authors and lines of research considered by a researcher are in most cases representatives of the same country and of the same research area as the author. This cultural specificity of research is particularly evident in the area of developmental disabilities. In this field discrepancies between areas and countries are particularly marked. Children defined by the American psychiatric manual DSM-IV (American Psychiatric Association, 1994) as having an attention deficit disorder are differently diagnosed and treated in other countries. Similarly, different types of learning difficulties are the object of different approaches throughout the world. With knowledge of different perspectives and procedures, intervention models can help to identify the limitations of a particular approach and to enlarge the spectrum of the phenomena under consideration. This approach can also help to increase communication between researchers from different countries and can help in the development of common procedures and models of analysis. The present book, by bringing together researchers from a variety of different countries and backgrounds, aims to contribute to the erosion of these barriers. The reader will find examples, not only of different approaches, but also of different procedures, criteria, and interventions. At the moment, we cannot know the precise influence of different languages on the development of reading comprehension difficulties, but it is possible that the development of cross-linguistic research using exactly the same methodologies with children of different languages could help to illuminate specific differences and inform theorizing. Cross-cultural research could explore whether differences in the numbers of children recognized as having a reading comprehension difficulty or differences in the established relationship found between reading decoding and reading comprehension are related to language transparency. For example, Italian children who read a highly transparent language could need lower decoding abilities in order to initiate the comprehension process, and this could increase the probability of finding a dissociation between decoding and comprehension.

THE ORGANIZATION OF THE BOOK

The different chapters of this book all examine reading comprehension difficulties. However, they consider the problem from different perspectives and with different focuses. We have divided the chapters into five sections. The first section is focused on factors which can produce a reading comprehension difficulty. The initial chapter by Gough, Hoover, and Peterson brings the reader to consider the main distinction between decoding and comprehension and their interaction in reading. Stanovich et al. consider the cultural environment and how literacy is related to success in reading. Ruffman raises the question of the nature of a comprehension monitoring difficulty, suggesting that it is related to a predisposition to derive single conclusions from a text.

The next section offers overviews of characteristics of children with poor comprehension. The chapter by Oakhill and Yuill reviews the large body of research they have conducted over more than 10 years on children with reading comprehension difficulties. Stothard and Hulme propose a direct contrast between young children with poor decoding but good comprehension and children with good decoding but poor comprehension, showing that these groups have distinct patterns of performance on a number of measures. Cornoldi et al. present the main results of a longitudinal study involving a group of adolescents with a reading comprehension problem. These data offer the possibility of recognizing typical characteristics of this group of subjects, but also the specific profile (and development of the ability) each of them can present. The chapter by Perfetti et al. extends the consideration of variables influencing reading comprehension to young adults.

The third section considers specific aspects of a reading comprehension problem. The chapter by Cain examines the role of story knowledge, Yuill considers riddle comprehension, and Ehrlich focuses on monitoring in the processing of anaphoric devices. The fourth section examines the cases of hydrocephalus (Barnes & Dennis) and deafness (Marschark & Harris), which appear particularly critical for the consideration of a reading comprehension problem in special populations. Finally, the last section is more directly related to the educational implications of research on reading comprehension difficulties, in a school (Lumbelli) or a social environment (Baker).

REFERENCES

American Psychiatric Association. (1994). *Diagnostic and statistical manual of mental disorders* (4th ed.). Washington, DC: Author.

Bakker, D. J., & Vinke, J. (1985). Effects of specific hemispheric stimulation on brain activity and reading in dyslexics. *Journal of Clinical and Experimental Neuropsychology, 1,* 505–525.

Coltheart, M., Masterson, J., Byng, S., Prior, S., & Riddoch, M. J. (1983). Surface dyslexia. *Quarterly Journal of Experimental Psychology, 35A,* 469–496.

Cornoldi, C. (1991). Metacognitive control processes and memory deficits in poor comprehenders. *Learning Disability Quarterly, 13,* 245–256.

Fletcher, J. M., & Morris, R. (1986). Classification of disabled learners: Beyond exclusionary definitions. In S. Ceci (Ed.), *Handbook of cognitive, social, and neuropsychological aspects of learning disabilities* (Vol. 1, pp. 55–80). Hillsdale, NJ: Lawrence Erlbaum Associates.

Fodor, G. (1983). *The modularity of mind.* Cambridge, MA: Harvard University Press.

Geary, A. (1993). Mathematical disabilities: Cognitive, neuropsychological and genetic components. *Psychological Bulletin, 114,* 354–362.

Hammill, D. D. (1990). On defining learning disabilities: An emerging consensus. *Journal of Learning Disabilities, 23,* 108–113.

Healy, J. R., Aram, D. M., Horwitz, S. J., Kessler, J. (1982). A study of children with hyperlexia. *Brain and Language, 17,* 1–23.

Lindgren, S. D., De Renzi, E., & Richman, L. C. (1985). Cross-national comparisons of developmental dyslexia in Italy and the United States. *Child Development, 56,* 1404–1417.

Perfetti, C. A. (1985). *Reading ability.* New York: Oxford University Press.

Shallice, T. (1988). *From neuropsychology to mental structure.* Cambridge, England: Cambridge University Press.

Stanovich, K., & Siegel, L. (1994). Phenotypic performance profile of children with reading disabilities: A regression-based method test of the phonological-core variable-difference model. *Journal of Educational Psychology, 86,* 24–53.

Thorndike, R. L. (1973). *Reading comprehension education in fifteen countries: An empirical study.* New York: Halsted.

Tramontana, M., Hooper, S., & Selzer, S. C. (1988). Research on the preschool prediction of later academic achievement: A review. *Developmental Review, 8,* 89–146.

Yuill, N. M., & Oakhill, J. V. (1991). *Children's problems in text comprehension: An experimental investigation.* Cambridge, England: Cambridge University Press.

CHAPTER ONE

Some Observations on a Simple View of Reading

Philip B. Gough
University of Texas at Austin

Wesley A. Hoover
Southwest Educational Development Laboratory

Cynthia L. Peterson
Southwest Texas State University

Only a fool would deny that reading is complex. Reading clearly involves many subprocesses, and those subprocesses must be skillfully coordinated.

There is first of all the control of eye movements. Reading begins with the fixation of the printed page. A quarter of a second later, a saccade to a new location takes place, and then the sequence is repeated, interrupted only by return sweeps and an occasional regression. Within each fixation, the reader must decide how long to maintain it and where to fixate next; because eye movements are ballistic, she must also program the eyes' musculature to carry out these decisions.

Then there is word recognition. On fixating a printed word, the reader must translate that meaningless set of letters into a recognizable object, locating or activating precisely the right word in a mental lexicon containing tens of thousands of items; she accomplishes this feat in less than one fifth of a second. At the same time, the reader is developing information about the form of the next word, and the location of the word after that.

Mere recognition of the word is not enough; the reader must also decide what the word means. Many words are ambiguous, and the reader must choose among those meanings; the reader must disambiguate the word.

Having selected the appropriate meaning for each word, the reader must then fit them together. She must determine the syntactic function of each word, and then determine the relations among them; she must decide which noun or noun phrase is the subject of each verb, which noun each adjective

1

modifies, and where each prepositional phrase is to be attached. In short, she must parse the sentence.

Once these relations are established, the reader must use this information to determine the meaning of the sentence. Often this will require inference: The reader will need to draw upon her knowledge of the world to construct a representation of the sentence's meaning.

Given a representation of the sentence's meaning, it must be related to meanings of previous sentences; it must be fitted into the reader's mental structure of the discourse.

Finally, the reader must decide what to do with this information. If she decides that it is true and valuable, she must incorporate it into her body of knowledge; she must learn.

All of these things must be accomplished by the reader. But we note that many of them must also be done by the auder, the person who is listening to language, not reading it. Beyond the point of word recognition, listening and reading appear to require essentially the same processes.

To be sure, the common processes are not exactly the same. Disambiguation is occasionally different, for the ambiguities of the spoken word and those of the printed word are not identical. Many spoken words (e.g., /sel/) are ambiguous; they must be disambiguated. But often their printed counterparts (e.g., *sail* and *sale*) are not ambiguous, at least not in the same way. In contrast, many printed words (e.g., *bow*) are polyphonic; they correspond to two different phonological forms (e.g., /bo/, /bau/) and those forms may or may not require disambiguation.

The process of parsing is also slightly different, for the two modalities convey information about syntax in different ways. Speech offers intonation and stress; print offers punctuation and capitalization.

The availability of the materials for integration differs as well. In print, the previous sentences remain on the page, and the reader can return to them at will. But speech is ephemeral, and the external evidence of previous sentences is lost; the auder must rely on memory.

But these differences pale in comparison to the similarities of processing in the two modalities. Virtually the same lexicon is used to read and aud. The vast majority of ambiguities are ambiguous in both modalities. In both modalities, the words are laid out linearly (printed words in space, spoken words in time), and word order plays a central role in parsing. Virtually the same grammar is employed in parsing both written and spoken sentences. The same background knowledge is brought to bear on printed and spoken words.

What this suggests, then, is that reading can be divided into two parts; that which is unique to reading, namely decoding, and that which is shared with auding, namely comprehension. The division is natural; we are cutting nature at its joint.

THE DISSOCIATION OF DECODING AND COMPREHENSION

Many students of reading would resist this division. They argue that reading is interactive, that decoding and comprehension are tightly interwoven.

The two are certainly correlated, and this correlation makes it difficult to separate the two. Skilled reading clearly requires skill in both decoding and comprehension. The most common sort of reading disability, which we call garden variety, involves deficits in both decoding and comprehension. In the general population, then, readers tend to be skilled in either both or neither. The result is a strong positive correlation between the two parts, and consequently, when researchers try to study differences in comprehension while matching on decoding, they are haunted by the problem of regression to the mean.

But decoding and comprehension can be separated, or at least dissociated. This is, we think, an important point, for neuropsychologists have offered such dissociation as evidence that the two skills are lodged in distinct mechanisms. In the case of decoding and comprehension, we think the dissociation is clear. To take one example, the typical 5-year-old Italian can understand Italian but not decode it; we, in contrast, can decode it (to a certain extent), but comprehend it very poorly.

Our favorite example is drawn from the life of John Milton. In his dotage, Milton wished to reread the Greek and Latin classics, but he was going blind. So he taught his daughters to decode Greek and Latin. They read the classics aloud while he listened to them. Between them, there was reading comprehension.

The dissociation of decoding and comprehension is also found in the dyslexic and the hyperlexic. The dyslexic can comprehend but not decode; the hyperlexic can decode but not comprehend. Between the two, there is double dissociation.

Decoding and comprehension, then, are the two halves of reading. But the two halves are not added together. Reading does not equal the sum of decoding and comprehension, for neither decoding in the absence of comprehension, nor comprehension in the absence of decoding, leads to any amount of reading. A child who cannot decode cannot read; a child who cannot comprehend cannot read either. Literacy—reading ability—can be found only in the presence of both decoding and comprehension. Both skills are necessary; neither is sufficient.

These observations led us to adopt a multiplicative hypothesis. If reading (r), decoding (d), and comprehension (c) are considered as skills that range from zero to one, then reading must be the product of decoding and comprehension. Put algebraically, $r = d \times c$. Reading takes place only when both d and c are greater than zero.

There is, then, only one way to read; by decoding and comprehending what you have decoded: There is only one kind of reading ability. But as we have seen, three kinds of reading disability can be distinguished; a deficiency in decoding (the dyslexic), a deficiency in comprehension (the hyperlexic), and a deficiency in both processes (the garden variety).

THE COMBINATION OF DECODING
AND COMPREHENSION

We hold, then, that reading ability consists of two distinct parts. Two major efforts to factor analyze the reading process have come to a conclusion that differs from ours.

Zwick (1987) analyzed the reading data collected in the 1983–1984 National Assessment of Educational Progress (NAEP). NAEP set up groups of seemingly dissimilar kinds of items, including items measuring general reading comprehension, items testing inference of word meanings from context, items having to do with everyday reading skills, and essay items. Both a full-information factor analysis and a test of unidimensionality developed by Rosenbaum (1985) supported the same conclusion: Despite their dissimilarities, the reading items used could be regarded as measures of a single dimension.

Rost (1989) gave 38 different reading tests, a spelling test, and a speed-of-information processing test to 220 German second graders, and intercorrelated them. His study yielded 780 correlation coefficients. A factor analysis of this matrix revealed only one broad general reading comprehension component, accounting for 61% of the total variance.

Carroll (1988) observed that multidimensionality is unlikely because as students progress, "different reading skills develop more or less in parallel" (p. 763). This argument seems to us to beg the question "Is reading unidimensional or multidimensional?" We think that a more convincing explanation of why Zwick and Rost failed to find two dimensions is because the tasks used in these studies all required decoding. As we see it, to separate the decoding and comprehension factors, we need tasks that measure each without involving the other.

What neither of these studies included were measures of listening comprehension, that is, measures of the comprehension component uncontaminated by decoding.

In 1990, we (Hoover & Gough) conducted a study that did obtain uncontaminated measures of each component skill. The Southwest Educational Development Laboratory (SEDL) measured separately the decoding, listening comprehension, and reading skills of 254 bilingual children in Texas each year for the first four grades. Decoding was assessed by asking the child to name pseudowords. Listening was measured by reading a story to the child, and then asking questions about the story. Reading comprehension was assessed in the same way, save that the child read the story.

It would surprise no one that we found both decoding ability and listening ability to correlate with reading comprehension. But we wanted to show that the multiplicative model accounted for the data better than the additive one. The problem we faced was that the two models make the same predictions almost everywhere: The best reader will be the child good at decoding and listening, the worst will be the child weak at both, and the intermediate reader will be the child intermediate at both skills. Where the two models differ is where the two skills are dissociated.

There was enough dissociation (i.e., enough children who were strong in one skill, but weak in the other) in the SEDL data to show that the product of decoding and listening comprehension correlated more highly with reading comprehension than did their sum. Those correlations were astonishingly high; .84 in the first grade, .85 in the second, and .91 in both the third and the fourth. Despite the fact that SEDL's measures of the three variables were not perfectly reliable, these correlations could not be closer to 1. These results offer an accurate description of reading ability: Reading is best described as the product of decoding and comprehension.

The Relationship of the Components to Reading

The simple view describes the joint relationship of decoding and comprehension to reading; it also helps us describe the separate relationships between the two components and reading.

In the typical kindergartner, comprehension is well developed; the typical 5-year-old can speak and understand her native language better than the typical foreign college student with four semesters in that language. The phonology and syntax of the language has been all but mastered, the child's vocabulary numbers in the thousands, and a great deal of knowledge about the world has been acquired. There is variability, to be sure, but we think that it is reasonable to assume that comprehension at school entry is normally distributed around a very substantial mean. The typical text that confronts the child at this age is very simple, with a difficulty level well beneath that mean. If the text were read to the child, it would be understood by almost every normal child. So, among beginning normal readers tested with typical materials, c approaches 1. In the multiplicative view, if $c = 1$, then $r = d$. Thus, we would expect to see that among beginning readers, the correlation between c and r would be negligible, whereas the correlation between d and r would be very high.

At the other end of the curriculum, the situation is just the reverse. The majority of college students can decode the vast majority of words they encounter; d approaches 1. But if $d = 1$, then $r = c$. So, although the correlation between c and r will be modest at best in the general population, among college students, we would expect it to be very high. Thus, the simple view leads us to expect that the correlation between decoding and reading will decrease across the grades, while the correlation between listening and reading will increase over the same time span.

Of course, in both cases above we presume that the materials used to assess c parallel those used to assess r. Although the language of print may indeed differ from that of speech (e.g., some syntactic devices used in the former rarely appear in the latter), this is not a necessary consequence of the medium, for anything that can be captured in language can be transmitted through either a written or oral form. Therefore, we must distinguish the message from the medium.

We looked for the trends predicted above in the relationships of reading to comprehension and decoding through a meta-analysis of existing research. We searched the published literature to identify investigations of normal reading in monolingual English speakers (first through sixth grade, and college level) where appropriate measures of the three variables were taken. By appropriate, we mean that (a) comprehension was measured free of decoding (i.e., using auding), and (b) auding and reading were measured in the same way. We found 10 such studies, reporting measures from 17 different samples.

Table 1.1 presents the correlations from these studies. The table displays the coefficients and tests of significance as well as the sample size; the data are grouped by grade level. In some cases, inverted scales were employed (e.g., latency was measured instead of accuracy), and for these scales, we reversed the signs of the coefficients so that a positive correlation indicates a direct relationship between two skills.

The simple vote-counting method applied to these data indicated that both relationships were positive: The 17 reported correlations between decoding and reading were all positive (15 of them significantly so), and 16 of the reported correlations between comprehension and reading were significantly positive as well (the sole exception being insignificant).

To obtain more precise estimates of these relationships, we conducted a series of statistical analyses using a standard meta-analysis package. Pooling the 17 correlations of decoding and reading yielded a highly significant (aggregate) correlation of .55; pooling the correlations of comprehension and reading yielded a value of .56. Within both analyses, the test for homogeneity was highly significant, indicating substantial differences among the 17 pooled coefficients.

Given the substantial differences between coefficients, an analysis of variance was conducted to test the hypothesis that grade level at the time of the test was an important determinant of such differences. For this purpose,

TABLE 1.1

Concurrent Correlations Between Reading and Its Components From Studies of English-Speaking Elementary Schoolchildren and Adults

Study	N	Time[a]	Group[b]	Zero-Order Correlations	
				DR[c]	CR[d]
Juel, Griffith, & Gough (1986)	129	1.8	1	.59*	.37*
Tunmer (1989)	100	1.8	1	.66*	.49*
Stanovich, Cunningham, & Feeman (1984)	56	1.9	1	.52*	.37*
Curtis (1980)	20	2.5	1	.54*	-.26
Juel, Griffith, & Gough (1986)	80	2.8	1	.59*	.43*
Tunmer (1989)	84	2.8	1	.66*	.54*
Dreyer & Katz (1991)	137	3.2	2	.62*	.38*
Curtis (1980)	40	3.5	2	.44*	.66*
Stanovich, Cunningham, & Feeman (1984)	18	3.9	2	.41	.52*
Stanovich, Nathan, & Vala-Rossi (1986)	33	3.9	2	.33*	.76*
Curtis (1980)	40	5.5	3	.47*	.74*
Stanovich, Cunningham, & Feeman (1984)	20	5.9	3	.83*	.59*
Stanovich, Nathan, & Vala-Rossi (1986)	35	5.9	3	.73*	.64*
Singer & Crouse (1981)	127	6.5	3	.36*	.76*
Jackson & McClelland (1979)	24	13.9	4	.49*	.70*
Cunningham, Stanovich, & Wilson (1990)	76	14.1	4	.55*	.54*
Palmer, MacLeod, Hunt, & Davidson (1985)	67	14.9	4	.18	.82*

Note. Entries are ordered by time of testing from youngest to oldest samples.

[a]Time of testing is represented in grade-level units using a grade–month coding with the integer portion representing the grade level and the decimal portion representing the month (.1 represents the month of September and .9 represents May). [b]1 = first and second grade; 2 = third and fourth grade; 3 = fifth and sixth grade; and 4 = college. For Group 4, precise time of testing for individual subjects was not reported; the entry is an estimate based on the information provided. [c]DR = Decoding and Reading. [d]CR = Comprehension (auding) and Reading.

*p < .05, two-tailed.

the studies were divided into four groups, combining studies of subjects in grades 1–2 (Group 1), grades 3–4 (Group 2), grades 5–6 (Group 3), and college (Group 4), respectively. For the correlations between decoding and reading, a significant between-group effect was found, indicating that the correlations differed depending on the grade level of the sample. Descriptively, the average weighted correlations obtained between decoding and reading were .61, .53, .48, and .39 for Groups 1, 2, 3, and 4, respectively. Each coefficient was found to be significantly positive, with the computed effect sizes declining in magnitude from Group 1 to Group 4 ($d = 1.51, 1.24, 1.09, .81$).

For the correlations between comprehension and reading, a highly significant between-group effect was found, again indicating the significant impact of grade level on the correlations. Descriptively, the average weighted correlations between comprehension and reading were .41, .50, .72, and .68 for Groups 1, 2, 3, and 4, respectively. Each coefficient was positive (significantly so), and the effect sizes for Groups 1 through 4 were .90, 1.13, 2.06, and 1.80. Note that in the three studies contained in Group 4, two found substantial correlational differences whereas the third, which was based on the largest sample size, reported almost identical coefficients. We note that the reliability of the comprehension measure employed in this last study was fairly low (.63), which might account for the correlational pattern found.

Overall, the results generally supported the pattern expected under the simple view. First, we found large positive, pooled correlations of reading with both decoding and comprehension. Second, the correlational trend between decoding and reading was consistent with the predicted decline with grade level, and the correlational trend between comprehension and reading was generally consistent with the predicted increase with grade level.

DECODING AND COMPREHENSION

We have observed that decoding and comprehension are positively correlated. The skilled decoder is also apt to be a skilled comprehender, and the child poor at either is likely to be poor at the other. But the simple view says that the relationship between decoding and comprehension must depend on reading level.

The skilled reader must be good at both decoding and comprehension; there can be little variation in either skill. Because the poor reader is generally poor at both, there is a positive correlation between decoding and comprehension in the total population.

But the poor reader can be poor in any of three ways; poor at decoding, poor at comprehension, or poor at both. What this entails is that, among poor readers, decoding skill and comprehension skill must be negatively correlated.

If you are a poor reader but good at decoding, then you must be poor at comprehension; if you are a poor reader but good at comprehension, then you must be poor at decoding. In other words, if $r = .1$, and if d is high, then c must be low, and vice versa. Hoover and Gough (1990) found that among the reading disabled, the correlation did indeed turn negative.

Multiple Literacies

Since ancient Rome, the term *literacy* (Latin *literatus*) has been ambiguous. It has always meant at least two things. In one sense, literacy (literacy$_1$) meant the ability to read and write; the other (literacy$_2$) meant cultured or educated. In recent years, it has been stretched even further, to the point where it may not even include the ability to read and write (see Kintgen, 1988). We read of computer literacy, Jewish literacy, musical literacy, and even visual literacy.

But a new and different ambiguity is being put forward. This is the claim that reading skill (literacy$_1$) is not one thing but many. For example, McLean and Goldstein (1988, p. 371) claimed that, "To predict with any accuracy which reading materials an individual will be able to comprehend, we must know that person's prior knowledge and cultural experiences" (p. 371). They claimed that, "In reality, reading achievement is not unidimensional" (p. 371). Instead, "People tend to exhibit different performances in different contexts, since interest, motivation, intention, and the like all play a role" (pp. 371–372).

The issue at stake is clearly empirical: To what extent do performances across "contexts" correlate? The evidence seems to indicate that these correlations are only moderate.

How are we to accommodate these data in terms of the simple view? We would agree with McLean and Goldstein that the reader's prior knowledge must influence his reading comprehension. But in the simple view, reading comprehension (literacy$_1$) is not one thing, but two. The question then becomes, where does background knowledge have its effect? Does background knowledge influence decoding, or comprehension, or both?

Background Knowledge, Decoding, and Comprehension

In her dissertation, Peterson (1993) endeavored to measure the interrelationships among background knowledge, reading, decoding, and comprehension. First, she assessed 135 naval reservists' knowledge of two unrelated subject matters, baseball and the personal computer (with the scope of background knowledge in each narrowed to knowledge of terminology and procedures). Next, she asked the reservists to read a passage from George

Will's recent book on baseball, and then to respond to literal and inferential questions about the passage. The reservists also listened to another passage from the same book, and again answered questions. Finally, each reservist read aloud a list of 100 content words drawn randomly from the reading passage. The reservists completed a parallel series of tasks for passages drawn from the personal computer magazine, *Byte*. They read part of an article and answered questions about it, listened to part of another article and again answered questions, and then read aloud a list of 100 words taken from those articles.

Peterson thus obtained eight measures from each subject, measures of their background knowledge, reading, listening, and decoding skill in each of two domains. Her results are presented in Fig. 1.1.

Peterson's data indicated that reading ability was only moderately correlated across the two domains: The correlation was somewhere between .35 (the observed correlation) and .53 (the correlation corrected for attenuation). But the moderation arose from the comprehension component: Baseball-listening comprehension and computer-listening comprehension correlated .40–.62. In striking contrast were her results with decoding: Baseball and computer decoding were correlated .88. Comprehension may not have been highly correlated across contexts, but decoding certainly was.

Peterson's data also made clear that background knowledge contributed primarily to comprehension, and not to decoding. Background knowledge correlated .60–.72 with listening comprehension in baseball, and .56–.82 with listening comprehension in computers. But it correlated much more modestly with decoding (.10 in baseball, .39 in computers) in the two subject matters.

These results suggest two answers to the question of whether there is a single, general literacy$_1$, or a collection of specific literacies. One component of reading is completely general; that is decoding. The other component of reading is more specific: Comprehension varies from subject matter to subject matter, and that variation is likely due to variation in background knowledge.

We conclude that the simple view of reading offers clear answers to two important questions. Reading is not unidimensional; it has two dimensions, decoding and comprehension. Reading (literacy$_1$) is both general and specific; decoding is general, and comprehension is specific.

TWO IMPLICATIONS

The simple view seems to us a sensible way of looking at reading; it seems like common sense. But we recognize that it is very much at odds with the current sense in education.

According to that sense, reading is whole; it cannot be broken down into subskills. Thus, we should not attempt to assess such subskills, nor should we attempt to teach them separately (International Reading Association, 1989).

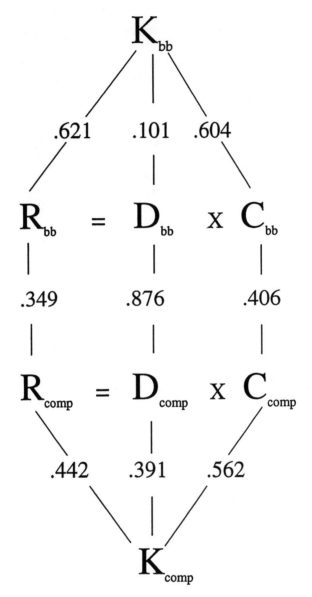

FIG. 1.1. The correlations between reading (R), decoding (D), comprehension (C), and background knowledge (K) in two domains, baseball (bb) and computers (comp).

If the simple view is correct, the IRA's position on assessment is wrong. If reading consists of two components, two skills, then it is surely important to separately assess those two skills. For example, if we encounter a disabled reader, then it is important to determine whether the disability results from a weakness in decoding, a weakness in comprehension, or (as is most likely) weaknesses in both, for the two disabilities call for very different types of remediation.

If the simple view is correct, then the IRA's stance on instruction may also be wrong. If reading consists of two isolable subcomponents, then we should at least consider the possibility that we might teach them in different ways. That reading consists of two skills does not imply that either one should be taught by drill. As we see it, both decoding and comprehension are primarily developed through reading, rather than through direct instruction. But we believe that decoding seldom begins without some form of instruction (Gough & Hillinger, 1980), and we hope that comprehension might benefit from it as well. The idea that the two skills are distinct suggests that they might best be taught in two different ways (a point convincingly developed by Stanovich, 1994). If reading has two parts, then we should determine whether optimal instruction should as well.

REFERENCES

Carroll, J. B. (1988). The NAEP Reading Proficiency Scale is not a fiction: A reply to McLean and Goldstein. *Phi Delta Kappan, 69,* 761–764.

Cunningham, A. E., Stanovich, K. E., & Wilson, M. R. (1990). Cognitive variation in adult college students differing in reading ability. In T. H. Carr & B. A. Levy (Eds.), *Reading and its development: Component skills approaches* (pp. 129–159). San Diego: Academic Press.

Curtis, M. E. (1980). Development of components of reading skill. *Journal of Educational Psychology, 72,* 656–669.

Dreyer, L. G., & Katz, L. (1991, December). *An examination of "The simple view of reading."* Paper presented at the meeting of the National Reading Conference, Palm Springs, CA.

Gough, P. B., & Hillinger, M. L. (1980). Learning to read: An unnatural act. *Bulletin of the Orton Society, 30,* 179–196.

Hoover, W. A., & Gough, P. B. (1990). The simple view of reading. *Reading and Writing, 2,* 127–160.

International Reading Association. (1989). Professional statements approved by the IRA Board of Directors. *Journal of Reading, 32,* 297.

Jackson, M. D., & McClelland, J. L. (1979). Processing determinants of reading speed. *Journal of Experimental Psychology: General, 108,* 151–181.

Juel, C., Griffith, P. L., & Gough, P. B. (1986). Acquisition of literacy: A longitudinal study of children in the first and second grade. *Journal of Educational Psychology, 78,* 243–255.

Kintgen, E. R. (1988). Literacy literacy. *Visible Language, 22,* 149–168.

McLean, L. D., & Goldstein, H. (1988). The U. S. National Assessments in Reading: Reading too much into the findings. *Phi Delta Kappan, 69,* 369–372.

Palmer, J., MacLeod, C. M., Hunt, E., & Davidson, J. E. (1985). Information processing correlates of reading. *Journal of Memory and Language, 24,* 59–88.

Peterson, C. L. (1993). *Background knowledge and the decomposition of literacy in skilled adult readers.* Unpublished doctoral dissertation, University of Texas, Austin.

Rosenbaum, P. R. (1985). Comparing distributions of item responses for two groups. *British Journal of Mathematical and Statistical Psychology, 38,* 206–215.

Rost, D. H. (1989). Reading comprehension: Skill or skills? *Journal of Research in Reading, 12,* 87–113.

Singer, M. H., & Crouse, J. (1981). The relationship of context-use skills to reading: A case for an alternative experimental logic. *Child Development, 52,* 1326–1329.

Stanovich, K. E. (1994). Constructivism in reading education. *Journal of Special Education, 28,* 259–274.

Stanovich, K. E., Cunningham, A. E., & Feeman, D. J. (1984). Intelligence, cognitive skills, and early reading progress. *Reading Research Quarterly, 19,* 278–303.

Stanovich, K. E., Nathan, R. G., & Vala-Rossi, M. (1986). Developmental changes in the cognitive correlates of reading ability and the developmental lag hypothesis. *Reading Research Quarterly, 21,* 267–283.

Tunmer, W. E. (1989). The role of language-related factors in reading disability. In D. Shankweiler & I. Y. Liberman (Eds.), *Phonology and reading disability* (pp. 91–131). Ann Arbor, MI: The University of Michigan Press.

Zwick, R. (1987). Assessing the dimensionality of NAEP reading data. *Journal of Educational Measurement, 24,* 293–308.

CHAPTER TWO

The Role of Inadequate Print Exposure as a Determinant of Reading Comprehension Problems

Keith E. Stanovich
University of Toronto

Richard F. West
James Madison University

Anne E. Cunningham
University of California, Berkeley

Jim Cipielewski
Oakland University

Shahid Siddiqui
University of Toronto

In the literature of cognitive developmental psychology, reading comprehension problems are typically analyzed in terms of cognitive processes operating in a suboptimal manner. In this chapter, we argue that cognitive developmental work on reading comprehension problems might benefit from searching for explanations at a more distal level than has been typical in our literature.

Researchers studying the cognitive psychology of reading comprehension have attempted to specify individual differences in the cognitive processes that support efficient reading performance (Carr & Levy, 1990; Daneman, 1991; Just & Carpenter, 1987; Perfetti, 1985; Rayner & Pollatsek, 1989; Stanovich & Cunningham, 1991). A popular research strategy has been the cognitive correlates approach (see Pellegrino & Glaser, 1979; Sternberg, 1990) in which investigators attempt to determine whether individual differences in particular cognitive processes or knowledge bases can serve as predictors of reading comprehension ability (e.g., Jackson & McClelland, 1979). The causal model implicit in such analyses locates individual differences in the cognitive subprocesses that determine comprehension ability.

In cognitive psychology, very little attention has been focused on what might be termed a form of reciprocal causation, or the possibility that individual differences in exposure to print (a side effect of differences in comprehension ability) affect both the development of cognitive processes and the declarative knowledge bases supportive of further gains in comprehension growth.

In contrast to cognitive psychologists, anthropologists and other social scientists have for decades been intensely preoccupied with speculations on how the exercise of literacy affects knowledge acquisition, belief systems, cognitive processes, and reasoning. Outside of psychology, the literature on the cognitive consequences of literacy is large and steadily growing (Akinnaso, 1981; Goody, 1977, 1987; Graff, 1986, 1987; Havelock, 1963, 1980; Kaestle, 1991; Olson, 1977, 1994; Ong, 1967, 1982; Stock, 1983).

It is not at all clear why the division of labor between cognitive psychologists and other social scientists in the domain of literacy developed in such an extreme fashion. Reading is a very special type of interface with the environment, providing unique opportunities to acquire declarative knowledge. Furthermore, the processing mechanisms exercised during reading receive an unusual amount of practice. For the avid reader, whatever cognitive processes are engaged over word or word-group units (phonological coding, semantic activation, parsing, induction of new vocabulary items) are being exercised hundreds of times a day. It might be expected that this amount of practice would have some cognitive effects. Nevertheless, the dominant framework in the cognitive psychology of reading continues to be the cognitive correlates approach, with its bias toward viewing cognitive processes as a determinant of reading ability which is almost exclusively conceived as an outcome variable.

The research we describe in this chapter challenges this causal priority by examining the extent to which differences in the exercise of reading skills may be viewed as determinants of individual differences in comprehension ability and of further growth in the cognitive abilities that underlie comprehension skill.

Reading comprehension is composed of a large number of subprocesses and component skills, and there is reason to expect that several of these processing subcomponents are enhanced by exposure to print. For example, automatic word recognition processes are known to be linked to higher levels of reading comprehension (Cunningham, Stanovich, & Wilson, 1990; Lesgold, Resnick, & Hammond, 1985; Perfetti, 1985; Stanovich, 1991), and the primary way in which word recognition becomes automatic is through extensive practice in recognizing words (LaBerge & Samuels, 1974; Perfetti, 1985; Stanovich, 1986). Similarly, levels of vocabulary knowledge are strongly correlated with reading comprehension ability (Anderson & Freebody, 1983). Later in this chapter we discuss evidence indicating that a substantial amount of vocabulary growth might occur by inferring the meaning of words from context during reading (Nagy & Anderson, 1984; Nagy & Herman, 1987). Likewise, rich bodies of declarative knowledge and large numbers of stored schemata are associated with higher levels of reading comprehension (Anderson & Pearson, 1984; Rumelhart, 1980). We argued in previous publications (Stanovich, 1993; Stanovich & Cunningham, 1993; West, Stanovich, & Mitchell, 1993) that print is a unique source of declarative knowledge, not replaceable by electronic media or oral sources.

We examine the evidence linking several of these reading subcomponents to print exposure in this chapter. However, we first address the more general question of whether individual differences in the global process of reading comprehension can be linked to individual differences in exposure to print.

DOES PRINT EXPOSURE PREDICT INDIVIDUAL DIFFERENCES IN COMPREHENSION GROWTH?

In a longitudinal investigation (Cipielewski & Stanovich, 1992), we addressed the question of whether individual differences in exposure to print can predict individual differences in the growth of reading comprehension over time. The participants were 82 children in the third grades (8- to 9-year-olds) who had been administered the comprehension subtest of the Iowa Tests of Basic Skills (ITBS). Two years later, as fifth graders, these same children were administered both the reading comprehension section of the Stanford Diagnostic Reading Test and the ITBS. Measures of exposure to print were also administered to the children in grade five.

A major part of our research program has involved the development of reliable and valid measures of individual differences in exposure to print. We have used diary methods (Allen, Cipielewski, & Stanovich, 1992), questionnaire methods (Stanovich & West, 1989), and we have developed our own unique recognition-checklist measures (Stanovich & West, 1989). Because we have described the instrument development issues extensively in many other publications (Allen et al., 1992; Stanovich, 1993; Stanovich & Cunningham, 1992, 1993; Stanovich & West, 1989), we will not dwell on this methodological issue other than to note that we used the recognition-checklist methods in most of the studies we discuss here. These measures involve having subjects recognize literacy-related items (authors of books, magazines, titles of books, newspapers, etc.) in the context of foils so that guessing can be easily detected. Scores on these instruments are then corrected for guessing (see Stanovich, 1993; Stanovich & Cunningham, 1993; Stanovich & West, 1989, for details).

Table 2.1 displays the results of a hierarchical forced-entry regression analysis in which fifth-grade reading comprehension was the criterion variable. Third-grade reading comprehension was entered first into the equation, followed by a measure of the children's exposure to print outside of school.

TABLE 2.1
Hierarchical Regressions Predicting Fifth-Grade Reading Comprehension

Step	Variable	R	R^2	R^2 Change	F to Enter
Fifth-grade Stanford reading comprehension					
1.	Iowa comprehension (3rd)	.645	.416	.416	54.06*
2.	Print exposure	.725	.526	.110	17.38*
Fifth-grade Iowa reading comprehension					
1.	Iowa comprehension (3rd)	.545	.297	.297	33.78*
2.	Print exposure	.609	.371	.074	9.25*

*$p < .01$.

Thus, the analyses essentially address the question of whether exposure to print can predict individual differences in growth in reading comprehension from third grade to fifth grade. In the first analysis, with the Stanford reading comprehension test as the criterion variable, the measure of print exposure accounted for 11% unique variance after the third-grade comprehension level had been partialed. In the second analysis, with the Iowa comprehension subtest as the criterion variable, print exposure accounted for 7.4% unique variance. In both cases, the unique variance accounted for by print exposure was statistically significant. Table 2.2 displays the results of a similar analysis conducted on these children as sixth graders. For a variety of reasons, we experienced substantial attrition prior to this analysis. Nevertheless, despite the smaller sample size, in both analyses, print exposure made a significant unique contribution to the prediction of sixth-grade reading comprehension.

Note the conservatism of these analyses. If print exposure did indeed contribute to growth in comprehension ability, then some of the effects of print exposure were already in the covariate (third-grade comprehension ability) because it is highly unlikely that the effects of print exposure begin only after the third-grade year. Nevertheless, we partialed third-grade comprehension ability entirely, knowing that it carried part of the previous print exposure variance with it. Thus, our analysis was focused on growth from

TABLE 2.2
Hierarchical Regressions Predicting Sixth-Grade Reading Comprehension

Step	Variable	R	R^2	R^2 Change	F to Enter
Sixth-grade Stanford reading comprehension					
1.	Iowa comprehension (3rd)	.548	.300	.300	11.13**
2.	Print exposure	.630	.396	.096	4.00*
Sixth-grade Iowa reading comprehension					
1.	Iowa comprehension (3rd)	.617	.380	.380	17.80**
2.	Print exposure	.712	.506	.126	7.15*

*$p < .05$. **$p < .01$.

third to fifth and sixth grade only. Longer time periods would probably apportion more variance to print exposure than did our analyses.

We continue to present relatively conservative analyses in the remainder of this chapter for the following reason. Levels of print exposure are correlated with many other cognitive and behavioral characteristics. Avid readers tend to be different from nonreaders on a wide variety of cognitive skills, behavioral habits, and background variables. Attributing any particular outcome solely to print exposure is extremely difficult. Thus, the explanatory ambiguities surrounding a variable such as print exposure have led us to continue to structure the analyses in a "worst case" manner as far as print exposure is concerned, because in certain analyses, we have actually partialed out variance in abilities that are likely to be developed by print exposure itself (Stanovich, 1986, 1993). It should be understood that the implied causal model in the analyses is deliberately misspecified. When the predictive power of print exposure survives such biased analyses, we begin to feel justified in advancing at least a tentative causal inference.

PRINT EXPOSURE AS A CONTRIBUTOR
TO VERBAL ABILITY AND DECLARATIVE KNOWLEDGE

The results presented in Tables 2.1 and 2.2 indicate a unique contribution of print exposure to the explanation of reading comprehension differences. But reading comprehension is an extremely broad skill. A large body of research has demonstrated that reading skill is linked to a wide range of verbal abilities: Vocabulary, syntactic knowledge, metalinguistic awareness, verbal short-term memory, phonological awareness, speech production, inferential comprehension, semantic memory, and verbal fluency form only a partial list (Cunningham, Stanovich, & Wilson, 1990; Gathercole & Baddeley, 1993; Gernsbacher, 1993; Kamhi & Catts, 1989; Oakhill & Garnham, 1988; Siegel & Ryan, 1988; Stanovich & Cunningham, 1991; Stanovich, Cunningham, & Feeman, 1984; Stanovich, Nathan, & Zolman, 1988; Vellutino & Scanlon, 1987). This raises the question of whether print exposure can be linked to any of these specific subcomponents of the global comprehension process, an issue that we have addressed in our research program.

In certain domains, reading is especially likely to be a substantial contributor to cognitive growth. For example, as a mechanism for building content knowledge structures (Glaser, 1984), reading seems to be unparalleled (Goody, 1987). The world's storehouse of knowledge is readily available to those who read, and much of this information is not usually attained from other media (Comstock & Paik, 1991; Huston, Watkins, & Kunkel, 1989; Postman, 1985; West, Stanovich, & Mitchell, 1993; Zill & Winglee, 1990).

Additionally, if we consider vocabulary to be one of the primary tools of verbal intelligence (Olson, 1986), then we have another mechanism by which print exposure may influence cognition because reading appears to be a uniquely efficacious way of acquiring vocabulary (Hayes, 1988; Hayes & Ahrens, 1988; Nagy & Anderson, 1984; Nagy & Herman, 1987; Stanovich, 1986, 1993).

There are sound theoretical reasons for believing that print exposure is a particularly efficacious way of expanding a child's vocabulary. These reasons derive from the differences in the statistical distributions of words found between print and oral language. Some of these differences have been illustrated in the results of research by Hayes and Ahrens (1988) who analyzed the distributions of words used in various contexts. Three different categories of language were analyzed: written language sampled from genres as difficult as scientific articles and as simple as preschool books, words spoken on television shows of various types, and adult speech in two contexts varying in formality. The words used in the different contexts were analyzed according to a standard frequency count of English (Carroll, Davies, & Richman, 1971). This frequency count ranks the 86,741 different words in English according to their frequency of occurrence in a large corpus of written English. For example, the word "the" is ranked number 1, the 10th most frequent word is "it," the word "know" is ranked 100, the word "pass" is ranked 1,000, the word "vibrate" is 5,000th in frequency, the word "shrimp" is 9,000th in frequency, and the word "amplifier" is 16,000th in frequency.

In Hayes and Ahrens' (1988) study, the average frequency rank of the words in children's books (after a small correction) was 627 in the Carroll et al. (1971) word count and the average frequency rank of the words in popular magazines was 1,399. What is immediately apparent, upon examining Hayes and Ahrens' (1988) data, is how lexically impoverished is most speech as compared to written language. With the exception of the special situation of courtroom testimony, the average frequency rank of the words in all of the samples of oral speech was quite high, hovering in the 400–600 range of ranks. The words in children's books were, in fact, rarer than those in adult conversation, except for the situation of courtroom testimony. Indeed, the words used in most children's books were considerably rarer than those in the speech on prime-time adult television. Adult reading matter was even more disparate from speech.

These relative differences in word rarity have direct implications for vocabulary development. If most vocabulary is acquired outside of formal teaching (Miller & Gildea, 1987; Sternberg, 1985, 1987), then the only opportunities to acquire new words occur when an individual is exposed to a word in either written or oral language that is outside their current vocabulary. That this will happen vastly more often while reading than while talking or watching television is illustrated in another statistic calculated by Hayes and Ahrens (1988). They reported how often a rare word occurred in their various categories of texts. A rare word was defined as one with a rank lower than

10,000; roughly, a word that is outside the vocabulary of fourth to sixth graders. For vocabulary growth to occur after the middle grades, children must be exposed to words that are rare by this definition. Again, it is print that provides many more such word-learning opportunities. Children's books had 50% more rare words in them than did adult prime-time television and the conversation of college graduates. Popular magazines had roughly three times more opportunities for new word learning than did prime-time television and adult conversation in the Hayes and Ahrens (1988) study. Assurances that "what they read and write may make people smarter, but so will any activity that engages the mind, including interesting conversation" (Smith, 1989, p. 354) are overstated, at least when applied to the domain of vocabulary learning. The data presented by Hayes and Ahrens indicate that conversation is not a substitute for reading.

The large differences in lexical richness between speech and print are a major source of individual differences in vocabulary development. These differences are created by the large variability among children in exposure to print. This was illustrated in a study of the out-of-school time use by fifth graders conducted by Anderson, Wilson, and Fielding (1988). From diaries that the children filled out daily over several months, the investigators estimated how many minutes per day the individuals were engaged in reading and other activities when not in school. Anderson et al. found that the child at the 50th percentile in amount of book reading was reading approximately 4.6 minutes per day, over six times as much as the child at the 20th percentile in amount of reading time (less than 1 minute daily). Or, to take another example, the child at the 80th percentile in amount of book reading time (14.2 minutes) was reading over 20 times as much as the child at the 20th percentile.

Anderson et al. (1988) estimated the children's reading rates and used these, in conjunction with the amount of reading in minutes per day, to extrapolate a figure for the number of words that the children at various percentiles were reading. These figures illustrated the enormous differences in word exposure generated by children's differential proclivities toward reading. For example, the average child at the 90th percentile in print exposure read almost 2.5 million words per year outside of school, over 46 times more words than the child at the 10th percentile, who was exposed to just 51,000 words outside of school during a year. Or, to put it another way, an entire year's out-of-school exposure for the child at the 10th percentile amounted to just 8 days of reading for the child at the 90th percentile. These are the differences that, when combined with the lexical richness of print, may act to create large vocabulary differences among children.

We attempted to provide empirical evidence for such a linkage in several studies (Cunningham & Stanovich, 1991; Stanovich & Cunningham, 1992, 1993). In a study of 134 fourth, fifth, and sixth graders (9- to 13-year-olds), we examined whether print exposure accounted for differences in vocabulary development once controls for both general and specific (i.e., vocabulary relevant) abilities were invoked. The analyses displayed in Table 2.3 illustrate some of the outcomes of this study. Three different vocabulary measures were employed as dependent variables: a word checklist measure of the written vocabulary modeled on the work of Anderson and Freebody (1983), a group-administered version of the Peabody Picture Vocabulary Test (PPVT), and a verbal fluency measure where the children had to output as many words as they could that fit into a particular category (e.g., things that are red, see Sincoff & Sternberg, 1987). Age was entered first into the regression equation, followed by scores on the Raven Progressive Matrices as a control for general intelligence.

As a second ability control more closely linked to vocabulary acquisition mechanisms, we entered phonological coding ability into the equation. A variable such as phonological coding skill may mediate the relationship between print exposure and a variable like vocabulary size in numerous ways. High levels of decoding skill—certainly a contributor to greater print exposure—may provide relatively complete verbal contexts for the induction of word meanings during reading. Decoding skill may also indirectly reflect

TABLE 2.3
Unique Print Exposure Variance After Age, Raven,
and Phonological Coding are Partialed

Written Vocabulary			
	R	R^2 Change	F to Enter
Age	.103	.011	1.41
Raven	.457	.198	32.57*
Phonological coding	.610	.163	33.49*
Print exposure	.683	.094	22.52*

Oral Vocabulary			
	R	R^2 Change	F to Enter
Age	.230	.053	7.29*
Raven	.393	.101	15.60*
Phonological coding	.403	.008	1.21
Print exposure	.516	.104	18.19*

Verbal Fluency			
	R	R^2 Change	F to Enter
Age	.043	.002	0.24
Raven	.231	.051	6.89*
Phonological coding	.477	.175	28.47*
Print exposure	.582	.111	21.02*

*$p < .01$.

differences in short-term phonological storage related to vocabulary learning, particularly in the preschool years (Gathercole & Baddeley, 1989, 1993). Thus, print exposure and vocabulary may be spuriously linked via their connection with decoding ability: Good decoders read a lot and have the best context available for inferring new words. This spurious linkage was controlled by entering phonological coding into the regression equation prior to print exposure. If print exposure was only an incidental correlate of vocabulary because of its linkage with phonological coding skill, then print exposure would not serve as a unique predictor of vocabulary once phonological coding was partialed out. The results of the analyses displayed in Table 2.3 indicate that for each of the vocabulary measures, print exposure accounted for a significant portion of the variance once the variance attributable to performance on the Raven and the phonological coding measure had been removed.

We conducted an even more stringent test of whether exposure to print is a unique predictor of verbal skill in a study of college students. Table 2.4 presents the results of this study. Here, two nonverbal measures of general ability, performance on a figural analogies test and on the Raven Matrices, were entered first in a hierarchical regression analysis. Next, performance on the Nelson–Denny reading comprehension test was entered subsequent to the two nonverbal ability tasks but prior to the measure of print exposure. By structuring the analyses in this way, we did not mean to imply that print exposure was not a determinant of reading comprehension ability—we showed in our longitudinal study that it is. Instead, we intended, as previously described, to separate the variance due to current level of comprehension ability from the variance due to current levels of the exercise of those abilities (i.e., self-chosen reading activities). We recognized that the reading comprehension variable carried some of the variance that should

TABLE 2.4
Unique Print Exposure Variance After Nonverbal Abilities and Reading
Comprehension Ability are Partialed Out

	R^2 Change					
	Dependent Variable					
Step	1.	2.	3.	4.	5.	6.
1. Figural analogies	.100*	.077*	.079*	.073*	.057*	.042*
2. Raven	.138*	.087*	.057*	.059*	.074*	.017
3. Comprehension	.230*	.129*	.222*	.227*	.208*	.045*
4. Print exposure	.076*	.180*	.100*	.286*	.052*	.075*

Note. Dependent variables are as follows; 1 = Nelson–Denny vocabulary, 2 = PPVT, 3 = history and literature knowledge (NAEP), 4 = cultural and literacy test, 5 = spelling composite, and 6 = verbal fluency.

*$p < .001$.

rightly be apportioned to print exposure (hence our characterization of these analyses as conservative with regard to the effects of print exposure).

The results presented in Table 2.4 indicate that print exposure accounted for additional variance in two measures of vocabulary (the Nelson–Denny vocabulary subtest and the PPVT), two measures of general knowledge (a measure of history and literature knowledge taken from the National Assessment of Educational Progress and a cultural literacy test), spelling, and verbal fluency even after reading comprehension ability had been partialed along with nonverbal ability. In some cases, the unique variance explained was quite substantial.

In this study, our sample size was large enough to allow us to explore the consequences—in a correlational sense—of pitting general comprehension ability against print exposure as predictors of cognitive outcomes in the verbal domain. The next analysis took advantage of the fact that, although print exposure was positively correlated with Nelson–Denny comprehension performance, the relationship was far from perfect. There were individuals who, despite having modest comprehension skills, seemed to read avidly; and there were other individuals who, despite very good comprehension skills, seemed not to exercise their abilities—the so-called aliterates.

What are the cognitive correlates of a mismatch between comprehension abilities and the exercise of those abilities? To investigate this issue, our sample of adults was classified according to a median split in performance on both the Nelson–Denny comprehension subtest and a composite print exposure variable. The resulting 2 × 2 matrix revealed 82 subjects who were discrepant; 38 subjects who were low in print exposure but high in comprehension (LoPrint/HiComp); and 44 subjects who were high in print exposure but low in comprehension (HiPrint/LoComp). These two groups were then compared on all the variables in the study (see Table 2.5). Despite

TABLE 2.5
Differences Between Subjects High in Comprehension Ability but Low
in Print Exposure ($N = 38$) and Subjects Low in Comprehension
Ability but High in Print Exposure ($N = 44$)

Variable	LoPrint/HiComp	HiPrint/LoComp	$t(80)$
N–D comprehension	25.3	20.9	−11.47**
Raven matrices	10.7	9.0	−2.44*
Nelson–Denny vocabulary	15.1	14.4	−0.94
Peabody vocabulary	10.6	12.1	2.06*
History & lit (NAEP)	12.7	13.4	0.99
Cultural literacy	.396	.483	3.86**
Spelling composite	.16	−.05	−1.12
Verbal fluency	31.6	32.0	0.30

*$p < .05$. **$p < .001$.

comprehension differences favoring the LoPrint/HiComp group, as well as nonverbal cognitive abilities favoring this group (they were also higher on the Raven), LoPrint/HiComp individuals were not significantly superior on any of the other variables assessed in the study. In fact, on one measure of vocabulary (the PPVT) and one measure of general knowledge (a cultural literacy test), the HiPrint/LoComp group performed significantly better. Although inferences from these correlational analysis must be tentative, the results do suggest that low ability need not necessarily hamper the development of vocabulary and verbal knowledge as long as the individual is exposed to a lot of print.

This is the glass half full part of the story of Matthew effects in education (see Stanovich, 1986; Walberg & Tsai, 1983)—that is, the rich get richer and the poor get poorer effects. The longitudinal study previously reported was the glass half empty part. Children with higher levels of reading comprehension ability tend to read more and hence develop further their already superior comprehension skill. However, the outlier analyses presented in Table 2.5 illustrate that there may be another part of the story. These analyses show that exposure to print is efficacious regardless of one's overall level of comprehension skill. If we can break the linkage between comprehension ability and exposure, low ability individuals who do begin to read more will develop the declarative knowledge bases and lexical tools that will bootstrap further comprehension gains (see Stanovich, 1993).

In another study, we tested the idea of experiential compensation (see Stanovich, West, & Harrison, 1995) by comparing the performance of 133 college students (mean age = 19.1 years) and 49 older individuals (mean age = 79.9 years) on two general knowledge tasks, a vocabulary task, a working memory task, a syllogistic reasoning task, and several measures of exposure to print. The older individuals outperformed the college students on the measures of general knowledge and vocabulary, but did significantly poorer on the working memory and syllogistic reasoning tasks. These results were consistent with the trend in the literature for crystallized abilities (knowledge and vocabulary) to continue to grow with age and for measures of fluid ability (e.g., working memory, syllogistic reasoning) to decline with age (Baltes, 1987; Horn, 1982, 1989; Horn & Hofer, 1992). However, a series of hierarchical regression analyses indicated that when measures of exposure to print were used as control variables, the positive relationships between age and vocabulary, and age and declarative knowledge, were eliminated; in contrast, the negative relationships between age and fluid abilities were largely unattenuated. The results suggest that, in the domain of verbal abilities, print exposure helps to compensate for the normally deleterious effects of aging.

In our more recent studies, we have been examining the role of print exposure in the development of linguistic sensitivity and decontextualized thinking. The development of one of our criterion measures was motivated by the work of Olson and Astington (1990; Astington & Olson, 1990) who argued that the acquisition of certain metalinguistic and metacognitive terms is uniquely tied to literacy and experience with print. They argued that one of the ways in which literacy has an impact on thought is by offering elaborating ways for talking about talk, about thought, and about knowledge. They pointed out that the massive borrowing of vocabulary from Latin into English in the 16th and 17th centuries contained as a conspicuous part "the speech act and mental state verbs that have come to play such a large part in psychology and philosophy of mind" (Olson & Astington, 1990, p. 712).

In his recent book, *The World on Paper*, Olson (1994) illustrated how many of these mental state and speech act verbs became necessary as writers strove to represent more and more of the illocutionary force and pragmatics of oral language in text. Olson argued that "writing is largely a matter of inventing communicative devices which can be taken as explicit representations of aspects of language which are expressed non-lexically in speech and thereby bringing those aspects of linguistic structure and meaning into consciousness" (p. 110). For example, Olson argued that an orator need not say "I insist that" because he can just use an insistent tone of voice. But to make writing serve the same function that speech serves, new verbs and new concepts have to be invented—concepts such as those expressed by terms like "insist," "imply," "concede," or "infer." In short, the writer must signal intentionality and illocutionary force to the reader and the writer needs tools to do so. According to Olson, these tools are mental state and speech-act verbs (and their nominalizations) that make more fine-grained intentional distinctions. Many of these words are more complex variants of their developmentally more primitive roots "think" (e.g., infer, confirm, assume), "know" (e.g., perceive, recall, comprehend), and "say" (e.g., concede, assert, imply).

In order to investigate the link between print exposure and the acquisition of a complex mental state and speech-act lexicon, we adapted a task developed by Astington and Olson (1990) and extended by Booth and Hall (1994). The task was designed to test whether students can choose the appropriate complex variant in a particular context. In describing the task, Astington and Olson (1990) stated that "we are not interested in simply discovering whether or not a student knows a particular word—that is, in simply producing a vocabulary test. We are interested in seeing whether students can distinguish between a set of <u>related</u> terms, sometimes quite closely related terms, by choosing appropriate ones for appropriate contexts" (p. 79). Two examples of items from the mental state verbs task are presented in Table 2.6. Thirty percent of a college sample chose an alternative other than the correct one in both of these problems.

Astington and Olson (1990) demonstrated that there is a developmental trend in items such as those in Table 2.6—that is, high schoolers scored better than eighth graders and college students scored better than high school

TABLE 2.6
Examples of Items From the Mental State Verbs Task

It's Adam's birthday tomorrow. Barbara is just sneaking out of the house to buy a present
for him when he sees her and asks her where she is going. Barbara says, "We're out of
milk. I'm going to the store."
A. Barbara *means* that she is going to buy milk.
B. Barbara *concedes* that she is going to buy milk.
C. Barbara *asserts* that she's going to buy milk.
*D. Barbara *implies* that she is going to buy milk.
69.3% correct

Kate was trying to retrieve a file from her floppy disk. She was not successful. She was
very upset. "Maybe there is some problem with my computer," she thought. She took the
disk to her friend's place and tried it in his computer but the result was the same. She
thought there must be something wrong with my floppy disk.
A. Kate *suggests* that there is something wrong with her floppy disk.
B. Kate *predicts* that there is something wrong with her floppy disk.
C. Kate *implies* that there is something wrong with her floppy disk.
*D. Kate *infers* that there is something wrong with her floppy disk.
66.4% correct

---

students. However, the key question raised in Olson's (1994) analysis concerned not merely the existence of developmental trends, which could arise for a variety of reasons, but whether exposure to print was specifically linked to performance on such items. Thus, we administered a set of these items to college students who also completed a battery of other tasks. Table 2.7 presents the results from two different regression analyses in which the criterion variable was the number of mental state and speech-act verb items answered correctly on a 38-item test. In the first regression analysis, performance on the Nelson–Denny comprehension subtest accounted for 18.7% of the variance in performance on the mental state verbs task. When entered

TABLE 2.7
Hierarchical Regression With Performance on the Mental State
Verbs Task as the Criterion Variable

	R	R^2 Change	F to Enter	Beta
Nelson–Denny comp	.432	.187	31.67*	.289*
Print exposure	.532	.096	18.38*	.342*
	R	R^2 Change	F to Enter	Beta
Year	.333	.111	16.49*	.154
Grade point avg	.419	.065	10.28*	.160
Nelson–Denny comp	.540	.116	21.29*	.271*
Print exposure	.574	.037	7.17*	.231*

*$p < .01$.

second, print exposure accounted for a statistically significant 9.6% unique variance. In fact, print exposure was a more potent predictor of performance than was comprehension ability as can be inferred from the last column, which displays the beta weight in the final equation. The beta weight for print exposure was higher than that for comprehension. An alternative way of expressing this relationship is to note that comprehension accounted for 6.9% unique variance after print exposure was entered into the equation, compared with 9.6% unique variance for print exposure when the reverse ordering was employed.

The ability of print exposure to account for unique variance was subjected to a more stringent test in the next hierarchical regression analysis where two additional covariates were added. Unlike our earlier college subjects, who were largely at a similar point in their university careers, the subjects in this sample ranged from first-year freshmen to fifth-year students in an education program. Therefore, we entered year in college first into the regression equation, followed by the students' college grade point average. Together, these two variables achieved a multiple R of .419. Nelson–Denny comprehension subtest performance accounted for 11.6% additional variance when entered third. Finally, print exposure was entered and accounted for 3.7% unique variance, considerably less than that obtained when only comprehension ability was entered prior, but still statistically significant. In the final equation, only the beta weights for comprehension ability and print exposure were significant. Again we have another situation in which we may be partialing too much. Year in college is probably in part a proxy for the type of text experience that leads one to induce the subtle distinctions between the mental state verbs necessary for good performance on this task.

CONCLUSION

Many of the results in this sampling of our studies may be seen as instances of what have been termed "Matthew effects" in literacy development; educational sequences in which early and efficient acquisition of reading skill yields faster rates of growth in reading achievement and other cognitive skills—that is, rich-get-richer and poor-get-poorer effects (see Stanovich, 1986; Walberg & Tsai, 1983). For example, children who are already good comprehenders may tend to read more, thus spurring further increases in the cognitive subcomponents, vocabulary, and knowledge bases that will underlie future increases in comprehension efficiency, thus increasing the achievement differences between them and their peers who are not good comprehenders and not avid readers. Thus, free reading choices may explain part of the puzzle and the pressing social problem of widening achievement disparities between the educational haves and the have-nots (Chall, Jacobs,

& Baldwin, 1990; Dreeben & Gamoran, 1986; Snow, Barnes, Chandler, Goodman, & Hemphill, 1991; Stanovich, 1993).

This, in a sense, is the glass half empty part of the story. But perhaps there is a glass half full part as well. We tested interaction terms (that is, ability by print exposure interactions) in all of our analyses and they were almost never significant. In short, exposure to print is efficacious regardless of the level of the child's cognitive and comprehension abilities. Even children with limited comprehension skills will build vocabulary and cognitive structures through immersion in literacy activities. An encouraging message for teachers of low-achieving children is implicit here. We often despair of changing "abilities", but there is at least one partially malleable habit that will itself develop "abilities"—reading.

The results summarized here suggest that, when studying comprehension deficiencies, volume of reading experience is a variable that might increase the explanatory power of our theories. Inadequate exposure to print prevents children from building important knowledge structures such as vocabulary, metalinguistic knowledge, and general world knowledge. These knowledge sources are necessary for efficient reading comprehension at the more advanced levels. Thus, early comprehension difficulties confer a twofold disadvantage. Ongoing reading is disrupted but, in addition, the child's exposure to some of the most linguistically rich stimuli—printed texts—is restricted. These potent feedback effects from self-exposure to literacy activities need to be integrated into current cognitive theories of reading comprehension difficulties.

ACKNOWLEDGMENTS

This research was supported by grant No. 410-95-0315 from the Social Sciences and Humanities Research Council of Canada to Keith E. Stanovich and a James Madison University Program Faculty Assistance Grant to Richard F. West.

REFERENCES

Akinnaso, F. N. (1981). The consequences of literacy in pragmatic and theoretical perspectives. *Anthropology & Education Quarterly, 12,* 163–200.

Allen, L., Cipielewski, J., & Stanovich, K. E. (1992). Multiple indicators of children's reading habits and attitudes: Construct validity and cognitive correlates. *Journal of Educational Psychology, 84,* 489–503.

Anderson, R. C., & Freebody, P. (1983). Reading comprehension and the assessment and acquisition of word knowledge. In B. Huston (Ed.), *Advances in reading/language research* (Vol. 2, pp. 231–256). Greenwich, CT: JAI Press.

Anderson, R. C., & Pearson, P. D. (1984). A schema-theoretic view of basic processes in reading comprehension. In P. D. Pearson (Ed.), *Handbook of reading research* (pp. 255–291). New York: Longman.

Anderson, R. C., Wilson, P. T., & Fielding, L. G. (1988). Growth in reading and how children spend their time outside of school. *Reading Research Quarterly, 23,* 285–303.

Astington, J. W., & Olson, D. R. (1990). Metacognitive and metalinguistic language: Learning to talk about thought. *Applied Psychology: An International Review, 39,* 77–87.

Baltes, P. B. (1987). Theoretical propositions of life-span developmental psychology: On the dynamics between growth and decline. *Developmental Psychology, 23,* 611–626.

Booth, J. R., & Hall, W. S. (1994). Role of the cognitive internal state lexicon in reading comprehension. *Journal of Educational Psychology, 86,* 413–422.

Carr, T. H., & Levy, B. A. (Eds.). (1990). *Reading and its development: Component skills approaches.* San Diego: Academic Press.

Carroll, J. B., Davies, P., & Richman, B. (1971). *Word frequency book.* Boston: Houghton Mifflin.

Chall, J. S., Jacobs, V., & Baldwin, L. (1990). *The reading crisis: Why poor children fall behind.* Cambridge, MA: Harvard University Press.

Cipielewski, J., & Stanovich, K. E. (1992). Predicting growth in reading ability from children's exposure to print. *Journal of Experimental Child Psychology, 54,* 74–89.

Comstock, G., & Paik, H. (1991). *Television and the American child.* San Diego: Academic Press.

Cunningham, A. E., & Stanovich, K. E. (1991). Tracking the unique effects of print exposure in children: Associations with vocabulary, general knowledge, and spelling. *Journal of Educational Psychology, 83,* 264–274.

Cunningham, A. E., Stanovich, K. E., & Wilson, M. R. (1990). Cognitive variation in adult students differing in reading ability. In T. Carr & B. A. Levy (Eds.), *Reading and development: Component skills approaches* (pp. 129–159). San Diego: Academic Press.

Daneman, M. (1991). Individual differences in reading skills. In R. Barr, M. L. Kamil, P. Mosenthal, & P. D. Pearson (Eds.), *Handbook of reading research* (Vol. 2, pp. 512–538). New York: Longman.

Dreeben, R., & Gamoran, A. (1986). Race, instruction, and learning. *American Sociological Review, 51,* 660–669.

Gathercole, S. E., & Baddeley, A. D. (1989). Evaluation of the role of phonological STM in the development of vocabulary in children: A longitudinal study. *Journal of Memory and Language, 28,* 200–213.

Gathercole, S. E., & Baddeley, A. D. (1993). *Working memory and language.* Hove, England: Lawrence Erlbaum Associates.

Gernsbacher, M. A. (1993). Less skilled readers have less efficient suppression mechanisms. *Psychological Science, 4,* 294–298.

Glaser, R. (1984). Education and thinking: The role of knowledge. *American Psychologist, 39,* 93–104.

Goody, J. (1977). *The domestication of the savage mind.* New York: Cambridge University Press.

Goody, J. (1987). *The interface between the written and the oral.* Cambridge, England: Cambridge University Press.

Graff, H. J. (1986). The legacies of literacy: Continuities and contradictions in western society and culture. In S. de Castell, A. Luke, & K. Egan (Eds.), *Literacy, society, and schooling* (pp. 61–86). Cambridge, England: Cambridge University Press.

Graff, H. J. (1987). *The labyrinths of literacy.* London: Falmer Press.

Havelock, E. A. (1963). *Preface to Plato.* Cambridge, MA: Harvard University Press.

Havelock, E. A. (1980). The coming of literate communication to Western culture. *Journal of Communication, 30,* 90–98.

Hayes, D. P. (1988). Speaking and writing: Distinct patterns of word choice. *Journal of Memory and Language, 27,* 572–585.

Hayes, D. P., & Ahrens, M. (1988). Vocabulary simplification for children: A special case of 'motherese'?. *Journal of Child Language, 15,* 395–410.

Horn, J. L. (1982). The theory of fluid and crystallized intelligence in relation to concepts of cognitive psychology and aging in adulthood. In F. I. M. Craik & S. Trehub (Eds.), *Aging and cognitive processes* (pp. 847–870). New York: Plenum Press.

Horn, J. L. (1989). Cognitive diversity: A framework for learning. In P. Ackerman, R. Sternberg, & R. Glaser (Eds.), *Learning and individual differences* (pp. 61–116). New York: W. H. Freeman.

Horn, J. L., & Hofer, S. (1992). Major abilities and development in the adult period. In R. J. Sternberg & C. A. Berg (Eds.), *Intellectual development* (pp. 44–99). Cambridge, England: Cambridge University Press.

Huston, A., Watkins, B. A., & Kunkel, D. (1989). Public policy and children's television. *American Psychologist, 44,* 424–433.

Jackson, M., & McClelland, J. (1979). Processing determinants of reading speed. *Journal of Experimental Psychology: General, 108,* 151–181.

Just, M., & Carpenter, P. A. (1987). *The psychology of reading and language comprehension.* Boston: Allyn & Bacon.

Kaestle, C. F. (1991). *Literacy in the United States.* New Haven, CT: Yale University Press.

Kamhi, A., & Catts, H. (1989). *Reading disabilities: A developmental language perspective.* Austin: PRO-ED.

LaBerge, D., & Samuels, S. (1974). Toward a theory of automatic information processing in reading. *Cognitive Psychology, 6,* 293–323.

Lesgold, A., Resnick, L., & Hammond, K. (1985). Learning to read: A longitudinal study of word skill development in two curricula. In G. MacKinnon & T. Waller (Eds.), *Reading research: Advances in theory and practice* (Vol. 4, pp. 107–138). London: Academic Press.

Miller, G. A., & Gildea, P. M. (1987). How children learn words. *Scientific American, 257*(3), 94–99.

Nagy, W. E., & Anderson, R. C. (1984). How many words are there in printed school English? *Reading Research Quarterly, 19,* 304–330.

Nagy, W. E., & Herman, P. A. (1987). Breadth and depth of vocabulary knowledge: Implications for acquisition and instruction. In M. McKeown & M. Curtis (Eds.), *The nature of vocabulary acquisition* (pp. 19–35). Hillsdale, NJ: Lawrence Erlbaum Associates.

Oakhill, J., & Garnham, A. (1988). *Becoming a skilled reader.* Oxford, England: Basil Blackwell.

Olson, D. R. (1977). From utterance to text: The bias of language in speech and writing. *Harvard Educational Review, 47,* 257–281.

Olson, D. R. (1986). Intelligence and literacy: The relationships between intelligence and the technologies of representation and communication. In R. J. Sternberg & R. K. Wagner (Eds.), *Practical intelligence* (pp. 338–360). Cambridge, England: Cambridge University Press.

Olson, D. R. (1994). *The world on paper.* Cambridge, England: Cambridge University Press.

Olson, D. R., & Astington, J. W. (1990). Talking about text: How literacy contributes to thought. *Journal of Pragmatics, 14,* 705–721.

Ong, W. J. (1967). *The presence of the word.* Minneapolis: University of Minnesota Press.

Ong, W. J. (1982). *Orality and literacy.* London: Methuen.

Pellegrino, J. W., & Glaser, R. (1979). Cognitive correlates and components in the analysis of individual differences. In R. J. Sternberg & D. K. Detterman (Eds.), *Human intelligence: Perspectives on its theory and measurement* (pp. 61–88). Norwood, NJ: Ablex.

Perfetti, C. A. (1985). *Reading ability.* New York: Oxford University Press.

Postman, N. (1985). *Amusing ourselves to death.* New York: Viking Penguin.

Rayner, K., & Pollatsek, A. (1989). *The psychology of reading.* Englewood Cliffs, NJ: Prentice-Hall.

Rumelhart, D. E. (1980). Schemata: The building blocks of cognition. In R. J. Spiro, B. C. Bruce, & W. F. Brewer (Eds.), *Theoretical issues in reading comprehension* (pp. 245–278). Hillsdale, NJ: Lawrence Erlbaum Associates.

Siegel, L. S., & Ryan, E. B. (1988). Development of grammatical-sensitivity, phonological, and short-term memory skills in normally achieving and learning disabled children. *Developmental Psychology, 24,* 28–37.

Sincoff, J. B., & Sternberg, R. J. (1987). Two faces of verbal ability. *Intelligence, 11,* 263–276.

Smith, F. (1989). Overselling literacy. *Phi Delta Kappan, 70*(5), 353–359.

Snow, C. E., Barnes, W., Chandler, J., Goodman, I., & Hemphill, L. (1991). *Unfulfilled expectations: Home and school influences on literacy.* Cambridge, MA: Harvard University Press.

Stanovich, K. E. (1986). Matthew effects in reading: Some consequences of individual differences in the acquisition of literacy. *Reading Research Quarterly, 21,* 360–407.

Stanovich, K. E. (1991). Word recognition: Changing perspectives. In R. Barr, M. L. Kamil, P. Mosenthal, & P. D. Pearson (Eds.), *Handbook of reading research* (Vol. 2, pp. 418–452). New York: Longman.

Stanovich, K. E. (1993). Does reading make you smarter? Literacy and the development of verbal intelligence. In H. Reese (Ed.), *Advances in child development and behavior* (Vol. 24, pp. 133–180). San Diego, CA: Academic Press.

Stanovich, K. E., & Cunningham, A. E. (1991). Reading as constrained reasoning. In S. Sternberg & P. Frensch (Eds.), *Complex problem solving: Principles and mechanisms* (pp. 3–60). Hillsdale, NJ: Lawrence Erlbaum Associates.

Stanovich, K. E., & Cunningham, A. E. (1992). Studying the consequences of literacy within a literate society: The cognitive correlates of print exposure. *Memory & Cognition, 20,* 51–68.

Stanovich, K. E., & Cunningham, A. E. (1993). Where does knowledge come from? Specific associations between print exposure and information acquisition. *Journal of Educational Psychology, 85,* 211–229.

Stanovich, K. E., Cunningham, A. E., & Feeman, D. J. (1984). Intelligence, cognitive skills, and early reading progress. *Reading Research Quarterly, 19,* 278–303.

Stanovich, K. E., Nathan, R. G., & Zolman, J. E. (1988). The developmental lag hypothesis in reading: Longitudinal and matched reading-level comparisons. *Child Development, 59,* 71–86.

Stanovich, K. E., & West, R. F. (1989). Exposure to print and orthographic processing. *Reading Research Quarterly, 24,* 402–433.

Stanovich, K. E., West, R. F., & Harrison, M. (1995). Knowledge growth and maintenance across the life span: The role of print exposure. *Developmental Psychology, 31,* 811–826.

Sternberg, R. J. (1985). *Beyond IQ: A triarchic theory of human intelligence.* Cambridge, England: Cambridge University Press.

Sternberg, R. J. (1987). Most vocabulary is learned from context. In M. G. McKeown & M. E. Curtis (Eds.), *The nature of vocabulary acquisition* (pp. 89–105). Hillsdale, NJ: Lawrence Erlbaum Associates.

Sternberg, R. J. (1990). *Metaphors of mind: Conceptions of the nature of intelligence.* Cambridge, England: Cambridge University Press.

Stock, B. (1983). *The implications of literacy.* Princeton, NJ: Princeton University Press.

Vellutino, F., & Scanlon, D. (1987). Phonological coding, phonological awareness, and reading ability: Evidence from a longitudinal and experimental study. *Merrill-Palmer Quarterly, 33,* 321–363.

Walberg, H. J., & Tsai, S. (1983). Matthew effects in education. *American Educational Research Journal, 20,* 359–373.

West, R. F., Stanovich, K. E., & Mitchell, H. R. (1993). Reading in the real world and its correlates. *Reading Research Quarterly, 28,* 34–50.

Zill, N., & Winglee, M. (1990). *Who reads literature?* Cabin John, MD: Seven Locks Press.

CHAPTER THREE

Reassessing Children's Comprehension-Monitoring Skills

Ted Ruffman
Sussex University

The ability to recognize mistakes and inconsistencies in texts and to understand that they impair a reader's comprehension is clearly an important skill for a budding reader. As a result, there has been a great deal of research aimed at uncovering how well children monitor their comprehension of a text. The results of this research are not encouraging. On the whole, children, and even adults, are surprisingly bad at such tasks (e.g., August, Flavell, & Clift, 1984; Baker, 1984a; Baker & Anderson, 1982; Beal, 1990; Beal, Garrod, & Bonitatibus, 1990; Markman, 1979; Markman & Gorin, 1981; Zabrucky & Ratner, 1986).

The aim of this chapter is fourfold. In the first section, I try to clarify what is required for a child to be credited with comprehension-monitoring skills and I examine whether previous tasks have been successful in measuring this. I argue that some tasks more clearly tap comprehension monitoring than others. In the second section, I discuss why children typically do so badly on comprehension-monitoring tasks. I consider six possible sources of difficulty. These are conceptual, metacognitive, low-confidence knowledge or nascent knowledge, information-processing limitations, a predisposition to derive a conclusion, and an absence of constructive processing. I argue that for the most part, children's difficulties in comprehension-monitoring tasks do not stem from conceptual or metacognitive deficits, nascent or low-confidence knowledge, or a failure to process the text constructively. Instead, I claim that information-processing limitations are likely contributors and that a predisposition to derive a conclusion is equally or more important.

In the third section, I present empirical evidence for my claims, and in the final section, I summarize these findings and discuss the wider implications.

SECTION I: WHICH TASKS MEASURE
COMPREHENSION MONITORING?

Comprehension monitoring occurs when one reflects on whether one has understood a text. This term implies a conscious awareness of a lack of understanding, although the child need not necessarily know what has led to a failure of comprehension. In a typical comprehension-monitoring task, children are asked to read or listen to a text containing logical (internal) inconsistencies, empirical (external) inconsistencies, ambiguities, and/or long, unknown words. They are then asked if the story makes sense or if there is anything wrong with it. Although it seems to be assumed that such procedures necessarily tap children's comprehension-monitoring skills, there is reason for suspecting that this might not always be the case. Asking the child whether there is anything wrong with the text (e.g., August et al., 1984; Baker, 1984a; Baker & Anderson, 1982; Harris, Kruithof, Terwogt, & Visser, 1981) requires the child to identify the problem but not to understand that the problem impairs comprehension. Asking the child whether the story makes sense seems to more clearly tap comprehension-monitoring skills because "making sense" means "understanding" or "comprehending." Granted, children could still misinterpret this question but our research in progress suggests that children do not treat the question "Which story makes more sense?" any differently than "Which story is easier to understand?."[1]

---

[1]Ackerman and Jackson (1991) argued that questions about whether a story makes sense are less likely to tap comprehension monitoring than questions about how easy a text was to understand. This claim was based on their finding that children asked to rate how well a text made sense were less likely to acknowledge a problem than children asked to rate how well they understood a text. However, besides our own finding of no difference in performance between a "sense" question and an "understand" question, there are at least four reasons for doubting whether Ackerman and Jackson's finding is meaningful. First, Ackerman gave one group of children the sense question and another group the understand question. Hence, any differences could very well reflect different levels of understanding in the two subject groups independent of the question form. Secondly, the sense question included the instruction "Rate how good the story is" before the instruction to rate how well the story made sense. The higher ratings given in response to the sense question (apparently indicating a reluctance to criticize the story) could easily reflect children's belief that the story was good (i.e., interesting) rather than their belief that it made sense. In contrast, this instruction was omitted from the understand question. Third, Ackerman, Spiker, and Glickman (1990, Experiment 1) found no difference in performance between a sense question and an understand question (where, incidentally, there was no "Rate how good the story is" instruction in either question). Fourth, a number of studies indicate that children as young as 6 do indeed identify logical inconsistencies as failing to make sense (Jorgensen & Falmagne, 1992; Ruffman, 1993; Vosniadou, Pearson, & Rogers, 1988; Zabrucky & Ratner, 1986, pilot study).

The type of textual problem employed could also affect the extent to which a task truly measures comprehension monitoring. Empirical inconsistencies are individual propositions that violate the child's general world knowledge (e.g., most dogs meow). Logical inconsistencies occur when two propositions asserted in a text contradict one another. Either of the propositions could be right on their own but it is logically impossible for both to be correct (e.g., most people I know like corn, most people I know do not like corn). Texts with empirical inconsistencies do not seem to tap comprehension monitoring as well as texts with logical inconsistencies. For instance, consider just one example from many in the literature. Markman and Gorin (1981, p. 321) included the following empirical inconsistency in their text, "They [Koalas] sleep on the tree tops where cool, soft grass grows." It is not clear whether one who came across such a passage would truly fail to comprehend the text. Although one would probably note the inconsistency and regard it as an error made by the author, it would not likely seriously threaten comprehension (i.e., it is at least debatable whether one would be tempted to believe that grass really grows on trees). It is a different case, however, for texts containing logical inconsistencies. Consider, for example, the following logical inconsistency from a text of Markman and Gorin, "[Koalas] will sleep only high up on the tops of trees. . . . They sleep on the ground in the cool, soft grass" (p. 321). Here, it really is unclear what conclusion should follow. In the absence of background knowledge to decide which claim is correct, one's ability to comprehend (i.e., reach a definite conclusion) is seriously compromised. It seems, then, that although there could be occasions when a child's comprehension might be genuinely threatened by empirical inconsistencies, texts which contain logical inconsistencies provide a better means of assessing comprehension monitoring.

Likewise, texts containing ambiguities or long, difficult words that the child does not understand, also tap comprehension monitoring more clearly than texts containing external inconsistencies because in each case, one's ability to form a definite conclusion about what the text is about is undermined. So-called "anomalous" texts may be an intermediate case in terms of how clearly they tap comprehension monitoring. For instance, Harris et al. (1981) gave children a text entitled "The Slide in the Pool" which went as follows, "Tom and Paul stand in line. When they are at the top, Tom sits down. Paul gives him a push and there goes Tom. At the bottom, he falls on the grass." Strictly speaking, this text contains a logical inconsistency because we do not know where the slide really is. However, the title serves a unique purpose by setting the tone for the rest of the story. Because it announces that the slide is in the pool, one might be tempted to treat the claim that "Tom falls on the grass" as an empirical inconsistency rather than a logical inconsistency. This is different from an untitled story containing a logical inconsistency where each of the contradictory propositions is given more equal status.

To sum up, then, if one's aim is to measure monitoring of comprehension, then texts with logical inconsistencies, ambiguities, or unknown words will be most appropriate, as will questions about whether the story makes sense or is understandable. Texts with empirical inconsistencies used to determine whether children find anything wrong with the text do not necessarily tap comprehension monitoring (the process by which a child reflects on how a textual problem impairs a reader's comprehension), but instead may simply tap problem monitoring (the awareness that a text contains a problem). In the next section, I consider why children might have fared so badly on comprehension-monitoring tasks.

SECTION II: WHAT ACCOUNTS FOR CHILDREN'S DIFFICULTY?

One of the problems in this field is taking the results of previous research at face value. The difficulty, once again, is that children and even adults are so bad at detecting blatant flaws in texts. The suspicion raised by some authors (e.g., Garner, 1987) is that errors in texts may go unreported rather than undetected. Although many factors that make tasks more or less difficult have been identified (e.g., Nesdale, Pratt, & Tunmer, 1985; Nesdale, Tunmer, & Clover, 1985; Tunmer, Nesdale, & Pratt, 1983; Vosniadou et al., 1988), there still remains some question as to why children often fail to detect inconsistencies. Next, I consider six possible reasons for children's difficulty with comprehension monitoring tasks; conceptual, metacognitive, nascent or low-confidence knowledge, information-processing limitations, a predisposition to derive an interpretation from a text, and an absence of constructive processing.

Conceptual

One possibility for children's difficulty with comprehension-monitoring tasks is simply that their concept of what constitutes "problematic text" does not include the types of deficiencies typically included in comprehension-monitoring tasks. Is there evidence for this? Clearly not, because quite young children explicitly recognize at least empirical inconsistencies, logical inconsistencies, and ambiguities as problematic. Pea (1980) showed that even 2-year-olds can identify empirically inconsistent statements. For instance, when shown an apple, they rejected the claim that the apple was a "biscuit." Research has also shown that by 6 years of age, children develop an explicit understanding of logical consistency (Braine & Rumaine, 1981; Jorgensen & Falmagne, 1992; Ruffman, 1993; Russell, 1982; Russell & Haworth, 1987). In one study (Braine & Rumaine, 1981), a puppet claimed that there was a dog in a box whereas a second puppet claimed that there was not a dog in the box. Most 6-year-olds recognized that both statements could not be right. As for ambiguity, research has shown that by as early as 4 years of age (Ruffman, Olson, & Astington, 1991) and certainly by 6 or 7 years of age (e.g., Sodian, 1988), children recognize that an ambiguous stimulus prevents one from knowing which of two conclusions is correct. So it seems, then, that children's problems with comprehension-monitoring tasks do not stem from an inadequate concept of what text is problematic or how it limits knowledge.

Metacognitive

Typically, two aspects of metacognition are identified, knowledge of reading comprehension processes and knowledge about whether one has understood a text (comprehension monitoring). Some research suggests that good and poor comprehenders differ in terms of the first aspect (see Ehrlich, this volume for a discussion of some of this research). My concern in this chapter, however, is with the second aspect. It is possible that even though children can identify a text as problematic, they may still fail comprehension-monitoring tasks because they lack metacognitive insight into how inconsistencies impair their understanding. That is, for comprehension monitoring to take place, it is not enough that the child merely recognizes that a text is wrong in some way; the child must also understand why it is wrong, in other words, that it is difficult to understand. Put differently, a child who monitors her comprehension must be able to distinguish between when she has guessed the meaning of a text (because it is unclear), and when she truly knows the meaning (because it is clear). Claims that children can monitor their comprehension in this way would seem more plausible if it were the case that they are generally good at understanding whether they really know something or whether they are just guessing.

Research indicates that by 5 or 6 years of age, children show some understanding of the know–guess distinction (Perner, 1991). Perner asked children what they thought was in a box. Sometimes the child had seen what the experimenter had placed inside the box and sometimes the child had not seen. Perner showed that by 5 or 6 years of age, children recognized that their correct statements about the contents of the box were knowledge only when they had seen inside the box and that correct statements when they had not were guesses. Children who can make this distinction are clearly able·to reflect on their conclusions and to recognize that a conclusion by itself does not constitute knowledge.[2]

If children understand by 5 or 6 years of age that inconsistent and ambiguous text is problematic, and the difference between knowing and guessing, then one might expect them to begin succeeding on comprehension-monitoring tasks around this time. In fact, under optimal circumstances,

---

[2]Also see Cornoldi (1990) for evidence that poor comprehenders are not impaired in all aspects of comprehension monitoring.

children do so; even 4- or 5-year-olds can detect empirical inconsistencies (Nesdale et al., 1985; Peterson & Marrie, 1988), and 5-year-olds can detect about half or more of the logical inconsistencies present (Baker, 1984b). Yet the bulk of results indicate that children and even adults very frequently have difficulties on comprehension-monitoring tasks. Thus, either children's understanding of when they don't know something continues to develop and does so very slowly, and/or some other factor contributes to their difficulties.

Low Confidence or Nascent Knowledge

A third reason I consider for children's difficulty on comprehension-monitoring tasks is that they are aware that a text is problematic (e.g., contains inconsistencies) but do not report a problem because they possess only low-confidence or nascent knowledge regarding the problem. Thus, when asked if there is a problem, children recognize that there might be one but are reluctant to commit themselves. Although Garner (1987) may have had some other reason in mind, this argument is consistent with her suspicion that problems in texts may go unreported rather than undetected.

Information-Processing Limitations

Many authors appeal to some form of information-processing limitation as the source of children's difficulties on comprehension-monitoring tasks. The general claim is that the demands on either memory or working memory are too great when passages are presented in a larger text and children fail the task as a result. For instance, Vosniadou et al. (1988) claimed that children's difficulty stems from an inability to remember the logically inconsistent propositions and that if children do remember the propositions, they have little difficulty detecting the inconsistency. Likewise, Wimmer (1979) found that children's ability to detect an empirical inconsistency was a function of their ability to remember the inconsistent premise. However, Yuill and Oakhill (1991, chapters 5 & 6) claimed that rather than an inability to store information (i.e., remember the propositions), children's difficulties may be more related to the simultaneous storage and processing of information (i.e., working memory). They found that the storage capacities of poor and good comprehenders were similar but that there was a significant correlation between reading comprehension and working memory (e.g., the ability to read a series of three digit numbers and retain for subsequent recall the last digit of each). Some form of memory or working memory was also implicated in Yuill and Oakhill's finding that poor comprehenders were significantly worse than good comprehenders at detecting inconsistencies when the inconsistencies were spread out in a text rather than when they were adjacent (see also Ackerman, 1984a, 1984b; Zabrucky & Ratner, 1986).

Another finding which fits well with this hypothesis is that without training or prior instruction, children are often better at detecting empirical inconsistencies than logical inconsistencies (Baker, 1984a, 1984b; Vosniadou et al., 1988). Inconsistencies are identified by comparing a given proposition to another proposition. In the case of an empirical inconsistency, the inconsistent proposition is compared to a known fact. If children read the empirically inconsistent proposition that "The dog has seven noses," they have a well-known standard ("Dogs have one nose") against which to evaluate the claim. This standard would make the inconsistent statement stand out and appear odd. Now consider the following logically inconsistent passage: "Albert's fur was all brown and as soft as could be. All the other dogs wished they had Albert's snow white fur." In this case children have a relatively weak standard ("Albert's fur was all brown and as soft as could be") for evaluating the second (inconsistent) proposition. The standard for identifying empirical inconsistencies would be much stronger because of the amount of exposure to empirical "facts" in contrast to just introduced propositions and because of the crucial importance of keeping track of facts as veridical representations of the world. Not surprisingly, children generally do better at spotting empirical inconsistencies.

It seems, then, that there is some good evidence in favor of the claim that information-processing limitations are partially to blame for children's difficulty on comprehension-monitoring tasks. However, the claim I am pursuing in this chapter is that there is often more to children's difficulty than memory or processing problems. I argue below that a predisposition to derive a conclusion from a text may often result in textual problems being missed.

Predisposition to Derive a Conclusion

In the typical comprehension-monitoring task, the child is presented with a problematic text and is then asked if she herself thinks the text makes sense. However, it may be that children will be less likely to succeed on comprehension-monitoring tasks when they are asked about their own comprehension than when they are asked about someone else's comprehension. Evidence from tasks investigating other aspects of cognitive development suggests that when presented with a number of possible conclusions, children tend to claim that they know the conclusion even though the evidence they have is not definitive. Yet, when asked about someone else's knowledge, conclusion, or view, children acknowledge that the other person does not know the conclusion. Children's good performance when asked about another person shows that they have at least some understanding of the concept being measured. Their performance when asked about themselves suggests either that this understanding is shaky or more simply that their understanding is masked on self-tasks.

It appears that when asked about themselves, children may simply check whether they have an answer to the question. If the evidence they have readily permits a conclusion, then they offer the conclusion or answer "yes." If no answer is readily apparent, then children answer "no." This notion is similar to what Wimmer, Hogrefe, and Sodian (1988, p. 177) called an "answer check procedure" in discussing children's understanding of their own knowledge. Importantly, the procedure applies only when children are asked about their own knowledge. When asked about another person's knowledge or interpretation of a contradictory text, the child has no direct access to the person's answer so the child's assessment is more likely to be based on a careful examination of the information to which the person had access.

One good example of the self–other phenomenon comes from children's understanding of visually ambiguous stimuli. In one such task (Olson & Astington, 1987), children aged 5 to 9 years were shown two blue animals (a pig and a dog). These animals were then secretly placed behind the windows of a cardboard cut-out barn so that the color but not the shape was visible. Even at 9 years of age children claimed incorrectly to know the identity of an ambiguous animal on 41% of the trials whereas children claimed the doll would know on only 6% of such trials. One explanation for such findings is that children are embarrassed to admit that they don't know something. However, this explanation is not plausible given the outcome on another condition in Olson and Astington's study. Here, children observed a yellow patch behind a window. This patch was not simply ambiguous but was completely unknown because children had not been previously shown a yellow animal. Averaging over all age groups, children claimed to know the identity of the unknown animal on only 21% of trials whereas they claimed to know the identity of the ambiguous animal on 65% of trials. Children's relatively good performance on the condition with the unknown animal shows that they were not simply reluctant to admit ignorance. Instead, it seems that when shown a blue patch, which, as a result of previous exposure to the blue pig and dog, readily admits two possible conclusions, children answered that they knew. Because the yellow patch was unknown and could not be identified as any of the animals previously seen, the incidence of errors (claims of knowledge) was fewer. Unlike the blue patches, the yellow patch did not readily invite an inference as to what it was.

The results of Mitchell and Robinson (1990, Experiment 4) also showed that children are not simply reluctant to admit ignorance. They asked 4- to 7-year-olds questions such as, "Do you know who Murkor (an invented character) is?" Children correctly acknowledged that they did not know 94% of the time. However, when presented with a number of pictures of potential targets, children acknowledged ignorance only 72% of the time. Indeed, this result was replicated in three other experiments by Mitchell and Robinson, and a similar result was obtained in Robinson and Mitchell (1994). My interpretation of these findings is that, as in Olson and Astington (1987), the pictures more readily invited an inference as to who Murkor was so there were fewer admissions of ignorance in this condition. Once again, children were not simply reluctant to admit ignorance because they did so under certain circumstances.

There is now a considerable body of research that shows when children err, they almost always do so by incorrectly attributing knowledge rather than ignorance to themselves. For instance, similar to Olson and Astington (1987), Ruffman et al. (1991) found that children aged 4 to 6 years were significantly more likely to recognize that another person would not know what an ambiguous stimulus was than to recognize that they themselves did not know. In another study, Robinson and Robinson (1982, Experiment 1) gave 5- to 7-year-olds ambiguous messages and drawings and asked them whether they had been told or shown enough to identify the referent of the message/drawing. Despite the ambiguity of the messages and drawings, a large proportion of the children (71%) claimed that they had been shown or told enough on every one of the four trials (two drawing, two message) and only 21% consistently recognized that they had not been shown enough. Likewise, in Experiment 2, 42% of the children (aged 5 to 6 years) claimed that they had been shown or told enough on every one of the six trials (three drawing, three message) and only 25% consistently recognized that they had not been shown enough. More support comes from Horobin and Acredolo's (1989) study of ambiguity. Although they asked children to withhold judgment if unsure and to identify all possible solutions, the 7- and 9-year-olds spontaneously opted for one particular solution.

In a study on children's deductive reasoning, Bereiter, Hidi, and Dimitroff (1979) also found evidence that children tended to spontaneously opt for one conclusion. Bereiter et al. gave children assertions such as, "If it is a hot day then Judy will wear her blue skirt." They were then given clues that were either insufficient ("Blue is Judy's favorite color") or sufficient ("It was a sizzling hot day") for inferring the conclusion ("Judy will wear her blue skirt"). Children had to decide when there was sufficient information to infer the conclusion. Bereiter et al. found that grade 2 children (approximately 7 to 8 years of age) answered the question at the earliest opportunity, frequently claiming that they had sufficient information to infer the conclusion even when the clue was insufficient.

In studies of scientific reasoning, adults tended to determine whether their own hypothesis or another hypothesis is correct by carefully testing each one experimentally. In contrast, children seemed to latch on to one hypothesis as preferred and then repeatedly tried to generate evidence for this hypothesis while ignoring evidence that was inconsistent with it (Klahr, Fay, & Dunbar, 1993; Schauble, 1990).

There is also more direct evidence to suggest that a similar phenomenon may be operating within the field of text understanding. For instance, Walczyk and Hall (1989) found that cognitively "reflective" children were more likely to spot inconsistencies than cognitively "impulsive" children. This finding is at least consistent with the inference hypothesis in that impulsive children may fail because they are quick to opt for one conclusion. More evidence indicating a tendency to infer the conclusion comes from Beal (1990) and Ackerman (1992), who found that children sometimes tended to infer a conclusion when reading a text, yet, they claimed that the conclusion was explicitly mentioned in the text rather than realizing that their conclusion was formed on the basis of their own inferences. Stronger evidence still comes from Ackerman and McGraw (1991) who presented children with stories in which a conclusion was either strongly supported by two "clues" or was indeterminate because there were no clues. When instructed to try to make sense of the story (Experiment 5), children often guessed the conclusion in both the zero clue and two clue conditions, but when instructed not to guess, children's tendency to infer the conclusion was significantly reduced (e.g., by about 27% for the 7-year-olds in the zero clue stories). A similar result was also obtained by Ackerman and Jackson (1991, Experiment 3) where guessing was reduced by about 16% to 20%. Furthermore, when Ackerman and Jackson specifically asked children to acknowledge whether they knew if a particular conclusion was true (Experiment 2) rather than simply allowing them to agree or disagree with the conclusion, the 7-year-olds did so 35% of the time and the 9-year-olds did so 56% of the time. Thus, guessing was reduced although not eliminated, as there was a sizable proportion of children in all experiments who continued to guess.

In sum, there is considerable evidence that when given a number of possible conclusions, children answer questions about their own knowledge by guessing the answer. This may occur because children check whether they have an answer. If a conclusion is readily suggested by the information at hand, they claim knowledge and opt for a preferred conclusion, even when the information permits more than one conclusion. In contrast, when assessing whether another person will know, the child has no direct access to the other person's conclusion so that their assessment is more likely to be based on the information accessible to the other person. Asking the child about whether another person would know may consequently reveal understanding that is not typically apparent. Because the question in a comprehension-monitoring experiment ("Does the story make sense?") has to do with whether the text is sufficiently clear that one could know (rather than guess) the conclusion, the self–other difference is relevant here as well.

An Absence of Constructive Processing

Constructive processing consists of efforts to build a mental model of the text by connecting the individual propositions together as one reads. Markman (1977, 1979) claimed that children might fail to detect inconsistencies in texts because they do not actively engage in constructive processing when reading the text. However, Harris et al. (1981) challenged this claim.

Recall that Harris et al. (1981) gave one group of children texts where the title was inconsistent with the fourth line. For instance, the title of one text was, "The slide in the swimming pool" and the text was as follows: 1. Tom and Paul stand in line. 2. When they are at the top, Tom sits down. 3. Paul gives him a push and there goes Tom. 4. At the bottom, he falls on the grass, and so forth. A second group of children was given the identical text but with a title that was consistent with the text ("The slide in the playground"). Harris et al. found that although the 11-year-olds were significantly better than the 8-year-olds at explicitly recognizing which line did not fit with the other lines, both groups of children spent more time reading the fourth line when it was inconsistent with the title than when it was consistent. The slower reading time on inconsistent lines led Harris et al. to conclude that the 8-year-olds processed the text constructively as they read it even if they were not able to explicitly identify problems. Harris et al. argued that the textual inconsistency seemed to cause an internal signal that led children to either reread the inconsistent line or to check the earlier text, even if they were not good at monitoring this signal. Subsequent research (August et al., 1984; Zabrucky & Ratner, 1986) using similar methodology was consistent with the work of Harris et al.

However, these studies are subject to limitations that threaten claims that children process a text constructively even when they do not spot inconsistencies. For instance, researchers have not treated children who fail the question about whether the story makes sense as independent from children who pass this measure. Recall that the strategy in previous research has been to (a) test two groups of children (e.g., 8- and 11-year-olds) and to show that the older children were significantly more likely to explicitly identify the inconsistent text as problematic, but that (b) the two groups do not differ in terms of reading time on this text. The problem with inferring constructive processing from such results in the absence of comprehension monitoring is that in each study, there was a substantial proportion of children in the younger group who recognized that the story did not make sense. As but one example of this, in Experiment 2 of Harris et al., 14 of 36 (38.9%) younger children showed at least some understanding that the story did not make sense (i.e., claimed that there was a line that did not fit in with the rest of the story). If so many of the younger group actually recognized that there was a problem with the text, then it is unclear that the younger group was engaging in constructive processing in the absence of comprehension monitoring. In other words, the slower reading times for the overall group may have been due exclusively to the children who recognized that the story did not make sense, and it is possible that children who failed this measure showed no reading time effect whatsoever.

The assumption followed by previous researchers when employing this strategy is that if the reading time effect for younger children was due to children recognizing the textual problem, then the effect should have been larger for the older children because more of these children would have spotted the problem. However, such an argument relies on the questionable assumption that the reading time effect for individual children would be identical in both the younger and older age groups. An older child, like an adult, might show much less in the way of a reading time effect because the inconsistency is so obvious there is no need to pause when it is encountered. In contrast, younger children might be sensitive to some kind of problem but would have to pause to determine what exactly is wrong and this would create longer individual reading times. If claims about constructive processing in the absence of comprehension monitoring are to be taken seriously, then an independent examination of the children who fail to monitor their comprehension is necessary, as is a demonstration of a reading time effect within this group. (See Ruffman, 1995, for other shortcomings of previous research.)

In the next section I discuss some of our own empirical evidence which addresses why children fail comprehension-monitoring tasks. The experiments examine several of the potential causes discussed earlier, including low-confidence or nascent knowledge, reluctance to admit a problem, information-processing limitations, a predisposition to derive a single conclusion, and an absence of constructive processing.

SECTION III: EMPIRICAL EVIDENCE FOR DIFFICULTIES IN COMPREHENSION MONITORING

In the first part of this section, I discuss two experiments drawn from Ruffman (1995) and then two experiments drawn from Ruffman, Billins, and White (1995). In Experiment 1, we examined whether children's problem on comprehension-monitoring tasks was due to low-confidence knowledge or nascent knowledge. In a standard comprehension-monitoring task, children are asked to listen to or read a text and are then asked if the text makes sense. In Experiment 1, this standard (one story) method was contrasted with a two story method where children were presented with two texts. The two texts were both five lines long and were identical except for the second line. In one story, the fourth line contradicted the second line whereas in the other story, the fourth line was consistent with the second line. Children read through both texts and were then asked which one made more sense. Whereas the one story task invited children to repair the text and not report a problem, the two story task compelled children to acknowledge that there was a problem, thereby making it more likely that a child who possessed nascent or low-confidence knowledge would succeed. If the child really understood that there was a problem, then she should be able to identify the story that did not make sense.

Low-Confidence Knowledge

Experiment 1

The subjects were forty 8-year-olds drawn from two classrooms in a small school. Twenty children were randomly assigned to either the standard one story condition (mean age: 8–6) or the two story condition (mean age: 8–4). The stories dealt with four topics, (a) the color of Albert the dog's fur, (b) whether Floppy the rabbit ever went out of the house, (c) whether most people like to eat corn, and (d) where Koalas sleep. The last story was new whereas the other stories were adapted from previous studies (Baker, 1984b; Markman & Gorin, 1981). The first two stories are included in Table 3.1. Children in the one story condition received the consistent version of two stories and the inconsistent version of the other two stories. Children in the two story condition received all four pairs of stories; a pair included both the consistent and inconsistent version of a story. The order of stories (consistent vs. inconsistent) was counterbalanced. For children who received the one story task, the version of a particular story was also counterbalanced (e.g., half the children received the consistent version of the Albert the dog story and half received the inconsistent version).

At the outset, the experimenter told children in the one story condition that some stories would make sense and some would not. Likewise, in the two story condition children were told that only one of the stories in each

TABLE 3.1
The Stories of Experiment 1

Albert:
1. Once there was a dog named Albert.
2. His fur was all shiny and as soft as could be. (Consistent)
2. His fur was all brown and as soft as could be. (Inconsistent)
3. He was very fluffy and had a beautiful tail.
4. All the other dogs wished they had his snow white fur.
5. Albert liked to play in Farmer Smith's garden.

Floppy:
1. Jack has a rabbit called Floppy.
2. Jack has had Floppy for one year now. (Consistent)
2. Floppy never goes out of the house. (Inconsistent)
3. Jack feeds Floppy lettuce and carrots.
4. Every day Floppy plays in the park and grass.
5. Jack really likes Floppy.

pair would make sense. Children read the stories on a portable computer so that a measure of reading time could be obtained (see the section on Constructive Processing below). The experimenter told the child how to read a story on the computer and then gave the child a practice story. The experimenter also told the child that she should try not to read as quickly as possible, but instead, should be sure that she understood the story so she could say whether it made sense. The child had to press the return key for the first line to appear. Further lines appeared with each subsequent key press. For example, the second key press resulted in the first line remaining on the screen and the second line appearing beneath. Eventually the whole story was visible on the screen so that the child could inspect it and detect inconsistencies. To encourage reading for understanding, children were instructed to read silently to themselves. Once a child had finished reading, the experimenter asked the makes sense question. In the one story condition this was, "Did the story make sense?" and in the two story condition, it was "Which story made more sense?"

Table 3.2 includes children's performance on the one story and two story tasks. The results suggests a slightly better performance in the two story condition. However, the results must be viewed with caution as the one story task was included primarily as a reference point to compare the two story task with the kind of task used in previous research and statistical comparisons between the one and two story tasks are subject to criticism. For instance, one could compare performance on the two inconsistent stories of the one story task with the performance on either (a) the first two story pairs of the two story task a child received, or (b) the last two such story pairs. If so, then the two story task appears to have been easier though not significantly so (Kolmogorov-Smirnov Test: $D_{16,16} = 48$, both p's > .20). Yet it is possible that had there been more subjects and therefore more statistical power, this result might have

TABLE 3.2
Number and Percentage of Children Correct on the Stories of Experiment 1

	One Story Task					
	Consistent			Inconsistent		
Number stories correct	0	1	2	0	1	2
	—	6	14	5	7	8
		85%			58%	
	Two Story Task					
	Conditions			Counterbalanced		
Number stories correct	0	1	2	3	4	
	1	2	4	5	8	
			71%			

attained significance. Perhaps the most sensible thing that can be said about these findings is that to avoid possible underestimations of children's understanding, the two story task is the more appropriate measure of comprehension monitoring.

The most important point to note about these findings might be that performance on the two story task was still well below ceiling. In this task, chance responding would lead to answering 50% of the test questions correctly. Thus, if many of the children were merely guessing but a few children really understood which story did not make sense, the percentage of correct responding should be above 50%. That the percentage was only 71% and well below ceiling is not very compelling evidence for claiming that 8-year-olds (as a group) are always aware of inconsistencies and how they impair a text's comprehensibility. The best evidence for such awareness would have been if the children had answered correctly on all four story pairs; yet only 8 children (45%) did this.

To sum up, we found little evidence for the claim that most children who fail one story tasks are aware of inconsistencies in texts but do not report them because their knowledge is fragile or held with limited confidence. Nor was there evidence for the claim that children are simply reluctant to admit that they don't understand a text. In the two story task of Experiment 1, children were compelled to accept that one story contained a problem, yet they still could not reliably identify the story that made better sense. If children really understood where the problem was, then they should have been able to identify it in these circumstances; however, many inconsistencies went unidentified.

However, before concluding that children failed the two story task due to genuine comprehension-monitoring problems, we found it necessary to rule out one other explanation for their difficulty on this task. It could be that children's difficulty on the two story task stemmed from a limitation of memory. In other words, when reading through the two stories, they may have been perfectly aware which one made sense. Yet, when subsequently asked the test question, they may have had difficulty remembering back to which story had struck them as more sensible. We investigated this possibility in Experiment 2. A second purpose of Experiment 2 was to examine the effect of other memory limitations on children's performance.

Experiment 2

Experimental Design. Children were given four different kinds of story pairs all within the framework of the two story task. The first type of story pair was identical to the story pairs of the two story task of Experiment 1. The two stories were five lines long. One of the stories made sense and the other did not because of a logical inconsistency (the fourth line contradicted the second line). Children read through each story once and were then asked which one made more sense. This story pair was called the long one-exposure pair, because each story was five lines long and because children read through each story only once (see Table 3.3).

Secondly, there was a control (empirical inconsistency) story pair. Both stories were five lines long with one story being consistent. Children read through each story once. However, rather than containing a logical (internal) inconsistency, one of the stories contained an empirical (external) inconsistency. Here, the second line conflicted with something that children knew to be true rather than with just another line in the story. For instance, in the inconsistent story about Albert the dog, the second line asserted that Albert had seven noses. Studies have shown that without training or prior instruction, children often are better at detecting empirical inconsistencies than logical inconsistencies (e.g., Baker, 1984a, 1984b; Vosniadou et al., 1988). Therefore, the empirical inconsistency story pair provided a good means of testing whether children's difficulty on the long one-exposure story pair was due to memory limitations. If children recognized which story did not make sense when given the empirical inconsistency story pair, then it would suggest that their difficulty on the long one-exposure story pair was not due to awareness at the time of reading and subsequent forgetting. That is, it would be clear that children could read two stories, store information about which story did not make sense, and then retrieve this information when asked the test question.

Remembering which of two stories did not make sense is a memory problem specifically tied to the two story task. However, memory limitations could account for children's difficulties in other ways (see also the two chapters by Cornoldi, De Beni, & Pazzaglia and by Oakhill & Yuill, this volume). That is, there are ways in which memory limitations could hamper children's ability to detect an inconsistency within a single story. The remaining two story pairs were aimed at determining whether such limitations could hinder a child's performance within a single story, despite evidence from the

TABLE 3.3
Experiment 2: Two Story Tasks

Condition	Consistency	# Lines	# Readings	Availability
Long one-exposure	1 consistent/ 1 inconsistent (logical)	5	1	no
Short one-exposure	1 consistent/ 1 inconsistent (logical)	2	1	no
Empirical inconsistency	1 consistent/ 1 inconsistent (external)	5	1	no
Long two-exposure	1 consistent/ 1 inconsistent (logical)	5	2	yes

child's performance on the empirical inconsistency stories that forgetting across two stories was not the source of their difficulty on the two story tasks. One potentially important limitation not specific to the two story task concerns the strength with which the contradictory propositions are represented in the child's mind. It is plausible that a second reading through each story and the ability to compare and contrast the two stories would improve a child's memory for the inconsistent propositions and subsequently, their ability to detect which story made sense. Another way memory limitations could have an effect is that a child might fail to detect a logical inconsistency because the two inconsistent sentences do not follow directly after one another (i.e., there is an intervening sentence). Recall that Ackerman (1984a, 1984b), Yuill and Oakhill (1991, chapter 6), and Zabrucky and Ratner (1986) found that children were better at spotting inconsistencies when they were adjacent. This was presumably because the gap in time or the intervening information weakened children's memory for the earlier proposition making it less likely that they would notice the contradiction with the inconsistent proposition. Once again, neither of these factors is specific to the two story paradigm; they could also affect children's performance when reading a single story.

The remaining two story pairs were included to examine each of these possibilities. In the long two-exposures story pairs, the stories were again five lines long and one story contained a logical inconsistency. Children read through each story twice before answering the test question. Furthermore, in this condition children had both stories available to compare and contrast when making their decision (each story being presented on a separate portable computer). In the short one-exposure story pair, the first, third, and fifth sentences were excluded leaving only two lines per story (i.e., two logically consistent or two contradictory lines). Children read through each story once and were then asked the test question.

If children still had problems on the long two-exposures and short one-exposure tasks, then an appeal to memory limitations (i.e., weak memory for the inconsistent propositions) as the cause of their difficulty on the long one-exposure task would be less straightforward. Given their good performance at detecting logical inconsistencies in isolation (see section II), memory limitations in a broad sense might still have something to do with children's difficulty in that unlimited study time might allow a sufficiently strong memory for the inconsistent propositions that the child would pick up the contradiction eventually. Nevertheless, difficulty on these tasks would suggest that some other factor contributed to children missing the inconsistency.

Participants. The subjects in Experiment 2 were sixty-nine 7- and 8-year-olds (mean age = 8-3 [8 years, 3 months]). The stories used in Experiment 2 were identical to those from Experiment 1, except of course that three lines were excluded in the case of the short one-exposure story pair. Each child read through all four story pairs and for each pair was asked,

"Which story made more sense?" The order of story types (long one-exposure, long two-exposures, etc.) and of stories within a story type (consistent vs. inconsistent) was counterbalanced.

Table 3.4 includes children's performance on the four types of story pairs. For the most part, children's problem was not in forgetting across the two stories because they did quite well on the empirical inconsistency pair (91% correct). Children's performance on the empirical inconsistency pair was examined relative to that on the long one-exposure pair because these two conditions were comparable; in each, the stories were five lines long and were repeated once. There were 16 children who passed the empirical inconsistency pair but not the long one-exposure pair and only four who obtained the opposite pattern [McNemar's Test: $\chi^2(1, n = 20) = 7.20, p < .01$].

Recall that Experiment 2 was also intended to examine two other ways in which memory limitations could hinder children's performance. These were insufficient study time leading to poor memory for the contradictory propositions, and too much of a gap between the contradictory propositions, again leading to poor memory. I pointed out earlier that neither of these factors is specific to the two story paradigm and they could have a similar effect when a child reads a single story. The long two-exposures story pairs and the short one-exposure story pairs were designed to test these factors. Table 3.4 shows that children did slightly better on these two story pairs than on the long one-exposure pair, yet in neither case was performance significantly better. The fact that both effects are in the same direction is consistent with the idea that memory limitations sometimes affect children's comprehension-monitoring abilities, but in neither instance is the case sufficiently strong to make clear claims. If such memory limitations do have an effect, then it may be either that they do not hamper all children (see Cornoldi, De Beni, & Pazzaglia, this volume), or that their effects can be reasonably weak. Regardless, the results suggest that there is more to children's difficulties.

In sum, Experiments 1 and 2 tested the idea that children are aware of inconsistencies but do not report problems because they have nascent or low-confidence knowledge. We found no evidence for such claims. In Experiment 3, we examined another possibility; that children fail comprehen-

TABLE 3.4
Number and Percentage of Children Correct
on the Story Pairs From Experiment 2

	Number/Percentage
Long one-exposure	51 (74)
External inconsistency	63 (91)
Long two-exposures	56 (81)
Short one-exposure	56 (81)

Note. $N = 69$.

sion-monitoring tasks because they are predisposed to opt for one conclusion as preferred.

Experiment 3

I previously suggested that when children are given a number of possible conclusions, they may answer questions about their own knowledge by checking on whether they have an answer. If a conclusion is readily suggested by a text, they opt for a preferred conclusion, even when more than one conclusion is possible. In Experiment 3, we examined the self–other contrast described earlier as a means of offsetting this tendency. That is, whereas in a typical comprehension-monitoring task children are asked about their own understanding of a text, in Experiment 3 we also asked the child whether the text would make sense to another person. Because the child has no direct access to the other person's answer, questions about another person's interpretation of a text are more likely to result in the child basing her answer on a careful analysis of the text's features and subsequent recognition that the text would not make sense.

Sixty-five children in grades 1, 2, and 3 of a local primary school were tested. These children were divided into four age groups. There were thirteen 5-year-olds (M = 5-7), twenty 6-year-olds (M = 6-7), twenty 7-year-olds (M = 7-4), and twelve 8-year-olds (M = 8-5). There were four stories about (a) whether a rabbit goes out of the house, (b) how Jane gets home from school, (c) how Mr. Smith gets to work, and (d) what Sally got for her birthday. As an example, Table 3.5 includes the first two stories. There was a consistent and an inconsistent version of each story. Each child received the consistent version of two stories and the inconsistent version of the other two stories. The order of stories (consistent vs. inconsistent) was counterbalanced, as

TABLE 3.5
The Stories From Experiment 3

Floppy:

1. Jack has a rabbit called Floppy.
2. When Jack gets home from school he lets Floppy run all around the garden.
3. Jack feeds Floppy lettuce and carrots.
4. Floppy likes to play in the garden but is afraid of the dog next door. (Consistent)
4. Floppy never goes out of his cage into the garden. (Inconsistent)

Jane:

1. Jane finishes school at 3:30 in the afternoon.
2. Jane's mom always comes to collect her from school in the car.
3. Jane has a best friend called Katy.
4. Sometimes Katy comes with Jane and Jane's mom in the car. (Consistent)
4. Jane always walks home from school in the afternoon. (Inconsistent)

was the order in which children were asked about both their own and the doll's interpretation.

To tap children's understanding of how another person would interpret the stories, we used a doll named "Sarah." An enormous body of research into children's "theory of mind" has shown that children readily accept the pretend premise that a doll is a person, and Sodian and Wimmer (1987) showed that there was no difference between children's assessments of a doll's knowledge versus a real person's knowledge. Because decoding abilities vary widely in the four age groups studied, children's listening rather than reading comprehension was examined. At the beginning of the session the child was told that some of the stories made sense and some did not. The experimenter read each story twice. For two stories (one consistent, one inconsistent), the experimenter read the story to the child alone and asked her whether it made sense ("Would you say that this story made sense or not?"). For the other two stories (one consistent, one inconsistent), the experimenter read the stories to the child and doll and asked whether it made sense to the doll ("Would Sarah say that this story made sense or not?").

Table 3.6 includes children's performance over both the consistent and inconsistent stories. The correct answer was to say "yes" when asked if the consistent story made sense (to both the self- and doll question), and "no" when asked if the inconsistent story made sense (to both the self- and doll question). The children who obtained this answer pattern are included in the first column of the self and doll sections of Table 3.6. The children who erred are included in the remaining three columns for each section. Only by 8 years of age were the majority of children correct on these questions when asked about themselves. However, when asked about the doll, even the 6- and 7-year-olds showed a good understanding of which story made sense. Indeed, children were significantly better on the question about the doll than they were on the question about themselves. There were 18 children who were correct on the makes sense question over both the consistent and inconsistent stories when asked about the doll, but who erred at least once when asked about themselves. In contrast, there were only 6 children who obtained the opposite pattern (Sign Test: $p < .03$).

The nature of children's errors is also of interest. I claimed that when asked about their own knowledge, children check whether they have an interpretation. If a text readily permits some kind of interpretation they claim knowledge (or that the text makes sense). If my claim was right, then children's errors should have been mostly overattributions of knowledge to themselves. In other words, children should have said yes to the makes sense question for both the consistent and inconsistent stories because in each case the child would have been able to infer a conclusion (i.e., an inconsistent text readily provides an interpretation, in fact, two interpretations). In contrast, this claim gave no cause for thinking that children should have overattributed knowledge to the doll because the child did not have

TABLE 3.6

Children's Answers to the "Makes Sense" Question for the Consistent and Inconsistent Stories in Experiment 3

	Self				Doll			
Age Group	Both Correct: Consis - Y Incons - N	Consistent Only Correct: Consis - Y Incons - Y	Inconsistent Only Correct: Consis - N Incons - N	Both Incorrect: Consis - N Incons - Y	Both Correct: Consis - Y Incons - N	Consistent Only Correct: Consis - Y Incons - Y	Inconsistent Only Correct: Consis - N Incons - N	Both Incorrect: Consis - N Incons - Y
5-year-olds (n = 13)	5 (38)	5 (38)	1 (8)	2 (15)	5 (38)	3 (23)	4 (31)	1 (8)
6-year-olds (n = 20)	8 (40)	8 (40)	3 (15)	1 (5)	16 (80)	—	2 (10)	2 (10)
7-year-olds (n = 20)	11 (55)	4 (20)	2 (10)	3 (15)	15 (75)	2 (10)	1 (5)	2 (10)
8-year-olds (n = 12)	10 (83)	1 (8)	—	1 (8)	10 (83)	—	1 (8)	1 (8)
	34 (52)	18 (28)	6 (9)	7 (11)	46 (71)	5 (8)	8 (12)	6 (9)

Note. Y = "yes," N = "no." Percentages are in brackets.

direct access to the doll's conclusion. Table 3.5 includes the errors children made on the questions for self and the doll. As expected, the predominant error when asked about themselves was to say that both stories made sense (column 2 of the self section), and this tendency was significantly different than what would have been expected by chance, $\chi^2(2, n = 33) = 8.58$, $p <$ .02. In contrast, Table 3.5 shows that children did not tend to overattribute knowledge to the doll (column 2 of the doll section). Another way to look at this is to directly compare children's errors on the questions for both self and the doll. Of particular interest again are children who obtained the "Y, Y" answer pattern (overattributed knowledge). There were 18 children who overattributed knowledge to themselves but not to the doll and only 5 who obtained the opposite pattern [McNemar's Test: $\chi^2(1, n = 23) = 6.86$, $p <$ .01].

In sum, Experiment 3 suggests that younger children's comprehension-monitoring abilities can be masked by asking them whether they think a text makes sense (the typical measure in previous research). Six- and 7-year-old children show little understanding of the comprehensibility of a text when asked about themselves but nevertheless show a good understanding when asked about someone else. I suggested that when children are asked about their own understanding of a text they claim to know whenever the text readily permits an answer. Inconsistent texts readily provide children with an interpretation and so they claim to understand. In contrast, when children are asked about another person, they are more likely to answer by evaluating the information the person has access to because the child has no direct access to another person's interpretation of a text. Thus, if children have any awareness of textual inconsistencies, it is more likely to be revealed when they are asked about another person rather than themselves. An alternative interpretation is that children are simply unwilling to admit that the text does not make sense when asked about themselves. Ultimately, it remains for future research to determine which interpretation is correct, or at least which contributes more to children's performance. Nevertheless, given children's willingness to admit ignorance in certain conditions of Olson and Astington (1987), Mitchell and Robinson (1990), and Robinson and Mitchell (1994) and the accumulating body of evidence that suggests a predisposition to opt for one conclusion as preferred, there is some suggestion that they are not simply reluctant to admit ignorance.

The results of Experiment 3 are notable for a second reason as well because they indicated unusually good performance by the 8-year-olds on the questions about the self. Recall that performance on comprehension-monitoring tasks by 8-year-olds is typically well below perfect. A likely explanation for the 8-year-olds' success in Experiment 3 is simply that the inconsistencies in the stories of Experiment 3 were more obvious than in the stories of Experiments 1 and 2 and in previous research.

In Experiment 4, we used a different means to test the idea that children's difficulty on comprehension-monitoring tasks stems from a predisposition to derive a conclusion from texts. I argued that consistent and inconsistent texts both readily provide an interpretation; that for a child, inconsistent texts might provide more in this way because they offer two interpretations rather than just one. If so, children might claim that an inconsistent text is actually clearer than a consistent text. In contrast, children should recognize that a consistent text which offers a clear conclusion regarding some matter is a clearer guide than one which offers no conclusion. In Experiment 4, we tested this possibility.

Experiment 4

Asking children to judge between a text containing no information about a topic and a text containing some (consistent) information is analogous to the condition from Olson and Astington (1987) in which children were asked whether they knew the identity of the "unknown" animal. Recall that children observed a yellow patch in one of the windows. Because children had not previously been shown a yellow animal, the patch did not invite conclusions as readily as a blue patch that could be identified as either of the blue animals the child had seen before. Similarly, the uninformative text would not invite conclusions as readily as an inconsistent text in which two possible conclusions are explicitly offered. If children's claims of knowledge or understanding hinge on how readily a text permits an answer, then they should find it much easier to identify the uninformative text as unclear than to identify the inconsistent text as unclear.

The subjects were sixteen 6- to 7-year-olds ($M = 6$-10) and sixteen 8- to 9-year-olds ($M = 9$-0). Subjects spoke English as their first language, and were from an elementary school serving a middle-class, predominantly white area of rural Britain. There were six basic stories (i.e., six types of story content). Two stories were based on the Albert and Koala stories of Experiments 1 and 2, and four were new stories. Furthermore, there were three versions of each story; inconsistent, consistent, and no information. Table 3.7 includes the three versions of the "school" story. A given child received either the consistent and no information versions or the consistent and inconsistent versions of each story. In total, each child received three consistent–no information story pairs and three consistent–inconsistent story pairs covering the six different stories. After hearing the two versions of a particular story, the child was asked which story was the clearest about some fact (e.g., "Which story was the most clear about how Mary gets to school?"), and why ("Why was that one clearer?"). The order of stories was counterbalanced as was the order in which the child received the versions and which story each version was paired with. Prior to reading the stories to the child, the experimenter cautioned that one story would be clearer than the other. For the younger children the experimenter

TABLE 3.7
The "School" Stories of Experiment 4

Inconsistent

---

1. Sarah goes to a big school.
2. Sarah's mom drives Sarah to school every day.
3. Most days, Sarah felt tired from her long walk to school.

Consistent

---

1. Sarah goes to a big school.
2. Sarah's mom helps Sarah with her homework.
3. Most days, Sarah felt tired from her long walk to school.

No Information

---

1. Sarah goes to a big school.
2. Sarah's mom helps Sarah with her homework.
3. Most days, Sarah liked school.

---

read the stories through once and then again. The older group read the stories twice themselves.

Table 3.8 includes children's performance on the consistent–inconsistent and consistent–no information story pairs. Their performance on the consistent–inconsistent story pair was about as expected with the younger children correctly identifying the consistent story as clearer 44% of the time and the older children doing so 54% of the time. Their performance on the consistent–no information pair was markedly better and near ceiling in both groups. Indeed, children in both age groups performed significantly better on the consistent–no information pair than on the consistent–inconsistent pair [younger children: $F(1, 15) = 9.29$, $p < .01$; older children: $F(1, 15) = 11.90$, $p < .01$]. Recall that this result was expected if children's claims of knowledge or understanding hinged on how readily a text permitted an answer because, in a sense, the inconsistent text more readily permitted an answer than either the consistent or no information text (i.e., it offers two conclusions rather than one or none).

Furthermore, if this was the reason for children's answers, then one would expect some converging evidence in their justifications for why the inconsis-

TABLE 3.8
Number and Percentage of Correct Responses
on the Story Pairs of Experiment 4

	Consistent–No Information					Consistent–Inconsistent				
	0	1	2	3	%	0	1	2	3	%
6- to 7-year-olds	—	2	4	10	83	4	6	3	3	44
8- to 9-year-olds	—	—	3	13	94	4	3	4	5	54

tent story was clearer. Of particular interest would be justifications where children claimed the inconsistent story said more about a topic (e.g., how Sarah gets to school) than the consistent story. In Experiment 4, children did this either explicitly (e.g., " 'Cuz [sic] this one says more"; " 'Cuz [sic] it says 'walks' in both stories but 'drives' here") or implicitly by only mentioning the extra proposition (e.g., " 'Cuz [sic] it says 'her mum [sic] drives' "). Of the 27 occasions on which the younger children claimed the inconsistent story was clearer, they offered justifications of this nature 19 times (70.4%). Of the 22 occasions on which the older children did so, they offered such justifications 17 times (77.3%). Nine of the 13 (69.2%) younger children who erred one or more times on a consistent–inconsistent story pair offered at least one such justification as did 9 of 11 (81.8%) older children. In other words, for many children, clarity and presumably comprehensibility were determined by the extent to which a text offered a conclusion rather than by the text's internal properties.

Besides providing support for this hypothesis, the results are notable in two other ways. First, like Experiment 3, they provide evidence of comprehension monitoring; children who fail to spot logical inconsistencies nevertheless understand something about a text's comprehensibility because they understand that a text which contains no information is less clear than a text which contains some (consistent) information. Secondly, they are important because they provide further evidence that children's difficulty in spotting logical inconsistencies on the two story task is not due to their being aware of the problem at the time of reading (or hearing) the texts and subsequently forgetting. In other words, memory does not seem to be the problem because children had no problem remembering across the two stories of the consistent–no information story pair.

Constructive Processing

In this part of Section III, I consider whether children engage in constructive processing of a text in the absence of comprehension monitoring. Recall that constructive processing consists of efforts to build a mental model of the text by connecting the individual propositions together as one reads. I argued that previous findings suggesting that children do constructively process a text in the absence of comprehension monitoring are suspect, for one reason, because children who failed to monitor their comprehension were not treated independently from children who did monitor their comprehension.

To examine this issue, we kept track of reading time in the two story tasks in Experiments 1 and 2. Recall that the stories in the two story condition were identical except for the second line. In one story, the fourth line contradicted the second line whereas in the other story, the fourth line was consistent. Our interest was in comparing reading time on the fourth line of each story as a percentage of reading time on lines 1, 3, 4, and 5 of the respective stories. That is, lines 1, 3, 4 and 5 were repeated in the consistent and inconsistent stories with only line 2 differing. Because line 2 was different across the consistent and inconsistent stories, it could lead to a misleading percentage when comparing the two stories and was excluded from the calculations. The question was whether children who were incorrect when asked which story made more sense would spend relatively more time on the fourth line of the inconsistent story than on the fourth line of the consistent story. First, I discuss the reading times from Experiment 1 and then I move on to Experiment 2.

In Experiment 1, children were correct on the "Which story made more sense?" question on 57 of the 80 story pairs (71.3% correct). Once the percentage reading times had been calculated for each story, a difference score was created by subtracting the percentage of time spent on the fourth line of the consistent story from the percentage of time spent on the fourth line of the inconsistent story. A difference score greater than zero meant that, proportionally, children spent more time on the inconsistent line than on the consistent line. To ensure that extreme scores did not exert undue influence we then checked for the presence of outliers (more than 3 standard deviations from the mean difference score). One outlier was identified (a positive difference score) and was eliminated from subsequent analyses.

Table 3.9 lists the mean percentage of time spent reading the fourth line of both the consistent and inconsistent stories in Experiment 1. The percentages for the consistent and inconsistent stories were compared with a 2 (story order) × 2 (percentage on consistent and inconsistent stories) analysis of variance. Story order (whether the child read the consistent or inconsistent story first)

TABLE 3.9

Mean Percentage of Time Spent Reading the Fourth Line of the Consistent and Inconsistent Stories in Experiments 1 and 2

	Percentage for Consistent Story	Percentage for Inconsistent Story	Difference (Inconsistent–Consistent)
Experiment 1:			
All 79 story pairs	28.05 (7.37)	31.59 (8.50)	3.54
Incorrect on makes sense question (23 occasions)	27.67 (6.98)	32.29 (11.09)	4.62
Correct on makes sense question (56 occasions)	28.20 (7.52)	31.30 (7.27)	3.10
Experiment 2 (long one-exposure and long two-exposure):			
All 135 story pairs	30.88 (9.28)	32.56 (8.80)	1.68
Incorrect on makes sense question (30 occasions)	29.17 (7.87)	32.19 (8.03)	3.02
Correct on makes sense question (105 occasions)	31.36 (9.51)	32.66 (8.83)	1.30

Note. Standard deviations are in brackets

was a between-cases variable whereas the percentage was of course a within-cases variable. Three separate analyses were carried out, one for all 79 stories, one for the 23 occasions where children failed the makes sense question, and one for the 56 occasions where children passed this question. Over all 79 stories, the main effect for percentage reading time was highly significant, $F(1, 77) = 11.29$, $p < .002$. This meant that over all stories, children spent proportionally more time on the inconsistent line than on the consistent line. This result is similar to those of previous studies where researchers included children who both passed and failed the makes sense question in their analyses. The question is whether such a finding was due primarily to those story pairs where children passed the makes sense question. I pointed out that this was a possible explanation for the significant result in previous research given that children who failed the makes sense question were not analyzed separately from those who passed. To examine this, we next carried out the same analysis on the 23 story pairs where children failed the makes sense question. Once again, the main effect for percentage reading time was significant, $F(1, 21) = 4.99$, $p < .04$. Likewise, the main effect for percentage reading time was also significant for the 56 stories where children were correct on the makes sense question, $F(1, 55) = 7.06$, $p < .02$. Table 3.8 shows that the magnitude of the difference between means was slightly (though not significantly) greater for the 23 story pairs where children failed the makes sense question than it was for the 56 story pairs where children passed this question. This effect is consistent with the claim I made earlier; more competent children might pause less when encountering an inconsistency because the problem is so obvious to them that they process the text without hesitation.

The results were similar for children in Experiment 2. First, I consider children's performance on the long one-exposure and long two-exposures story pairs and then I consider their performance on the short one-exposure pairs. Over the long one-exposure and long two-exposures story pairs, three outliers on the difference scores were identified (two negative, one positive) and were eliminated from subsequent analyses. Table 3.8 lists the mean percentage of time spent reading the fourth line of the consistent and inconsistent stories. As in Experiment 1, the percentage of time spent reading the fourth line of the inconsistent story was significantly greater for all 135 stories, $F(1, 133) = 4.24$, $p < .05$, and for the 30 stories where children failed the makes sense question, $F(1, 28) = 5.65$, $p < .03$. In addition, the effect for the 105 stories where children passed the makes sense question was in the same direction (see Table 3.8) but failed to reach significance, $F(1, 103) = 1.74$, $p = .19$. Thus, consistent with the results of Experiment 1, the difference score was greater for children who failed the makes sense question than it was for children who passed this measure although, again, not significantly so.

Children's performance on the short one-exposure story pair provides converging evidence. Recall that these stories were only two lines long. As a result, it made no sense at all to compute a percentage measure. Because the first line of one story of a given pair was different from the first line of the other story, it would have been necessary to exclude this line when calculating the percentage of time children spent on the key line (in this case the second line) relative to the whole story. But this would have made each percentage equal to 1 (i.e., the only line left is the key line). Consequently, it was necessary to examine actual reading time although this measure was imperfect because there was a general tendency for children to spend more time reading the first story than the second story (presumably because the bulk of the decoding work had been done the first time around) and the variance accounted for by this tendency detracted from the overall result. Table 3.10 lists the reading times for the consistent and inconsistent lines. Two outliers (both positive) were eliminated from the analyses. Once again, the results were consistent with earlier results in that the effect was clearest for children who failed the makes sense question, although the effect for this group did not reach significance, $F(1, 11) = 0.68, p = .42$. That the effect failed to reach significance was not surprising because the analysis was based on only the 13 children who failed the makes sense question for these story pairs and because a percentage measure (which minimizes unrelated variance) could not be used. That it was in the same direction and of a reasonable magnitude provides converging evidence for constructive processing in the absence of comprehension monitoring.

In sum, the results of both experiments indicate that children spend more time reading a line that contradicts an earlier line than they do reading a consistent line. This result is consistent with previous findings but provides a much stronger test because the effect was clearly evident in those children who were incorrect when asked which story made more sense. Consequently, the effect could not have been due to children who spotted the problem in one text.

It is important to be careful in interpreting this result however. For instance, although August et al. (1984, p. 47) claimed that a reading time effect likely

TABLE 3.10
Mean Time (in Seconds) Spent Reading the Second Line
of the Consistent and Inconsistent Stories of the
Short One-Exposure Story Pairs in Experiment 2

	Time for Consistent Story	Time for Inconsistent Story	Difference (Inconsistent–Consistent)
All 67 story pairs	7.52 (4.19)	8.80 (4.62)	0.56
Incorrect on makes sense question (13 occasions)	9.64 (4.61)	12.06 (6.29)	2.42
Correct on makes sense question (54 occasions)	7.01 (4.01)	7.13 (3.95)	0.12

Note. Standard deviations are in brackets.

indicated an unconscious sensitivity to logical inconsistency, it is possible that children had no such sensitivity whatsoever. That is, the result could simply reflect the occurrence of an integration process. Presumably, in both the consistent and inconsistent stories, children would have attempted to integrate the second proposition (e.g., line 4) into the model they had built up when reading the story. The reading time effect could reflect the fact that irrespective of their consistency, some propositions are more difficult to integrate than others. A proposition that addresses the same concept expressed in an earlier proposition could be more difficult to integrate than a proposition that addresses a new concept because the former requires more in the way of restructuring of the mental model. Thus, integrating "white fur–brown fur" could be more difficult than integrating "shiny fur–brown fur" because the first two propositions both comment on the color of the fur whereas the second two propositions comment on different properties of fur. In other words, one might get the same reading time effect if the propositions in question were logically consistent (e.g., "brown fur–chocolaty fur"). So the reading time effect could simply reflect integration difficulties rather than sensitivity to logical inconsistency.

A second caution is that children in our experiments were instructed to read the texts for understanding. These instructions may have induced them to read the text more carefully than they ordinarily would and hence slowed them down more than usual. It is possible, then, that a reading time effect would not be found in spontaneous reading. Yet despite these cautions, it seems clear that the reading time effect we obtained does indicate that children who failed to identify the sensible story were engaging in constructive processing because integration attempts would clearly reflect an attempt to connect the propositions and build a mental model of the text. Thus, it appears that in this instance Markman (1977, 1979) was wrong and that children's failure to spot inconsistencies or monitor their comprehension is not necessarily due to a failure to engage in some form of constructive processing. This conclusion is at odds with that reached by Oakhill (1982; Oakhill, Yuill, & Parkin, 1986) whose findings suggested that good comprehenders were more likely to engage in constructive processing than poor comprehenders. One way around this apparent contradiction is to posit that both groups might be equally involved in attempts to build a mental model of the text but that good comprehenders are more likely to succeed. (See Ruffman, 1995, for other interpretations of this contradiction.)

SECTION IV: SUMMARY AND IMPLICATIONS

In this chapter, I tried to take a closer look at what is involved in comprehension monitoring and what causes children's difficulties. I argued that for the most part their difficulty is not likely due to conceptual limitations, limitations in metacognitive knowledge of when they understand a text (although metacognitive knowledge of reading processes may be a factor), low-confidence or nascent knowledge, or a failure to process the text constructively. On the other hand, I argued that information-processing limitations likely play a role in some children's failures and I suggested that a primary cause is that children are predisposed to derive a single interpretation from a text.

The notion that information-processing limitations play a role in children's difficulties is not new. However, information-processing limitations are not likely to be the sole cause for several reasons. First, children's difficulty on the long two-exposure and short one-exposure tasks of Experiment 2, where the memory and information-processing demands were substantially reduced, suggests that some other factor is also at work. Children's performance in Experiment 3 underlines this point particularly well. Memory and information-processing problems are an unlikely cause for children's difficulty on the self-questions because they were perfectly able to remember and process the inconsistent propositions when judging that a story would not make sense to the doll. Likewise, there is other evidence that children sometimes remember the inconsistent propositions yet fail to report a problem (Markman, 1979; Zabrucky & Ratner, 1986).

As for the claim that children's failures are partially due to a predisposition to derive a single interpretation from the text, I argued that when asked if the text makes sense children check on whether they have been able to derive an interpretation. Claims of knowledge (or that the text makes sense) hinge on the extent to which the text permits such an interpretation. Texts that are ambiguous, inconsistent, or that contain an unknown word all readily allow an interpretation (in the latter case because of the contextual information) and so the child claims the text makes sense. Experiment 3 showed that children's default strategy when asked about their own understanding of a text can sometimes be overcome by asking them about another person's understanding. My argument was that children have no direct access to another person's interpretation and must consequently answer the question on different grounds. This makes it more likely that they will consider the text's internal features. I backed up these claims by discussing similar findings in research concerning children's understanding of both texts and ambiguity.

It is important to point out that children are unlikely to always be superior when asked about someone else's understanding of a text. This manipulation will yield such results only when children have some understanding that a text does not make sense. Children's relatively poor performance on the two story tasks of Experiments 1, 2, and 4 suggests that inconsistencies often go unreported not just because children are asked about their own understanding, but because of a real difficulty in detecting a problem. My guess is that children are so inclined to derive an interpretation when reading a text that they fail to notice the contradiction.

The results of Experiment 4 are also consistent with the idea that children are predisposed to derive an interpretation. Children often claimed an inconsistent text was clearer than a consistent text and justified their answer by claiming that the inconsistent text provided more information to a particular question (e.g., how Sarah gets to school). Once again, it seems that for many children, clarity and comprehensibility are determined not by a text's internal properties, but by the extent to which the text provides a conclusion.

Children's tendency to opt for one conclusion as preferred could be understood as the product of a process in which the child's aim when reading is to construct a mental model of the text (e.g., Garnham, 1989, chapter 7). So far as is possible, children seem to prefer a single uncluttered model of the world, that is, a model free from ambiguity and uncertainty. An important question is what motivates children to do this. It is possible that children might opt for one of the inconsistent (or ambiguous) propositions as preferred because of an implicit sensitivity to the fact that it is logically impossible for both interpretations to be veridical, because it is important to derive models of the world that allow clear predictions and actions, and because as Johnson-Laird (1983) pointed out, a single model frees up space for subsequent mental operations. In Ruffman et al. (1995) we provided a more detailed account of what other possible reasons there are and why we think these unlikely.

Interestingly, it may be that the mutual exclusivity bias (the tendency to identify objects with a single label) represents another manifestation of a more general tendency to opt for one conclusion. For instance, Golinkoff, Hirsh-Pasek, Lavallee, and Baduini (as cited in Markman, 1989) presented children with three familiar objects and a novel object. They found that when children as young as 2½ years heard a novel noun they picked up the novel object. Markman explained this finding quite plausibly by stating that children prefer to identify objects with a single label to avoid redundancy when learning the meanings of category terms. This strategy generally serves children well and seems to indicate sensitivity to inconsistent labelling (e.g., calling a cow both a "cow" and a "horse"). Thus, a child presented with two possible labels ("cow" and "glok") for the animal they know as a cow prefers just the first label. This is sensible because unless glok is a superordinate category label (like "animal") or a subordinate label (like "Guernsey cow"), the cow can't be both. In the same way a child given two possible descriptions of Albert the dog's fur (dark brown and all white) prefers just one description because both cannot be true.

This raises the question of what changes with age. That is, if children do have a general tendency to treat one description as preferable, then what accounts for increased competence at monitoring comprehension? Besides possible improvements in memory or working memory, such changes may also be due either to a decline in the tendency to opt for one proposition or to an increase in some other skill that offsets this tendency. As for the mutual exclusivity bias, Markman (1989, p. 215) suggested that although the bias might be relaxed with age it does not likely disappear because adults would most probably perform like children in mutual exclusivity experiments. Given adults' difficulty detecting logical inconsistencies in some tasks (Baker & Anderson, 1982) a similar argument might apply to comprehension monitoring. That is, it is possible that at least some trace of the tendency to prefer one conclusion lingers into adulthood as well. Countering this tendency and helping improve comprehension-monitoring skills might be increased knowledge of and attention to a text's internal properties, including its consistency. As Olson (1977) suggested, such knowledge and attention may develop as a result of the child becoming part of a literate culture. It may also develop as a function of schooling (Scribner & Cole, 1981). In addition, we argued above that certain manipulations (i.e., asking the child about someone else's understanding rather than their own) might offset children's default tendency to derive a single conclusion making it more likely that they will take a text's internal properties into consideration.

Remediation

I argued that children's failure to recognize when texts make sense is in large part due to a predisposition to derive a single conclusion from a text. If this is right, then one might expect poor comprehension monitors to show similar response patterns over a variety of tasks, for instance, ambiguity tasks. It remains to be seen whether future research will bear out such predictions. Furthermore, if my claims are right, then remediation should be directed at least partly toward helping children to become aware of their tendency to derive single conclusions when several alternatives are possible. On the one hand, there seems reason to be hopeful about the prospects of helping children to monitor their comprehension because they seem to have the requisite conceptual and metacognitive skills (see section I). On the other hand, because the predisposition to derive a single conclusion seems to be a very pervasive disposition displayed over a wide variety of tasks (see section II), remediation might be difficult. Many questions still remain unanswered.

REFERENCES

Ackerman, B. P. (1984a). Storage and processing constraints on integrating story information in children and adults. *Journal of Experimental Child Psychology, 38,* 64–92.

Ackerman, B. P. (1984b). The effects of storage and processing complexity on comprehension repair in children and adults. *Journal of Experimental Child Psychology, 37,* 303–334.

Ackerman, B. P. (1992). The source of children's errors in judging causal inferences. *Journal of Experimental Child Psychology, 54,* 90–119.

Ackerman, B. P., & Jackson, M. (1991). When is a guess a guess: Children's sensitivity to inference constraint in assessing understanding of story information. *Journal of Experimental Child Psychology, 52,* 117–146.

Ackerman, B. P., & McGraw, M. (1991). Constraints on the causal inferences of children and adults in comprehending stories. *Journal of Experimental Child Psychology, 51,* 364–394.

Ackerman, B. P., Spiker, K., & Glickman, I. (1990). Children's sensitivity to topical discontinuity in judging story adequacy. *Developmental Psychology, 26,* 837–844.

August, D. L., Flavell, J. H., & Clift, R. (1984). Comparison of comprehension monitoring of skilled and less skilled readers. *Reading Research Quarterly, 20,* 39–53.

Baker, L. (1984a). Spontaneous versus instructed use of multiple standards for evaluating comprehension: Effects of age, reading proficiency, and type of standard. *Journal of Experimental Child Psychology, 38,* 289–311.

Baker, L., (1984b). Children's effective use of multiple standards for evaluating their comprehension. *Journal of Educational Psychology, 76,* 588–597.

Baker, L., & Anderson, R. I. (1982). Effects of inconsistent information on text processing: Evidence for comprehension monitoring. *Reading Research Quarterly, 27,* 281–294.

Beal, C. R. (1990). The development of text evaluation and revision skills. *Child Development, 61,* 247–258.

Beal, C. R., Garrod, A. C., & Bonitatibus, G. J. (1990). Fostering children's revision skills through training in comprehension monitoring. *Journal of Educational Psychology, 82,* 275–280.

Bereiter, C., Hidi, S., & Dimitroff, G. (1979). Qualitative changes in verbal reasoning during middle and late childhood. *Child Development, 50,* 142–151.

Braine, M., & Rumaine, B. (1981). Development of comprehension of "or": Evidence for a sequence of competencies. *Journal of Experimental Child Psychology, 31,* 46–70.

Casteel, M. A. (1993). Effects of inference necessity and reading goal on children's inferential generation. *Developmental Psychology, 29,* 346–357.

Cornoldi, C. (1990). Metacognitive control processes and memory deficits in poor comprehenders. *Learning Disability Quarterly, 13,* 245–255.

Garner, R. (1987). *Metacognition and reading comprehension.* New Jersey: Ablex.

Garnham, A. (1989). *Psycholinguistics: Central topics.* London: Routledge.

Guttentag, R. E. (1985). Memory and aging: Implications for theories of memory development during childhood. *Developmental Review, 52,* 1216–1233.

Harris, P. L., Kruithof, A., Terwogt, M., & Visser, T. (1981). Children's detection and awareness of textual anomaly. *Journal of Experimental Child Psychology, 31,* 212–230.

Horobin, K., & Acredolo, C. (1989). The impact of probability judgments on reasoning about multiple possibilities. *Child Development, 60,* 183–200.

Johnson-Laird, P. N. (1983). *Mental models.* Cambridge, MA: Harvard University Press.

Jorgensen, J. C., & Falmagne, R. J. (1992). Aspects of the meaning of *If . . . Then* for older preschoolers: Hypotheticality, entailment, and suppositional processes. *Cognitive Development, 7,* 189–212.

Klahr, D., Fay, A. L., & Dunbar, K. (1993). Heuristics for scientific experimentation: A developmental study. *Cognitive Psychology, 25,* 111–146.

Markman, E. M. (1977). Realizing that you don't understand: A preliminary investigation. *Child Development, 48,* 986–992.

Markman, E. M. (1979). Realizing that you don't understand: Elementary school children's awareness of inconsistencies. *Child Development, 50,* 1216–1223.

Markman, E. M. (1989). *Categorization and naming in children.* Cambridge, MA: MIT Press.

Markman, E. M., & Gorin, L. (1981). Children's ability to adjust their standards for evaluating comprehension. *Journal of Educational Psychology, 73,* 320–325.

Miller, G. E. (1985). The effects of general and specific self-instruction training on children's comprehension monitoring performances during reading. *Reading Research Quarterly, 20,* 616–628.

Mitchell, P., & Robinson, E. J. (1990). When do children overestimate their knowledge of unfamiliar targets? *Journal of Experimental Child Psychology, 50,* 81–101.

Nesdale, A. R., Pratt, C., & Tunmer, W. E. (1985). Young children's detection of propositional inconsistencies in oral communications. *Australian Journal of Psychology, 37,* 289–296.

Nesdale, A. R., Tunmer, W. E., & Clover, J. (1985). Factors influencing young children's ability to detect logical inconsistencies in oral communications. *Journal of Language and Social Psychology, 4,* 39–49.

Oakhill, J. (1982). Constructive processes in skilled and less skilled comprehenders' memory for sentences. *British Journal of Psychology, 73,* 13–20.

Oakhill, J., Yuill, N., & Parkin, A. J. (1986). On the nature of the difference between skilled and less-skilled comprehenders. *Journal of Research in Reading, 9,* 80–91.

Olson, D. R. (1977). From utterance to text: The bias of language in speech and writing. *Harvard Educational Review, 47,* 257–281.

Olson, D. R., & Astington, J. W. (1987). See and knowing: On the ascription of mental states to young children. *Canadian Journal of Psychology, 41,* 399–411.

Pea, R. D. (1980). The development of negation in early child language. In D. R. Olson (Ed.), *The social foundations of language and thought: Essays in honour of Jerome S. Bruner* (pp. 156–186). New York: Norton.

Perner, J. (1991). *Understanding the representational mind.* Cambridge, MA: MIT/Bradford Books.

Peterson, C., & Marrie, C. (1988). Even 4-year-olds can detect inconsistency. *The Journal of Genetic Psychology, 149,* 119–126.

Robinson, E. J., & Mitchell, P. (1994). Children's judgements of ignorance on the basis of absence of experience. *British Journal of Developmental Psychology, 12,* 113–129.

Robinson, E. J., & Robinson, W. P. (1982). Knowing when you don't know enough: Children's judgements about ambiguous information. *Cognition, 12,* 267–280.

Ruffman, T. (1993, September). *Internal consistency: When do children come to understand that claims or beliefs should be logically consistent?* Paper presented at the British Psychological Society Annual Meeting, Birmingham.

Ruffman, T. (1995). *Constructive processing and comprehension monitoring.* Unpublished manuscript, University of Sussex, Brighton.

Ruffman, T., Billins, Z., & White, D. (1995). *Another look at children's comprehension-monitoring skills.* Unpublished manuscript, University of Sussex, Brighton.

Ruffman, T., Olson, D. R., & Astington, J. W. (1991). Children's understanding of visual ambiguity. *British Journal of Developmental Psychology, 9,* 89–102.

Russell, J. (1982). The child's appreciation of the necessary truth and the necessary falseness of propositions. *British Journal of Psychology, 73,* 253–266.

Russell, J., & Haworth, H. M. (1987). Perceiving the logical status of sentences. *Cognition, 27,* 73–96.

Schauble, L. (1990). Belief revision in children: The role of prior knowledge and strategies for generating evidence. *Journal of Experimental Child Psychology, 49,* 31–57.

Scribner, S., & Cole, M. (1981). *The psychology of literacy.* Cambridge, MA: Harvard University Press.

Sodian, B. (1988). Children's attributions of knowledge to a listener in a referential communication task. *Child Development, 59,* 324–335.

Sodian, B., & Wimmer, H. (1987). Children's understanding of inference as a source of knowledge. *Child Development, 58,* 424–433.

Tunmer, W. E., Nesdale, A. R., & Pratt, C. (1983). The development of young children's awareness of logical inconsistencies. *Journal of Experimental Child Psychology, 36,* 97–108.

Vosniadou, S. P., Pearson, D., & Rogers, T. (1988). What causes children's failures to detect inconsistencies in text? Representation versus comparison difficulties. *Journal of Educational Psychology, 80,* 27–39.

Walczyk, J. J., & Hall, V. C. (1989) Is the failure to monitor comprehension an instance of cognitive impulsivity? *Journal of Educational Psychology, 81,* 294–298.

Wimmer, H. (1979). Processing of script deviations by young children. *Discourse Processes, 2,* 301–310.

Wimmer, H., Hogrefe, J., & Sodian, B. (1988). A second stage in children's conception of mental life: Understanding informational accesses as origins of knowledge and belief. In J. W. Astington, P. L. Harris, & D. R. Olson (Eds.), *Developing theories of mind* (pp. 173–192). Cambridge, England: Cambridge University Press.

Yuill, N., & Oakhill, J. (1991). *Children's problems in text comprehension: An experimental investigation.* Cambridge, England: Cambridge University Press.

Zabrucky, K., & Ratner, H. (1986). Children's comprehension monitoring and recall of inconsistent stories. *Child Development, 57,* 1401–1418.

Zacks, R. T., & Hasher, L. (1988). Capacity theory and the processing of inferences. In L. L. Light & D. M. Burke (Eds.), *Language, memory, and aging* (pp. 154–170). New York: Cambridge University Press.

CHAPTER FOUR

Higher Order Factors in Comprehension Disability: Processes and Remediation

Jane Oakhill
Nicola Yuill
University of Sussex

This chapter is primarily an overview of our own work on children who have comprehension difficulties, though we outline other theoretical perspectives, and discuss how they relate to our own work. We have been concerned with the problems of young children who have developed good word recognition and can understand sentences and read aloud apparently fluently, but who, nevertheless, have a poor understanding of what they read. In our studies, we excluded children who might have comprehension difficulties associated with word recognition problems. We chose to do so not because we think that such children's problems are uninteresting, or that they do not exist—Perfetti's work (e.g., 1985) showed unequivocally that they do—but because we were interested in looking at children who have a specific comprehension problem. We start with a brief summary of some of the skills that might be needed for successful comprehension, and outline three main areas that we consider to be important—inference making, understanding text structure, and comprehension monitoring—before going on to describe some of our own research in each of these areas. A fuller list of possible sources of comprehension failure can be found in Perfetti's chapter (this volume).

The first area is inference making. To understand the full meaning of a text, readers need to go beyond what is explicitly stated, to link up ideas within the text, and to bring their general knowledge to bear on their understanding of it. Authors necessarily leave some of the links and expansions of a text implicit. A fully explicit text would not only be very long and boring, but it would destroy the reader's pleasure in imposing meaning on the text or making it "their own." However, skilled readers need to assess which inferences are needed, and not let their inferential machinery run wild! Second, readers need to understand the structure of a text: In the case of stories, this might include identifying the main character(s) and their motives, following the plot, and extracting the main theme of the text. Third, readers need to monitor their comprehension. Poor comprehenders may not realize that they don't understand a particular text or portion of text, and may not know what to do about their poor understanding, even if they do realize.

In this chapter, we focus on these three areas, and consider how deficits in each might be related to processing limitations. We do not wish to imply that poor comprehenders might not have difficulties in other areas, but these are the ones we focused on in our research.

The children we studied have a specific comprehension problem, in that their single-word reading and vocabulary was normal for their age, but their ability to understand the text they had just read was considerably behind what have been predicted from their chronological age and word reading accuracy. In our studies, we compared the performance of such children with that of skilled comprehenders of the same age. Typical groups of subjects are shown in Table 4.1. The groups were selected using the Neale Analysis of Reading Ability and the Gates–MacGinitie Vocabulary Test (see Gates & MacGinitie, 1965, and Neale, 1989). The Neale Analysis provides measures of both reading accuracy (word recognition in context) and comprehension (assessed by ability to answer a series of questions about each passage). The test consists of a series of passages presented in a small booklet, each with an accompanying picture. The passages increase in difficulty as the test progresses. The test is administered individually. The child reads a passage, and is told any words that she does not know, or misreads. When the end of the passage is reached, the tester asks the child set questions about it. These questions are a mixture of factual and inferential ones. The child then goes on to the next passage, and so on, until she makes a prescribed number of word-reading errors on a passage, at which point testing is discontinued. This is the point at which the reading is felt to be too difficult for the child, and it is assumed that, beyond this level, the test would become one of listening rather than reading comprehension. The child receives two scores for the test; a word-reading accuracy score and a

TABLE 4.1
Characteristics of Groups of Skilled and Less Skilled Comprehenders

	Chronol. Age/Yrs	Accuracy Age/Yrs	Compreh. Age/Yrs	Gates–MacGinitie (Score / 48)
Less skilled	7.9	8.4	7.3	38.0
Skilled	7.9	8.4	9.1	38.3

comprehension score. The Gates–MacGinitie test requires the child to select one of four words to go with a picture. Thus, it acts as a measure of silent word recognition, and provides an index of the child's vocabulary. In all our studies, the groups of skilled and less skilled comprehenders were matched for word recognition ability (Neale Accuracy and Gates–MacGinitie) and chronological age, but differed in Neale Comprehension scores. In general, all children were above average at word recognition; one group comprised very good comprehenders, the other group were poor comprehenders, particularly relative to their ability to recognize words. Unless otherwise mentioned, all of the children who participated in the studies described in this chapter were 7 or 8 years old.

Some theories of poor comprehension, for example, that of Perfetti (1985), have proposed that comprehension problems stem from difficulties at the level of single words. Indeed, because word-decoding accuracy and comprehension are generally highly correlated, it is likely that many poor comprehenders will also have difficulties at the level of single words. Proponents of this perspective argue that accuracy of word recognition is not sufficient for good comprehension: Recognition must also be fast and automatic so that, in a limited capacity system, the lower level (word recognition) processes do not use up the resources needed for higher level (comprehension) processes. However, we found no differences between our good and poor comprehenders in decoding speed for high or low frequency words, or in automaticity of decoding, as measured by a picture/word interference task (see Yuill and Oakhill, 1991). So, although we do not deny that such factors are likely to lead to comprehension problems in some children, we argue that poor comprehenders exist who do not have difficulties at the word level. In addition, comprehension was clearly not limited by slow and labored decoding in some of our sample of poor comprehenders: Many of them read with great facility and fluency even though they were very poor at answering questions about what they had just read. Conversely, some good comprehenders showed very slow and laborious decoding. Another possibility is that poor comprehenders have difficulties at the level of single sentences, failing to understand certain syntactic constructions. However, when we tested the children on Dorothy Bishop's (1983) *Test for Reception of Grammar,* we found no clear differences between the groups. Let us turn now to the areas in which we have found differences.

INFERENCES

One consistent finding is that poor comprehenders are not skilled at making inferences. Here, we outline one experiment to illustrate the point. This study (Oakhill, 1984) stemmed from the idea that, because tests such as the Neale Analysis require children to answer questions from memory, poor comprehenders might do badly on such tests, not because of problems making inferences, but simply because they have generally deficient memories. Although there is no evidence that skilled and less skilled comprehenders differ in ability on digit span and other short-term memory tasks (Yuill & Oakhill, 1991), they might differ in longer term memory for sentences and text. In this experiment, therefore, there were two main conditions: Either the children had to answer questions about a text from memory, or they could refer back to the text to find the answers to the questions. An additional variable was whether the questions could be answered using literal information from the text, or whether they required an inference.

Each child was seen individually, and read four passages out loud (with help with decoding, if needed) and then tried to answer a set of questions about them. When they had completed all the questions for one passage, they were asked to go back to the passage and look for the correct answers, or to check their answers. The children were given as long as they needed and, in this second session, could reread the passage if they wanted to. A sample passage, with examples of the questions, is shown in Table 4.2.

The results (shown in Table 4.3) demonstrated that, as expected, the skilled comprehenders were better overall at answering questions than were less skilled comprehenders, and that questions that could be answered from the literal content of the passages were easier than questions requiring inferences. However, what was of particular interest was the significant three-way interaction between comprehension skill, passage availability, and type of question. Without the passage available, the skilled comprehenders were globally better; with the passage to refer to, they were only better on the inference questions. Even when a text is available for them to look over, the

TABLE 4.2
Example Passage and Questions From Inference Experiment

Linda was playing with her new doll in front of the house. Suddenly she heard a strange noise, coming from under the bushes. It was the flapping of wings. Tears came to Linda's eyes because she did not know what to do. She ran inside and got a shoe box from the cupboard. Then Linda looked inside her desk until she found eight sheets of yellow paper and some scissors. When she had finished she put the little pieces of paper in the box. Linda gently picked up the helpless creature and took it with her. Her teacher knew what to do.

Literal questions (examples):

What was Linda doing when she heard the strange noise?
What color was the paper?

Inference questions (examples):

What creature was making the noise?
What did Linda do with the paper before she put it in the box?

TABLE 4.3
Percentages of Errors on Literal and Inferential Questions

	Unseen		Seen	
	Literal	Inferential	Literal	Inferential
Less skilled	29.2	45.8	3.6	35.4
Skilled	10.9	15.6	1.0	9.9

less skilled comprehenders are still unable to answer a high proportion of the questions that require an inference. However, this conclusion should be treated with some caution because the data from the literal, seen condition are subject to a floor effect. Had it been possible to make the task harder, the poor comprehenders might have performed more poorly in this condition too, so an explanation based on the quality of their representation of literal information in the text cannot be ruled out (though some of our other work showed that poor comprehenders are relatively good at remembering information verbatim).

There are several reasons for the particular difficulties that poor comprehenders have with inferences, some of which are discussed in the following pages. First, poor comprehenders might simply lack the general knowledge to make the inferences. Such an explanation seems unlikely (we would expect a 7-year-old to know that a creature that flaps its wings is likely to be a bird) and, indeed, was ruled out in a subsequent study in which similar differences were shown, even though the poor comprehenders had the relevant knowledge available to them (Cain, 1994). A second possibility may be that poor comprehenders realize that inferences are legitimate, but may have difficulty accessing relevant knowledge and integrating it with what is in the text because of processing limitations. Third, poor comprehenders may not realize that inferences are necessary or even permissible—perhaps they focus too much on getting the literal meaning from the text. We argue later that there is some evidence supporting both the second and third of these possible explanations.

Our research indicated that poor comprehenders have difficulties with other types of inference; such as those that need to be made to provide cohesion in a text (even without the inclusion of any general knowledge) and those about the particular meanings of words, based on the context in which they occur (see Oakhill, 1982, 1983).

UNDERSTANDING TEXT STRUCTURE

Now we turn to another aspect of our research which illustrates some of the difficulties that good and poor comprehenders have in understanding the structure of a text, but which also, incidentally, illustrates the generality of their comprehension difficulties. This area of research is discussed in more detail in Cain's chapter (this volume).

Our work in this area explored children's ability to retell stories, aided by picture sequences. Our previous research gave the general picture that less skilled children construct rather poorly integrated mental models of texts: They are poor at providing the gist of what they have read or heard, even though they can recall verbatim information quite well. We might expect that an inability to appreciate how stories cohere would carry over to the production of text. We assessed production in various studies by asking children (aged 7 to 8) in the two skill groups to narrate stories from picture sequences. Previous work showed that, even from the age of 4, children have some means of introducing coherence into stories. For instance, when given picture sequences in the appropriate order rather than in a scrambled order, they are more likely to mention the essential points of the story as determined by adults (Poulsen, Kintsch, Kintsch, & Premack, 1979). There are further changes with age in the way that noun phrases, verbs, and connectives are used to establish cohesion in stories (e.g., see Stenning & Michell, 1985). In a pilot study, we told a simple illustrated story to skilled and less skilled children, and asked them to reproduce it immediately. Although less skilled children were able to recall the connective terms (e.g., *and, then, because*) used in the original stories, skilled comprehenders were much more likely to add new connective terms to increase the cohesion of their retellings.

It is possible that this difference reflects different perceptions of the task: Less skilled children may have felt that verbatim accuracy was important, and so kept to the original wording. To assess in closer detail any differences in narrative production, we showed children correctly ordered picture sequences from the Wechsler Picture Arrangement Test and asked the children to tell the story from the pictures. We presented the picture sequences in two different ways; serially, where the pictures were bound together in a book and children told the stories as they leafed through, or simultaneously, where the pictures were laid out from left to right and the children could see all the pictures while telling the story. We scored the resulting narratives for stylistic features of reference, tense, and connective terms.

We gave each story production an overall rating according to how referential ties were used, based on the coding scheme developed by Stenning and Michell (1985). They identified two styles, called "naive" and "sophisticated," which we (in common with others) termed "embedded" and "disembedded," respectively. A disembedded style does not require the listener to know the content of the pictures in order to understand the story; references are varied, but unambiguous (e.g., "Once a man saw a table . . . he went into the shop to buy it." An embedded style, by contrast, requires the listener to have access to the pictures in order to understand the story properly. Thus, stories of this sort contain ambiguous or otherwise infelicitous references (e.g., "He saw the table . . . he went into the shop," where the antecedent of the pronoun he has not been introduced). Approximately 12% of the stories, evenly divided between skill groups, contained clear (unambiguous), but repetitious references (e.g., "The man saw the table. The man went into the shop"). These were felt to reflect an inadequate grasp of reference and, for the purposes of scoring, were put in the same category as the embedded stories.

We were particularly interested in how children's referential style varies as a function of the presentation condition: In serial presentation, the children did not know what would happen next. This type of presentation makes it quite difficult to plan a strategy for the coherent use of referring expressions because you do not know who is the main character, or who will appear in the next picture. Both groups tended to use an embedded style in this condition. In the simultaneous condition, though, the children had an opportunity to plan a coherent way of referring to the characters, for example, by using pronouns more frequently to refer to the main character. This mode of presentation made no difference to the poor comprehenders, who tended to use an embedded style in both presentation conditions. Skilled comprehenders, however, benefited in this condition: They were more likely to use the disembedded style, resulting in an interaction between skill group and method of presentation for this measure of felicity of reference. Verb tense, too, differentiated the groups: Skilled comprehenders were more likely to use the past tense than less skilled ones, and this contributed to the more "story-like" quality of their productions. Contrary to our findings from the pilot study, there were no differences between the two skill groups in their use of connectives such as because.

The difference between the groups might be described in stylistic terms, because the less skilled children told stories that were more like running commentaries. In some cases, this may have been an effective stylistic device, but in others, it seemed more to reflect the fact that the children were describing a series of apparently unrelated events (what Yussen, 1982, called a "reactive chain"), rather than constructing an integrated sequence of statements. For some of the poor comprehenders, it did seem that every picture tells a story.

We are not suggesting that these differences in language use simply reflect children's general linguistic competence. For example, less skilled children are quite capable of producing verbs in the past tense. The differences between the groups lie in both the choice of language forms for narrating stories, and the flexibility of styles of narration in different presentation conditions. The stories in the two skill groups differed on a range of features as well as those features we picked out here, and these differences can perhaps be illustrated more vividly by comparing two typical stories from a poor and a good comprehender, respectively:

A man and a lady is walking along and the doggie is behind them and there's some chicken hanging out of their bag and the dog bites it and they have a picnic and all the food is gone.

Once there was a man and a lady and a dog and they went for a walk to have a picnic and they took two [chicken] legs with them. When they came near the spot they were gonna have their picnic, the dog was trying to get their food because he thought the food was for him so he ate the food, and when they got to their picnic spot they looked in and everything was gone and they were so surprised they went home and got their dinner at home.

As well as illustrating some of the differences between skill groups in language use (e.g., choice of verb tense), these stories show the contrast between a typical reactive chain story (the first example, above) and a more cohesive narrative style. The second narrator seemed to have some general plan in mind, as she mentioned the couple's intention to have a picnic and their approach to the picnic spot, which only appeared in the final picture of the sequence. This planning required the narrator to look ahead, and to modify the description of the current picture with respect to what would be said about subsequent ones. This more complex style presumably makes more demands on working memory during production. The first narrator merely described one or two aspects of each picture, and was probably focusing on each picture in sequence to provide an external place marker of where she was in the story. It may be that less skilled children, despite having some knowledge of cohesive devices, are constrained by working memory limitations in the sorts of stories they can produce. It is also notable that the central point of the story was not made explicit by the poor comprehender. There was no indication that the couple were surprised at the disappearance of the chicken, and it was not even clear why "all the food is gone": Without seeing the pictures, a listener might assume that the couple ate the food themselves. Some of our other work suggested that poor comprehenders are not very good at picking out the main point of stories. When asked to pick (from four options) the statement that best described what a story (in the form of a picture sequence) was about, the good comprehenders far outperformed the poor ones (see Yuill & Oakhill, 1991).

COMPREHENSION MONITORING

The third main area that we mentioned in the introduction was comprehension monitoring. This topic is also discussed extensively by Linda Baker and by Ted Ruffman in their chapters in this volume. In an initial experiment (Yuill, Oakhill, & Parkin, 1989) to explore whether good and poor comprehenders differ in their ability to keep track of their own comprehension, we used an anomaly resolution task (adapted from Ackerman, 1984). The children were read short stories describing an adult's apparently inconsistent response to a child's action. Information to resolve the inconsistency was contained somewhere within the story. There were other types of stories, consistent ones and unresolved ones, which acted as controls. For example, a mother praised her son for not allowing his brother to have a turn riding a bike. The apparent inconsistency was either preceded by or followed by the resolving information (in the example above, that the brother had a sprained ankle, and was not supposed to ride on the bike). We expected that resolving information would be harder to use when it followed, rather than preceded, an inconsistency because it would require retrospective resolution. The difficulty of using the resolving information was also manipulated by varying the distance between the anomaly and its resolution. After hearing each story, the children were asked three types of questions. First, they were asked about whether the adult in the story should have acted as he or she did, and why. This first question was the crucial one: It could only be answered correctly if the anomaly was correctly resolved and, thus, it acted as a crucial index of whether or not the child had integrated the anomaly with the resolving information. Second, they were asked a question to test their memory for a crucial aspect of the story. Third, they were asked a question about the rule on which the inconsistency was based, for example, in the case above, "Would someone usually be praised or blamed for not giving their brother a turn on their bike?" If children answered this question incorrectly, this indicated that they did not agree with the behavioral norms, and should not find the story inconsistent.

Very few children in either skill group answered the memory and rule questions incorrectly. The ability of the children to resolve the anomalies in the crucial inconsistent, resolving condition is shown in Table 4.4. An ANOVA showed an interaction between comprehension skill and the memory demands of the task. The groups were equally good at resolving the inconsistencies when the inconsistency and the resolving information were in adjacent sentences, but the less skilled children performed much worse when the two pieces of information were separated in the text. This is an interesting finding because it demonstrates that the poor comprehenders do not have any general deficit in comprehension monitoring: They are highly competent at the task when the memory demands are small. Both groups

TABLE 4.4
Percentages Correct in Anomaly Resolution Task

	Near	*Far*
Less skilled	72.2	16.7
Skilled	66.7	66.7

found it harder to use resolving information when it followed, rather than preceded, the inconsistency, and this difference was slightly, though not significantly, larger for the less skilled comprehenders.

The experiment described above tested for ability to integrate information in text, and did not test comprehension monitoring directly. We now turn to some more recent work on monitoring that used more traditional monitoring tasks (Oakhill, Hartt, & Samols, 1995). In the first of these experiments, the children were required to read short passages containing nonsense words and phrases. Slightly older children (9- to 10-year-olds) were used than in the experiments described above, as they were more likely to notice problems in texts, and to comment on them sensibly. The children were selected in the same way as described earlier. Both "spontaneous" and "directed" monitoring were measured, as described below.

To assess spontaneous monitoring, the children were simply asked to read two passages out loud (with no indication that there were any problems in them), and were tape-recorded. The tapes were later transcribed, and readers' hesitations, repetitions, and self-corrections were noted. No differences between the groups were found on any of the measures of spontaneous monitoring behavior, though perhaps this is not surprising because the measures were rather insensitive. However, when the children were asked, after they had finished reading, if they had noticed anything that did not make sense in the texts, significantly more (67%) of the skilled comprehenders commented on problems than did the less skilled comprehenders (17%).

In the directed monitoring condition, the children were presented with two different texts, and were told that some parts of the passages may not make sense. They were asked to underline any words or phrases that they did not understand. The data were scored in two ways. First, the total number of words and phrases underlined was calculated. On this measure, there were no differences between the skilled and less skilled comprehenders. This finding indicates that both groups were equally willing to indicate problems in the texts. Second, the number of problematic words and phrases as a proportion of the total number of words and phrases underlined was calculated. Separate calculations were made for words and phrases for each group. The results are shown in Table 4.5. As can be seen, there were large, and significant, differences between the groups in their ability to correctly detect the problem areas in the texts.

TABLE 4.5
Correct Monitoring Responses as a Percentage
of Total Words/Phrases Underlined

	Words	Phrases
Less skilled	17.5	24.7
Skilled	51.0	56.3

After both the spontaneous and the directed monitoring conditions, the children were asked questions about the passages. As we expected, the skilled comprehenders were better than the less skilled ones at answering these questions. However, there was no improvement in question answering in the directed monitoring condition, even though the children were, presumably, being induced to attend more closely to the text in that condition.

In a further experiment, we again assessed monitoring using an error detection paradigm, but in this case the errors were internal inconsistencies within the text, that is, contradictory statements. This had the advantage of allowing us to manipulate the intrinsic memory load of the task because the inconsistencies were either in adjacent sentences, or were separated by several sentences. An example passage is shown in Table 4.6. The children were presented with two passages in each of the memory load conditions. They were also asked to read and make judgments about two passages without any inconsistencies so that we could make sure that they really could discriminate between passages with problems and those without. Once again, 9- to 10-year-olds were used as subjects.

The children read the passages aloud, and were asked to identify any problems with them, defined as "something that doesn't make sense." They were given an example of the sort of blatant inconsistency that occurred in the test passages. The children read the passages at their own pace, and underlined any problems they encountered in them. At the end of each passage, they were asked to indicate their overall assessment of the passage (as shown in Table 4.6). If they indicated a problem, they were asked to explain it. If the child did not immediately identify a problem, they were told that there was a problem, and were given another chance to find it. If they still failed to locate it, the experimenter underlined the two inconsistent sentences, and asked the child if they made sense together. For each of the inconsistent passages, each child obtained a minimum score of 0 (if they did not identify a problem, despite all prompting) and a maximum of 3 (if

TABLE 4.6
Example Passage From Comprehension Monitoring Experiment

Gorillas are clever animals that live together in groups in Africa.
Gorillas sleep on the ground on a bed of leaves and they like to eat different types of fruit.
They are shy and gentle and they hardly ever fight with each other.
Gorillas have flat noses and a very poor sense of smell but their eyesight is very good.
They move about the ground on their hands and feet.
Gorillas sleep in trees and they often build a shelter out of leaves above them, to keep the rain out.

___ This passage makes sense, it does not need to be changed.
___ This passage does not make sense, it needs to be changed.

Note. In the adjacent condition, the italicized sentence occurred after "They move about the ground on their hands and feet."

TABLE 4.7
Mean Scores on Detection Task (Max = 6)

	Condition	
	Adjacent	Distant
Less skilled	4.3	3.2
Skilled	5.2	5.0

they ticked the correct option on first reading, and correctly identified the problem). The mean scores for the groups in the two conditions are shown in Table 4.7.

An analysis of these data showed that the skilled comprehenders were better overall, and that there was a distance effect: The inconsistencies were harder to detect when they were separated by several sentences. However, there was also an interaction between the distance and the skill variables: The less skilled comprehenders were more affected by the distance manipulation than were the skilled ones. Performance on the nonproblematic passages was uniformly high.

WORKING MEMORY IN TEXT PROCESSING

Our research on comprehension monitoring, anomaly detection, and inferences, suggests that the integration of information from different parts of a text is very much harder for poor comprehenders. Such problems may well be related to working memory. Many recent models of reading emphasize the importance of various aspects of memory. Short-term memory is needed for temporary storage and integration of information, and long-term memory is needed for more permanent storage and as a source of background knowledge (for example, in making inferences). Both, therefore, play an important part in comprehension, but in this section, we focus on short-term and working memory.

Studies of the relation between short-term memory and comprehension skills have produced mixed results (see Perfetti & Goldman, 1976; Perfetti & Lesgold, 1979; Torgeson, 1978–1979). Several studies have shown that, where good and poor readers do differ on memory span tasks, these differences can largely be accounted for by differences in the efficiency of phonological coding in working memory (see Stanovich, 1986a; Wagner & Torgeson, 1987). Some of our own work has addressed the issue of whether children with a specific comprehension problem, as opposed to some more general reading problem, have deficiencies in short-term memory (see Oakhill, Yuill, & Parkin, 1986). We investigated whether skilled and less skilled comprehenders who were matched on word recognition skill differed in their use of phonological coding, using a technique developed by Hitch and Halliday (1983). The children were required to remember short lists of one-, two- and three-syllable spoken words. Sensitivity to word length in this condition would indicate that the children were rehearsing the words in the articulatory loop. Both skilled and less skilled comprehenders recalled more short than long words, but there were no differences between the groups. The children were also asked, on a different occasion, to remember a series of pictures that corresponded to the words in the lists. Sensitivity to word length in this condition would indicate that the children were coding the picture names in a phonological (rather than purely visual) form. Again, there was a main effect of the length of the pictures' names, but no differences between the groups: Both showed evidence of verbal recoding of the picture names. These results supported the idea that there are no general differences in short-term memory capacity or encoding strategies between the groups.

However, the tests we used in this experiment were primarily tests of storage capacity. Perfetti and Goldman (1976) proposed that good and poor comprehenders differ in functional memory, rather than short-term capacity *per se*, and Oakhill, Yuill, and Parkin (1988) suggested that good and poor comprehenders might differ on a task that makes heavier demands on working memory, a limited capacity system for the simultaneous storage and processing of information. Recent research with adults has shown that comprehension skill is related to performance on tests of working memory (for a review, see Daneman, 1987). Daneman and Carpenter (1980, 1983) showed that various aspects of skilled comprehension (remembering facts, detecting inconsistencies, resolving pronouns) were related to a verbal test of working memory (the sentence span task). In this test, the subjects were required to read and understand a series of sentences (the processing requirement) while simultaneously trying to remember the final word in each (the storage requirement). Because Daneman and Carpenter's reading span test involved reading and understanding sentences, we felt that the skilled comprehenders might be at an advantage in performing it. We therefore developed an analogous task using digits rather than words. The children were presented with lists of numbers to read aloud (the processing requirement) and had to remember the final digit in each group (storage requirement). The memory load was varied by increasing the number of sets of digits and, therefore, the number of final digits to be recalled (2, 3 or 4). So, for example, in a two-digit case, the child might read the sets 7–4–2 and 1–3–9 and then have to recall 2 and 9. We found that, although there were no differences between the groups in the easiest version (two-digit recall), there were differences in the three- and four-digit versions of the task. We replicated this finding several times with both 7- to 8-year-olds and 9- to 10-year-olds. These levels of the task were appropriate for all children in this age range; even the skilled older children were performing at only about 50% correct in the most difficult, four-digit condition. So, one obvious suggestion is that skilled comprehenders are better at making inferences, monitoring their understanding, interpreting anaphors, and deriving the structure of stories because they have more efficient working memories. Indeed, the idea of a working memory deficit fits in nicely with our studies of anomaly detection and comprehension monitoring described earlier, where we showed that it was only when the crucial pieces of information were nonadjacent in the text that the less skilled comprehenders had particular difficulties. As yet, however, we have no data on the direction of the link. It may be the case, as Tunmer (1989) suggested, that practice at reading with understanding increases working memory capacity, rather than the reverse. Verbal working memory, in particular, might be influenced in this way. Perhaps practice in reading and in attempting to understand long and/or complex sentence constructions increases the efficiency of verbal working memory.

In the final part of this chapter, we turn to two other areas of research which suggest that, even if working memory was found to be causally linked to comprehension skill, it is very unlikely to be a complete explanation of individual differences in skill. The reason for this caution is that certain experiences that do not have working memory as an obvious mediating link, have been shown to be related to reading comprehension. These are the positive effects on comprehension of reading and being read to at home, and the effects of short periods of training on improving comprehension. These topics are discussed in turn below.

READING AT HOME

Kate Cain (1994) recently assessed the home reading habits of 7- to 8-year-old good and poor comprehenders. Through questionnaires, she obtained data from both parents and children about the extent to which the children read at home, are read to, the number of books owned, library membership, and so forth. The number of subjects was fairly small, but interesting patterns emerged. The data about how often parents or guardians read to children are shown in Table 4.8. There is a significant relation, in both sets of data, between skill group and how frequently the children are read to: Skilled comprehenders are read to more frequently at home. In addition, more skilled than less skilled comprehenders had visited a library, or were members of a library, though in this case the relation between skill level and library attendance did not reach significance. These findings may mean that the poorer comprehenders have not had the same level of exposure to stories and story structures from a very early age that skilled comprehenders might have had. Thus, they might have missed out on hundreds or even thousands of hours of story reading and book sharing from a very early age, and this experience, if it proves to be crucial to later reading comprehension skill, would be exceedingly difficult to compen-

TABLE 4.8
Home Reading Study

Parents' Questionnaire: "Do you ever read to your child now?"		
	Skilled (n = 9)	Less skilled (n = 6)
One or more times a week	8	1
Less than once a week	1	5
Children's Interview: "Does anyone at home read you stories?"		
	Skilled (n = 10)	Less skilled (n = 12)
One or more times a week	8	2
Less than once a week	2	10

sate for (even if such compensation were found to be effective at a later age). Of course, it could be that poorer comprehenders are read to less because they are poor comprehenders, and perhaps don't enjoy being read to, or are not rewarding to read to. We end this chapter on a more optimistic note, because we have found that even relatively short-term training studies can be very effective in improving comprehension.

REMEDIATION STUDIES

In this section, we consider how children can be taught to apply more efficient processing strategies as they are reading. Most studies of remediation techniques have concentrated on teaching strategies that children will be able to apply to any text.

The aim of the studies we describe in this section was to see if less skilled readers' comprehension could be improved by relatively short periods of training. The rationale was that, if less skilled children can be trained in the skills they are supposed to lack, then their comprehension should improve. If the poor comprehenders' understanding is deficient because they lack the skills in which they are being trained, then we would expect that the less skilled comprehenders might improve to the same level as the skilled ones following training, but the skilled ones would benefit relatively little from training (because they already have the skills being trained).

The aim of the first study we describe here (Yuill & Oakhill, 1988) was to try to engage children more actively in their own comprehension, to encourage inferencing and comprehension monitoring. The children were 7- to 8-year-old good and poor comprehenders, who were allocated to one of three groups, with equal numbers of good and poor comprehenders in each. These groups included the training group (which we describe shortly), and two control groups who spent the same amount of time with the experimenter doing activities that were not expected to improve their comprehension. All three groups spent a total of seven sessions of about 30 minutes each with the experimenter. One of the control groups simply spent their time answering questions about a series of short passages (there were 14 children in this group). The other control group had training in rapid word decoding (there were 12 children in this group). As we mentioned earlier, one theory of poor comprehension suggests that accurate word recognition is not sufficient for efficient comprehension, but that words must also be recognized quickly and automatically. If they are not, then the resources devoted to word recognition will not be available for comprehension processes, which will suffer as a consequence. This group read the same texts as the other group, and practiced decoding lists of words from them. Thus, the improvement of the trained group could be compared with that of the control groups.

The group who received training was also seen in seven separate sessions of about 30 minutes each (there were 26 children in this group). There were three components to the training. First, they received training in making *lexical inferences.* This training was included in all seven sessions. The children were encouraged to say what they could work out about a sentence or story from the individual words, for instance, the setting, or what a particular character was like. The children were given practice in applying this technique, first with sentences, and then with short abstract stories of the sort shown below. Second, in four of the sessions, the chidren engaged in *question generation.* They were invited to generate questions such as "Where was Lucy?" and "What was she trying to do?" for the passage shown in Table 4.9 (the questions shown in the table were not presented in this training condition). The children took turns generating questions. Third, in

TABLE 4.9
Inference Training

Example text

Lucy saw the ground below her. It seemed very far away. She heard the cat and tried to move, but she realized it was unsafe. What could she do? Then she saw her father walking toward the house. She called loudly to him. Father looked up and saw Lucy, then he ran toward the tree.

Example questions (exercise group only):

Where was Lucy?
Why was she there?
Why couldn't she move?
Who did she see from the tree?
Where did her father go?

---

one session, they were encouraged to engage in *prediction*. In this session, part of the text was covered, and the children were encouraged to guess at what was missing. After they had done so, the text was revealed and the appropriateness of their guesses was discussed with them.

The control group who did comprehension exercises shared the reading of the text, and took turns at attempting to answer the set questions on it. Examples of the questions supplied in this condition are shown in Table 4.9. The children were given minimal feedback on their answers by the experimenter, except that obvious errors were corrected. However, they often discussed their answers and errors among themselves which, as we shall see later, may have influenced the results in this control condition. The children in the other control group, who were given training in rapid decoding, practiced reading words from the same texts as quickly as possible.

The training took place over about 2 months, and then the children were retested on a different form of the Neale Analysis. The improvement scores for the six groups are shown in Table 4.10. As can be seen, the very smallest average increase in improvement was 6 months. However, the absolute differences in improvement probably mean very little because either the different forms of the Neale are not exactly parallel, or because the children just happened to have made rapid progress in reading at the time of year the testing was done. What is notable, though, are the relative differences in improvement in the various groups. The less skilled comprehenders benefited from inference training more than the skilled comprehenders, and the less skilled group who received inference training improved more than those given decoding practice. Training did not differentially affect reading speed or accuracy of word decoding—there were no differences between the groups on these measures. The gains in comprehension scores after this relatively short period of training were impressive. However, it was surprising that the group given inference training did not improve more than those given comprehension exercises. One possible explanation for this result is that the children in the latter group discussed their answers, and often argued with one another about their answers. These discussions may have had the effect of increasing both their awareness of comprehension, and of the processes involved in inference making. In addition, as can be seen from

TABLE 4.10
Inference Training Study: Mean Improvement in Comprehension Ability (Months) as a Function of Skill Group and Type of Training

	Rapid Decoding	Comprehension Exercises	Inference Training
Less skilled	6.00	13.71	17.38
Skilled	10.33	5.43	5.92

the example text, the texts used were rather abstract and obscure to provide suitable material for the group given inference training and this in itself may have encouraged more inferential processing and reflection than would have occurred with more traditional stories.

We also explored the effects of training in generating mental images of the events in a text on comprehension (Oakhill & Patel, 1991). Michael Pressley's work (1976) showed that imagery can be successful as a way of improving children's comprehension of stories. We explored whether less skilled comprehenders might benefit from imagery training, and also addressed the issue of whether imagery might be particularly suitable for aiding memory for particular sorts of information. The children were asked three different sorts of question. The first type, "factual" questions, tapped memory for facts that were explicit in the texts. The second type, "inferential," asked about information that could only be inferred from the story, and the third, "descriptive," asked about details that might be particularly likely to come to the reader's attention if an image had been formed. An example text, with the three types of question is shown in Table 4.11.

The good and poor comprehenders were slightly older in this study ($M =$ 9.7). Older children were used as subjects because Pressley (1976) showed that it is not until about 8 that children can use self-generated images. Each group was divided into two subgroups, one of which was given training in imagery. The imagery training took place in small groups (4 or 5 children) over three sessions on different days. The children were told that they would be learning to "think in pictures" as they read stories, to help them to answer questions about them. Four stories were used for training, and five in the test session. In the first training session, the children read one of the stories, and the experimenter then produced two drawings: One was a cartoon-like sequence of four pictures representative of the main sequence of events in the

TABLE 4.11
Imagery Training Study: Example Story and Questions

The stepladder was put away safely behind the door which was just to the right of the cooker. The three shelves were up at last and, even with a sore thumb, Terry Butcher was happy. The hammer that had caused the pain was put away in the toolbox with the other tools.
Linda, Terry's wife, came into the room with a box of crockery. "The shelves are for my little model airplanes," said Terry, in a stern voice. "We'll see," was the reply from Linda.
A little while later, when Terry was putting away the toolbox, he heard a loud scream and the sound of breaking glass and china. Terry walked back into the room and was angry. "I warned you about those shelves," he said to Linda.

Example questions:

How many shelves had been put up? (factual)
Why did Terry have a sore thumb? (inferential)
Describe the scene in the room when Linda screamed. (descriptive)

story. The other was a single picture representative of the main event in the story. The children were shown how each of the pictures related to the story, and were encouraged to use these "pictures in their minds" to help them to answer questions about the stories. For a second story in this session, the children were not shown pictures but were encouraged to formulate their own mental images. They discussed their images and received feedback and suggestions from the experimenter. In a second session, a similar procedure was followed. In the final training session, the children were not shown any drawings. The imagery procedure was reiterated, and the children read and answered questions about a new story and discussed their "mental pictures," as in the first two sessions.

The groups who did not receive imagery training saw the same stories, also in three sessions. They read the stories and answered the questions. Their answers were then discussed with them. The children in these groups spent as long with the experimenter as had those in the imagery training groups. In the test phase, the groups who had received the imagery training were reminded of this strategy before they read the test stories, and reminded to use their mental pictures to help them to answer the questions. The children in the control condition were told to read the stories very carefully, and to answer the questions in as much detail as possible.

The data from this experiment are shown in Table 4.12. Overall, the good comprehenders answered more questions correctly than did the poor ones, and the children given imagery training performed better than the control group. As predicted, the poor comprehenders given imagery training showed a marked improvement in memory for the passages: They performed significantly better on the test questions than did the control group of poor comprehenders. There was no such difference between the groups of good comprehenders. Imagery training did not have a differential effect for the different types of questions. Where there was improvement, it was general, and not related to particular question types. These results show that imagery training was especially beneficial for those children who do not possess adequate comprehension skills. Poor comprehenders may show a particular benefit from imagery training because it enables them, or forces them, to integrate information in the text in a way that they would not normally do. Of course, the finding that the comprehension of the good group did not improve

TABLE 4.12
Imagery Study: Mean Posttraining Scores as a Function of
Comprehension Skill, Training Group, and Question Type (Max = 15)

	Imagery Training	Control
Less skilled	9.61	7.27
Skilled	10.17	9.50

with imagery does not necessarily mean that they already use imagery. It may be that they have some equally efficient strategy for remembering information from text, and that training in imagery gives them no additional advantage. Imagery may help poor comprehenders by giving them a strategy to help them overcome some of the limitations of their comprehension skills. For instance, it may give poor comprehenders a way to help circumvent their memory limitations by enabling them to use a different, and perhaps more economical, means of representing information in the text.

In conclusion, we showed that two very different types of training can have substantial effects on the comprehension scores of less skilled comprehenders, at least in the short term. However, further work is needed to establish the long-term effects of such training. Although these findings give us cause for optimism, we conclude this section with two notes of caution. First, most methods of improving comprehension (including the ones we have described here) assume that poor comprehenders will benefit from being taught the skills that good readers use. However, the picture might not be so simple. The fact that poor readers lack some skills might indicate that, at least in some cases, they are unable to use them. Second, some forms of instruction might need to wait until after the beginning stages of learning to read, until decoding skills are fairly well-established. A related point is that young readers may find learning to use skills such as imagery and comprehension monitoring very difficult—it is not until about 9, for instance, that children are typically able to understand and use imagery (Pressley, 1976). Of course, these reservations about specific training in comprehension skills should not be taken to mean that reading for meaning should not be encouraged from the very beginning, but just that deliberate training of comprehension skills may be more useful later.

CONCLUSIONS AND FUTURE DIRECTIONS

The general picture that emerges of less skilled comprehenders is of children who are poor at making inferences and connecting ideas in a text. Their problem seems not to be restricted to understanding the written word as they also have difficulties with listening comprehension and with understanding narrative picture sequences. Working memory may play a part in such skills. Our work has shown that less skilled comprehenders perform poorly on a test of working memory. Such a deficit could readily explain the less skilled comprehenders' problems in making inferences, in understanding story structure, and in monitoring their comprehension. We have assumed that, because we showed a relation between a nonverbal working memory test and children's comprehension, poor comprehenders have a general deficiency (rather than a verbal deficiency) in working memory skills. However, we did not test the children on a verbal working memory test, so it may be the case that verbal working memory is an even better predictor of comprehension skill in children than the test we used. We are currently developing a variety of working memory tests (verbal, numerical, and spatial) for use with children, and are exploring these issues, and also investigating how the relation between working memory and comprehension changes with age.

However, patterns of causality between working memory skills and text comprehension have yet to be established. Lower working memory capacity might be either a cause or a consequence of poor comprehension. In any case, a deficient working memory seems unlikely to be a complete explanation of the less skilled children's problem because inference skills can be trained, and one would not expect working memory to be susceptible to indirect training over so short a period. The training might increase children's awareness of the need to make inferences, but is unlikely to improve their working memory. This is not to deny that working memory might be susceptible to training, perhaps instruction in use of task specific strategies, and other metacognitive abilities, might be helpful in improving working memory performance. One possibility that reconciles these two sets of findings is that less skilled comprehenders do have a basic deficit in working memory, which affects their comprehension, but they can be taught general comprehension strategies that help them to circumvent their memory limitations. In addition, some findings are emerging to show that extensive experience of being read to may be important. It may be that being read to from an early age turns out to be a crucial factor in the development of comprehension skills. The investigation of this possibility would require a large-scale longitudinal study. Some recent work by Dickinson and Tabors (1991) and by Reese (1994), however, shed some light on the relation between reading to children and later comprehension skills. Reese, for example, showed that it is not so much the amount of reading that parents and children engage in that is important but, rather, the extent to which parents comment on the stories. Nonreading activities were also important predictors of later literacy. The extent to which parents engaged their children in decontextualized talk about past events, and encouraged metacognitive reasoning in their children was important.

The work on the relation between metacognitive skills and comprehension is one that we hope to explore further, especially as it may be an area that provides opportunities for training, at least in older children who are able to understand the concept of monitoring. We hope to assess whether metacognitive awareness can successfully be trained, and the extent to which such training improves not only monitoring, but also comprehension skills more generally.

In a further project, we intend to map the progress of poor comprehenders as they progress through junior school (from ages 7 to 10+), to examine the effects of being a poor comprehender at age 7 on later reading development. There are two distinct possibilities. Children identified as poor comprehenders at age 7 might spontaneously "recover" by the time they are 8 or 9, as they belatedly develop comprehension skills; alternatively, children who are poor comprehenders at 7 may find reading a fairly unrewarding activity because they understand little of what they read, and might read less than good comprehenders of the same age, thus becoming poorer readers more generally (a form of "Matthew effect," Stanovich, 1986b). The results of this longitudinal study could have important implications for remediation. If the first scenario is more accurate, then intensive remediation might prove unnecessary; children might simply need some facilitation at the appropriate time to bring their comprehension skills into line with their decoding ability. If the second scenario proves to be the case, however, then remediation of comprehension disability at an early age is likely to be essential, in the hope of preventing more global reading problems later.

We shall also look at possible patterns of causality between the skills and abilities outlined above, and comprehension ability. If there is a difference between good and poor comprehenders on some measure (inferences, metacognitive skills), the poor comprehenders' lower performance might be either a cause or a consequence of their poor comprehension. For example, poor comprehenders might not adequately understand a text because they do not make the right inferences, or they might fail to make inferences because they have had less experience of reading text and, therefore, less practice at making inferences. Thus far, our studies have not addressed the issue of causality, except indirectly in training studies. We intend to do this in two main ways. First, we intend to use a "comprehension age match" (analogous to the "reading age match" used by Bryant and associates, see Goswami & Bryant, 1991). In this design, the poor comprehenders are matched not only with children of the same age and reading ability who have superior comprehension skills, but also with younger children who have a similar level of comprehension ability, but whose comprehension is commensurate with their word recognition skills and their chronological age. In this way, we can compare groups with the same absolute level of comprehension, one of which (the older poor comprehenders) has more experience of reading text. If poor comprehenders are worse on tasks than younger children with the same level of comprehension skill, then we can infer that the particular skill deficit does not arise from less experience of reading, because the younger children perform better, even though they would be expected to have had less reading experience. Thus, a causal link is a possibility. The other way in which we intend to investigate causal factors is by exploring, in a longitudinal study, how well later comprehension can be predicted by various skills in which poor comprehenders are deficient (e.g., inference making, working memory, verbal IQ, metacognitive skills) and compare that with how well comprehension predicts performance on tasks that measure those skills at a later age. The relative strengths of these relations will throw light on the direction of causal links between comprehension skill and the other variables.

REFERENCES

Ackerman, B. P. (1984). The effects of storage and processing complexity on comprehension repair in children and adults. *Journal of Experimental Child Psychology, 37,* 303–334.

Bishop, D. (1982). *Test for the Reception of Grammar.* Manchester, England: Chapel Press.

Cain, K. (1994). *An investigation into comprehension difficulties in young children.* Unpublished doctoral dissertation, University of Sussex, England.

Daneman, M. (1987). Reading and working memory. In J. R. Beech & A. M. Colley (Eds.), *Cognitive approaches to reading.* Chichester, England: Wiley.

Daneman, M., & Carpenter, P. A. (1980). Individual differences in working memory and reading. *Journal of Verbal Learning and Verbal Behavior, 19,* 450–466.

Daneman, M., & Carpenter, P. A. (1983). Individual differences in integrating information between and within sentences. *Journal of Experimental Psychology: Learning Memory and Cognition, 9,* 561–584.

Dickinson, D. K., & Tabors, P. O. (1991). Early literacy: Linkages between home, school and literacy achievement at age five. *Journal of Research in Childhood Education, 6,* 30–44.

Gates, A. I., & MacGinitie, W. H. (1965). *Gates-MacGinitie Reading Tests.* New York: Columbia University Teachers' College Press.

Goswami, U., & Bryant, P. E. (1991). *Phonological skills and learning to read.* Hove, England: Lawrence Erlbaum Associates.

Hitch, G. J., & Halliday, M. S. (1983). Working memory in children. *Philosophical Transactions of the Royal Society, Series B,* 325–340.

Markman, E. (1977). Realizing that you don't understand: A preliminary investigation. *Child Development, 48,* 986–992.

Neale, M. D. (1989). *The Neale Analysis of Reading Ability* (rev.). Windsor: NFER-Nelson.

Oakhill, J. V. (1982). Constructive processes in skilled and less-skilled comprehenders. *British Journal of Psychology, 73,* 13–20

Oakhill, J. V. (1983). Instantiation in skilled and less-skilled comprehenders. *Quarterly Journal of Experimental Psychology, 35A,* 441–450.

Oakhill, J. V. (1984). Inferential and memory skills in children's comprehension of stories. *British Journal of Educational Psychology, 54,* 31–39.

Oakhill, J. V., & Garnham, A. (1988). *Becoming a skilled reader.* Oxford, England: Basil Blackwell.

Oakhill, J. V., Hartt, J., & Samols, D. (1995, April). *Comprehension monitoring and working memory in good and poor comprehenders.* Paper presented at the Experimental Psychology Society meeting, Cambridge, England.

Oakhill, J. V., & Patel, S. (1991). Can imagery training help children who have comprehension problems? *Journal of Research in Reading, 14,* 106–115.

Oakhill, J. V., & Yuill, N. M. (1991). The remediation of reading comprehension difficulties. In M. J. Snowling & M. Thomson (Eds.), *Dyslexia: Integrating theory and practice* (pp. 215–235). London: Whurr Publishers Ltd.

Oakhill, J. V., Yuill, N. M., & Parkin, A. J. (1986). On the nature of the difference between skilled and less-skilled comprehenders. *Journal of Research in Reading, 9,* 80–91.

Oakhill, J. V., Yuill, N. M., & Parkin, A. J. (1988). Memory and inference in skilled and less-skilled comprehenders. In M. M. Gruneberg, P. E. Morris, & R. N. Sykes (Eds.), *Practical aspects of memory* (vol. 2, pp. 315–320). Chichester, England: Wiley.

Perfetti, C. A. (1985). *Reading ability.* Oxford, England: Oxford University Press.

Perfetti, C. A., & Goldman, S. R. (1976). Discourse memory and reading comprehension skill. *Journal of Verbal Learning and Verbal Behavior, 15,* 33–42.

Perfetti, C. A., & Lesgold, A. M. (1979). Coding and comprehension in skilled reading and implications for reading instruction. In L. B. Resnick & P. Weaver (Eds.), *Theory and practice of early reading* (vol. 1, pp. 57–84). Hillsdale, NJ: Lawrence Erlbaum Associates.

Poulsen, D., Kintsch, E., Kintsch, W., & Premack, D. (1979). Children's comprehension and memory for stories. *Journal of Experimental Child Psychology, 28,* 379–401.

Pressley, G. M. (1976). Mental imagery helps eight-year-olds remember what they read. *Journal of Educational Psychology, 68,* 355–359.

Reese, E. (1994, August). *Relations between memories and the word: Past event narratives and children's emergent literacy.* Poster presented at the Practical Aspects of Memory Conference, Washington, DC.

Stanovich, K. E. (1986a). Cognitive processes and reading problems of learning disabled children: Evaluating the assumption of specificity. In J. K. Torgeson & B. Wong (Eds.), *Psychological and educational perspectives on learning disabilities.* New York: Academic Press.

Stanovich, K. E. (1986b). Matthew effects in reading: Some consequences of individual differences in the acquisition of literacy. *Reading Research Quarterly, 21,* 360–407.

Stenning, K., & Michell, L. (1985). Learning how to tell a good story: The development of content and language in children's telling of one tale. *Discourse Processes, 8,* 261–279.

Torgeson, J. K. (1978–1979). Performance of reading disabled children on serial memory tasks: A selective review of recent research. *Reading Research Quarterly, 14,* 57–87.

Tunmer, W. (1989). The role of language-related factors in reading disability. In D. Shankweiler & I. Y. Liberman (Eds.), *Phonology and reading disability: Solving the reading puzzle.* Ann Arbor, MI: University of Michigan Press.

Wagner, R., & Torgeson, J. K. (1987). The nature of phonological processing and its causal role in the acquisition of reading skills. *Psychological Bulletin, 101,* 192–212.

Yuill, N. M., & Oakhill, J. V. (1988). Effects of inference awareness training on poor reading comprehension. *Applied Cognitive Psychology, 2,* 33–45.

Yuill, N. M., & Oakhill, J. V. (1991). *Children's problems in text comprehension: An experimental investigation.* Cambridge, England: Cambridge University Press.

Yuill, N. M., Oakhill, J. V., & Parkin, A. J. (1989). Working memory, comprehension ability and the resolution of text anomaly. *British Journal of Psychology, 80,* 351–361.

Yussen, S. R. (1982). Children's impressions of coherence in narratives. In B. A. Hutson (Ed.), *Advances in reading/language research* (Vol. 1, pp. 245–281).

CHAPTER FIVE

A Comparison of Reading Comprehension and Decoding Difficulties in Children

Susan E. Stothard
University of Newcastle Upon Tyne

Charles Hulme
University of York

Reading can be considered to comprise two component skills; word recognition and comprehension. The skilled reader needs to identify the individual words of a text and integrate the meaning of these words and sentences to comprehend what is being read. This view was described by Gough and Tunmer's (1986) simple model of reading (see also Gough, Hoover, & Peterson, this volume; Hoover & Gough, 1990). Gough and Tunmer proposed that reading comprehension is determined by decoding and language comprehension skills. Each of these components is assumed to be necessary, but not sufficient, for success in reading. According to this theory, the ability to recognize the printed words of text is essential to understanding what is written, but, good decoding is not sufficient for reading; comprehension is also required, the ultimate goal of reading being the extraction of meaning.

Gough and Tunmer's simple model proposed that reading ability is determined by the product of decoding and language comprehension skills, or $r = d \times c$, where r represents reading comprehension, d equals decoding ability, and c equals language comprehension skill; and each variable ranges from 0 (nullity, or no skill) to 1 (perfection). This multiplicative model captures the idea of necessity and nonsufficiency; progress in reading requires skill in both components, that is, both components must be nonzero. So although decoding is necessary for efficient reading, it is not sufficient. Children who can decode accurately but with little understanding are clearly not skilled readers ($c = 0$, therefore $r = 0$ whatever the value of d). Similarly, comprehension is necessary but not sufficient; even the most skilled comprehenders will be very poor readers if they are unable to decode (d = 0, therefore r = 0). From this model, it follows that reading difficulties can arise from either decoding problems, comprehension problems, or a combination of the two.

There is now a large volume of research concerned with the processes underlying the acquisition of decoding skills and the deficits associated with difficulties in acquiring decoding skills (see Hulme & Snowling, 1992, for a review). It is generally accepted that there is a close relationship between phonological skills and the development of decoding skills. The evidence for this relationship comes from studies of both normal and atypical development. Longitudinal studies of unselected groups of children have shown that preschool phonological skills predict later decoding skill (Bradley & Bryant, 1983) even after controlling for the substantial effects of IQ (see Rack, Hulme, & Snowling, 1993, for a review). Furthermore, it appears that this relationship may be a causal one. Training studies have shown that training in phonological awareness enhances the reading (decoding) skills of children in comparison with children from control groups (Bradley & Bryant, 1983; Hatcher, Hulme, & Ellis, 1994).

Further support for the view that phonology is central to the development of decoding skills comes from the observation that children with specific decoding difficulties (i.e., dyslexia) exhibit phonological processing deficits (see Hulme & Snowling, 1992, for a review). Studies comparing dyslexic children with normal readers have generally revealed problems with phonological awareness (Wagner & Torgesen, 1987) and with verbal memory (Brady, Shankweiler, & Mann, 1983; Johnston, Rugg, & Scott, 1987). It has also been reported that these children have difficulties with speech perception (Reed, 1989), speech production (Snowling, 1981; Snowling, Goulandris, Bowlby, & Howell, 1986) and naming (Snowling, van Wagtendonk, & Stafford, 1988).

Moreover, there is now good evidence that phonological impairments are directly related to these children's reading difficulties. Many dyslexic children show nonword reading deficits (see Rack, Snowling, & Olson, 1992 for a review) indicating that their ability to use phonological strategies to decode unfamiliar words (e.g., GROMP, TEGWOP) is out of line with their lexical reading skills. Taken together, these studies provide convincing evidence that phonological impairments play a key role in the development of decoding difficulties.

In contrast to our knowledge of the nature and causes of decoding difficulties in children, much less is known about the causes of reading comprehension problems. The majority of studies investigating reading comprehension problems in children have examined generally poor readers. Such children had deficits on a variety of tasks including inefficient decoding skills (Perfetti, 1985), global language comprehension problems (Smiley, Oakley, Worthen, Campione & Brown, 1977), and poor metacognitive skills

(Paris & Myers, 1981). However, these studies confound decoding and comprehension difficulty and therefore cannot address the causes of reading comprehension problems.

A more appropriate way to investigate reading comprehension problems is to select children whose decoding skills are normal, but whose reading comprehension skills are poor. This approach has been adopted by Oakhill and her colleagues in a series of studies that have attempted to identify the causes of reading comprehension problems in children (see Yuill & Oakhill, 1991, for a recent review).

It is well established that comprehension is a constructive, integrative process. When presented with a story, the skilled reader spontaneously draws inferences to link together ideas and to fill in information that is only implicit. Oakhill and colleagues claimed that children with comprehension problems are less likely to engage in constructive processing during reading. Specifically, poor comprehenders are less able than good readers to draw inferences and to use relevant general knowledge when reading a story (e.g., Oakhill, 1984). They also have difficulty making inferences about the meanings of specific words in sentences (instantiation) and are poor at understanding pronouns (e.g., Oakhill & Yuill, 1986; Yuill & Oakhill, 1988). Associated problems with text comprehension arise because these children do not naturally monitor their comprehension and they have considerable difficulty in resolving apparent inconsistencies in texts (Yuill, Oakhill, & Parkin, 1989).

A number of studies have investigated whether these difficulties might be related to poor comprehenders' poor verbal memory skills. To understand prose it is necessary to hold information in memory so that the semantic and syntactic relationships among successive words, phrases, and sentences may be computed and a meaningful representation of the passage constructed. It is reasonable, therefore, to suggest that a memory deficit might contribute to reading comprehension difficulties.

There is, however, little support for this proposal. Several studies have reported that children with specific comprehension difficulties have normal verbal short-term memory spans (e.g., Oakhill, Yuill, & Parkin, 1986; Stothard & Hulme, 1992). It appears that limited short-term memory capacity is not a major causal factor in the development of reading comprehension difficulties in children. Yuill et al. (1989) argued that comprehension difficulties are related to more complex impairments in functional working memory capacity (see Oakhill & Yuill, and Cain chapters for a more detailed discussion). However, we have been unable to find evidence of a working memory deficit in our group of poor comprehenders (Stothard & Hulme, 1992). Further research is clearly needed to assess what role working memory deficits might play in reading comprehension difficulties.

In summary, research has indicated that children with reading comprehension problems have a wide range of difficulties. However, because virtually all of these studies have failed to measure and control for general intellectual differences between normal and poor comprehenders, it is impossible to tell whether the sorts of deficits reported have a specific association with reading comprehension problems or are simply associated with differences in general intelligence. Furthermore, most previous studies have failed to employ a control group of younger normal children matched to the poor comprehenders for reading comprehension level. However, this design is now beginning to be used in investigations of children's comprehension skill (see, e.g., Cain's study of story production in good and poor comprehenders, this volume). The omission of a comprehension-age match control group makes it difficult to determine whether any deficits observed in the poor comprehenders were a consequence or a cause of their reading comprehension difficulties.

ASSESSING THE COGNITIVE SKILLS OF CHILDREN WITH READING COMPREHENSION DIFFICULTIES

The aim of the first study was to clarify the nature of the deficits associated with reading comprehension difficulties in children (see Stothard & Hulme, 1992, 1995 for further details). Three groups of children were studied; a group of poor comprehenders (children with relatively severe reading comprehension problems in the presence of normal decoding skills), a group of normal age-match controls with equivalent decoding skills, and a younger group of normal readers matched for comprehension age to the poor comprehenders. This latter control group was important because it allowed us to determine the extent to which deficits found in the poor comprehenders were in line with their level of reading comprehension skills. If the poor comprehenders were worse on any tasks than the younger comprehension-age match controls, then this would be important. It would show that the deficits were not simply a consequence of comprehension difficulties, because the two groups had a similar level of reading comprehension skills. Rather, it would appear that the differences were likely to be a cause of the poor comprehenders' difficulties.

The children were selected by administering a standardized test of reading ability, the Neale Analysis of Reading Ability (Revised), Form 1 (Neale, 1989). The Neale is a test of prose reading; the child is required to read aloud a series of short stories and at the end of each is asked a set of comprehension questions. This test provides age-related measures of reading accuracy, reading comprehension, and reading speed.

To be classified as a poor comprehender, a child had to show a deficit of at least 6 months between comprehension age and chronological age and also a deficit of at least 6 months between comprehension age and reading accuracy age. In addition, only those children with adequate reading accuracy skills (accuracy age no more than 12 months below chronological age) were selected. Using these selection criteria, 9.5% of the initial sample of 7- to 8-year-old children (n = 147) were classified as having specific comprehension difficulties. The chronological age controls were individually matched to the poor comprehenders for chronological age and reading accuracy age. However, the two groups showed a marked discrepancy between their comprehension scores. The comprehension-age match control group comprised younger children whose reading skills were developing normally, that is, their reading accuracy and reading comprehension skills were in line with their age. The comprehension-age match controls were individually matched with the poor comprehenders for comprehension age. The poor comprehenders were also matched to the control groups for gender, giving 7 boys and 7 girls in each group. The characteristics of the three groups are shown in Table 5.1.

It should be noted that the Neale is discontinued when a prescribed number of reading (decoding) errors have been made. Therefore, young children with relatively weak reading accuracy skills read fewer passages than older children who are better decoders. Hence, the poor comprehenders actually read more passages than the younger comprehension-age match controls. It might be argued that the comprehension-age match controls would obtain higher comprehension scores if the later passages were presented. However, this seems unlikely for a number of reasons. First, the comprehension-age match controls' comprehension skills were in line with their chronological age. The later passages, which were not presented, contain information that is more difficult to understand and is likely to exceed the comprehension skills of these children. Second, in an unpublished study I (Stothard, 1992) showed that the poor comprehenders and comprehension-age match controls did not differ in their ability to answer comprehension questions when given identical passages to read. Finally, our results indicated that these two groups of children have equivalent listening comprehension skills. Therefore, we were confident that the poor comprehenders and younger comprehension-age match controls were accurately matched for comprehension skills.

TABLE 5.1
Characteristics of the Subject Groups

Group (N = 14)	Chronological Age	Accuracy Age	Comprehension Age	Reading Rate (wpm)
Poor comprehenders	8.0 (4 mths)	8.4 (16 mths)	6.8 (5 mths)	75.93 (19.91)
Chronological age controls	7.10 (3 mths)	8.4 (12 mths)	8.9 (6 mths)	78.07 (16.15)
Comprehension age controls	6.9 (5 mths)	6.8 (5 mths)	6.9 (4 mths)	57.14 (19.33)

Note. Ages are in years.months. Standard deviations are in parentheses.

Speed and Automaticity of Decoding

It has been suggested that reading comprehension problems might be attributable to inefficient decoding processes. The main version of this theory is Perfetti's decoding bottleneck or verbal efficiency hypothesis (e.g., Perfetti, 1985). According to this theory, if readers do not recognize words sufficiently quickly and automatically, the processing required for word recognition will place an additional burden on memory and will reduce the resources available for comprehension. Therefore, even when decoding is not inaccurate, if it is slow and effortful, it may use resources important for comprehension. It should, however, be noted that Oakhill (1981, as cited in Yuill & Oakhill, 1991) reported that her sample of children with reading comprehension problems were not slow at decoding.

Reading speed in the present study was assessed by the Neale. For each child a reading speed, in words per minute (wpm), was calculated. As can be seen in Table 5.1, the poor comprehenders read at a rate similar to the chronological age controls. However, they read more quickly than the younger, comprehension-age match controls. It is clear that slow and inefficient decoding is not an adequate explanation of the comprehension difficulties observed in the present group of poor comprehenders.

General Intellectual Characteristics

Intelligence was assessed by administering a short form of the Wechsler Intelligence Scale for Children-Revised (WISC-R; Wechsler, 1974). Verbal IQ was measured by the Vocabulary and Similarities subtests, and performance IQ was assessed by the Block Design and Object Assembly subtests. These subtests were chosen because each shows a strong correlation with the component of intelligence it is designed to measure (Sattler, 1982). The Similarities subtest assesses general knowledge and verbal reasoning skills. In this task, children are required to explain in their own words how pairs of words (e.g., wheel, ball) are similar. The Vocabulary task measures knowledge of word meanings; here, children are asked to give definitions for words of increasing difficulty. The Block Design and Object Assembly subtests are measures of nonverbal problem-solving skills. The former task involves recreating a geometric pattern using small patterned blocks and the latter task requires the child to arrange several "jigsaw-like" puzzle pieces into the shape of a common object.

Table 5.2 shows the intelligence profiles of the three groups. As can be seen, the poor comprehenders obtained lower verbal IQ scores than either of the two control groups. An ANOVA confirmed that there was a significant difference between the verbal IQ scores of the three groups, $F(2, 39) = 9.24$, $p < .005$. The poor comprehenders obtained significantly lower verbal IQ scores than either the chronological age or comprehension-age match controls, $HSD = 15.21$, $df = 39$, $p < .01$. In contrast, there was no significant difference between the performance intelligence scores obtained by the three groups.

TABLE 5.2
Verbal IQ and Performance IQ Scores of the Three Subject Groups

Group (N = 14)	Verbal IQ	Performance IQ
Poor comprehenders	91.79 (13.26)	102.43 (14.03)
Chronological age controls	110.57 (11.99)	111.79 (11.18)
Comprehension age controls	108.86 (13.08)	109.71 (12.96)

Note. Standard deviations are in parentheses.

Furthermore, the poor comprehenders showed a marked discrepancy between their verbal and performance IQ scores, $t(13) = 2.64$, $p < .05$. In these children, verbal IQ was consistently lower than performance IQ. In contrast, neither the chronological age controls nor the comprehension-age match controls showed any marked difference between their verbal and performance IQ scores.

The poor comprehenders' impaired verbal intellectual skills were further examined by analyzing the raw scores on each of the WISC-R subtests. The absolute level of performance (not adjusted for chronological age) of the poor comprehenders could therefore be examined in comparison to both chronological age and comprehension-age match controls. As can be seen in Table 5.3, there was a marked difference between the Vocabulary and Similarities raw scores obtained by the three groups, $F(2, 39) = 6.45$, $p < .005$ and $F(2, 39) = 5.18$, $p < .05$, respectively. The poor comprehenders obtained similar raw scores to the younger comprehension-age match controls, but obtained significantly lower raw scores than the chronological age controls on Vocabulary, $HSD = 3.56$, $df = 39$, $p < .05$ and on Similarities, $HSD = 2.75$, $df = 39$, $p < .05$. In contrast, all three groups performed at a similar level on the two performance subtests.

These findings indicate that the poor comprehenders exhibited a specific deficit in verbal skills. They had below average verbal IQ scores. Furthermore, in contrast to the two control groups, they showed a marked discrepancy between their verbal and performance IQ scores. However, the raw scores obtained by the poor comprehenders on the verbal subtests did not differ from those of the comprehension-age match control group. The poor

TABLE 5.3
Raw Scores Obtained on the WISC-R Subtests

Group (N = 14)	Vocabulary	Similarities	Block Design	Object Assembly
Poor comprehenders	20.29 (4.51)	8.36 (3.15)	19.14 (8.93)	16.71 (4.18)
Chronological age controls	25.21 (3.58)	11.43 (3.01)	23.14 (5.84)	18.43 (3.94)
Comprehension age controls	21.36 (3.25)	8.29 (2.67)	17.29 (7.88)	16.00 (4.51)

Note. Standard deviations are given in parentheses.

comprehenders thus showed similar comprehension and verbal-semantic skills to a group of younger children whose comprehension was normal for their age. It seems that the low level of comprehension skills exhibited by the poor comprehenders were actually in line with their other verbal skills.

Language Comprehension Skills

The findings just presented suggest that the poor comprehenders' difficulties do not reflect a specific deficit in reading comprehension, but rather that their reading problem may be viewed as part of a general verbal deficit. From this it might be hypothesized that the poor comprehenders should show deficits on tasks that measure language comprehension skills but that do not involve reading, such as listening comprehension.

Language comprehension skills were assessed by administering a non-standardized test of listening comprehension. This test involved listening to a series of short stories and answering questions based on them. The stories and questions were taken from the parallel form of the Neale (Revised) which had not been used to measure the children's reading comprehension skills.

Receptive language comprehension skills were examined by using Bishop's Test for the Reception of Grammar (TROG, 1983). This test is comprised of a series of 80 four-choice items. For each item, four colored pictures are presented and the child's task is to select the picture that depicts a test sentence read aloud by the experimenter. For each item, there are three distractors of either a lexical or grammatical nature. The test assesses the understanding of a range of grammatical contrasts, such as masculine/feminine personal pronoun, comparative/absolute, and neither X nor Y. Because the test sentences are presented aurally, TROG may be considered to be a measure of listening comprehension skill.

As can be seen in Table 5.4, the poor comprehenders exhibited difficulties on both measures of language comprehension. On the listening comprehension task, they answered fewer questions correctly than did the chronological age controls, $F(2, 39) = 24.97$, $p < .001$; $HSD = 3.63$, $df = 39$, $p < .01$. However, their performance did not differ from that of the younger comprehension-age match controls. Similarly, on the TROG, the poor compre-

TABLE 5.4
Language Comprehension Skills of the Three Subject Groups

Subject Group (N = 14)	Listening Comprehension (Max = 28)	TROG (Max = 80)
Poor comprehenders	11.93 (3.47)	71.29 (4.65)
Chronological age controls	18.6 (2.53)	76.50 (2.21)
Comprehension age controls	11.29 (3.07)	70.93 (3.63)

Note. Standard deviations appear in parentheses.

henders obtained lower scores than their age-match controls, performing at a level similar to the younger children matched for reading comprehension level, $F(2, 39) = 10.31$, $p < .001$; $HSD = 4.32$, $df = 39$, $p < .01$.

It is clear that the comprehension problems experienced by these poor comprehenders are not restricted to reading, because on both measures of listening comprehension they performed at a level lower than their chronological age controls. However, they did not differ from a group of younger children matched for reading comprehension skills. Yuill and Oakhill (1991) also reported that there was a tendency for children with poor comprehension skills to make more errors on the TROG than age-matched controls. However, the differences observed in their study were relatively small and failed to reach significance. We conclude that these poor comprehenders have general language comprehension difficulties which are a product of their weak verbal-semantic skills.

 Phonological Skills

If reading comprehension is dependent upon verbal-semantic skills, then it is quite possible that other aspects of the reading process will be normal. The other major component of reading ability is decoding skill. As noted above, there is now a vast amount of evidence linking variations in decoding skills to variations in underlying phonological skills. Given that the poor comprehenders were selected to have age-appropriate decoding skills, a strong hypothesis is that they should show normal phonological skills for their age. The children's phonological skills were assessed by three tasks; a spoonerism task, a nonword reading test, and a spelling test.

Phonological awareness skills were examined by administering a spoonerism task in which the children were required to transpose the initial sounds from the beginning of two spoken words (e.g., "Rice Pudding" → /paɪs rʊdɪŋ/, "Shopping List" → /lɒpɪŋ ʃɪst/). The ability to use phonological decoding strategies in reading was assessed using the Graded Nonword Reading Test (Snowling, Stothard, & McLean, in press). This test is comprised of 10 one-syllable nonwords (e.g., mosp, gromp) and 10 two-syllable nonwords (e.g., tegwop, molsmit). The nonwords are typed in lower case letters on separate cards and presented individually to be read aloud. Spelling skills were assessed with the Vernon Graded Word Spelling Test (Vernon, 1977). In this test, children are required to spell a series of dictated words presented in a sentence context.

Table 5.5 shows the performance of the three groups on the phonological tasks. The poor comprehenders and chronological age controls gained similar scores on the spoonerism task, both groups performing at a significantly higher level than the comprehension-age match controls, $F(2, 39) = 6.82$, $p < .005$; $HSD = 9.69$, $df = 39$, $p < .05$. Thus, the poor comprehenders were

TABLE 5.5
Phonological Skills of the Three Subject Groups

Subject Group (N = 14)	Spoonerism Task Number Correct (Max = 48)		Nonword Reading Number Correct (Max = 20)	Vernon Spelling Number Correct
Poor comprehenders	34.29	(6.76)	15.79 (2.69)	29.21 (6.55)
Chronological age controls	37.50	(7.69)	16.36 (3.00)	31.07 (6.02)
Comprehension age controls	23.64	(14.79)	12.00 (3.37)	20.43 (5.58)

Note. Standard deviations appear in parentheses.

able to segment and transpose the beginning phonemes of words, indicating that explicit phonological awareness was normal.

Furthermore, the poor comprehenders were able to use these phonological skills in both reading and spelling. They read a similar number of nonwords correctly as the chronological age controls, but obtained significantly higher scores than the younger comprehension-age match controls, $F(2, 39) = 9. 22$, $p < .001$; $HSD = 3.61$, $df = 39$, $p < .01$. Thus, the poor comprehenders were able to use phonological recoding skills when reading. A similar pattern of results was observed on the Vernon Spelling Test. The poor comprehenders and chronological age controls spelled a similar number of words correctly, both groups performing at a higher level than the comprehension-age match controls, $F(2, 39) = 12.30$, $p < .001$; $HSD = 7.21$, $df = 39$, $p < .01$. It is clear that the poor comprehenders' spelling skills were normal for their age. Furthermore, their spelling errors indicated the use of a phonological strategy. Sixty-seven percent of their misspellings were accurate phonetic representations of the target words, errors such as "hoos" for "whose" and "onist" for "honest" being common. It may be concluded that the poor comprehenders have normal phonological skills for their age and that their phonological skills are commensurate with their decoding skills.

Summary

To summarize, these findings indicate that reading comprehension problems (in the presence of normal decoding skills) are associated with impaired verbal-semantic skills. The poor comprehenders were found to have selective deficits in verbal IQ. They also showed marked impairments on tests of language comprehension. However, their performance was similar to that of a group of younger control children matched to the poor comprehenders for reading comprehension skills. Therefore, their reading comprehension difficulties might be thought of as a manifestation of a more global deficit in general language skills (while in contrast their phonological skills are normal). In line with this finding, the poor comprehenders were also found to have listening comprehension problems. In sum, the comprehension deficit experienced by the poor comprehenders is clearly not specific to reading, but rather represents a general language comprehension limitation. In contrast to their impaired general language skills, the poor comprehenders showed absolutely normal phonological skills for their age.

These findings suggest that the development of reading comprehension skills is dependent upon intact underlying general language skills, whereas the development of decoding skills appears to depend upon the existence of intact phonological skills. According to this hypothesis, the poor comprehenders had been able to learn to decode words at a normal rate because this skill was heavily dependent upon their normal phonological skills. In contrast, although these children could decode words normally in reading, their comprehension was impaired by their weak underlying general language skills which were also manifest in their poor performance on tests of spoken language comprehension.

This hypothesis makes a clear prediction. Children with decoding problems in the absence of language comprehension problems should show a contrasting pattern of characteristics to poor comprehenders. Poor decoders might be expected to show impaired phonological skills but relatively normal general language skills. This prediction was tested in the following study.

ASSESSING THE COGNITIVE SKILLS OF CHILDREN WITH DECODING DIFFICULTIES

The vast majority of research on children's decoding difficulties has focused on processes associated with the development of word recognition skills. As noted earlier, this work has shown that poor decoding skills in children are closely associated with phonological impairments (see Hulme & Snowling, 1992, for a recent review). In contrast, relatively little research has examined the comprehension skills of children with specific decoding difficulties. It is, however, generally assumed that these children are characterized by a primary deficit in word recognition, not comprehension, and this idea has been embodied formally in the phonological-core variable-difference model of Stanovich (1988). In line with this model several studies have reported that children with specific decoding difficulties typically have comprehension skills that are superior to their decoding skills (e.g., Conners & Olson, 1990; Frith & Snowling, 1983).

The aim of the following study was to provide an assessment of comprehension ability and phonological skills in children with decoding difficulties. It was predicted that children with specific decoding difficulties would have impaired phonological skills but relatively normal language comprehension skills. Further details of this study are given in Stothard and Hulme (1995).

Two groups of children participated in this study, 14 poor decoders and 14 reading-age match controls. The children were selected on the basis of their performance on the Neale Analysis of Reading Ability (Revised). To be classified as a poor decoder, a child had to show a deficit of at least 12 months between reading accuracy age and chronological age and 6 months between reading accuracy age and reading comprehension age. In most cases the poor decoders experienced a decoding deficit that was much greater than the baseline criterion of 12 months. The reading-age match control group was comprised of younger children whose reading skills were developing normally for their age. The reading-age match controls were individually matched to the poor decoders for reading accuracy age. Because of the low reading ages of the poor decoders, three of the reading-age match controls were 5 years old. In England, children start school at 4 years and most have a measurable reading age at 5 years.

There were 10 boys and 4 girls in the group of poor decoders, and 7 boys and 7 girls in the reading age-match control group. The preponderance of boys in the former group reflects the bias towards males in groups of children with specific decoding difficulties (Rutter & Yule, 1975). The characteristics of the subject groups are presented in Table 5.6.

As can be seen in Table 5.6, the poor decoders' primary reading difficulty was weak reading accuracy skills. Reading accuracy age lagged behind chronological age and reading comprehension age. Nevertheless, although this group's reading comprehension skills were in advance of their decoding ability, reading comprehension was still low for their age. It is, however, highly probable that the Neale provided a conservative estimate of these children's reading comprehension skills. The Neale is discontinued when a prescribed number of reading errors has been made. Thus, children with poor decoding skills did not progress past the early passages, and their reading comprehension scores were limited.

To check that the poor decoders' low comprehension skills could be explained in this way, a group of children matched to the poor decoders for chronological age were also given the Neale. For each chronological age control, a new comprehension score was computed based on the number of questions answered correctly on only those passages that had been read by the matched poor decoder. The chronological age controls answered an

TABLE 5.6
Characteristics of the Subject Groups

Group (n = 14)	Chronological Age	Accuracy Age	Comprehension Age	Reading Rate (wpm)
Poor decoders	8.5 (7 mths)	6.6 (10 mths)	7.7 (8 mths)	46.71 (20.41)
Reading age controls	6.8 (7 mths)	6.7 (10 mths)	6.8 (11 mths)	53.71 (27.46)

Note. Ages are in years.months. Standard deviations appear in parentheses.

average of 12.86 questions correctly compared with 13.64 questions correct for the poor decoders (the reading age controls answered 9.64 questions correctly). It is clear that there was no difference between the performance of these two groups.

Speed and Automaticity of Decoding

Table 5.6 gives the reading rates of the two groups. As can be seen, the poor decoders read at a rate similar to the younger reading-age match controls. In fact, the poor decoders' reading speed was equivalent to an average reading rate age of 7 years, 1 month (Neale Manual). Thus, the poor decoders had impaired decoding speed as well as poor accuracy.

Intellectual Characteristics and Language Comprehension Skills

As in the first study, intelligence was assessed by administering a short form of the WISC-R (Wechsler, 1974). Three of the children in the reading age-match control group fell outside the age range of the WISC-R. All of these children were 5 years old. The Wechsler Preschool and Primary Scale of Intelligence Test (WPPSI, Wechsler, 1967) was used to obtain an estimate of IQ for these children. Language comprehension skills were examined by administering the listening comprehension test and the TROG.

For each child, a prorated verbal IQ and performance IQ were calculated. These are shown in Table 5.7. It is clear that the poor decoders and reading age-match controls obtained similar IQ scores. T tests confirmed that the poor decoders and their reading age-match controls did not differ in either verbal IQ or performance IQ. Furthermore, neither group showed a marked discrepancy between verbal and performance IQ scores. Matched samples t tests confirmed that there were no within-subject group differences between verbal and performance IQ scores.

As three of the reading age-match controls received the WPPSI rather than the WISC-R, it was not possible to examine the raw scores obtained on the individual subtests. We were unable to compare the absolute level of performance of the two groups. However, because both groups obtained

TABLE 5.7
Verbal IQ and Performance IQ Scores of the Two Subject Groups

Group (N = 14)	Verbal IQ	Performance IQ
Poor decoders	101.07 (13.50)	108.21 (11.14)
Reading age controls	107.57 (11.90)	111.71 (13.53)

Note. Standard deviations appear in parentheses.

TABLE 5.8
Language Comprehension Skills of the Subject Groups

Subject Group (N = 14)	Listening Comprehension (Max = 28)	TROG (Max = 80)
Poor decoders	17.79 (3.38)	75.64 (1.78)
Reading age controls	9.93 (3.63)	70.93 (5.03)
Chronological age controls	17.93 (3.38)	76.57 (2.03)

Note. Standard deviations appear in parentheses.

age-appropriate IQ scores, it is clear that the poor decoders were performing at a higher intellectual level than the younger reading-age match controls.

As can be seen in Table 5.8, the poor decoders were also found to have age-appropriate language comprehension skills. On the listening comprehension task, they consistently answered more questions correctly than did the reading-age match control group, $t(26) = 5.93$, $p < .001$. Thus, the poor decoders' listening comprehension skills were superior to their decoding skills. To check that the poor decoders obtained age-appropriate comprehension scores, their performance was compared with that of a group of children matched for chronological age. These chronological age controls had normal reading skills for their age. The poor decoders and chronological age controls answered a similar number of questions correctly.

A similar pattern of results was obtained on the TROG. The poor decoders scored higher than the reading-age match controls, $t(26) = 3.31$, $p < .005$. However, they obtained similar scores to a group of age-match controls.

These findings indicate that the poor decoders had age-appropriate verbal-semantic skills. They obtained normal verbal IQ scores and performed at a level similar to age-match controls on two measures of language comprehension. Explanations of the poor decoders' difficulties must, therefore, look to processes specific to reading, rather than to general cognitive factors such as intelligence.

Phonological Skills

Phonological skills were examined by administering the spoonerism task, the Graded Nonword Reading Test, and the Vernon Spelling Test. The results obtained on the phonological tasks are shown in Table 5.9.

The poor decoders were found to have severely impaired phonological skills. They exhibited marked difficulties on the spoonerism task, obtaining considerably lower scores than the reading-age match controls, $t(26) = 3.84$, $p < .001$. Thus, the poor decoders had phonological difficulties even in comparison to younger normal children matched for decoding skill. This finding is consistent with the idea of phonological skills being a cause of these children's reading difficulties.

TABLE 5.9
Phonological Skills of the Subject Groups

Subject Group (N = 14)	Spoonerism Task Number Correct (Max = 48)	Nonword Reading Number Correct (Max = 20)	Vernon Spelling Number Correct
Poor decoders	11.14 (6.40)	7.64 (3.89)	12.50 (4.43)
Reading age controls	27.29 (14.38)	9.93 (5.48)	20.43 (8.86)

Note. Standard deviations appear in parentheses.

The poor decoders were also found to have difficulty using a phonological strategy during reading. On the Graded Nonword Reading Test they read, on average, only 7 nonwords correctly. This performance was slightly lower than the younger reading-age match controls, and considerably poorer than chronological age controls ($M = 15.21$). In fact, the poor decoders obtained significantly lower nonword reading scores than did the age-match controls, $t(26) = 5.69$, $p < .001$. In other words, the poor decoders' nonword reading skills were consistent with their level of decoding ability but much weaker than expected given their chronological age.

Phonological skills were also assessed by administering the Vernon Spelling Test. Once again, the poor decoders exhibited difficulties on this task. In fact, they spelled significantly fewer words correctly than did the younger reading-age match controls, $t(26) = 2.99$, $p < .01$. Furthermore, approximately half (48%) of the poor decoders' spelling errors were dysphonetic. For example, one poor decoder wrote "rolel" for "royal," "lenfle" for "length," and "sutdel" for "suitable." Errors such as these indicate that the poor decoders had difficulty using phoneme-to-grapheme correspondences in spelling. It seems reasonable to infer that the poor decoders' spelling difficulties are a product of their phonological deficits.

The pattern of results obtained here confirms the prediction that children with specific decoding deficits will show impaired phonological skills but normal general language skills. This supports the idea put forward earlier that there are two separate components in reading, decoding, and comprehension, and these skills can develop independently. The development of decoding skills appears to depend critically upon intact phonological skills whereas the development of comprehension skills appears to depend upon general language skills.

GENERAL DISCUSSION

The two studies presented here have identified two contrasting and highly distinctive groups of poor readers, children with comprehension problems and children with decoding problems. It is clear that reading problems are not homogeneous; children may develop reading difficulties because they have poor decoding skills or poor comprehension skills (or in some cases both). These findings are very much in line with Gough and Tunmer's (1986) simple model of reading which proposed that reading ability can be divided into two component skills, reading accuracy and language comprehension. Typically, these two component skills are highly correlated so that children who are good decoders also have good comprehension skills (see Juel, Griffith, & Gough, 1986). However, the present research demonstrates that the two components are separable. Deficits can occur in one subcomponent independently of the other, resulting in the development of different forms of reading difficulty. Furthermore, these different categories of reading problems appear to have different underlying causes and so require different forms of treatment.

Consistent with previous work, our findings show that children with decoding difficulties have impaired phonological skills. It is a reasonable hypothesis that this phonological deficit is a direct cause of these children's decoding difficulties. These poor decoders do not, however, have a general language impairment. They have normal verbal IQ scores and normal language comprehension ability. It appears that these children's proficient verbal-semantic skills support the comprehension of what they read.

Characterizing the reading impairment of the poor comprehenders is more difficult. These children have general language comprehension difficulties that are evident on tests of both reading and listening comprehension. In fact, these children do not have an impairment of reading, but can be more accurately described as having general language comprehension difficulties. The skills that underlie reading comprehension appear to have much in common with general language comprehension processes (see Palmer, MacLeod, Hunt, & Davidson, 1985). It seems that poor verbal-semantic skills contribute to these children's difficulties. The poor comprehenders do, however, have normal phonological skills which have enabled them to develop proficient decoding skills.

Why is low verbal ability related to reading comprehension problems? Previous research has identified two major characteristics of individuals with high verbal ability; fast access to overlearned codes in long-term memory (e.g., Goldberg, Schwartz, & Stewart, 1977; Hunt, Lunneborg, & Lewis, 1975) and the ability to learn from context (see Sternberg, 1982, 1985, for reviews). It may be of particular relevance here that high verbal ability facilitates vocabulary learning (Sternberg & Powell, 1983).

It has been reported that the ability to learn vocabulary from context is closely related to IQ and to reading comprehension ability (Sternberg & Powell, 1983; van Daalen-Kapteijns & Elshout-Mohr, 1981). Sternberg and Powell (1983) asked a group of high-school students to read passages containing a number of extremely low-frequency words. At the end of each passage they had to define the meaning of each low-frequency word. Subjects with high verbal ability obtained higher scores than subjects with low verbal ability, and there were substantial correlations between vocabulary learning scores and verbal ability. It would appear that an important component of verbal ability is the ability to acquire new verbal knowledge. Given that vocabulary knowledge is an important component of intelligence and verbal comprehension (Jensen, 1980), it seems reasonable to suggest that vocabulary knowledge might help to explain the relationship between verbal intelligence and comprehension ability. Subjects with high verbal ability are able to learn the meanings of words more easily than those with low verbal ability. High verbal ability may therefore aid reading comprehension in at least two ways. In the first place, people of high verbal ability simply know the meanings of more words than subjects of low verbal ability. Secondly, when subjects of high verbal ability encounter words they do not understand in reading they are better able to infer the meanings of the unknown word and retain this new knowledge.

The argument presented here suggests that verbal intelligence is related to comprehension such that high verbal IQ leads to good comprehension skills. However, it must also be pointed out that other factors might mediate this relationship. For example, Stanovich, West, Cunningham, Cipielewski, and Siddiqui (this volume) showed that exposure to print increases both intelligence and vocabulary knowledge.

The proposal for a developmental separation between decoding and comprehension skills in reading is not new. Frith and Snowling (1983) reported evidence for a dissociation of comprehension and decoding ability. They assessed phonological reading skills and comprehension skills in autistic children, dyslexic children, and younger normal controls, matched for reading age. The autistic children were able to read nonwords as well as younger reading-age match controls and also showed a regularity effect in reading, correctly reading more regular than irregular words. Thus, the autistic children's phonological recoding skills were generally in line with their decoding level. The dyslexic children, however, showed an abnormal pattern of performance on these tasks. They read significantly fewer nonwords correctly than did reading age-match controls and also failed to show a regularity effect in reading. These findings suggest that the dyslexics have difficulty using a phonological strategy for reading. A contrasting pattern of results was obtained when the children's semantic processing skills were assessed. Here, the autistic children exhibited deficits. Compared with younger reading-age match controls, the autistic children showed impaired ability to utilize sentence context to pronounce homographs and also showed deficits on a cloze reading task. Conversely, the dyslexic children showed a high level of performance on these tasks in comparison to their reading-age level. Thus, the autistic children had normal phonological skills but poor semantic skills, whereas the dyslexic children showed impaired phonological reading skills but normal semantic skills (given their decoding level).

To conclude, these findings indicate that reading ability comprises two major components, comprehension and decoding skill. These two facets of reading skill are subserved by different language mechanisms (verbal ability and phonology, respectively) allowing for dissociations between them during childhood.

REFERENCES

Bishop, D. (1983). *Test for the Reception of Grammar.* Manchester, England: Chapel Press.

Bradley, L., & Bryant, P. E. (1983). Categorizing sounds and learning to read: A causal connection. *Nature, 301,* 419–421.

Brady, S., Shankweiler, D., & Mann, V. (1983). Speech perception and memory coding in relation to reading ability. *Journal of Experimental Child Psychology, 35,* 345–367.

Conners, F. A., & Olson, R. K. (1990). Reading comprehension in dyslexic and normal readers: A component-skills analysis. In D. A. Balota, G. B. Flores d'Arcais, & K. Rayner (Eds.), *Comprehension processes in reading* (pp. 557–579). Hillsdale, NJ: Lawrence Erlbaum Associates.

Frith, U., & Snowling, M. (1983). Reading for meaning and reading for sound in autistic and dyslexic children. *British Journal of Developmental Psychology, 1,* 329–342.

Goldberg, R. A., Schwartz, S., & Stewart, M. (1977). Individual differences in cognitive processes. *Journal of Educational Psychology, 69,* 9–14.

Gough, P. B., & Tunmer, W. E. (1986). Decoding, reading and reading disability. *Remedial and Special Education, 7,* 6–10.

Hatcher, P. J., Hulme, C., & Ellis, A. W. (1994). Ameliorating early reading failure by integrating the teaching of reading and phonological skills: The phonological linkage hypothesis. *Child Development, 65,* 41–57.

Hoover, W. A., & Gough, P. B. (1990). The simple view of reading. *Reading and Writing, 2,* 127–160.

Hulme, C., & Snowling, M. (1992). Phonological deficits in dyslexia: A "sound" reappraisal of the verbal deficit hypothesis. In N. Singh & I. Beale (Eds.), *Current perspectives in learning disabilities* (pp. 270–301). New York: Springer-Verlag.

Hunt, E., Lunneborg, C., & Lewis, J. (1975). What does it mean to be high verbal? *Cognitive Psychology, 7,* 194–227.

Jensen, A. R. (1980). *Bias in mental testing.* New York: Free Press.

Johnston, R., Rugg, M., & Scott, T. (1987). Phonological similarity effects, memory span and developmental reading disorders: The nature of the relationship. *British Journal of Psychology, 78,* 205–211.

Juel, C., Griffith, P. L., & Gough, P. B. (1986). Acquisition of literacy: A longitudinal study of children in first and second grade. *Journal of Educational Psychology, 78,* 243–255.

Neale, M. D. (1989). *The Neale Analysis of Reading Ability* (Rev. British Edition). Windsor, England: NFER-Nelson.

Oakhill, J. (1984). Inferential and memory skills in children's comprehension of stories. *British Journal of Educational Psychology, 54,* 31–39.

Oakhill, J., & Yuill, N. (1986). Pronoun resolution in skilled and less-skilled comprehenders: Effects of memory load and inferential complexity. *Language and Speech, 29,* 25–37.

Oakhill, J., Yuill, N., & Parkin, A. (1986). On the nature of the difference between skilled and less-skilled comprehenders. *Journal of Research in Reading, 9,* 80–91.

Palmer, J., MacLeod, C. M., Hunt, E., & Davidson, J. (1985). Information processing correlates of reading. *Journal of Memory and Language, 24,* 59–88.

Paris, S. G., & Myers, M. (1981). Comprehension monitoring, memory, and study strategies of good and poor readers. *Journal of Reading Behavior, 13,* 5–22.

Perfetti, C. A. (1985). *Reading ability.* Oxford, England: Oxford University Press.

Rack, J. P., Hulme, C., & Snowling, M. J. (1993). Learning to read: A theoretical synthesis. In H. Reese (Ed.), *Advances in child development and behavior* (Vol. 24, pp. 99–132). New York: Academic Press.

Rack, J. P., Snowling, M. J., & Olson, R. K. (1992). The nonword reading deficit in developmental dyslexia: A review. *Reading Research Quarterly, 27,* 28–53.

Reed, C. (1989). Speech perception and the discrimination of brief auditory cues in reading disabled children. *Journal of Experimental Child Psychology, 48,* 270–292.

Rutter, M., & Yule, W. (1975). The concept of specific reading retardation. *Journal of Child Psychology and Psychiatry, 16,* 181–197.

Sattler, J. M. (1982). *Assessment of children's intelligence and special abilities* (2nd ed.). Boston: Allyn & Bacon.

Smiley, S. S., Oakley, D. D., Worthen, D., Campione, J. C., & Brown, A. L. (1977). Recall of thematically relevant material by adolescent good and poor readers as a function of written versus oral presentation. *Journal of Educational Psychology, 69,* 381–387.

Snowling, M. J. (1981). Phonemic deficits in developmental dyslexia. *Psychological Research, 43,* 219–234.

Snowling, M. J., Goulandris, N., Bowlby, M., & Howell, P. (1986). Segmentation and speech perception in relation to reading skill: A developmental analysis. *Journal of Experimental Child Psychology, 41,* 489–507.

Snowling, M. J., Stothard, S. E., & McLean, J. (in press). *Graded Nonword Reading Test.* Suffolk, England: Thames Valley Test Company.

Snowling, M., van Wagtendonk, B., & Stafford, C. (1988). Object-naming deficits in developmental dyslexia. *Journal of Research in Reading, 11,* 67–85.

Stanovich, K. E. (1988). Explaining the differences between the dyslexic and the garden-variety poor reader: The phonological-core variable-difference model. *Journal of Learning Disabilities, 21,* 590–604.

Sternberg, R. J. (Ed.). (1982). *Handbook of human intelligence.* Cambridge, England: Cambridge University Press.

Sternberg, R. J. (Ed.). (1985). *Human abilities: An information processing approach.* San Francisco: Freeman.

Sternberg, R. J., & Powell, J. S. (1983). Comprehending verbal comprehension. *American Psychologist, 38,* 878–893.

Stothard, S. E. (1992). *Reading difficulties in children: Problems of decoding and comprehension.* Unpublished doctoral dissertation, University of York, England.

Stothard, S. E., & Hulme, C. (1992). Reading comprehension difficulties in children: The role of language comprehension and working memory skills. *Reading and Writing, 4,* 245–256.

Stothard, S. E., & Hulme, C. (1995). A comparison of phonological skills in children with reading comprehension difficulties and children with decoding difficulties. *Journal of Child Psychology and Psychiatry, 36,* 399–408.

van Daalen-Kapteijns, M. M., & Elshout-Mohr, M. (1981). The acquisition of word meanings as a cognitive learning process. *Journal of Verbal Learning and Verbal Behavior, 20,* 386–399.

Vernon, P. E. (1977). *Graded Word Spelling Test.* London: Hodder & Stoughton.

Wagner, R. K., & Torgesen, J. K. (1987). The nature of phonological processing and its causal role in the acquisition of reading skills. *Psychological Bulletin, 101,* 192–212.

Wechsler, D. (1967). *Wechsler Preschool and Primary Scale of Intelligence.* New York: Psychological Corporation.

Wechsler, D. (1974). *Wechsler Intelligence Scale for Children-Revised.* New York: Psychological Corporation.

Yuill, N., & Oakhill, J. (1988). Understanding of anaphoric relations in skilled and less skilled comprehenders. *British Journal of Psychology, 79,* 173–186.

Yuill, N., & Oakhill, J. (1991). *Children's problems in text comprehension.* Cambridge, England: Cambridge University Press.

Yuill, N., Oakhill, J., & Parkin, A. (1989). Working memory, comprehension ability and the resolution of text anomaly. *British Journal of Psychology, 80,* 351–361.

CHAPTER SIX

Profiles of Reading Comprehension Difficulties: An Analysis of Single Cases

Cesare Cornoldi
Rossana De Beni
Francesca Pazzaglia
Department of General Psychology
University of Padova

Over the years, studies on comprehension difficulties have utilized different methodologies, moving from general, correlational studies to more specific analyses matching groups of good and poor comprehenders. The analysis of group patterns has given a strong impulse to the research, stressing the role of some cognitive and metacognitive variables in comprehension and comprehension difficulties. On the other hand, it has also presented some problems, due both to the complexity of the comprehension task, and to some methodological points. The present chapter aims at examining some theoretical and methodological issues in the studies on reading difficulties, and the role played by some cognitive and metacognitive variables in reading comprehension difficulty. In particular, we compared the results derived from two different methodologies, one contrasting groups of poor and good readers, and the other separately analyzing single cases of poor readers.

Reading comprehension is a complex ability that requires the involvement of several specific cognitive components. Moreover, some of these components are likely to be central, that is, involving a number of attentional resources as well as a general executive function. This therefore places it in a general mental framework that is quite difficult to trace back to clear and specific cognitive and neuropsychological deficits (Baddeley, 1990; Moscovitch & Umiltà, 1991). Given the complexity of the task, it is not surprising that research, including that reported in this volume, that compared subjects with comprehension difficulty to matched control subjects has found in the former a high variety of deficits in areas such as vocabulary, lexical access,

113

retrieval from long-term memory, syntactic processing, inferences, text integration, working memory, metacognition, linguistic awareness, use of cohesive devices, language production, narrative comprehension and production, listening, and so forth. One deduction that can be made from this massive amount of research is that (a) subjects with reading comprehension difficulty are characterized by all these deficits. From an operational viewpoint, a further deduction is that (b) because subjects with reading comprehension difficulty are lacking in these characteristics, they will benefit from an intervention in one or more of them. However, a further analysis of the problem is sufficient to understand that deduction (a) can be read in two different ways and consequently, deduction (b) can be totally wrong. Deduction (a) can be taken to mean that either subjects with text comprehension difficulty present on the whole the deficits described in the literature or that each subject presents those deficits. The fact that in subjects with reading comprehension difficulty the distribution of ability scores (related to a component hypothesized as underlying the comprehension process) significantly differs from the distribution of the same ability scores in control subjects is often interpreted as a sign that all subjects of the disabled group present this difference. Given the very large number of variables associated with reading comprehension, if every subject with text comprehension difficulty had a deficit in each of them, the situation would indeed be depressing and a considerable number of cases would present devastating cognitive profiles.

Some methodological caution must be taken into account when the analysis is confined to comparison between groups. For instance, Baron and Treiman (1980) warned against three types of error that can be made in such cases. First, if, due to a different performance in one task and a similar one in another, subjects are inferred to differ in the former and not in the latter, this conclusion may be affected by the different discriminative power of the two tasks. Secondly, the difference between the two groups of subjects may be affected by other elements associated with the task, such as greater motivation, ability to understand instructions, familiarity with the material, or the task itself, which help the performance of one group over the other. Thirdly, it must be taken into account that a task is unlikely to measure only what it sets out to measure: The poorer performance in a given test (e.g., use of cohesive devices) could be due to a lesser ability which, although not directly measured by the test, nevertheless plays a part in it (e.g., reasoning). These methodological cautions are related to another one concerning the interpretation of the difference between groups (Ehri, 1979). A cognitive component in which subjects experiencing problems with text comprehension might obtain a significantly lower score could be considered in four different ways, that is as a prerequisite of comprehension ability, as a facilitator, as a consequence, or, lastly, as an incidental correlate of reading comprehension ability. For example, among the components typically associated with reading comprehension, a sufficient working memory ability or good listening comprehension could be considered almost essential prerequisites; good metacognitive knowledge of the reading process a facilitator; a good study ability a consequence; and success in a syllogistic reasoning task an incidental correlate (due to the fact that reasoning and comprehension are tied to a common source).

These methodological considerations can lead to different theoretical frameworks of comprehension difficulty. In particular, going back to the two deductions mentioned earlier, (a) may simply be read in the sense that some subjects with text comprehension difficulty, and not necessarily all of them, will present a deficit in an ability underlying their reading comprehension ability. If this is so, deduction (b) may be incorrect, as it assumes that the whole group of subjects will benefit from training in that underlying ability, even the subjects who are not lacking in it.

These general reflections have considerable repercussions on the kinds of intervention carried out on subjects with text comprehension difficulty. There is a long-standing debate between those who support a, let us call it, "global" position and maintain that the intervention must cover the process as a whole, and, those who believe that it is better to single out the process components in which the subjects are particularly lacking and work on them. If the profiles of subjects with text comprehension difficulty are shown to be highly differentiated, the global position turns out to be rather weakened by proposing the same intervention for subjects who are actually different.

The opportunity to directly test subjects with text comprehension difficulty was given to us by the Consiglio Nazionale Italiano delle Ricerche (Italian National Research Council) when it accepted a project of ours for a systematic analysis on learning disabilities. The project involved over 1,000 children between ages 11 and 14, who underwent a series of tasks designed to identify subjects with text comprehension difficulty and other tasks either involved in the underlying processes or related to reading abilities. Moreover, it was envisaged to follow a number of younger subjects for a period of over 2½ years. Thus, conditions were created to establish the number and the characteristics of subjects with text comprehension difficulty and, further, to analyze some individual cases to determine the relationship between text comprehension difficulty and other variables, also measured, which were hypothesized to be related to text comprehension difficulty. Starting from our premise that a number of abilities are tied to the reading comprehension process, but that not all subjects who have text comprehension difficulty will have deficits in each of them, we hypothesized that a disabled group and a control group matched for decoding and intelligence, should present different overall scores in all the considered variables. We further hypothesized that the analysis of single cases would show diversified typologies, where the reading comprehension difficulty was related to a greater or smaller number of variables, according to the extent of the deficit and the relevance of that variable to reading comprehension. In particular, if a measured ability was an essential prerequisite, we should find subjects whose text comprehension difficulty was related to a deficit in that ability only. Moreover, we expected disabled subjects to share common profiles as concerned interdependent variables, but present remarkably different ones as concerned other variables. We would need a population far larger than that we had available for testing in order to establish common typologies.

WORKING MEMORY, METACOGNITION, AND LISTENING IN READING

Considerable evidence in the literature based on the matched groups' analysis, has pointed to a series of cognitive variables as discriminating between good and poor comprehenders, like decoding, lexical knowledge, previous knowledge, ability to activate adequate schema of knowledge and change the wrong schema (Blachowicz, 1984), ability to make inferences (Yuill & Oakhill, 1988) and ability to organize the material just read (Golinkoff, 1976; Ryan, 1981). Furthermore, good and poor comprehenders differ in some aspects of short-term memory, particularly working memory (Yuill, Oakhill, & Parkin, 1989), and the ability to do a syntactic analysis (Norman, Kemper, & Kynette, 1992; Penning & Raphael, 1991). Other studies, focused on the study of metacognitive variables, have highlighted bad comprehenders' poorer performance in a number of metacognitive aspects involved in reading, such as the awareness of reading goals, knowledge of strategies, text sensitivity, and control of comprehension (Brown, Armbruster, & Baker, 1986; Garner, 1987; Garner & Kraus, 1981–1982). Among the variables just mentioned, working memory, metacognition, and listening comprehension are addressed in the present work.

The relationship between working memory and reading comprehension has been shown in a series of studies, and the best advocates of this line of research are also included in this volume (Perfetti, 1985; Yuill et al., 1988). These studies found differences between good and poor comprehenders in a number of working memory tasks. On the other hand, some correlational studies failed to find a relationship between short-term memory and comprehension. For instance, several researchers (Daneman & Carpenter, 1980; Dixon, LeFevre, & Twilley, 1988; Masson & Miller, 1983; Turner & Engle, 1989) found that both digit and verbal span had a low correlation with reading comprehension, whereas some working memory tests had a higher correlation with reading proficiency (Daneman & Carpenter, 1980; Yuill et al., 1988). According to Baddeley (1992), working memory can be divided into different subsystems. The most important one is the central executive, involved in attention-demanding activities and not specifically related to information modality. Two others, the articulatory loop and the visuospatial sketchpad, are specifically involved in maintaining and processing either auditory–articulatory or visuospatial information. If in the comprehension process it is mainly the central executive system that is involved, we should expect different measures of working memory to be similarly related to comprehension difficulty, as they also involve the activity of a central executive system. Our data bank made it possible to examine this issue, because three different measures of working memory were available. One of them (the Figure Intersection Test) is completely nonverbal but is hypothesized to involve a central working memory component (Pascual-Leone & Ijaz, 1989).

Also as concerns metacognition, the relationship between reading comprehension failure and metacognitive deficits is well established in the literature (see Garner, 1987, for a review). It has been shown that poor readers present less adequate knowledge both about reading (Myers & Paris, 1978) and about other cognitive processes (Papetti, Cornoldi, Pettavino, Mazzoni, & Borkowsky, 1992) and have trouble in controlling the reading process (Pazzaglia, Cornoldi, & De Beni, 1995). According to the literature, poor comprehenders seem less aware of the importance of giving meaning to a text, and stress decoding to the detriment of comprehension (Baker & Brown, 1984). Moreover, they sometimes do not realize when they do not understand (Garner & Reis, 1981), they rarely use reading strategies (Brown et al., 1986), and they have more difficulty in adjusting the strategy to the task (Palincsar & Brown, 1987). Also the ability to evaluate the complexity of a text, to detect text structures, to control comprehension, and to detect text anomalies discriminate between good and poor comprehenders (August, Flavell, & Cliff, 1984; Brown et al., 1986; Garner, 1980, 1981).

Listening comprehension can also be studied in relation to reading comprehension (see Gough, Hoover, & Peterson, this volume). Reading and listening comprehension seem to reflect common cognitive processes related to word identification, syntactic and semantic processing of the sentence, integration of information, and so forth (Townsend, Carrithers, & Bever, 1987). Furthermore, the relationship between reading and listening comprehension seems to become stronger as children develop their reading skills (Curtis, 1980). However, some differences do exist. For example, listening requires a sequential process (reading is both sequential and parallel), relies more strongly on attention and memory (it is not possible to go back to preceding parts of the text), and depends on an externally determined presentation rate. These differences are made stronger by the fact that, typically, texts and contexts of listening tasks have different semantic and syntactic structure compared to reading. In conclusion, as reading and listening comprehension share similarities and differences, we might expect a poor reading comprehender to present a listening problem, although this would not necessarily be the case.

The Research

For a comprehensive evaluation of the characteristics of reading comprehension disabilities, we carried out a longitudinal research project in order to investigate the roles of both working memory and of listening and metacognitive variables in comprehension disabilities. This was done by comparing carefully selected groups of poor and good comprehenders. The poor comprehenders were repeatedly evaluated over a period of 3 years, considering other variables such as writing under dictation, math and verbal abilities, and decoding.

We also wanted to analyze single cases of poor comprehenders. This was done by comparing their performance in numerous cognitive and metacognitive abilities with the performance of a sample of subjects of the same age; and by following the evolution of the deficit during the 3-year period.

On the basis of the considerable evidence in the literature, we hypothesized that the analysis made on the matched groups would reveal a general inferiority of the poor comprehenders in all the considered variables. Furthermore, we expected a different outcome from the analysis of the single cases, with more specific deficits peculiar either to each case, or, to a number of cases.

The research project was articulated in three parts; selection of a sample of poor comprehenders, attending sixth and eighth grade; analysis of matched groups of good and poor comprehenders; and analysis of single cases of poor comprehenders.

In the present chapter, we briefly discuss the first two points, described elsewhere in depth (De Beni, Palladino, & Pazzaglia, 1995; Lumbelli & Cornoldi, 1994; Palladino, De Beni, & Cornoldi, 1995; Pazzaglia et al., 1995), and deal extensively with the analysis of single cases.

Specification of the Criteria for the Selection of the Sample of Poor Comprehenders

Subject selection was made within a strategic research project on learning disabilities in children between the ages of 11 and 13, chaired by Cesare Cornoldi, and financially supported by the CNR (Consiglio Nazionale della Ricerca). The first phase of the research consisted of the administration of a battery of tests to 1,285 boys and girls (589 sixth graders and 696 eighth graders) attending schools of different sociocultural background in Northeastern Italy. The test was administered at the beginning of the school year.

In our study a student was classed as a poor comprehender when she or he met the following three criteria.

1. Normal or good intelligence defined by a total score above the 45th percentile in a combined score obtained by summing the scores on the arithmetic, visuospatial, and verbal fluency subscales of the Primary Mental Abilities intelligence test (Thurstone & Thurstone, 1941)

2. Normal or good "decoding," we could not individually test subjects' performance in reading aloud; therefore we used a group procedure that tested language ability at the word-level. The chosen test battery, devised by Bisiacchi and Colombo (1996), included a syllable division task (12 three-syllable words divided in syllables) and a search for hidden words (10 words embedded in 10 pseudowords, for example the subject had to find the word "OCA" hidden in the pseudoword "SCOCATA"). Subjects' total score was above the 45th percentile.

3. Poor reading comprehension defined by a score lower than −0.4 *SD* from the mean in a reading comprehension test (Cornoldi, Colpo, & Gruppo MT, 1981) based on the presentation of a one-page text and on a series of multiple choice questions (fewer than 4 out of 10 correct for sixth graders and 6 out of 13 correct for eighth graders). In order to have a sufficiently large group of subjects we had to adopt a lenient criterion, assuming that less severe cases should share a similar pattern of difficulties with the most severe cases.

Thirty-four sixth graders and 33 eighth graders, approximately 5% of our initial sample, met these criteria. The control group was matched for sex, age, school, grade, "decoding," intelligence, but had a good level of comprehension (a score of > 5 and > 7 respectively obtained on the first two comprehension tests).

As already stated, the entire research project also included specific studies, where we offered a more detailed report of methodology and data. Some of the studies underlined the metacognitive aspects involved in comprehension (Pazzaglia et al., 1995), others focused on the working memory variables (De Beni et al. 1995), or on the relationship between reading comprehension and television comprehension (Lumbelli & Cornoldi, 1994). Finally, a recent study (Palladino et al., 1995) developed a longitudinal analysis of reading comprehension difficulty. In the next section we report the overall pattern of data, including those obtained by the previously cited studies on different subsamples of poor comprehenders. For this reason, our data on matched groups of good and poor readers relates in one case to the whole sample of older and younger good and poor comprehenders, and in the other cases to more or less limited subgroups of subjects from the younger group, that is the subjects who could be retested during the two following school years (seventh and eighth grade).

The Battery of Tests

During the school years 1991–1992, 1992–1993, 1993–1994 good and poor comprehenders were compared on a wide range of cognitive and metacognitive variables, by administering the following tests.

Reading Comprehension Tests. The reading comprehension tests consisted of two specific multiple choice comprehension subtests taken from a standardized reading comprehension battery (MT-advanced, Cornoldi, Rizzo, & Pra Baldi, 1991); the incongruencies subtest (inc1 and inc2) required the detection and/or explanation of incongruencies in the text, and the story grammar subtest (story1 and story2) required the comprehension of episodes and characters of a story. They were presented twice in the two parallel forms in both the sixth (inc1 and story1) and eighth grades (inc2 and story2).

Television Comprehension Tests (TV Speech and Images). The television comprehension tests consisted of two tests which evaluated the comprehension and the immediate recall of both the verbal text (TV-text1, TV-text2) and the images (TV-images1, TV-images2) of two TV news programs on high-speed trains and Iraq's war. Each program lasted approximately 5 minutes and was presented on a TV screen. Each projection was stopped after about 30 seconds. Just after the stop, the subject was required to answer to two written multiple choice questions on the information just presented. Then the representation continued. One question regarded visual information, and the other concerned implications of the verbal message of the news. Whereas the visual questions were mainly about explicitly presented aspects (e.g., what color were the train seats? Was the land visible from the train mountainous, coastal, flat, partly hilly?), the verbal questions required the subject to create connections and produce inferences (why do travelers prefer the train to the airplane?). The tests were administered in the 1991–1992 school year.

Listening Comprehension and Memory. A listening comprehension and memory test (listening) was taken from a test prepared by Molin (1993). The subjects had to listen to a tape recorded 4-minute radio news bulletin, presenting six different news items. At the end of the presentation the subject was requested to answer 14 multiple choice written questions on facts (e.g., what event was mentioned? a firemen's strike? air-travel problems? dismissal of protest by air travelers? a union crisis?). It was administered during the 1993–1994 school year.

Metacognition. A reading metacognition test (metac2) by Pazzaglia, De Beni, and Cristante (1994), comprised of 32 items was used. The test is composed of four subtests evaluating knowledge about both reading goals and strategies, text sensitivity, and control of comprehension. For this reason the test has four different scores; awareness of goals (metac2–goals) and strategies (metac2–strat), text sensitivity or the ability to evaluate text difficulty and to detect text structure (metac2–sens), and control (metac2–control). It was administered in the 1992–1993 school year.

School Achievement. School achievement was measured by a mathematics achievement test (math) based on a selection between the multiple choice items from the standardized Emme + battery (Soresi & Corcione, 1991), administered at the beginning of the 1991–1992 school year. The test includes items about problem solving, calculation, and geometry.

A reading aloud accuracy test (accuracy) from the standardized passage of the MT reading battery-basic (Cornoldi et al., 1981), administered during the 1992–1993 school year provided a second measure of school achievement. The task required subjects to read aloud a one-page passage, while the experimenter took note of reading mistakes on a paper.

A third measure of school achievement was a writing under dictation task (dictation) from the Tressoldi and Cornoldi (1991) writing battery and it was administered in the 1991–1992 school year. Children were requested to write under dictation some tape-recorded tongue twisters. The score was the number of errors.

Mental Abilities. Mental abilities was measured by the other two PMA subtests; a lexical knowledge task (pma – vm = primary mental abilities – verbal meaning), requiring the finding of the appropriate synonym for a word within a series of five alternatives, and a logic ability task (pma – r = primary mental abilities – reasoning) requiring the detection of the rule organizing a series of elements (e.g., which letter follows the series "cadaeafa" or the series "abmcdmefmghm"). They were administered during the 1991–1992 school year.

Working Memory. Working memory was measured verbally and nonverbally. From the verbal working memory test (Daneman & Carpenter, 1980), we used the Reading Span Test (reading test). Participants had to memorize the last word of each of a series of sentences which required semantic processing (makes sense judgment). The test was administered in the 1993–1994 school year.

For the nonverbal working memory test (Yuill et al., 1989), the Digit Working Memory Span Test (digit test), requiring the memorization of the last digit of each of a series of digit sequences, was used. Subjects were presented with series of 4, 5, and 6 sequences. The scoring criteria were modified in order to adapt them to the subjects' age (De Beni et al., 1995).

We used a test to evaluate the central executive functioning (Baddeley, 1966), the random generation of letters (random gener.). Subjects were requested to randomly generate letters at different rates (one letter every half, 1, and 2 seconds).

All these working memory tests were administered in the 1993–1994 school year.

Finally, a visuospatial working memory test was used. It was the Figure Intersection Test (F.I.T.) by Pascual-Leone (1970), requiring subjects to find the intersection between a series of geometrical figures. The test was administered in the 1991–1992 school year.

Comparisons Between Reading Comprehension Disabled Subjects and Controls

A first analysis was based on a comparison between the overall performance of girls and boys with reading comprehension difficulty and controls. The analysis was intended to replicate and extend data previously obtained, by matching groups of poor and good comprehenders (see for a review Garner, 1987; Yuill & Oakhill, 1991), and to offer a basis for a comparison with a single case approach. Table 6.1 shows the mean performance of the two groups on the battery of tests. The table shows both poor comprehenders' and good comprehenders' mean scores, number of subjects, and standard deviation; t values, and probability level. Oral comprehension/memory tests were administered both to younger and older children (56 poor comprehenders and 54 good comprehenders). The other tests were administered to different subgroups of younger poor and good comprehenders, who could be retested in the following two school years. The results indicate that the two groups differed in many of the variables considered, with some distinctions within them.

As concerns metacognitive proficiency, poor readers obtained lower scores on all four subtests measuring control, strategies, text sensitivity, and goals. The working memory performance of poor comprehenders was also lower than that of good readers, particularly in the verbal working memory test, in the letter random generation task, and in the visuospatial working memory test. As concerns the digit working memory test, we did not find a significant difference between the two groups in the total span score, but they did differ in two other indices supplied by the test; the span at the level of five digit sequences [mean for the experimental group = 3.68; mean for the control group = 5.89; $t(38) = 3.25$, $p = .003$), and the total number of digits recalled on the entire test (mean for the experimental group = 22.2; mean for the control group = 26.5; $t(38) = 2.43$, $p = .02$]. This meant that the two groups gave the same performance on the most difficult and on the easiest trials of the test, and that only the intermediate level could discriminate between groups (see for example Turner & Engle, 1989). An analogous result was found in the random letter generation test, where we found

TABLE 6.1
Scores Obtained by Poor Comprehenders and Control Subjects in the Tests
Administered in the 1991–1992, 1992–1993, and 1993–1994 School Years

| | Groups | | | | | |
| | Experimental | | Control | | | |
Tests	M(n)	sd	M(n)	sd	t	p
1991-1992						
Oral Compr./Memory						
TV-text1	1.93(56)	1.04	2.40(54)	1.07	2.33	.21
TV-images1	2.60(56)	0.97	2.63(54)	1.04	0.11	.91
TV-Text2	3.22(56)	1.30	3.77(54)	0.91	2.58	.011
TV-images2	2.79(56)	0.78	2.98(54)	0.92	1.12	.26
General Skills						
Dictation	12.19(26)	7.06	9.61(26)	5.15	1.50	.14
PMA-VM	7.96(26)	3.25	11.88(26)	5.14	3.29	.002
PMA-R	7.53(26)	3.92	11.26(26)	3.95	3.42	.001
Comprehension						
Inc1	3.03(26)	1.99	5.11(26)	2.08	3.67	.001
Story1	3.50(26)	1.67	5.30(26)	1.51	4.07	.001
Working Memory						
F.I.T. corr (visuosp)	22.11(26)	4.16	24.92(26)	5.09	2.18	.035
F.I.T. level (visuosp)	4.53(26)	1.02	5.23(26)	1.21	2.22	.031
1992–1993						
Metacognition						
Metac2-total	35.83(34)	4.66	39.92(34)	2.78	4.39	.001
Metac2-cont	10.97(34)	2.00	12.01(34)	1.44	2.46	.017
Metac2-strat	7.23(34)	1.55	8.23(34)	1.04	3.11	.003
Metac2-sens	8.88(34)	2.22	10.41(34)	1.81	3.11	.003
Metac2-goals	8.75(34)	1.11	9.26(34)	0.80	2.18	.033
General Skills						
Accuracy	4.50(34)	2.36	2.66(34)	1.50	3.82	.001
1993–1994						
Working Memory						
Digit test	3.42(20)	0.67	3.71(20)	0.82	1.19	.24
Reading Span	2.22(20)	0.80	2.87(20)	0.60	2.89	.006
Random gener.	4.36(20)	0.08	4.26(20)	0.15	2.57	.014

a difference between the two groups with a presentation rate of one letter per second; but there was no difference both in the most difficult case (one letter every half second), and the easiest (one letter every 2 seconds). As for the two comprehension tests and the PMA subtests, a significant difference was again found between experimental and control groups. On the TV-comprehension tests, good and poor comprehenders' performance differed only in the task requiring them to answer some questions about the verbal message of the news (TV-text2), but no differences were found for memory of images (TV-images1 or 2).

Analysis of the Single Cases

General Logic in Presentation of Single Cases

Table 6.2 presents data from 12 children who underwent all the above tests plus a standard comprehension test given during the third year, and indicates when they were deemed to have failed (criteria below).

Some tests were standardized, whereas others had been constructed for our goals. Consequently, the confidence intervals might undergo wide variability due to the size of the reference sample. For this reason, we decided to assume as a large discrepancy from typical performance (indicated with *) when the subject's score was 1 *SD* from the mean, and a very large discrepancy (indicated with **) when the score was 1.5 *SD* lower (for the Metacognitive Questionnaire and the span tests, where the range of scores is limited, only one critical value, falling in between −1 and −1.5 *SD*, was defined). A "+" was given when the performance of the subject was remarkably higher than the mean value of the normative group (approximately 1 *SD* above the mean). The indices are preceded by a parenthesis only when they approach the critical values.

A Short Look at the Cases: Severe Comprehension Difficulty Persisting Also After 2 Years.
The cases seem to show very little overlap in their patterns of deficit.

First, the longitudinal analysis, carried out on 12 poor comprehenders (see also Palladino, De Beni, & Cornoldi, 1995), revealed that only 7 subjects showed a severe comprehension difficulty after 2 years. Second, the subjects still having a comprehension deficit showed very different profiles from each other. We briefly examine them one by one:

PL (female) had the greatest difficulties in comprehending a story and in indicating flexible strategies in reading;

VG (female), on the contrary, exhibited a more pervasive comprehension difficulty over all aspects of comprehension, including TV text listening (but not the comprehension and memory of the radio passage), and the working

TABLE 6.2
Analysis of Single Cases

Tests	Cases											
	PL	VG	FM	TL	AN	NL	LD	FC	MM	DM	CL	CM
Reading Compr.												
Comp2	**	**	**	**	**	**	**	(*	(*			(*
Inc1		**										
Inc2		**										
Story1	**	**		*		**		**	**		*	**
Story2	*	**	**			**		**	**			
Oral Compr./ Memory												
TV-text1+2		**	**	**	**			**		**		
TV-images1+2				**								
Listening			+					+				
Metac.												
Metac2-cont		*	*	*	*		*	*	(*		*	*
Metac2-strat	*			*			*	*	(*		*	
Metac2-sens	*		*				*		(*	*		
Metac2-goal									(*			
Working Memory												
F.I.T.				+			**			*	*	
Digit test	*					*		*				
Reading test	*	*	*	*	*		*	*	*			
Random gener.		*		*	**		*	*	*	*		
General Skills												
Math	+			+					*		(*	
PMA-VM			*	(*		*	*		*	*		
PMA-R			+	(+	*	**	**		*	*		
Accuracy		+								(+		
Dictation	(*	+				**		(*	*			*

Note. Tests where single poor comprehenders presented a strong (*) or a very strong (**) failure or particular success (+). The indices are preceded by a parenthesis only when they approach the critical values.

memory tests. Her metacognitive difficulties, also related to control, were reflected in her difficulty with the Incongruencies subtest.

FM (male) exhibited failures related to text processing and metacognition, but had high levels of performance in some tasks. Particularly remarkable was his very high performance in the dictation with only one error (mean performance of the normative group = 12.6 errors) and in the comprehension and memory of the radio passage.

TL (female) presented comprehension difficulty, but high competence in both PMA reasoning and math. Her difficulty could be related to sentence processing as she had problems with the reading span test (but not with the other working memory measures) and in the control subtest of the metacognitive questionnaire, typically requiring the detection of errors in sentences. She was also the only case who had difficulty in processing both aspects of the TV passages.

AN (male) had some similarities with VG (failures with the TV-text and working memory tests), but with a smaller number of failures.

NL (female) had difficulty with the story comprehension subtest, with the digit working memory test (score = 2.5), with the two PMA subtests, and with the dictation (25 errors). This girl presented similarities to PL: Both had problems with the stories, but neither had a listening problem. However, in this case, other language problems were present (see dictation and PMA).

LD (female), as in the preceding case, had low scores on the PMA subtests and no listening problems. She differed in other aspects, having no trouble with the stories and presenting metacognitive problems. She was also the only case out of seven having the lowest score on the F.I.T. test. It is interesting to mention that she and TL were the only cases presenting a low score in the PMA-spatial subtest (not shown in Tables 6.1 and 6.2 because the test was used in the initial exclusion criteria). However, her overall intelligence score (which justified her inclusion in the group) was high.

Cases With Minor Difficulty After 2 Years. At the final reading comprehension test, the other five cases followed up from sixth to eighth grade presented a minor difficulty in comprehension. It must be stressed that, in order to be included in the initial group of poor comprehenders, the subjects had to fail more than one comprehension test, and that the tests were administered in different circumstances. Therefore their initial difficulty was not due to specific difficulties with a particular material, but was constant across materials. Although the improvement was modest in some cases, the change in these 5 subjects (and especially in 2 of them) cannot be attributed simply to fluctuations in performance. After 2 years, 3 of the 5 subjects had a comprehension score slightly higher than one negative standard deviation, whereas the other 2 had a score either slightly lower (DM) or slightly higher (CL) than the mean score of the normative group.

The deficit, partially shared by these subjects and the 7 who maintained a severe comprehension deficit, was the difficulty with story comprehension. Four of them had difficulty as sixth graders and 2 of them maintained the difficulty until the eighth grade. Further, all these subjects presented some metacognitive difficulty on the questionnaires, as was the case for 6 out of the 7 most severe cases. The similarities between these five cases end here, as they present different patterns in working memory tests, in the PMA subtests, and in other aspects of school achievement (math, reading accuracy, and writing).

Some General Observations

The longitudinal individual case analysis showed that only some poor comprehenders maintained their deficits across a 30-month period. The partial improvement of 5 out of these 12 subjects could be interpreted either as a spontaneous remediation for at least some poor comprehenders, or as a positive effect of a teaching activity focused on that problem. Using a larger group of the initial sample (20 subjects), Palladino et al. (1995) carried out a comparative analysis between poor comprehenders who had a remediation and those who did not. The analysis showed that the two groups significantly differed in the TV comprehension test (both in the questions concerning verbal text and images). These results suggest that a more general comprehension ability is the most predictive variable for the maintenance of the comprehension deficit (see also Gough, Hoover & Peterson, this volume).

Relationship (and Lack of it) Between Variables Derived From the Analysis of Single Cases

We now examine the issue of the relationship between reading comprehension and other hypothesized processes on the basis of the pattern of data obtained in the analysis both of the disabled and control groups and of the single cases. In the following sections, we consider the relationship between oral and written comprehension, and the relationship between reading comprehension, metacognition (control and awareness), working memory, and some more general measures.

Relationship Between Oral and Written Comprehension

The two procedures we used to test oral comprehension concerned partially similar new information, but they involved the subjects' memory resources to different degrees. That the two tests were different could be the explanation for the surprising fact that children failing one of them did not fail the other, or that two cases (FM and FC) who failed the TV text test, had a very high score with the broadcast text. In fact, the broadcast listening test was the only procedure we used whose discriminative capacity between good and poor comprehenders was not good. In the present study, not one poor comprehender failed the test. This test difficulty seems related to memory for specific information presented, rather than to extraction of meaning from the text. Our data suggest that remembering specific information, presented either visually or verbally, is not a typical poor comprehenders' problem. These data contrast with the hypothesis that general comprehension factors can predict memory for broadcast messages (Berry, 1988), whereas they are consistent with Larsen's (1988) assumption that news must be treated as a particular example of a different, autobiographical memory system. As the broadcast listening test was not given to the control group, we cannot say whether it could differentiate between our groups. On the contrary, the ability to understand a TV text seems critically related to reading comprehension ability, significantly discriminating between groups and being the best predictor of reading comprehension ability 2 years later (Palladino et al., 1995). This seems an important result because it confirms the existence of a relationship between written and oral comprehension (Curtis, 1980). Because television is very popular with boys and girls of this age, television comprehension difficulty cannot be linked to a lack of experience with the medium, but, rather, either to a typical exposure to television programs which are poorer in content and language (see Stanovich, West, Cunningham, Cipielewski, & Siddiqui, this volume), or to a more general comprehension difficulty.

At the same time, the popularity of the medium and the fact that many poor comprehenders are good at processing visual information offer important suggestions for a remedial approach. Poor comprehenders could be more motivated to participate in remedial interventions based on the presentation of television texts rather than of written texts. As some subjects had difficulty both with oral and written comprehension, and these aspects share common mechanisms, an improvement in television comprehension may extend to written comprehension. However, this consideration can only be applied to poor reading comprehenders who also have television comprehension difficulty. In fact, some of the subjects did not fail in this area, suggesting that there was not necessarily a relationship between oral and written comprehension. The relationship mentioned in the literature between oral and written comprehension could have been emphasized by overlapping aspects in texts and testing procedures. However, Curtis (1980) found that listening comprehension was more closely related to reading comprehension in better readers than in less skilled readers.

Further, some subjects failed both the TV texts and working memory tests. In fact, the television texts involved a memory variable, presumably a working memory one, but they also required more complex comprehension operations where the poor comprehenders could be at a disadvantage even when they have a sufficient working memory span (see the case of DM). Clearly, the comprehension problems were partly different as some poor comprehenders did not have any difficulty with the television text.

This last result confirms that oral and written comprehension, although partly overlapping, cannot be considered identical, at least when typical oral and written texts are used for the two kinds of tests. In fact, most of these differences could be due to the textual and procedural differences typically associated with the two kinds of tests.

Metacognition and Reading Comprehension Difficulty

The subject's ability to detect incongruencies or ambiguities in the text was examined in two ways, through a specific subtest (Inc) of a reading comprehension standardized battery which presents a text including incongruencies and a series of ambiguous sentences where the subject is invited to find and/or explain a semantic incongruency; and through an area of the metacognitive questionnaire presenting eight sentences with a variety of semantic, syntactic, and orthographic errors that the child is invited to spot.

If we consider the second administration of the metacognitive questionnaire, we can see that a large number of our subjects failed to detect the text errors and one of them also failed in the other metacognitive test (Metac1, which, being devised for younger subjects, might not discriminate less severe cases). As the errors presented in the questionnaire were at different levels (orthographic, syntactic, and semantic), it seems logical to conclude that poor comprehenders have a general difficulty in detecting errors.

In the questionnaire, the part related to the goals of reading is very simple for the 13-year-old subjects and, probably for this reason, it was not possible to look for specific failures at the individual level. Five subjects had a lower score in strategy knowledge and 4 in text sensitivity. Pazzaglia et al. (1995) found that the different areas of the test were highly correlated in a large pool of normal children, while a significant correlation was not found between the same variables when they considered the original group of 34 poor comprehenders of the CNR project. Furthermore, matching the group composed of 34 poor comprehenders to the control group, they found that some items evaluating knowledge and use of different reading strategies were particularly good at discriminating between good and poor comprehenders. Those items required the understanding of what must be done when speed reading is required, when a single piece of information must be searched for, and when different tasks are presented. All these items are related to the awareness that reading must be a flexible activity. Furthermore, in a research project carried out on a large group of subjects, ages 8 to 14 (Pazzaglia et al., 1994), subjects with different levels of reading comprehension were found to differ in their metacognitive test performance, both on total scores and on the four subtest scores. Taken together, these data seem to confirm that reading comprehension ability is related to high metacognitive ability (Garner, 1987).

Working Memory and Reading Comprehension Difficulty

Our results also confirm the existence of a pervasive working memory deficit in poor comprehenders, as suggested by many studies. This is also borne out by the matched group analysis: Poor and good comprehenders differed on almost all the working memory tests, with the exception of the digit span test. In that case the experimental and control group presented the same total span score, but differed in the 5th level span and in the total number of recalled digits.

Another important outcome is that only one case failed the F.I.T. test and one of the span tests. This is despite the idea that working memory may be considered as a single component (Pascual-Leone & Ijaz, 1989), or that the F.I.T. test and the other two working memory tests measure a central executive component. On the contrary, the relationship between the two span tests (digit and verbal) was high: Many children failed both tests (many subjects had a score of 3 on the digit test which approached the critical predefined score of 2.5). It must be noticed that the correlation (calculated on a sample of 38 good and poor comprehenders) between the total number of digits and words recalled in the digit span test and in the reading span test respectively was significant ($r = .50$, $p < .001$). However, the three tests were also measuring different aspects of working memory, related not only to a central executive component (Baddeley, 1986) but also to its visuospatial components (FIT) and auditory–articulatory components (the other two). The two cases presenting the worst failure on the span tests also had very low scores on the story comprehension subtests, suggesting that working memory is critical in storing a sequence of events.

General Measures and Reading Comprehension Difficulty

Our results show that the use of strict inclusion criteria reduces the apparent generality of a learning difficulty. For example, we found that only one poor comprehender (MM) presented math disorders, contrasting with the data from other research studies which found a relationship between comprehension and math abilities (Goodman & Mann, 1976). On the contrary, two of our cases' performance was very good in the math test (PL and TL). The two cases do not share many similarities but both show the same working memory preference, that is, failing the sentence test but not failing the visuospatial one (at which TL was particularly good). In fact, it has already been shown that visuospatial ability may be related to success in mathematics (e.g., Rourke & Finlayson, 1978).

The fact that not one of the subjects failed the accuracy test of oral reading suggests that the decoding score used as an inclusion criterion was also related to performance on the accuracy test and probably to other decoding abilities which could only be tested individually. However, another aspect, often related to decoding abilities (e.g., Tressoldi & Cornoldi, 1991), such as writing under dictation, presented a very heterogeneous pattern. NL, the only case with severe difficulty in writing, had a low score in the auditory nonlinguistic working memory measure, suggesting a relationship between the two aspects. She also had difficulty with story comprehension, but a relationship between writing and story comprehension does not seem to be a general case. FM, showing poor story comprehension, had a particularly high score on the writing test. In general, writing and comprehension were not strongly related. This is confirmed by the fact that writing and reading comprehension are not highly related in the overall population ($r = .36$ for 507 sixth graders and .34 for 664 eighth graders of the initial sample) and even less related in the disabled subgroup.

GENERAL CONCLUSIONS

Thanks to the opportunities offered by a National CNR program that enabled us to administer a large battery of tests to a substantial number of subjects, we were able to have a multifaceted survey of adolescents presenting specific reading comprehension difficulties. Approximately 5% of subjects tested presented poor performance in reading comprehension, but had good performance in intelligence and decoding tests. Many of them maintained their problem during a 30-month period.

The group of poor comprehenders was contrasted with a control group (matched for intelligence and decoding) in a series of tasks testing abilities related to reading comprehension, and typically showed lower performance in them. In particular, we focused on oral comprehension (listening), working memory, and metacognition, finding poorer performance in the group of poor comprehenders. These data replicate previous studies which have shown that subjects with a specific reading comprehension difficulty may also show problems in those areas (for a review, Yuill & Oakhill, 1991). In our study, all the metacognition measures significantly differentiated between groups, confirming their strong connection with reading comprehension and distinguishing the metacognitive deficit with reference to control, strategies, text sensitivity, and knowledge of the goals. For what concerns oral comprehension and working memory, the greater part of the measures also indicated significant differences between groups. In the case of the television test, however, the majority of poor comprehenders appeared able to capture visual information, suggesting that their problem is restricted to some (linguistic) aspects of the television message. Further, the good performance of single cases who were tested with a broadcast listening task suggests that poor comprehenders may be adequate when memory for broadcast information is involved, but that they experience listening problems only when the message is complex and requires difficult inferences, a case which is not frequent in everyday life, but which can be typical of school lectures.

Poor comprehenders also failed, as a group, in a series of working memory tasks, either testing, with reference to the Baddeley's (1992) model, the central executive component of (the random generation task), or the auditory (span) and spatial (F.I.T.) components. The digit test was not able to significantly differentiate between groups, as had been observed by Yuill et al. (1989), a result perhaps due to the fact that our poor comprehenders had good number-manipulation abilities (see exclusion criteria), and were also much older. However, the same digit test was critical in determining the deficit of a subsample of poor comprehenders. This subsample was different from the subsample failing the visuospatial working memory test, suggesting that the two tests measure different components.

The fact that poor comprehenders had good performance on the tests used for the exclusion criteria (whose discriminative capacity has been demonstrated) and on some of the battery tests, decreases the probability that the group differences we found were due to methodological artifacts or to general intellectual abilities involved in all tasks. However, the direction of the relationship between hypothesized underlying abilities and reading comprehension remains unclear. No underlying ability we tested could be considered a necessary prerequisite (unless the prerequisite cutoff, i.e., the level of the prerequisite ability required for comprehension, should be put so low so as to be met by all subjects), nor a necessarily related ability. In fact, we could also find some control subjects with good comprehension but low performance on some of the battery tests. Further, not all the poor comprehenders failed in all the tests. A plausible conclusion in this respect can be that the abilities we measured are necessary prerequisites, at a minimum level, and together contribute, at higher levels, as facilitators of reading comprehension ability. In other words, a child with no listening, working memory, and metacognition abilities at all could not pass a reading comprehension task; a child with a modest level in these abilities could be disadvantaged during comprehension. Conversely, low reading comprehension could affect some or all of these abilities.

From a theoretical point of view, two main conclusions can be drawn from the individual analysis of the individual cases.

The cases share very few common traits: No unique pattern of difficulties emerges from the comparison of the 12 cases or even of the 7 most severe cases. When the comparisons are made between cases described by different researchers or clinical services, the lack of similarity may also be due to differences in procedure (criteria for inclusion, tests used), but this does not seem to apply to our study as the procedures were exactly the same for all the subjects. A possible explanation may be that many factors are related to reading comprehension difficulty, and for each case some of them are related, and sometimes even crucially so, to the subject's difficulty.

Comprehension difficulty does not seem to be necessarily due to listening problems, to metacognition, or to other aspects that sometimes appear strongly related to comprehension (working memory, lexical knowledge, math, incongruencies explanation, etc.). In fact, we can find dissociations between all these aspects. According to our first conclusion, we can say that all the tested aspects are related to reading comprehension and can indeed affect the reading process, but they are not necessarily part of all comprehension difficulties (at least of the difficulties found through our inclusion criteria), as other aspects are sufficient to produce difficulty at this level.

A counterargument to our conclusions could be that we have not chosen the appropriate procedures to test the aspects hypothesized to underlie reading comprehension difficulty, and that the cognitive functions measured by our battery of tests has no relation to reading comprehension. Nevertheless, the comparisons between poor comprehenders and controls carried out by us as well as by other researchers (following a similar procedure) show that the tests were really discriminative between the two groups and that a relation does exist between those tests and comprehension ability. However, what a group comparison procedure cannot show is how general a deficit related to a reading comprehension problem is. Sometimes a misunderstanding of results from matched-group analysis can lead people working in clinical settings (e.g., psychologists and speech therapists) to think that, if the poor comprehenders' performance is significantly worse in a test, all poor comprehenders should present a deficit in the area measured by the test and should need a treatment program in that area. Our data suggest that this is not the case.

ACKNOWLEDGMENTS

The present research was supported by a national CNR Grant to the first author. We are greatly indebted to Drs. P. Palladino, R. Bruschi, A. Ferretti, and R. Santagata who helped in collecting and analyzing data.

REFERENCES

August, D. L., Flavell, J. H., & Cliff, R. (1984). Comparison of comprehension monitoring of skilled and less skilled readers. *Reading Research Quarterly, 20,* 39–53.

Baddeley, A. D. (1966). The capacity for generating information by randomization. *Quarterly Journal of Experimental Psychology, 18,* 119–129.

Baddeley, A. D. (1986). *Working memory.* London: Oxford University Press.

Baddeley, A. D. (1990). *Human memory: Theory and practice.* Hove, England: Lawrence Erlbaum Associates.

Baddeley, A. (1992). Is working memory working? The fifteenth Bartlett lecture. *The Quarterly Journal of Experimental Psychology, 1,* 1–31.

Baker, L., & Brown, A. L. (1984). Metacognitive skills of reading. In D. Pearson, R. Barr, M. Kamil, & P. Monsenthal (Eds.), *Handbook of reading research* (pp. 353–394). New York: Longman.

Baron, J., & Treiman, R. (1980). Some problems in the study of differences in cognitive processes. *Memory and Cognition, 8,* 313–321.

Berry, C. (1988). Memory studies and broadcast messages. In M. M. Gruneberg, P. E. Morris, & R. N. Sykes (Eds.), *Practical aspects of memory: Current research and issues* (vol. 1, pp. 434–439). New York: Wiley.

Bisiacchi, P., & Colombo, L. (1996). *A battery of tests to evaluate phonological awareness and decoding ability.* Manuscript in preparation.

Blachowicz, C. L. Z. (1984). Reading and remembering. *Visible Language, 4,* 391–403.

Brown, A. L., Armbruster, B. B., & Baker, L. (1986). The role of metacognition in reading and studying. In J. Orasanu (Ed.), *Reading comprehension: From research to practice* (pp. 49–75). Hillsdale, NJ: Lawrence Erlbaum Associates.

Cornoldi, C., Colpo, G., & Gruppo, M. T. (1981). *La verifica dell'apprendimento della lettura* [How to verify reading achievement]. Firenze, Italy: Organizzazioni Speciali.

Cornoldi, C., De Beni, R., & Gruppo, M. T. (1989). *Guida alla comprensione del testo* [Reading comprehension]. Bergamo, Italy: Walk Over.

Cornoldi, C., Rizzo, A., & Pra Baldi, A. (1991). *Prove avanzate MT di comprensione nella lettura* [MT-Advanced comprehension tests]. Firenze, Italy: Organizzazioni Speciali.

Curtis, M. (1980). Development of components of reading skill. *Journal of Educational Psychology, 72,* 656–669.

Daneman, M., & Carpenter, P. A. (1980). Individual differences in working memory and reading. *Journal of Verbal Learning and Verbal Behavior, 19,* 450–466.

De Beni, R., Palladino, P., & Pazzaglia, F. (1995). Influenza della memoria di lavoro e abilita' metacognitive e sintattiche nei disturbi specifici di comprensione [Influence of working memory, metacognition and syntactic analysis on reading comprehension difficulties]. *Giornale Italiano di Psicologia, 22,* 615–640.

Dixon, P., LeFevre, J., & Twilley, L. C. (1988). Word knowledge and working memory as predictors of reading skill. *Journal of Educational Psychology, 80,* 465–472.

Ehri, L. C. (1979). Linguistic insight: Threshold of reading acquisition. In T. G. Waller & G. E. MacKinnon (Eds.), *Reading research: Advances in theory and practice* (pp. 63–116). New York: Academic Press.

Garner, R. (1980). Monitoring of understanding: An investigation of good and poor readers' awareness of induced miscomprehension of text. *Journal of Reading Behavior, 12,* 55–64.

Garner, R. (1981). Monitoring of passage inconsistency among poor comprehenders: A preliminary test of the "piecemeal processing" explanation. *Journal of Educational Research, 74,* 159–162.

Garner, R. (1987). *Metacognition and reading comprehension.* Norwood: Ablex.

Garner, R., & Kraus, C. (1981–1982). Good and poor comprehender differences in knowing and regulating reading behaviors. *Educational Research Quarterly, 6,* 5–12.

Garner, R., & Reis, R. (1981). Monitoring and resolving comprehension obstacles: An investigation of spontaneous text lookbacks among upper-grade good and poor comprehenders. *Reading Research Quarterly, 16,* 569–582.

Golinkoff, R. (1976). A comparison of reading comprehension in good and poor comprehenders. *Reading Research Quarterly, 11,* 623–659.

Goodman, L., & Mann, L. (1976). *Learning disabilities in the secondary school.* New York: Grune & Stratton.

Larsen, S. F. (1988). Remembering reported events: Memory for news in ecological perspective. In M. M. Gruneberg, P. E. Morris, & R. N. Sykes (Eds.), *Practical aspects of memory: Current research and issues* (vol. 1, pp. 440–445). New York: Wiley.

Lumbelli, L., & Cornoldi, C. (1994). Interaction between verbal and visual information in audio-visual text comprehension. In F. P. C. M. De Jong & B. H. A. M. van Hout-Wolters (Eds.), *Process-oriented instruction and learning from text* (pp. 183–193). Amsterdam: VU University Press.

Masson, M. E. J., & Miller, J. A. (1983). Working memory and individual differences in comprehension and memory of text. *Journal of Educational Psychology, 75*, 314–318.

Molin, A. (1993). Prova di ascolto (Listening test). In C. Cornoldi, G. Colpo, & C. Vocetti (Eds.), *Dimensione lettura. Introduzione all'antologia* [Introduction to the anthology "Reading Dimension"] (pp. 108–109). Novara, Italy: Istituto Geografico De Agostini.

Moscovitch, M., & Umiltà, C. (1991). Conscious and nonconscious aspects of memory: A neuropsychological framework of modules and central systems. In R. G. Lister & H. J. Weingarter (Eds.), *Perspective on cognitive neuroscience* (pp. 229–266). Oxford, England: Oxford University Press.

Myers, M., & Paris, S. G. (1978). Children's metacognitive knowledge about reading. *Journal of Educational Psychology, 70*, 680–690.

Norman, S., Kemper, S., & Kynette, D. (1992). Adults' reading comprehension: Effects of syntactic complexity and working memory. *Journal of Gerontology: Psychological Sciences, 4*, 258–265.

Palincsar, A. S., & Brown, D. A. (1987). Enhancing instructional time through attention to metacognition. *Journal of Learning Disabilities, 20*, 76–85.

Palladino, P., De Beni, R., & Cornoldi, C. (1995). *L'evoluzione di difficolta' specifiche di comprensione del testo: uno studio longitudinale* [The time course of specific reading comprehension difficulties: A longitudinal study]. *Archivio di Psicologia, 5*, 3–20.

Papetti, O., Cornoldi, C., Pettavino, A., Mazzoni, G., & Borkowsky, J. (1992). Memory judgments and allocation of study times in good and poor comprehenders. *Advances in Learning and Behavioral Disabilities, 7*, 3–33.

Pascual-Leone, J. (1970). A mathematical model for transition in Piaget's developmental stages. *Acta Psychologica, 32*, 301–345.

Pascual-Leone, J., & Ijaz, H. (1989). Mental capacity testing as a form of intellectual-development assessment. In R. Samuda, S. Jong, J. Pascual-Leone, & J. Lewis (Eds.), *Assessment and placement of minority students* (pp. 143–171). Toronto: Hogrefe.

Pazzaglia, F., Cornoldi, C., & De Beni, R. (1995). Knowledge about reading and self-evaluation in reading disabled children. *Advances in Learning and Behavioral Disabilities, 9*, 91–117.

Pazzaglia, F., De Beni, R., & Cristante, F. (1994). *Prova di metacomprensione* [A metacomprehension test]. Firenze, Italy: Organizzazioni Speciali.

Penning, M. J., & Raphael, T. E. (1991). The impact of language ability and text variables on sixth-grade students' comprehension. *Applied Psycholinguistics, 12*, 397–417.

Perfetti, C. A. (1985). *Reading ability*. New York: Oxford University Press.

Rourke, B. P., & Finlayson, N. A. J. (1978). Neuropsychological significance of variations in patterns of academic performance: Verbal and visuo-spatial abilities. *Journal of Abnormal Child Psychology, 6*, 121–133.

Ryan, E. B. (1981). Identifying and remediating failures in reading comprehension: Toward an instructional approach for poor comprehenders. In T. G. Walker & G. E. MacKinnon (Eds.), *Advances in reading research* (pp. 9–50). New York: Academic Press.

Soresi, S., & Corcione, D. (1991). *Prove oggettive di matematica* [Mathematic achievement tests]. Firenze, Italy: Organizzazioni Speciali.

Thurstone, N. L., & Thurstone, T. G. (1941). Factorial studies of intelligence. *Psychometric Monographs, 2*.

Townsend, D. J., Carrithers, C., & Bever, T. G. (1987). Listening and reading processes in college- and middle school-age readers. In R. Orowitz & S. J. Samuels (Eds.), *Comprehending oral and written language* (pp. 217–242). New York: Academic Press.

Tressoldi, P. E., & Cornoldi, C. (1991). *Batteria per la valutazione della scrittura* [Battery for writing evaluation]. Firenze, Italy: Organizzazioni Speciali.

Turner, M. L., & Engle, R. W. (1989). Is working memory capacity task dependent? *Journal of Memory and Language, 28*, 127–154.

Yuill, N., & Oakhill, J. (1988). Understanding of anaphoric relations in skilled and less skilled comprehenders. *British Journal of Psychology, 79,* 173-186.

Yuill, N., & Oakhill, J. (1991). *Children's problems in text comprehension.* Cambridge, England: Cambridge University Press.

Yuill, N., Oakhill, J., & Parkin, A. (1989). Working memory, comprehension ability and the resolution of text anomaly. *British Journal of Psychology, 80,* 351-361.

CHAPTER SEVEN

Sources of Comprehension Failure: Theoretical Perspectives and Case Studies

Charles A. Perfetti
Maureen A. Marron
Peter W. Foltz
University of Pittsburgh

The possibilities for comprehension failure seem to be endless. "Comprehension," after all, is a word that we use to cover a range of complex processes involved in language, any of which can fail. In this chapter, we examine the possibilities for comprehension problems with the goal of learning whether some of these possibilities might be more likely than others.

We begin our examination with a brief text, drawn from a syndicated newspaper column by George Will that was reprinted in the *Pittsburgh Post-Gazette* (1993) on August 30. This text unexpectedly exposed a rich stew of comprehension failure:

> Amid the genteel tinkle of restaurant lunch sounds, Mark Weber is having difficulty doing justice to his salmon, such is his passion for justice, as he pretends to understand it. He is trying to persuade me that the Holocaust never happened. It is not going well. (p. B-2)

This paragraph began the column, and as a beginning paragraph, it has all of the special difficulties characteristic of beginnings. The reader really doesn't know what this column is going to be about. (A headline to the column would certainly give some cues. The headline to this column as it appeared was "Ignorance, Anti-Semitism and 'Scholarship'." Of course the headline would have been different in other newspapers that carried this column.)

What the reader tries to do, of course, is to make some connection between the words of the text and some piece of knowledge he or she has

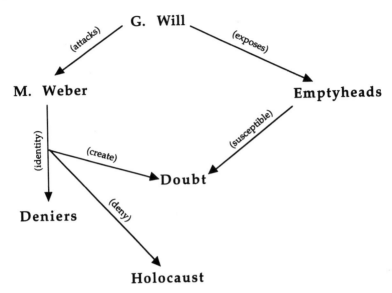

FIG. 7.1.   The Will text: A macrorhetorical schema.

about the world. In making these connections, the reader builds a mental model, or what we call, following van Dijk and Kintsch (1983), a "situation model," a representation of the situation described in the text. Of course, building this model is slow going at first, because it is not clear which kinds of knowledge are most relevant. However, roughly speaking, what can be constructed on the basis of this one paragraph is something like the follow- ing: The writer and someone named Mark Weber are having lunch. Weber is trying to persuade the writer that the event known as the Holocaust did not happen. In addition, we infer from the last sentence that the writer, George Will, is not easily persuaded to accept this argument. This situation is the foundation for the argumentative text that develops over the next 12 paragraphs of the Will column (see Appendix A for the entire Will column). The lunch situation and the two characters turn out to be mere backdrop for the rhetorical heart of the Will article. Its macrorhetorical structure is schematically represented in Fig. 7.1.

   Mark Weber, the reader learns, is a Holocaust "denier," a propagandist occupied with creating doubt about the Holocaust. George Will is having none of it, and in this column he sets out to debunk the deniers, taking note of their pseudoscholarship and their anti-Semitic motivations, two trade- marks of their "revisionist" effort.

   We were interested in studying the reasoning processes of college students as they read both Will's editorial and a reply by Weber. We wanted to learn the extent to which students would adopt a doubting position when intro- duced to the mere hint of argument, that is, whether they would incorrectly assume that a genuine controversy existed after they were exposed to a text (Weber's, not Will's) raising doubts against a historically validated conclusion.[1] But our attempt to learn more about this kind of reasoning will have to wait, because in the course of studying our subjects' reasoning attempts, we learned a hard lesson. Most of our subjects could not comprehend the texts. It is not possible to examine someone's reasoning if their comprehension is as negligible as was our subjects'. So we started to ask "why." Why was the comprehension of at least 3 out of our first 4 subjects so miserable?

Let us examine briefly one possibility. It might be the case that a University of Pittsburgh undergraduate is not prepared to read an opinionated syndicated newspaper column, or at least not one written by George Will, the Princeton-educated writer of lively politically conservative critical prose. If so, this is a startling state of affairs. Presumably George Will does not write his column only for Princeton graduates. Whether he would be disappointed at learning that his columns cannot be understood by more typical college undergraduates, we don't know. It is possible he hopes only for an elite audience. But even if Will doesn't care about reaching a typical college student, it is widely assumed that higher education should prepare students to want to read such columns or at least to understand them. We expect students to become reasoning, critical-thinking adults. A simpler text probably would have been better understood by our subjects, at least superficially, but this would mask genuine comprehension problems that could be exposed by still other texts.

We take the Will column as an example of a demanding text that can expose comprehension problems. Psychological research has other examples in which difficult texts are used to expose factors that operate in ordinary comprehension, but that are invisible unless high demands are placed on the reader. A well-known example of this is Bransford and Johnson's (1972) famous experiment demonstrating the importance of prior knowledge in interpreting texts about washing clothes. Like the Will text, although for different reasons, it was the intentional difficulty of the text that revealed the value that prior knowledge might have in interpretation. In a similar manner, we might say that parsing research initially demonstrated the ordinary importance of syntactic processes by the creation of very difficult garden path sentences (e.g., "the horse raced past the barn fell"). So we offer these observations about our subjects in the same spirit. These were challenging texts for our subjects and we think they exposed problems in comprehension that are potentially quite general.

Before returning to our observations on these subjects, we discuss the range of possibilities that we see for comprehension problems.

---

[1]Deniers of the Holocaust trade on this apparent willingness of people to assume that things are controversial, merely because someone says they are. Will referred to the failure to distinguish open-mindedness from empty-headedness as a common failure of the ignorant.

THINGS THAT CAN GO WRONG IN COMPREHENSION

Virtually everything that logically can be identified as a component of comprehension has been identified as a source of comprehension failure. We believe indeed that comprehension is complex enough that the number of potential sources of comprehension failure is limited primarily by the grain size of our descriptions and by our imagination. However, we also believe that theoretical considerations make some components of comprehension more likely as sources of failure than others. In earlier work with children's comprehension, one of us developed a theory of individual differences in comprehension that we called the "verbal efficiency theory" (Perfetti, 1985; Perfetti & Lesgold, 1977, 1979). The central claim of this theory was that certain processes were good candidates for becoming relatively resource free and that a failure to have such processes become resource free was a substantial cause of reading comprehension difficulties. The theory identified two particular sources of comprehension failure: (1) working memory limitations and (2) lexical processes.

1. *Working memory limitations.* Our work pointed to clear evidence in both written and spoken language comprehension that skilled comprehenders had better working memories than less skilled comprehenders (Perfetti & Goldman, 1976), a hypothesis that has been confirmed and elevated to a privileged position in the explanation of comprehension difficulties (Carpenter & Just, 1988; Daneman & Carpenter, 1980; Just & Carpenter, 1992; Yuill, Oakhill, & Parkin, 1989).

2. *Lexical processes.* The second empirical pillar of this theory was the strong association between comprehension and measures of lexical processing, including both pseudoword and real word naming speed. So pervasive is this association that it is found in studies of adults as well as children (Bell & Perfetti, 1994; Bruck, 1988, 1990; Cunningham, Stanovich, & Wilson, 1990). The lexical processing difficulties include sublexical processing, such as knowledge of orthographic structure, phonological mappings to orthography, and so forth.

Because both of these components of comprehension difficulty are identified through correlations, albeit very consistent correlations across many studies, causal conclusions have never been completely warranted. They have, however, been made more credible on theoretical grounds. A processing theory based on a general understanding of how comprehension works dictates that these two components, lexical processes and the limited capacity of working memory, are inevitable sources of comprehension difficulty. The real question in our minds was, what else is involved?

TABLE 7.1
Six General Sources of Comprehension Failure
and Observed Failures in Three Subjects

	Subject 1	Subject 2	Subject 3
Processes			
Lexical	x	x	x
Working memory	x	x	x
Inference making	x	x	x
Comprehension monitoring	?	?	?
Knowledge			
Word meanings	x	x	x
Domain knowledge	x	x	x

Let's take a look at an expanded but still theoretically coherent listing of possible causes of comprehension difficulty. (These are shown in Table 7.1.) Our list begins with the two we have already identified, working memory limitations and lexical processing.

3. *Inference making.* Because texts, even single sentences, cannot be fully explicit, comprehension involves the drawing of inferences. Inferences come in many varieties and we will not try to list them and demark them here. For our purposes, the important point is simply the possibility that individuals might differ in their ability to make inferences. An inability to make an inference would lead to a comprehension failure.

4. *Comprehension monitoring.* Comprehension monitoring refers to a set of metacognitive processes that a reader can call upon to assess whether he or she is understanding a text. An effective monitoring of comprehension can lead to steps to repair miscomprehensions.

Like inferences, comprehension strategies, including monitoring, come in many varieties. The most general-level strategy is an orientation toward the text that refers to the reader's goal of obtaining meaning. To put it in its most general terms, comprehension strategies in general, and comprehension monitoring in particular, are associated with an active process in which the reader attempts to construct a coherent representation. Good comprehension monitoring is consistent with this active process.

These first four potential components of comprehension failure (lexical processes, working memory, inference making, and comprehension monitoring) can be grouped together as "processes." That is, they are ordinarily assumed to be generalized processing components as opposed to the second major category, 5 and 6 below, which is knowledge.

5. *Word meanings.* Although word meanings could be considered part of lexical processing, we list them separately here because they are so important that they deserve separate consideration.[2]

6. *Domain knowledge.* The second major knowledge category refers not to specific vocabulary but to the concepts that are a part of the background of any text. Thus, a text on psychology requires specific knowledge of its domain, and so does a text on physics, biology, or history. This domain knowledge is a critical ingredient in the construction of a situation model. It links the reader's superficial, linguistically based representation of the text to a richer inference-based representation of the situation. To be clear, vocabulary knowledge is intimately connected with domain knowledge. A generalized vocabulary deficit, for example, translates into a large number of component domain deficits. Concepts in a domain are expressed in a vocabulary (thus, word meanings and domain knowledge are highly correlated).

An additional source of reading comprehension failure sometimes has been suggested, namely, the limits set by oral language comprehension. Indeed we believe, in general, that reading comprehension is limited primarily by oral language ability; however, most of the six components listed here apply equally well to spoken language comprehension and reading comprehension. Spoken language comprehension ability and written word identification in combination should predict reading comprehension ability rather well. Gough and Tunmer (1986) proposed a simple multiplicative function for this combination, that is, decoding × spoken language comprehension = reading comprehension. This is a sound view that does a good job accounting for data. However, we note that it is possible, at least in principle, that failures in inference making, for example, or in comprehension monitoring, might be restricted to print. There are significant differences between printed language and spoken language (Perfetti, 1985) and although one can do very well by combining decoding ability and spoken language comprehension ability to predict reading comprehension, it remains possible that for some individuals, not everything transfers from the oral language situation.

We believe that these six components (working memory limitations, lexical processes, inference making, comprehension monitoring, word meanings, and domain knowledge) comprise a fundamental list of potential sources of reading comprehension failure. These sources can be theoretically motivated; that is, they can be explicitly tied to models of reading comprehension.

---

[2]In separating these components into knowledge and process, we do not wish to claim that this distinction is psychologically real. It is, however, a convenient distinction. The role of vocabulary is obvious enough. A failure to understand words in texts will cause problems in understanding the text. Although readers can infer word meanings, there is a limit to the usefulness of this strategy.

How Likely Are Each of These Components as Sources of Comprehension Failure?

There is evidence for each of these components in the literature on children and adult comprehension. The evidence shows that measures of working memory capacity separate better from lesser comprehenders (Carpenter & Just, 1988; Daneman & Carpenter, 1980; Just & Carpenter, 1992; Yuill et al., 1989). Similarly, the evidence that children who are less skilled in comprehension have problems with word decoding is substantial (Perfetti, 1985; Stanovich, 1980). Less-skilled comprehenders show poorer inference making than do more-skilled comprehenders (Yuill & Oakhill, 1991). And the ability to monitor one's comprehension also varies by comprehension skill (Baker, 1979, 1984, 1985; Baker & Anderson, 1982; Garner, 1980). For vocabulary, we have direct evidence from a study by McKeown, Beck, Omanson, and Perfetti (1983; Beck, Perfetti, & McKeown, 1982) which showed that children who learned relevant vocabulary understood passages containing the key vocabulary. Numerous studies (Anderson, Reynolds, Schallert, & Goetz, 1977; Anderson, Spiro, & Anderson, 1978; Spilich, Vesonder, Chiesi, & Voss, 1979) provided evidence on how differences in domain knowledge influence comprehension. We turn to a discussion of some of this evidence.

Comprehension Monitoring and Inference Making

We discuss comprehension monitoring and inference making together. Both are high-level processes that a reader uses to form a coherent mental representation. Although the case can be made that these processes are frequent sources of comprehension failure, this case may be overstated.

Evidence that comprehension monitoring distinguishes good from poor readers has come from numerous investigations (Baker, 1979, 1984, 1985; Baker & Anderson, 1982; Garner, 1980; Oakhill, 1993; Otero & Kintsch, 1992; Vosniadou, Pearson, & Rogers, 1988). To test for the presence of comprehension-monitoring processes, an experimenter introduces an inconsistency into a (typically) short text and then observes whether the reader can detect (explicitly comment on or recall) the inconsistency. The type of inconsistency often varies—scrambled words, contradictory statements in different paragraphs, statements that contradict a reader's prior knowledge (see Baker, 1985, for a listing of inconsistency types).

The typical pattern of results from these studies has been that some readers can detect the inconsistencies and some cannot. This division of readers into detectors and nondetectors occurs with both adults (Baker, 1979, 1985; Baker & Anderson, 1982) and children (Baker, 1984; Garner, 1980). Not surprisingly, the detectors, those who show greater comprehension-monitoring skill and use varied strategies to detect inconsistencies, are usually either high-ability readers or older readers (compared to younger readers), whereas the nondetectors are either low-ability or younger readers.

Although some low-ability readers are classified as nondetectors, they often detect local inconsistencies that interfere with the formation of a text-based representation. Noticing scrambled words and commenting on the semantic meaningfulness of individual sentences are within the processing capabilities of low-ability readers. In contrast, high-ability readers detect global inconsistencies that interfere with their formation of a situation model, such as whether the different paragraphs present unrelated topics.

There are at least two explanations for why less-skilled readers might show "lower level" but not "higher level" comprehension-monitoring strategies. One is that less-skilled readers may have misconceptions about reading goals, believing that reading is about decoding words rather than about obtaining meaning from text. There have been some indications that some readers, particularly younger children, have this misconception (Myers & Paris, 1978).

The second explanation is that less-skilled readers have difficulties with the component processes of representing a text. This second interpretation, although not typically favored by researchers in this area, deserves attention. If the text representation is impoverished, there is little for the monitoring skills to operate on. Comprehension cannot be monitored or evaluated if no comprehension has taken place. Equally serious is that there may be little a reader can do about a feeling of noncomprehension absent the skills to construct a representation of the text. When asked to verbalize comprehension difficulties, a reader must respond on the basis of that text information he or she has been able to represent in memory. For the low-ability reader, the representation is limited in ways that have their most visible impact on indicators of more global text understanding; but the representation failure may be quite general, local in critical parts as well as global. More recent evidence in fact has suggested that the problems with nondetectors do arise from lower level sources, either unequal or inappropriate weighting of propositions during the construction of a mental model (Otero & Kintsch, 1992) or the inability to simultaneously represent inconsistent information (Vosniadou et al., 1988).

Making inferences and integrating information across sentences have this same problem of explanation. Like monitoring, they both contribute to and depend on text representations. Oakhill and colleagues (Oakhill, 1993; Oakhill & Garnham, 1988; Oakhill & Yuill, 1986; Yuill & Oakhill, 1988, 1991; Yuill et al., 1989) found, for example, that more-skilled comprehenders make correct anaphoric references and integrate information in stories better than do less-skilled comprehenders.

Although differences in inferencing and integration performance are difficult to interpret, one possibility is that lack of these skills is an underlying source of comprehension failure. A reader thus could develop a situation model that is inferentially poor, despite having good word identification skills, working memory, and other lower level abilities. It is such a reader that Oakhill and colleagues claimed to have identified. In their account, the difference between skilled and less-skilled readers was in whether inferences are made and information integrated across sentences. Skilled comprehenders have inferentially rich representations. Less-skilled comprehenders are poor inference makers. Thus, they create weak situation models and show incomplete comprehension of a passage.

An alternative explanation is that the problem originates in lower level processing, a failure of word-level and proposition-building skills to produce a representation sufficient to promote needed inferences. This is not to say that reading is a sequential process in which a reader first builds a text-based representation (with minimal inferences being made) and then uses that representation to conduct higher level processes (such as elaborative inferences). Inferences of some kind are made as part of immediate comprehension. But the number of inferences that can be made, either immediately or later, has to be limited by the quality of the propositional representation that is being constructed. Questions about the mechanisms of inferencing and their relationship to other text processes make conclusions about their causal role in comprehension skill very difficult (Perfetti, 1989). Before we can conclude that some inability to make inferences is a problem, we must be sure that the foundational elements of text understanding are effective.

These foundational elements include lexical processing. Thus, controlling for lexical processing is critical in order to make the claim that higher level processes are sources of comprehension failure. Many inference studies have simply ignored lexical processing. Oakhill and colleagues have made serious efforts to control for lexical processing differences, attempting to match groups differing in comprehension on decoding (see discussion in Yuill & Oakhill, 1991).

There remains some doubt, however, judging by their measures of lexical processing. Typically, their studies matched readers on word reading by the Neale Analysis of Reading Ability. But the Neale Analysis measures reading words aloud *in context*. The evidence is clear in showing that context reduces the word identification differences between skilled and less-skilled readers (Perfetti, 1985; Stanovich, 1986). Thus, the Neale may overestimate the basic word recognition capability of less-skilled readers. Context gives them exactly what they need to perform similarly to the way skilled readers perform without context. Word reading is an autonomous, resource-free process in skilled readers; it is a context-dependent, resource-demanding process in less-skilled readers. To be clear, skilled readers are good at using context, and this adds to the methodological problem. Skilled readers use context in higher level processes such as inferences. In effect, the Neale controls for context use in word identification, thus equating more and less skilled readers, and allows for variation in the use of inferences.

The most direct solution to these problems is to produce matches on the accuracy and speed of reading words and pseudowords in isolation. The ability to read pseudowords is the clearest demonstration of a reader's knowledge of the writing system. Yuill and Oakhill (1991) reported one experiment (Experiment 3.3 in chap. 3) that used isolated word reading and pseudoword reading. They found no differences in speed or accuracy of reading isolated real words, but they did find a difference between their subjects' pseudoword reading performance. Thus, the observed difference in inference making was not independent of the kind of basic decoding skill tapped by pseudoword reading.

We believe that comprehension monitoring and inference making are important characteristics of successful learning from text. Furthermore, in agreement with Oakhill and colleagues, we accept that comprehension monitoring and inference making are less characteristic of less-skilled comprehenders. But there are many things that are characteristic of poor comprehension, and figuring out how all these characteristics interconnect around a few fundamental causal processing problems is difficult. Granting privileged causal status to a higher level characteristic requires careful attention to components whose foundational contribution has been established both theoretically and empirically. Basic reading ability, combined with text-relevant knowledge, is required to form an integrated, interpreted representation (see discussion in Perfetti, 1989).

Knowledge

The component that may be both the most important and the least interesting is domain knowledge. There have been ample demonstrations that knowledge in a domain is associated with text comprehension in that domain (e.g., Anderson et al., 1977; Anderson et al., 1978; Chiesi, Spilich, & Voss, 1979; Spilich et al., 1979). However, it has been typically assumed that this knowledge is an extra component, not intrinsically part of comprehension. Indeed, we have made exactly this claim, trying to argue for a concept of general language comprehension that is completely free of knowledge (Perfetti, 1989). In explanations of comprehension, knowledge is often considered a nuisance factor.

But there is a more interesting perspective on the role of knowledge. We can think of knowledge as the component, that, when aggregated, is associated with intellectual habits. To be a little more precise, knowledge arises from learning and education. The role of knowledge as a product of education is especially driven home when we see students like those reading the George Will column struggle with individual words, with concepts, and indeed with the entire critical perspective required for understanding. In the past, we have been inclined to treat these knowledge components as a nuisance, something that if it were only otherwise then we could study specifically the language comprehension factors. To a significant extent, we continue to think that is the case. However, what has been overlooked perhaps is the important role that knowledge plays in triggering processes important for comprehension. In particular, knowledge is required for controlling such things as comprehension monitoring and for triggering inference making.[3]

The other important thing about knowledge is that lack of it is a marker of poor comprehension. It is a mistake to imagine that a person who is low in knowledge of some domain will compensate by being high in some other domain. Certainly we can arrange experimental situations to demonstrate that some piece of text comprehension is connected with specific domain knowledge. But the facts of life are probably a bit more cruel. People who don't know anything about the Holocaust and anti-Semitism also don't know very much about a host of other topics that they might encounter in political, social, and cultural texts. They are at risk for failing in comprehension for a wide range of texts dealing with the ordinary discourse of educated persons. Furthermore, their difficulties in knowledge will associate with difficulties in lexical processing and working memory constraints. Stanovich (1986) in applying the Matthew effect (Merton, 1968; Walberg & Tsai, 1983) to reading made a telling point: Students who are ineffective in basic reading processes will read less and ultimately learn less, feeding into a vicious cycle of low achievement. In short, reading skill begets reading which begets reading skill. We can substitute the phrase "comprehension skill" for reading skill and we get the same story. It really doesn't matter all that much whether we focus on word recognition as a defining event, as we would in dyslexia, or on comprehension "disability." In both cases, the rich get richer and the poor get poorer. We have observed moderately successful college students, for example, whose difficulties in comprehending oral and written texts go hand-in-hand with difficulties in pronouncing pseudowords (Bell & Perfetti, 1994). We can argue about which comes first, the basic skill or the comprehension ability. And for some purposes the right answer matters. But for purposes of understanding and characterizing poor comprehension, it is not quite as critical as it once seemed. People who don't know the structure of their writing system, and so show lexical processing failures in pronunciations of pseudowords, or rapid decoding of low-frequency regular words, and so forth, are also going to have difficulty in comprehension. They have failed to engage effectively in the kind of reading activity that practices simultaneously all of the components of comprehension.

---

[3]There is much more required than content knowledge. Knowledge of text types (genres) and the structures of texts within a type are important in comprehension strategies, for example.

CASE STUDY OBSERVATIONS ON ADULT
COMPREHENSION FAILURE

We now examine the protocols of 3 of the 4 students who tried to read and understand the column by George Will with which we began our chapter and a rebuttal by Mark Weber, the Holocaust denier. The students we examine here are adults rather than children. But the comprehension problems we observed are characteristic of children as well as adults, provided allowances are made for the peculiar difficulties of one of our texts (the Will text). The texts read by children would not have rhetorical structures in which arguments are layered in webs of specialized background knowledge. However, there would be analogous demands of text structure, knowledge, and vocabulary.

The two texts were read in succession with the idea that we could engage the subject in some reasoning about the controversy that was being played out between them. The George Will text was 774 words long and the rebuttal by Mark Weber, published as a letter to the editor in many of the newspapers that carried the Will syndication, was 369 words long. The Flesch–Kincaid grade level for the Will text was 12th grade, whereas for the Weber text, it was 17th grade.[4]

The subjects were chosen by screening a group of 50 introductory psychology students on their knowledge of history and their habits of reading newspapers and editorials. It may be interesting to note that of the 50 students screened, only one could generate the name of any newspaper editorial columnist and only half said that they regularly read a newspaper. (We think this turns out to be important in accounting for their low level of comprehension.) The subjects we chose were, by design, not especially high in their knowledge of history. Our goal was to study how people would reason with texts when they lacked background knowledge.

The three subjects who are the focus of the present discussion scored in the 25th, 49th, and 19th percentile on the Nelson–Denny reading test and scored around 25% on tests of specific knowledge of World War II, the Nazi regime, the Holocaust, and history in general. Thus, these three subjects could be characterized as low in comprehension skill and low in history knowledge. (A fourth subject, who fared better in reading the Will text had similar low scores on the history knowledge test.) The important fact about all three subjects was that all failed to understand critical parts of the essay by George Will, the rebuttal by Mark Weber, or both. We focus here on the George Will essay.

---

[4]It is interesting to note that subjects had much less difficulty with the Weber text than with the Will text, despite the "easier" readability index of the Will text. Thus, these readability scores are likely not a good indication of actual readability. This is consistent with a variety of findings that have shown that readability formulas are not highly effective for predicting comprehension (e.g., Bruce, Rubin, & Starr, 1981; Klare, 1974/1975).

Subjects were instructed that they were going to read some editorials out loud and be required to think out loud about the writers' arguments and use of evidence as they read through the editorials. Each paragraph of the editorials was printed on an individual index card and after reading through each paragraph, the subject was prompted to say what he or she thought. In addition, after each paragraph, the experimenter asked the subject various scripted questions to assess the subject's understanding of the paragraph and the text in general. The questions ranged from facts that were mentioned in the paragraph (e.g., *What is revisionism?*) to more general issues, such as what was the author's motivation (e.g., *What do you think Weber's purpose was with this paragraph?*). In order to make subjects more comfortable with the task of reading out loud and providing verbal protocols, before reading the two editorials on the Holocaust, they practiced the same procedure with a short (four paragraph) editorial about gambling in Pittsburgh. During reading, the experimenter provided assistance with definitions of words if the subjects asked for help, but provided no feedback on the subjects' comprehension or help with understanding the paragraphs.

The combination of oral reading and verbal protocols provided a rich record of the reading process. Accordingly, we had information about the subjects' ability in recognizing words, in knowing the meaning of words, and in understanding what they read. We were not able to separate clearly cases in which a subject merely failed to produce correctly a word he or she might have known (e.g., "persuade" misread as "pursue") from those in which the subject neither knew nor pronounced the word correctly (e.g., "deconstructionist").

Subject 1, whose reading comprehension test result was in the 25th percentile, made 46 uncorrected word-reading errors on the Will passage, a rate of approximately 6%. For example, in the first paragraph, in which Will refers to the "genteel tinkle of restaurant lunch sounds," Subject 1 read "gentle trickle," and misread "persuade" as "pursue." This 6% error rate does not include a number of occasions on which Subject 1 misread a word or a phrase, then backtracked and read it more or less correctly. (To help make sense of how our subjects performed, the entire text from the Will column and the Weber rebuttal are presented in the appendices.)

Subject 2, whose reading comprehension score was in the 49th percentile, had far fewer explicit troubles in word recognition, making only one uncorrected error along with seven or eight corrected errors. It was clear that reading aloud was a problem for him as he stumbled on the text multiple times, but he performed much better than Subject 1. However, he shared with Subject 1 serious misapprehensions of the article.

Subject 3, who had a reading comprehension score in the 19th percentile, made 26 uncorrected errors (about 3%), intermediate between Subjects 1 and 2. Like Subject 1 and Subject 2, Subject 3 also had profound misunderstandings of the text. Moreover, the kinds of misunderstandings that the three subjects showed tended to be shared among them. We use Subject 3 to illustrate the problems.

One Subject's Comprehension Problems

Ideally, one would like to identify the kinds of problems exhibited by a subject by referring to the six theoretical possibilities outlined previously. But this strategy makes the arguable assumption that errors can be reliably classified, and the even more arguable assumption that, once classified, they comprise an account of the reader's comprehension problems. A more illuminating approach may be to go through the text with the reader, paragraph by paragraph, and try to see the comprehension problems she faced. We refer to categories of errors for descriptive purposes, and, because they were so pervasive, we first examine lexical errors over the entire text.

Lexical Errors

In the first paragraph, Subject 3 needed help with the word "salmon." Unfortunately we do not know whether the word "salmon" was in her vocabulary, that is, whether this is a decoding error or a vocabulary error. But it illustrates a disturbing and common problem: Students have trouble with what many would consider ordinary, nonspecialized words. (She also could not pronounce correctly "genteel" in the first paragraph.) In the second paragraph, she said that she could not pronounce the words of the death camps (Auschwitz–Birkenau, Majdanck, Treblinka), which, of course, is quite understandable. Only one of our three subjects pronounced even Auschwitz correctly. The assumption that Auschwitz is synonymous in the public mind with the Holocaust may be mistaken; many students in the United States appear not to know what Auschwitz refers to. In that paragraph, our subject also had trouble with "extermination," and jumping to paragraph 4, she could not read "pseudo-scholarship," "anti-Semitism," "rigors," and "martyrdom." In paragraph 5, she stumbled on "annihilation" and "hyperbole." In paragraph 6, she couldn't handle "partisanship," pointing out to us that it was a big word. In paragraph 7, she had trouble with "fascist," "rehabilitize," "delegitimizing," and "vilifying," all words critical to understanding the paragraph. In paragraph 8, she stumbled on "anti-Semitic," "hierarchical," and "racial." In paragraph 9, she stumbled on "sundered"; in paragraph 10 on "farragoes," "sequiturs," and "cynics." In paragraph 11, it was "amnesia" and "skepticism." And finally, in paragraph 12 it was, naturally, "epistemological indeterminacy."

Now let us put these errors in perspective. The errors occurred on low-frequency words that are unfamiliar to many students. On the one hand, for an American student to be able to pronounce a German name, perhaps even to pronounce Auschwitz, is too much to expect. On the other hand, one might expect words like "salmon," "racial," "rigor," "partisanship," to be within the reach of a college undergraduate, even a freshman. We don't wish to belabor, as many do, the ignorance of our students. The point is not to document ignorance but to illuminate their comprehension problems. The fact that these texts were challenging, including the fact that the vocabulary was a step above the mundane, exposed some problems of comprehension. Not only was Subject 3 not able to read about 3% of the words in the text, she was unable to grasp the essential message of the column.

Conceptual Muddles in the Situation Model

During the first two paragraphs, we can characterize Subject 3 as being a bit lost. She does not know what salmon means, she does not know what this lunch is all about, she cannot pronounce the names of the death camps, and we suspect she does not know that they are death camps either. So when we ask her questions about those paragraphs, she has very little to say. But by paragraph 3, a general kind of comprehension problem becomes visible. She is asked who Mark Weber is. This is an interesting question, because to know who Mark Weber is, is to have established the beginnings of a situation model. That is, Mark Weber is not known to anyone at the beginning of this article and the whole point is for George Will to tell the reader about who Mark Weber is. And it is critical in all of this to understand that Mark Weber is a Holocaust denier and that George Will is exposing him and deniers generally as anti-Semitic frauds. So when Subject 3, after reading the third paragraph, is asked who Mark Weber is, and she responds, "I guess he's Jewish," one has the impression that there is a failure of understanding. This conceptual muddle will help prevent her from constructing a coherent representation of both the situation and the unfolding of the macro-rhetorical structure of the text.

Paragraph 3 can provide a clue as to the nature of the misunderstandings. This paragraph establishes that Weber edits the *Journal of Historical Review*, that this journal has advertised a book saying "that the Jews benefited" from Crystal Night, and that this outlandish claim is characteristic of Holocaust revisionism. It is safe to say that our subject lacks a critical piece of knowledge, namely, what Crystal Night refers to.[5] This gap allows her to not apprehend the sarcastic sense being employed by Will. However, notice that the subject has had now three paragraphs to catch on to the fact that Mark Weber is a Holocaust denier. Will has already established that Weber

---

[5]Crystal Night ("Kristallnacht") refers to Nazi-led, anti-Jewish riots that took place in the Third Reich in November 1938. It was a night of violence against Jews in which tens of thousands were arrested, synagogues destroyed, and Jewish-owned shops looted. It is referred to as "Crystal Night" because of the breaking glass from the shops.

is a Holocaust denier, and further made clear that he himself is not one to be persuaded by a denier. Guessing that Weber is Jewish is not merely lack of knowledge, but an expression of an unfiltered association that something in this text is Jewish.

Failures of Inference and Working Memory

If we were to try to explain this misapprehension in terms of our candidate components of comprehension failure, there are several possibilities. One is that our subject is failing to make inferences. When Will says, "If you guessed that the Jews benefited, you have got the drift of Holocaust 'revisionism,' " there should be an inference process that leads to the conclusion that (the author believes) Weber is anti-Semitic, or at least not Jewish. A second possibility is the working memory hypothesis. Subject 3 has a limited working memory, one that can hold only a few words at a time, constrained especially by processing costs charged by this text to her processing capabilities. She extracts some propositions from the key sentences in paragraph 3, but she does not carry over enough information from the preceding paragraph to allow her to connect the current sentence to the preceding sentence. Accordingly, although after paragraph 2 she might have (in some sense) understood (inferred) who Mark Weber was, by paragraph 3, having to handle these quotes about Crystal Night and other things that she knew nothing about was an overload, and she simply could no longer retrieve what she once knew.

This working memory problem would be part of a Verbal Efficiency explanation (Perfetti, 1985). Several words have been incorrectly recognized by Subject 3, suggesting that even those correctly recognized are demanding too many processing resources, resulting in a failure to assemble the needed propositions. Sentences and parts of sentences would be misunderstood. There would be a failure, on this account, not merely of inference making, but of local text representation.

Examining the situation in terms of hypothesized possibilities, of course, is a kind of confirmation strategy. Such a strategy is bound to show reasonable possibilities without identifying a single best account of these comprehension problems.

Further Muddles in the Rhetorical Structure

Despite her mistake about Weber's identity, Subject 3 does seem to infer that Will's attitude toward Weber is negative. She was asked specifically what Will thought about Weber, and responded, "It's kind of negative, I think." So, there is at least a piece of relevant rhetorical structure being represented, although it is a mystery as to what Subject 3's mental model of this text is after three paragraphs.

After paragraph 4, where Subject 3 stumbles over "pseudo-scholarship," "anti-Semitism," and a couple of other words, she asks the experimenter who the denier is and whether Weber is the denier. The questions indicate that she is trying to understand this piece of text and indeed is monitoring her own difficulty in understanding the text. After paragraph 5 in which Subject 3 indicates she does not know "annihilation" and does not know "hyperbole," she distorts the meaning to the simple message that, "They're saying they don't believe the Nazis really hurt them." There is no sense that she knows who the "they" are, nor that the text in the preceding paragraph concerns the *form* of the deniers' arguments rather than their claim that the Nazis didn't "hurt them." This illustrates the problems in her situation model. First, she fails to establish adequate *discourse referents*, that is, representations of the people and their arguments. From this failure comes confusion that is never repaired. Second, she fails to represent the developing rhetorical structure of the text. She is forced to misrepresent the nature of the argument between the author and the deniers.

Perhaps the extent of Subject 3's misunderstanding of the entire text is seen in her answer to the question following paragraph 6 when she is asked what she thinks George Will meant by writing, "such a person tortures the past in the hope of making the future safe for torturers." The subject observes that this does not make sense and wonders "whether they mean the people getting tortured or the people who's torturing." When she was informed that the sentence refers to the people who were torturing, she still does not get it, answering the question very literally as "like might try to make it safe for them. They're the ones being, they're the ones making it dangerous."

We skip now to paragraph 11 to see an example of a comprehension problem for Subject 3. Whereas the first 10 paragraphs can be characterized as exposing the arguments of the deniers and shining a light on their motivations, paragraph 11 gets at the heart of the essay. It expresses Will's explanation of why Holocaust deniers meet with some success (see Fig. 7.1). People who lack knowledge substitute skepticism, assuming legitimate controversy where, in fact, none exists. The key event explained in paragraph 11 concerns a reporter who asks Deborah Lipstadt, author of a book about Holocaust deniers, about proof for the existence of the Holocaust that Lipstadt might have included in her book. Will's comment is that the reporter "passed through college unmarked by information about even the largest events of the century, but acquired the conventional skepticism of the emptyheaded." This hypothesis about the relation between ignorance and skepticism is completely missed by Subject 3. She incorrectly summarizes the point of the paragraph by saying the reporter does not believe in the Holocaust.

Where does such misunderstanding come from? Is it because the subject didn't know the word "amnesia" and the word "skepticism" in that paragraph? Or is it that even though the subject could decode the word "emptyheaded,"

she didn't know what it meant? To put it another way, why did the subject
make the inference that the reporter didn't believe in the Holocaust? One
possibility is that she had only recently figured out that this text was about
Holocaust deniers and the point of confrontation was between the deniers
and the author of the column. This hard-won achievement couldn't be jeop-
ardized by moving to a new and equally unfamiliar level. But this, of course,
is not much of an explanation.

After paragraph 12 the subject gets another chance. Paragraph 12 expands
this notion of ignorance spawning doubt. Unfortunately for the subject,
George Will elaborates this idea with esoterica, such as "epistemological
indeterminacy," "deconstructionism," and so forth. The subject surely must
be excused for wondering what in the world the author was talking about
in referring to life as a mere "narrative." On the other hand, even someone
unfamiliar with literary deconstructionism and epistemological indeterminacy as academic attitudes might at least understand a distinction between
the author and his subject. It ought to be clear that George Will is saying
something rather negative about a variety of "academic theories" explicitly
mentioned in line three of the paragraph.

For a brief moment Subject 3 appeared to have grasped the "macro
message" of the column. After paragraph 12, she was asked what George Will
thought about the deniers and she answered, "It's kind of negative." At this
point she appears to have understood at least the author's attitude, which,
generously, might be said to be the main point of the article.[6] But illustrating
the confusion that one can discover by further probing, the subject was asked
what she thought the purpose of Will's column was. After a long pause, her
uncertain response was that the purpose was to "first make people believe
that the Holocaust didn't happen?" This opinion, tentative though it was, was
clearly inconsistent with her conclusion that Will's attitude toward the deniers
was negative. It is likely that she continued to fail to grasp the concept of
denier. Alternatively, it might be an extreme example, a caricature, of the kind
of failures of comprehension monitoring in which subjects fail to detect
inconsistencies (Baker, 1979, 1984, 1985; Baker & Anderson, 1982; Garner,
1980; Oakhill, 1993; Otero & Kintsch, 1992; Vosniadou et al., 1988).

Problems With a Simpler Text

If Subject 3's problems in comprehension were specific to the demanding
style of Will's prose, then she should have done better on the Mark Weber
column that was directed against Will's essay. The prose in Weber's column

---

[6]Will's column, representative of literate argumentative prose, should give pause to the
assumption that identifying "main ideas" is the critical high level goal of comprehension. There
is no single main idea in the Will column, but two interconnected rhetorical goals, as shown
in Fig. 7.1.

is simple, direct, and, as one can see in the text given in Appendix B, rather easy to understand compared with Will's.[7] In fact, Subject 3 made far fewer reading errors, only five uncorrected errors out of 385 words (about 1%).

Working Memory Again. Nevertheless, Subject 3 continued to show comprehension problems. An interesting example of what appears to be a parsing problem occurred in paragraph 2. The point of Weber's paragraph 2 is to convince the reader that deniers are highly credible sources, including "historians and former concentration camp inmates, and a gas chamber specialist," and to convince the reader that these people deny the Holocaust not because of evil motives, but on the basis of "a sincere and thoughtful evaluation of the evidence." Thus, the paragraph asserts the motives for their denial while presupposing the denial itself. When asked what the purpose of the paragraph was, Subject 3 responded that (the people mentioned) "were not rejecting the Holocaust extermination story." The source of this serious error appears to be that the predicate "did not decide to reject the Holocaust extermination story" actually occurred in the paragraph. The subject completely missed the following "because" clause, which should have signaled that the deniers in fact had rejected the Holocaust, while asserting why they had rejected it. This kind of comprehension problem ordinarily suggests the limitations of working memory in retaining sentence information during subsequent demanding processing.

Subject 3, despite the easier prose in the Weber text, went merrily down a comprehension garden path. After paragraph 3, she is asked what Weber is trying to say, and she answers, "the deniers are wrong," a complete reversal of the text argument. Again, it is tempting to look at a very local comprehension event. Line 4 of paragraph 3 states, "his (Will's) portrayal of the arguments of Holocaust deniers is grotesquely inaccurate." Is it possible that the subject's limited working memory allows her to grasp only something about "deniers" and "grotesquely inaccurate," thereby interpreting the paragraph as an argument against deniers? It's an interesting possibility. One cannot appreciate a layered text, one layered not only in its syntax but in the relation of its syntax to the author's voice, with a seriously limited working memory capacity made functionally more limited by processing demands.[8]

---

[7]We have produced the Weber text as an appendix only so that the reader can follow the comprehension example in this section. We do so with considerable reservation. We risk the possibility that an uninformed reader will approach these texts with what Will referred to as the "conventional wisdom of the emptyheaded," taking them as somehow equivalent in the legitimacy of their basic historical argument. There is no genuine controversy about the central facts of the Holocaust. We recommend Lipstadt (1994) for an informed perspective on the phenomenon of Holocaust denial.

[8]Another possibility is that she did retain her incorrect situation model of the first text that Will's purpose was to "make people believe the Holocaust didn't happen." This could have led her to believe that Weber is against deniers.

Even in the simpler text, Subject 3 never really does catch on to very much. After reading the seventh paragraph of the Weber text, she is still unclear about what the revisionist view is and asks the experimenter to help her with it. There is very little inferring of meaning from context here. Again, the failure to construct a clear situation model from the first text leads to a misunderstanding of the critical rhetorical (argumentative) structures of both texts.

Knowledge, Inferences, and Comprehension Monitoring

At this point it is tempting to simply dismiss all this by saying we have a demanding text and a subject who has all kinds of problems, so we can't shed any light on the sources of comprehension failure. Although we do believe that a subject's failures with a difficult task can be exposed with other texts if they are sufficiently challenging, there is a serious problem in constraining the possible explanations for the comprehension problems. However, this problem may be more general across research methods rather than confined to the kind of single-subject analysis we have carried out here. It exists as well in the typical style of research in which two groups of subjects are selected to be different in overall comprehension skill. The researcher then tests a single, or perhaps at most two, hypothesized components of their comprehension differences, typically finding confirmation of the one or two that the researcher has hypothesized. The research strategy is seldom to test every theoretically motivated source of difference. We have made, as near as we can tell, practically no progress in isolating, relatively speaking, the components of comprehension failure. In this respect there might be a rather general lesson from a protocol like this. We can see the problems in comprehension and we can describe them without being exactly sure about how to explain them.

Nevertheless, we do not want to imply that no constraints can be placed on the kind of explanations one might offer. In particular, we do not think that failures to draw inferences and failures to monitor comprehension are likely to be general problems in comprehension, and are not problems in these protocols, except insofar as they depend on knowledge. To illustrate with our subjects we move to Subject 1 and Subject 2, both of whom had somewhat richer protocols than Subject 3.

Subject 1 was generous with statements indicating his awareness of his level of comprehension. He not only observes that he does not understand something, but also that the reason for his problem is that "they don't give enough information." (This follows paragraph 3 where he tries to come to grips with the claims that the Jews benefited from Crystal Night.) A particularly clear statement of this kind occurs after paragraph 5. Subject 1 remarks that "I'm like confused about these topics. Cause they like give me a brief thing about each one and like I got a lot of questions in my mind like I want to ask but . . ." We don't want to make too much of this kind of metacognitive statement, but there is an important point. The subjects know very well they are not understanding this. They are not having trouble monitoring their comprehension in that sense. What they are having trouble with is understanding.

If what one means by comprehension monitoring instead refers to the ability to detect inconsistencies in texts, then it is less clear what to conclude. There were no inconsistencies in our texts. Instead, our subjects appeared to create inconsistencies in their mental models. (See Subject 3 for a clear example.) But where do such inconsistencies come from? Are they some highly general and stable characteristic failure to monitor comprehension? Perhaps. But it is at least equally plausible that our subjects tolerated inconsistencies, even created them, because of insufficient knowledge. A subject who knows nothing about the Holocaust might be expected to construct incompatible elements in his mental model from reading texts about this topic, such as the Weber and Will texts. Or to give a more specific example, Subject 3 did not know what "skepticism" was, or at least was unable to read it. It is quite reasonable for her then to think that the reporter who, according to Will's text, has the "skepticism of the ignorant" merely fails to believe in the Holocaust, rather than being prone to skepticism. The inconsistencies and the inaccuracies in the mental model arise not because of a failure to monitor inconsistencies, but from a lack of knowledge. We suggest that knowledge is what triggers the kind of comprehension activity we normally ascribe to some general monitoring process. Inconsistencies with real knowledge will be noticed.

We think much the same can be said of inferences. Is a failure to make inferences a general processing characteristic of individuals in much the same way as, say, lexical access or working memory is? Perhaps there are some people who go through life without making inferences and others who always make inferences. We can't rule that out and there is evidence that seems to link comprehension skill to inference making. But we're not sure that everyone who talks about inference making has a shared understanding of what it is. Making an inference depends on the knowledge and goals of the reader, in connection with properties of the text. The assumption that such a process is a stable, individual characteristic is patently dubious. Moreover, the evidence that people make inferences during reading, at least inferences of a certain kind, is not very strong. Debates about "online inferences" continue in full force and attempts to demonstrate such inferences have been forced to become increasingly sophisticated, because they are difficult to demonstrate.[9] It is not, in other words, even clear that a failure to make inferences is a marker of poor comprehension.

---

[9]See for example McKoon and Ratcliff (1992) and Graesser, Singer, and Trabasso (1994), as well as Trabasso and Suh (1993), Graesser and Kreuz (1993), Perfetti (1993), and other papers in a collection edited by Graesser (1993).

Even if it is a marker of poor comprehension, there remains a question of whether it is an individual characteristic or a characteristic of knowledge representation. A reader motivated to construct a coherent representation of a text and who has necessary knowledge to represent the information from a text may make the needed inferences. A reader lacking the knowledge may be the reader who fails to make the inferences. We can't demonstrate clearly in our subjects failures to make inferences, although there are several candidate examples, including one already described for Subject 3. But our suggestion is that if we could isolate an inference failure in a subject, we would be hard-pressed to attribute it to a general processing characteristic. We would be much more likely to connect it to a knowledge gap.

The quest for individual differences in processing should not blind us to the possibility that these individual differences are intimately connected with knowledge; knowledge of word meanings, knowledge of concepts, knowledge of domains in general, and even knowledge of how language works. We can go so far as to rewrite all of the claims about decoding and working memory deficits into knowledge deficits. It is clear that the idea of a functional working memory depends on knowledge of whatever it is that is used to test memory. And decoding processes can be rephrased to refer to knowledge of words and word constituents. We don't necessarily wish to do this complete revamping of a process-oriented deficit description, but it is not obvious that we can understand these processes, especially working memory, as content-blind processing machinery. It is even more evident in the case of inferences, comprehension monitoring, and the like that knowledge is involved. Knowledge of domains is intrinsically relevant to the construction of a situation model, and to mental models in general. And failures in knowledge will be manifest as failures in comprehension monitoring or inference making or perhaps something else.

CONCLUSIONS: IMPLICATIONS FOR CHILDREN'S COMPREHENSION PROBLEMS

What do our observations about a few cases of adult comprehension failure have to do with children's comprehension disability? Before answering this question, we need to consider real reading disability. Two things seem increasingly clear: First, children who have reading disabilities, carefully defined by exclusionary criteria, have basic problems in language processing that center around phonology. These problems are manifest in a range of tasks—phonological awareness, pseudoword reading, spelling, speech perception, and others—although not in all tasks for all disabled subjects; second, such children do not necessarily differ qualitatively from garden variety poor readers. The same set of lexical processing problems, often including phonological processing, along with working memory problems, characterize low-achieving readers, whether or not low achievement is defined with respect to IQ.[10]

It is important to emphasize these basic processing deficits as pervasive in reading disability, and we have argued for the centrality of these language processing abilities in previous work (e.g., Perfetti, 1985, 1989, 1994). It is also important to recognize that these processing problems apply to children whose low achievement is defined by reading comprehension. Reading comprehension is limited by the operation of basic processes that identify words, activate their meanings, configure phrases (parsing), assemble meanings, and so forth. Convincing evidence that children have comprehension problems *in the absence of problems in these lower level components* has been limited. It remains for those who claim that children have distinctive problems in inference making and comprehension monitoring beyond basic lexical and working memory problems to demonstrate such problems under conditions that remove doubt about the children's abilities in the basic components.

Against this background, our suggestion is that we need to reconsider the importance of knowledge, including knowledge of word meanings, as a source of comprehension failure. Again, it is not that there has been inadequate attention to knowledge factors in comprehension. The research on higher level comprehension processes is replete with demonstrations of knowledge factors. The importance of knowledge in comprehension, however, is not merely a matter of background or domain knowledge. Drawing an appropriate inference depends on having relevant knowledge activated when it is needed. Monitoring comprehension depends on having a sufficient base of knowledge so that an occasional "signal" of misapprehension is detectable against a low noise background of adequate comprehension. Similarly, noticing text inconsistency is a signal detection task, in which a mainly coherent representation of the text is a prerequisite.

Is knowledge sufficient for inference making and comprehension monitoring? Probably not. The reader's goals, including especially a willingness to expend effort at "deep" comprehension are critical. This is why both inferences and comprehension monitoring are unlikely to be routine parts of reading. Only when a reader has both adequate knowledge and sufficient motivation will inferences be drawn and comprehension monitored in any useful sense. (This argument has been made for inferences in more detail in Perfetti, 1993.)

---

[10]This is not to say that there are no differences between garden variety poor readers and disabled readers. One expects a wider range of problems in the garden variety poor reader, but the core components of phonological processing, and, especially lexical processing remain important. We also need to emphasize that evidence allows the possibility that some disabilities may arise from other sources connected to visual processing. The main point is that, overall, most reading problems are characterized by basic lexical and phonological weaknesses.

The fact is that a fairly passive reading machinery is sufficient for some levels of comprehension. The problem is that a reader who engages only the passive machinery most of the time is at risk for not acquiring two important things: further knowledge and good habits of intellect.

The latter refers to an acquired characteristic of critical thinking as part of reading, part of a generalized attitude toward learning and knowledge. It is clear that genuine individual differences exist in habits of intellect as well as in knowledge. To the extent that such things as comprehension monitoring and inference making are stable general characteristics of individuals, they are examples of habits of intellect. But we should resist the temptation to assume they are stable and general characteristics until the evidence warrants this conclusion. If these higher level features of comprehension arise from interactions of specific texts with the reader's reading ability, knowledge, and motivation, then we should expect the higher-level comprehension factors not to be simple characteristics of individuals.

Thus, the connection between our cases of adult failures in comprehension and children's comprehension disability is this: Knowledge of words and concepts is critical in building a representation of a text for all readers. We observe all manner of problems in children's reading, just as we did for our adult readers when they were given a challenging text. Some of these problems can be readily attributed to lower level lexical processing difficulties. To the extent they cannot, we should not necessarily conclude that higher level strategic skills are somehow the critical issue. It is exactly these processes that are most vulnerable to specific knowledge failures. We think these processes are important, but we suspect that they develop ordinarily in tandem with the gradual accumulation of knowledge and in the context of text understanding. It is the understanding itself that is critical. Thus, training a child in detecting text inconsistencies is probably effective to the extent that it helps direct attention to the understanding of the text. It can help compensate for low knowledge and low reading skill, and especially for low motivation to understand. But it may not substitute, in the long run, for the knowledge and skill that are acquired over years of learning and that promote the habits of intellect one would like to see in college students.

APPENDIX A

Ignorance, Anti-Semitism and 'Scholarship'
George F. Will

NEWPORT BEACH, California. Amid the genteel tinkle of restaurant lunch sounds, Mark Weber is having difficulty doing justice to his salmon, such is his passion for justice, as he pretends to understand it. He is trying to persuade me that the Holocaust never happened. It is not going well.

I am a hard sell, having visited death camps (Auschwitz-Birkenau, Majdanck, Treblinka) with survivors. But the fact that some Jews survived is part of the Holocaust deniers "proof" that the Nazis never intended extermination.

Weber edits *The Journal of Historical Review,* a recent issue of which advertises a book "that dares to ask: Who Benefited from the 'Crystal Night'?", the Nov. 6, 1938, anti-Jewish rioting. If you guessed that the Jew benefited, you have got the drift of Holocaust "revisionism."

Revisionism is a term of scholarship hijacked by pseudo-scholarship in the service of anti-Semitism. Holocaust deniers present any conflict among, or amendment of, survivors' testimonies, or any historical refinement of previous understandings, as "proof" that the Holocaust is a myth. Weber allows as how maybe a million Jews were victims—of the rigors of confinement, and of excessive Nazi security concerns. But Holocaust deniers say victims exaggerate, and after the war Nazis made false confessions to appease their captors, who were serving the myth-makers—Jews fabricating martyrdom for political and financial gains.

The deniers' "arguments" always return to what Weber, like the Nazis, calls "the Jewish question" (*Judenfrage*). The gas chambers were really showers. Zyclon-B gas was too weak to kill. Or too powerful to use for mass murder—it would have killed those who emptied the "alleged" gas chambers. When Hitler promised "the annihilation of the Jewish race in Europe" (Jan. 30, 1939) he was, says one denier, merely using heroic hyperbole—"the kind of defiance that was hurled by ancient heroes." And so on.

For some people, historical partisanship, such as defending Richard III against the charge that he ordered the murder of the princes in the Tower, is a hobby. But what kind of person makes a career of denying the reality of an almost contemporary event that was recorded graphically, documented bureaucratically and described in detail by victims, bystanders and perpetrators? Such a person tortures the past in the hope of making the future safe for torturers.

In her new book *Denying the Holocaust: The Growing Assault on Truth and Memory,* Deborah Lipstadt of Emory University argues that the deniers' work "is intimately connected to a neo-fascist political agenda." She says the deniers' aim is to rehabilitize Nazism and reevaluate its victims, thereby delegitimizing Israel and vilifying Jews.

Hitler, says Weber at lunch, was "the most philosophical" figure of the 20th century, and "his understanding of this century was more on the mark than any of his contemporaries." And "Hitler has the 'rep' he has because he opposed the whole development of the 20th century." Anti-Semitic and anti-democratic, Hitler understood the necessity for severely hierarchical and racially homogenous nations.

Applying these ideas, Weber says that America "has two ways to go." It can become a "Third World" chaos of tribes, or it can be sundered into racially pure entities.

The Webers of the world are few and their "arguments" are farragoes of dizzying nonsequiturs and mock-scientific analyses of a sort concocted only by lunatics or sinister cynics. But the deniers' increasing echoes, and their ability to insert themselves into the conversation of society, are cultural symptoms.

Holocaust deniers play upon contemporary society's tendency toward historical amnesia, and its fuzzy notion of "tolerance" that cannot distinguish between an open mind and an empty mind. Thus a young reporter for a respected magazine interviewing Lipstadt (without reading her book) asked this question: "What proof do you include in your book that the Holocaust happened?" That reporter passed through college unmarked by information about even the largest events of the century, but acquired the conventional skepticism of the emptyheaded: When in doubt, doubt.

People as ignorant as that reporter know nothing, so they doubt everything except how sophisticated they are when they assume that nothing is certain. This assumption is irrigated in the badly educated by fashionable academic theories of epistemological indeterminacy. The vocabulary and mentality of literary "deconstruction" seeps everywhere, relativizing everything, teaching that history, like all of life, is a mere "narrative," a "text" with no meaning beyond what any individual reads into it. No event, no book, nothing has a fixed content, the individual's "perception" or "reaction" to it is everything.

That is the bad news. The good news is that this year two million people will pass through Washington's new Holocaust Memorial Museum, which will survive the survivors and be their testimony.

APPENDIX B

Will Is Ignorant of Basic Facts of the Holocaust
Mark Weber
Editor, Journal of Historical Review
Institute for Historical Review
Newport Beach, California[11]

George F. Will's claim that I, and other "Holocaust deniers, torture the past in the hope of making the future safe for torturers" is contemptible ("Ignorance, Anti-Semitism and 'Scholarship,'" Perspectives, Aug. 30).

University professors such as Arthur Butz and Robert Faurisson, historians such as David Irving and Harry Elmer Barnes, former concentration-camp

---

[11]Originally appeared as a Letter to the Editor in the September 18, 1993, *Pittsburgh Post-Gazette*, page B-2. The text, including the headline, was taken directly from the paper.

163

inmates such as Paul Rassinier and American gas-chamber specialist Fred Leuchter did not decide to reject the Holocaust extermination story—thereby risking public censure, and worse—because their motives are evil, but rather on the basis of a sincere and thoughtful evaluation of the evidence.

In his mean-spirited polemic, Will attributes words to me that are either invented or are crass distortions of remarks ripped from their context. Similarly, his portrayal of the arguments of Holocaust "deniers" is grotesquely inaccurate. I do not contend—as Will so simplistically puts it—that "the Holocaust never happened." Every serious revisionist readily acknowledges that Europe's Jews endured a terrible catastrophe during World War II.

Will seems to think that his visits to the sites of three wartime camps, and a reading of some secondary literature, make him something of an expert on this subject. As he revealed during our Aug. 19 luncheon meeting, though, he is remarkably ignorant of the basic facts of Holocaust history.

Will was not aware, for example, that Anne Frank—along with others in her family—had "survived" Auschwitz internment (she later died in Bergen-Belsen, a victim of typhus). He was completely unfamiliar with the Einsatzgruppen—the special German security police units that operated in the occupied Soviet territories.

Will told me that he accepts as accurate and reliable the "testimony" of Auschwitz commandant Rudolf Hess, unaware that this important piece of Holocaust evidence was obtained by torture, and that, on a number of key points, it is not even consistent with the current version of the Auschwitz extermination story. Will also acknowledged his ignorance of the many German wartime documents that plainly show that the "Final Solution" policy was not one of extermination.

Will's attempt to portray Holocaust revisionism as part of a vast anti-Semitic conspiracy is not only inaccurate, it is an insult to the growing number of Jews who support the revisionist view.

REFERENCES

Anderson, R. C., Reynolds, R. E., Schallert, D. L., & Goetz, E. T. (1977). Frameworks for comprehending discourse. *American Educational Research Journal, 14*, 367–381.

Anderson, R. C., Spiro, R. J., & Anderson, M. C. (1978). Schemata as scaffolding for the representation of information in connected discourse. *American Educational Research Journal, 15*, 433–440.

Baker, L. (1979). Comprehension monitoring: Identifying and coping with text confusions. *Journal of Reading Behavior, 11*, 365–374.

Baker, L. (1984). Spontaneous versus instructed use of multiple standards for evaluating comprehension: Effects of age, reading proficiency, and type of standard. *Journal of Experimental Child Psychology, 38*, 289–311.

Baker, L. (1985). Differences in the standards used by college students to evaluate their comprehension of expository prose. *Reading Research Quarterly, 20*, 297–313.

Baker, L., & Anderson, R. I. (1982). Effects of inconsistent information on text processing: Evidence for comprehension monitoring. *Reading Research Quarterly, 22,* 281–294.

Beck, I. L., Perfetti, C. A., & McKeown, M. G. (1982). The effects of long-term vocabulary instruction on lexical access and reading comprehension. *Journal of Educational Psychology, 74,* 506–521.

Bell, L., & Perfetti, C. A. (1994). Reading skill: Some adult comparisons. *Journal of Educational Psychology, 86,* 244–255.

Bransford, J. D., & Johnson, M. K. (1972). Contextual prerequisites for understanding: Some investigations of comprehension and recall. *Journal of Verbal Learning and Verbal Behavior, 11,* 717–726.

Bruce, B., Rubin, A., & Starr, K. (1981). *Why readability formulas fail* (BBN Report No. 4715). Urbana-Champaign, IL: University of Illinois at Urbana-Champaign, Center for the Study of Reading.

Bruck, M. (1988). The word recognition and spelling of dyslexic children. *Reading Research Quarterly, 23,* 51–69.

Bruck, M. (1990). Word-recognition skills of adults with childhood diagnosis of dyslexia. *Developmental Psychology, 26,* 439–454.

Carpenter, P. A., & Just, M. A. (1988). The role of working memory in language comprehension. In D. Klahr & K. Kotovsky (Eds.), *Complex information processing: The impact of Herbert A. Simon* (pp. 31–68). Hillsdale, NJ: Lawrence Erlbaum Associates.

Chiesi, H. L., Spilich, G. J., & Voss, J. F. (1979). Acquisition of domain-related information in relation to high and low domain knowledge. *Journal of Verbal Learning and Verbal Behavior, 18,* 257–274.

Cunningham, A. E., Stanovich, K. E., & Wilson, M. R. (1990). Cognitive variation in adult students differing in reading ability. In T. H. Carr & B. A. Levy (Eds.), *Reading and its development: Component skills approaches* (pp. 129–159). New York: Academic Press.

Daneman, M., & Carpenter, P. A. (1980). Individual differences in working memory and reading. *Journal of Verbal Learning and Verbal Behavior, 19,* 450–466.

Garner, R. (1980). Monitoring of understanding: An investigation of good and poor readers' awareness of induced miscomprehension of text. *Journal of Reading Behavior, 12,* 55–63.

Gough, P. B., & Tunmer, W. E. (1986). Decoding, reading, and reading disability. *Remedial and Special Education, 7,* 6–10.

Graesser, A. C. (Ed.). (1993). Inference generation during text comprehension [Special issue]. *Discourse Processes, 16*(1–2).

Graesser, A. C., & Kreuz, R. J. (1993). A theory of inference generation during text comprehension. *Discourse Processes, 16,* 145–160.

Graesser, A. C., Singer, M., & Trabasso, T. (1994). *Constructing inferences during narrative text comprehension.* Manuscript submitted for publication.

Just, M. A., & Carpenter, P. A. (1992). A capacity theory of comprehension: Individual differences in working memory. *Psychological Review, 99,* 122–149.

Klare, G. (1974/1975). Assessing readability. *Reading Research Quarterly, 10,* 62–102.

Lipstadt, D. E. (1993). *Denying the Holocaust: The growing assault on truth and memory.* New York: Free Press.

McKeown, M. G., Beck, I. L., Omanson, R., & Perfetti, C. A. (1983). The effects of long-term vocabulary instruction on reading comprehension: A replication. *Journal of Reading Behavior, 15,* 3–18.

McKoon, G., & Ratcliff, R. (1992). Inference during reading. *Psychological Review, 99,* 440–466.

Merton, R. (1968). The Matthew effect in science. *Science,* 56–63.

Myers, M., & Paris, S. G. (1978). Children's metacognitive knowledge about reading. *Journal of Educational Psychology, 70,* 680–690.

Oakhill, J. (1993). Children's difficulties in reading comprehension. *Educational Psychology Review, 5,* 223–237.

Oakhill, J., & Garnham, A. (1988). *Becoming a skilled reader.* New York: Basil Blackwell.

Oakhill, J., & Yuill, N. (1986). Pronoun resolution in skilled and less-skilled comprehenders: Effects of memory load and inferential complexity. *Language and Speech, 29,* 25–36.

Otero, J., & Kintsch, W. (1992). Failures to detect contradictions in a text: What readers believe versus what they read. *Psychological Science, 3,* 229–235.

Perfetti, C. A. (1985). *Reading ability.* New York: Oxford University Press.

Perfetti, C. A. (1989). There are generalized abilities and one of them is reading. In L. Resnick (Ed.), *Knowing, learning and instruction: Essays in honor of Robert Glaser* (pp. 307–335). Hillsdale, NJ: Lawrence Erlbaum Associates.

Perfetti, C. A. (1993). Why inferences might be restricted. *Discourse Processes, 16,* 181–192.

Perfetti, C. A. (1994). Psycholinguistics and reading ability. In M. A. Gernsbacher (Ed.), *Handbook of psycholinguistics.* Orlando, FL: Academic Press.

Perfetti, C. A., & Goldman, S. R. (1976). Discourse memory and reading comprehension skill. *Journal of Verbal Learning and Verbal Behavior, 14,* 33–42.

Perfetti, C. A., & Lesgold, A. M. (1977). Discourse comprehension and sources of individual differences. In P. A. Carpenter & M. A. Just (Eds.), *Cognitive processes in comprehension* (pp. 141–183). Hillsdale, NJ: Lawrence Erlbaum Associates.

Perfetti, C. A., & Lesgold, A. M. (1979). Coding and comprehension in skilled reading and implications for reading instruction. In L. B. Resnick & P. A. Weaver (Eds.), *Theory and practice in early reading* (Vol. 1, pp. 57–84). Hillsdale, NJ: Lawrence Erlbaum Associates.

Spilich, G. J., Vesonder, G. T., Chiesi, H. L., & Voss, J. F. (1979). Text processing of domain related information for individuals with high and low domain knowledge. *Journal of Verbal Learning and Verbal Behavior, 18,* 275–290.

Stanovich, K. E. (1980). Toward an interactive-compensatory model of individual differences in the development of reading fluency. *Reading Research Quarterly, 16,* 32–71.

Stanovich, K. E. (1986). Matthew effects in reading: Some consequences of individual differences in the acquisition of literacy. *Reading Research Quarterly, 21,* 360–407.

Trabasso, T., & Suh, S. (1993). Understanding text: Achieving explanatory coherence through online inferences and mental operations in working memory. *Discourse Processes, 16,* 3–34.

van Dijk, T. A., & Kintsch, W. (1983). *Strategies of discourse comprehension.* New York: Academic Press.

Vosniadou, S., Pearson, P. D., & Rogers, T. (1988). What causes children's failures to detect inconsistencies in texts? Representation versus comparison difficulties. *Journal of Educational Psychology, 80,* 27–39.

Walberg, H. J., & Tsai, S-L. (1983). Matthew effects in education. *American Educational Research Journal, 20,* 359–373.

Weber, M. (1993, September 18). Will is ignorant of basic facts of the Holocaust. *Pittsburgh Post-Gazette,* p. B-2.

Will, G. (1993, August 30). Ignorance, anti-semitism, and 'scholarship.' *Pittsburgh Post-Gazette,* p. D-2.

Yuill, N., & Oakhill, J. (1988). Effects on inference awareness training of poor reading comprehension. *Applied Cognitive Psychology, 2,* 33–45.

Yuill, N., & Oakhill, J. (1991). *Children's problems in text comprehension.* Cambridge, England: Cambridge University Press.

Yuill, N., Oakhill, J., & Parkin, A. (1989). Working memory, comprehension ability, and the resolution of text anomaly. *British Journal of Psychology, 80,* 351–361.

CHAPTER EIGHT

Story Knowledge and Comprehension Skill

Kate Cain
University of Sussex, Brighton

Stories play an important role in the lives of young children. Fictional narratives, as opposed to expository texts, are the most popular choice of reading material for both preschoolers and children in the first few grades (e.g., Guthrie & Greaney, 1991; Maxwell, 1977). However, despite the extensive exposure to narratives that most young children have had before they actually begin reading them for themselves, young children's understanding of and knowledge about stories is still developing during their first few years of reading. Children's knowledge about stories will assist their understanding of the stories they read or hear and there is now a wealth of research detailing how a child's concept of a story becomes refined with age (e.g., Applebee, 1978; Peterson & McCabe, 1983; Spinillo & Pinto, 1994; Stein & Glenn, 1979, 1982; Stein & Policastro, 1984). However, little is known about how comprehension skill is related to such knowledge.

Children with a specific comprehension deficit, that is, children who are fluent readers but who do not understand what they have just read, not only experience comprehension difficulties for stories that they have read, but they also have a poor understanding of stories that they have just heard (Oakhill, Yuill, & Parkin, 1986). In addition, such less skilled comprehenders show deficits in their oral story-telling abilities. Yuill and Oakhill (1991) asked children to retell a story from a picture sequence that was first narrated by the experimenter. They found that, although skilled and less skilled comprehenders were equally likely to reproduce the connectives used in the original story, the skilled comprehenders were more likely to include

167

additional connectives to those used in the experimenter's version. A subsequent experiment requiring children to plan stories from picture sequences found that the less skilled comprehenders were less consistent in their use of causal connectives and were more likely to use referential ties, such as pronouns, ambiguously or repetitiously. These studies have demonstrated that the problems of such less skilled comprehenders are not just restricted to reading, but are part of a more general comprehension deficit. However, because these studies were not designed to investigate story-specific knowledge such as the overall structure of the stories and certain conventional story features, we do not know if the differences in story-telling ability were due simply to general differences in the ability to use cohesive links and anaphors, or whether differences in the concept of a story also underlie these differences.

The purpose of the research reported in this chapter was to investigate this issue further, to see whether comprehension skill was related to story knowledge, and if so, how. Two different methods were employed to address the first part of this aim. A story production task was used to investigate how the concept of a story was related to comprehension skill. As well as this indirect measure of story knowledge, guided interviews were used to assess children's explicit awareness of particular features of stories. The design of these studies addressed the second part of the aim, the direction of the relationship between story knowledge and comprehension skill: Does good reading comprehension experience promote story knowledge, or does story knowledge facilitate comprehension skill? The design is discussed in the next section, followed by a report of the experimental work.

THE RESEARCH DESIGN: INVESTIGATING THE NATURE OF THE RELATIONSHIP BETWEEN COMPREHENSION SKILL AND STORY KNOWLEDGE

In order to establish the direction of causal relationships, most researchers agree that evidence is required from both longitudinal studies and interventionist designs. However, these sorts of design are time consuming and, therefore, only worth pursuing once a particular skill has been identified as a candidate cause. The design of the research reported in this chapter enabled identification of potential causal factors by adopting a design that was similar in logic to the reading-age match design pioneered by Bryant and colleagues in their work on phonological awareness and early reading skill (see Goswami & Bryant, 1990, for a review). In the work reported in this chapter the performance of less skilled comprehenders was compared to two groups; same-age skilled comprehenders, and younger children at the same level of comprehension ability as the less skilled group, that is, a comprehension-age match group. First, it is necessary to explain how the different subject groups were selected and then the crucial comparisons between these groups will be discussed.

Subject Selection

Although different cohorts of subjects were selected to participate in the different experiments reported in this chapter, the same procedure and matching criteria were always used to select the three different subject groups. The subjects were all young children between the ages of 6–8 years who were, therefore, in the early stages of reading development. The children were all resident in England and would, therefore, have had between 1–3 years of formal reading instruction depending on their chronological age.

Two tests, the Gates–MacGinitie Primary Two Vocabulary Test (Gates & MacGinitie, 1965) and the Neale Analysis of Reading Ability—Revised British Edition (Neale, 1989), were used in the selection process. The Gates–MacGinitie is a test of sight vocabulary, in which children have to select one of four words that goes best with an accompanying picture. The Neale test consists of a series of short self-contained passages which are graded in difficulty. For the age range used in this work, the passages that children read were short narratives, although expository texts are included at the more difficult levels of the test. In this test, children read each story aloud and are corrected with any word reading errors. After each story they are asked a series of questions tapping both factual and inferential information from the passage. Testing stops after the child has made a prescribed number of reading accuracy errors. The Neale test provides two measures; a reading accuracy age based on the number of word pronunciation errors that a child makes, and a reading comprehension age based on the number of questions that the child answers correctly. The two older groups, the skilled and less skilled comprehenders, read an average of three stories (before testing ceased) and each child was, therefore, asked a minimum of 20 comprehension questions to assess their comprehension. The comprehension-age match group were younger and consequently had a lower level of decoding skill. This group read an average of two stories and each child was asked at least 12 comprehension questions. The children in each group who successfully completed more stories were asked a greater number of questions. Table 8.1 shows the characteristics of the three groups who participated in experiment one. All of the children spoke English as their first language and had no known behavioral or learning difficulties.

The subject group of primary interest was a group of children with a reading comprehension deficit, who were called the *less skilled comprehenders*. These children were 7–8 years of age. They did not have any obvious decoding problems; they all read fluently and had age-appropriate

TABLE 8.1
Means and Standard Deviations (in Parentheses) of Characteristics of
Groups Who Participated in the Story Production Task

Measure	Less Skilled Comprehenders (n = 16)	Skilled Comprehenders (n = 12)	Comprehension- Age Match (n = 15)
Age	7;9	7;8	6;10
	(3.06)	(2.39)	(3.37)
Sight vocabulary	36.94	38.33	34.13
	(2.96)	(2.90)	(4.09)
Reading accuracy	7;10	7;8	6;8
	(8.67)	(5.04)	(4.56)
Reading comprehension	6;6	8;3	6;8
	(4.03)	(6.87)	(3.80)

Note. Ages are given as years and whole months, so that 7;6 indicates 7 years and 6 months, with standard deviations in months. Otherwise, raw scores are provided.

reading accuracy ability. However, they all had comprehension ages that were at least 6 months below their reading accuracy age. Their performance was compared to that of two control groups.

The first was a group of *skilled comprehenders* whose mean comprehension level was significantly better than that of the less skilled comprehenders. Because these two groups were selected to differ in their ability to understand written text, it was important that this comprehension difference was not the result of some other reading difficulty, which could affect comprehension. It has generally been agreed that out of the various sources of comprehension failure, lexical-based problems with decoding or vocabulary are the most pervasive (e.g., Perfetti, 1985). Inefficient or nonautomatic word decoding can use up limited processing capacity at the expense of higher level comprehension processes. Unknown or difficult vocabulary will also disrupt comprehension. Therefore, these two groups were selected to ensure that there was no difference with respect to either reading accuracy (measured by the Neale test) or sight vocabulary (measured by the Gates–MacGinitie). In this way, we could assume that the less skilled comprehenders' performance, relative to the skilled group, was not poorer due to some other reading difficulty, but was a specific comprehension deficit in the absence of other obvious reading problems. It is of interest to note that because early reading instruction emphasizes word recognition rather than comprehension, the less skilled comprehenders' difficulties generally go unnoticed by their classroom teachers.

The other comparison group consisted of younger children who were progressing normally in both reading accuracy and comprehension for their chronological age. This group was selected because their mean comprehension age was not significantly different from the mean comprehension age of the less skilled comprehenders, and for this reason they will be referred to as the *comprehension-age match* group (or CAM group) in this chapter.

Issues of Causality

If the same-age skilled and less skilled comprehenders were found to differ in their concept of a story, there are two possible explanations. This difference could be a consequence of the comprehension differences that exist between the two groups: It may be that the skilled comprehenders' greater experience of understanding, and therefore following, a narrative thread has resulted in a more mature concept of a story. Alternatively, any differences between the two groups on this task could be causally related to their comprehension differences: It may be that the less skilled comprehenders' poorer concept of a story has caused (in part) their poorer comprehension. The comparison group of younger children, who were matched to the less skilled comprehenders for comprehension age (CAM group), was used in the current research to determine which of these two explanations was the more plausible. If the less skilled comprehenders were found to have a poorer concept of stories than the comprehension-age match group, this difference could not simply be the result of differences in reading experience, because these younger children would have had far less experience of reading and understanding stories. Instead, it would posit knowledge about stories as a candidate cause of good comprehension.

ASSESSING STORY KNOWLEDGE
THROUGH STORYTELLING

Previous research described earlier has demonstrated that less skilled comprehenders' problems extend beyond reading: They have difficulty in the use and interpretation of local cohesive devices such as pronouns and connectives in reading, listening, and production tasks. It has been proposed that another reason for their story comprehension difficulties may be due to a poorly developed concept of a story. It may be that they do not appreciate that stories consist of a series of related events which have an overall point, message, or theme, helping to make the whole coherent. Yuill and Oakhill's (1991) finding that less skilled comprehenders were poorer at selecting the main point of both an aurally presented story and a picture sequence story, lends some support to this suggestion. Because these difficulties were found in tasks that did not require reading, this work demonstrated that less skilled comprehenders' problems are not specific to reading and, in addition, this work indicated that these children may have a general story concept deficit.

Although research investigating the relationship between story production and comprehension skill is limited, numerous investigations into the developmental pattern of story production looking at a variety of story features have been conducted. As well as looking at the use of referential and cohesive devices (e.g., Hickmann, 1985; Stenning & Michell, 1985), attention has been focused on story-specific features such as conventional features (e.g., Applebee, 1978), the overall story structure (e.g., Applebee, 1978; Peterson & McCabe, 1983; Stein & Glenn, 1979; see Stein & Trabasso, 1981, for a review) and a combination of elements from the latter two (e.g., Spinillo & Pinto, 1994).

Conventional Features in Stories

Characteristic beginnings and endings occur in most stories. As well as indicating the start of a story, conventional beginnings serve to set the action in a particular time, for example, "*Once upon a time . . . ,*" and are usually expanded to introduce the location and the main protagonist(s) of the tale, for example, "*in a far off land, there lived an old, gray wizard. . . .*" These conventional features are useful for providing a context or framework in which to place subsequent events. In addition to familiar beginnings, we all know the formulaic "*and they all lived happily ever after*" to signal the end of a story, often preceded by the moral or lesson to be learned from the tale. These features are not just useful for children: They are recognized literary conventions we expect, and which can be flouted for effect as in Joyce's (1964) *Finnegans Wake* where the book begins abruptly in midsentence.

Several studies have investigated the use of story conventions by young children. Applebee (1978) looked at the use of temporal beginnings, endings, and the past tense in Pitcher and Prelinger's (1963) corpus of young children's oral narratives. He found that by the age of 5, 47% of the stories contained all three elements. Similarly, Mandler and Johnson (1977) found that 6-year-olds were highly likely to remember the beginnings, settings, and outcomes of stories, although they were very poor at remembering the actual endings. More recently, Spinillo and Pinto (1994) found that only 42.5% of the 8-year-olds in their sample produced stories that included both beginnings and endings, fewer than in Applebee's younger sample. On the basis of the performance by Applebee's 5-year-olds, one might expect a higher proportion of Spinillo and Pinto's sample to include such features in their stories. However, there are reasons that may account for these inconsistent findings. For instance, although the stories analyzed by Applebee, and Spinillo and Pinto, were all elicited in oral production tasks, different prompts were used in these tasks. Applebee used a "tell me a story" prompt, whereas Spinillo and Pinto used this and three other prompts, single pictures, short picture sequences, and dictating a story (for someone else to read). Mandler and Johnson's study utilized a recall paradigm, which may account for the high use of these salient conventional features that they found. Furthermore, the children who participated in the work reported by Applebee and by Mandler and Johnson were American, whereas the children who participated in Spinillo and Pinto's study were English and Italian. Therefore, these different groups had very different early schooling experiences. However, in the context of the research reported in this chapter, Spinillo and Pinto's study demonstrated that the particular story conventions apparent in the beginnings and endings of stories were not used consistently by all English children, even after several years' reading instruction.

The Event Structure of Stories

Many investigations into developmental changes in story concept have focused on the overall structure of narratives, often using story grammars to analyze the stories generated by children. Story grammars are based on the assumption that there is an underlying structure to stories, which can be specified in rewrite rules similar to those of a sentence structure grammar. Evidence from memory, production, and judgment tasks has been used to argue for the psychological reality of these grammars: Recall of particular story events is related to their grammar category as opposed to their propositional content (Stein & Glenn, 1979); with increasing age, children incorporate more of the necessary grammar categories into their narrative productions to produce more "complete" stories (Stein & Glenn, 1982); stories which conform to specified grammars are judged to be more storylike (e.g., Mandler & Johnson, 1977). There are many criticisms of story grammars as an explanation of these empirical findings (Garnham, 1983). Other, more general, non-story-specific explanations include the proposal that the subjects in these tasks were using some sort of goal-directed event sequence plan to make sense of a character's actions (Brewer & Lichtenstein, 1982) or that causality between events and their position in a causal network of the text was the basis for these findings (e.g., Trabasso & Sperry, 1985; Trabasso & van den Broek, 1985).

Central to all of these approaches is the concept that a story consists of a sequence of causally related events, a concept that is empirically supported. It is one of the common defining features of narrative organization and structure used by researchers (Stein & Trabasso, 1981). In addition, 7- to 8-year-olds regard some type of causal relationship between events as a necessary feature of stories (Stein & Policastro, 1984). Moreover, Day, Stein, and Trabasso (as cited in Stein & Glenn, 1982) found that children as young as 4 were able to produce a structured, ordered sequence of events in a story recall task. This finding suggests that very young children already have a fairly stable and internalized concept of a story. However, different tasks, such as nonrecall tasks, reveal a different view of young children's competence.

Production studies demonstrate a gradual shift from character or temporally bound narratives at age 4 to causally related, integrated event sequences. Four- and 5-year-olds tend to produce original narratives with the same central character as the binding between events, rather than a directed plot (Applebee, 1978). The ability to produce a coherent, plot-directed narrative develops between the ages of 4 and 8 (e.g., Haslett, 1986; Spinillo & Pinto, 1994) and continues to undergo refinement between the ages of 8 and 10 (Fitzgerald, Spiegel, & Webb, 1985). A study by Stein and Glenn (1982) suggested that narrative concept is still developing in 10-year-olds, although Fitzgerald (1984) found little difference between 9- and 11-year-olds' story knowledge. An analysis by Peterson and McCabe (1983) of narratives produced by 3½- to 9½-year-olds revealed that this development is not necessarily consistent across subjects. They used three different structural analyses, which provided generally comparable patterns of development in that there was a steady progression toward more structurally complex, integrated narratives with age. Their analyses captured the importance of causal linkage between events in stories. One type, the *high point* analysis, revealed that the narratives of 48% of the 7-year-olds and 62% of the 8-year-olds consisted of a sequence of causally related events, which built up to a high point in the action, followed by a resolution. However, a sizeable proportion of these children's narratives (25% and 21% for each age group, respectively) were simply a listing of events, whose common link was that they all happened at the same place and time as each other, such as events at a party. Structural integration between the events was lacking, a style similar to the stories by 5-year-olds that Applebee (1978) analyzed.

The Effect of Story Prompts

One factor influencing performance may be the nature of the task itself, that is, the way in which the story was elicited may affect the quality of story productions. This factor, in turn, may account for some of the age differences at which certain story features have been found to appear in children's narratives. Various methods have been used by researchers to elicit such narratives including topic prompts (Peterson & McCabe, 1983), simply requesting subjects to tell a story (Pitcher & Prelinger, as cited in Applebee, 1978; Spinillo & Pinto, 1994), film (Hickmann, 1985) or picture sequences (Spinillo & Pinto, 1994; Stenning & Michell, 1985; Yuill & Oakhill, 1991), and subject-drawn pictures (Spinillo & Pinto, 1994). One study investigating the effect of different story prompts on storytelling was conducted by Spinillo and Pinto (1994). They found that stories tended to have more mature structures when elicited without a picture prompt than when such a prompt was used. Intuitively, it seems that a picture prompt might be an aid to story production by providing a narrative structure that provides implicit causal links and thereby minimizes the demands on the working memory system. Indeed, picture prompts have been shown to benefit the recall and comprehension of written texts (see Rusted, 1984, for a review). However, this was not the conclusion reached by Spinillo and Pinto. It may be that the sorts of picture prompts that they used in their study resulted in the children focusing on the individual pictures themselves, describing the pictures rather than telling a story from them: One picture prompt was a subject-drawn picture and the other a three-picture sequence. However, a different sort of picture prompt, with a greater number of pictures, may be found to facilitate story quality. Indeed, Yuill and Oakhill (1991) found satisfactory story production by 7- to 8-year-olds with sequences comprising up to 5 pictures.

Summary

This brief and selective review of the literature demonstrates that the ability to produce a simple narrative is a skill still developing in 8-year-olds. This has been confirmed in a variety of studies investigating different story features and using different types of analysis. As already mentioned, story skill continues to develop at this age in spite of the fact that these children have had stories read to them for many years and have also been reading (and writing) stories on their own for some time. There is also evidence that the sort of prompt used to elicit stories can affect the sophistication of the story produced.

EXPERIMENT TO INVESTIGATE THE RELATION BETWEEN COMPREHENSION SKILL AND STORYTELLING

Method and Design

This study was designed with two questions in mind. The first was whether the quality of story generated by young children is related to comprehension skill and if so, how. As the preceding review demonstrated, research in this area has focused on the relation between story knowledge and age. So, although feasible, it is not known whether there is a relationship between story knowledge and comprehension skill. The second question to be looked at was whether the amount of structural information provided by the prompt affects story production.

The three groups of children who participated in this work, less skilled comprehenders, skilled comprehenders, and a comprehension-age match group, were selected according to the criteria outlined previously. Table 8.1 presents the groups' reading and comprehension profiles. There were 16 less skilled, 12 skilled, and 15 comprehension-age match children. In order to manipulate the amount of structural information provided, two different sorts of prompt were used to elicit narratives from the children. One type of prompt was a sequence of six pictures, which provided a basic structure and plot for a story. The other prompt type comprised a topic title, for example, "Pirates," for the subjects to plan a story around. The children's task was to tell the experimenter three fictional stories in each prompt condition. The stories were told in two sessions with one sort of prompt used in each, and the order of session was counterbalanced. There was one practice story, for the relevant prompt, at the beginning of each session. (Further methodological details can be found in Cain & Oakhill, in press).

Predictions

The less skilled comprehenders were expected to produce poorer stories in general, because it was proposed that they had a poorly developed story concept. The stories elicited with a picture sequence prompt were expected to be better than those in the topic prompt condition, because the picture sequence provided information and a clear structure around which to base the story. In addition, the sort of prompt was expected to affect the groups differently in the following ways. It was expected that in the topic condition, the skilled comprehenders would produce higher scoring stories than the less skilled comprehenders, but that this difference would be reduced or eliminated in the picture condition, because the story structure was readily apparent in this condition. In addition to this, if knowledge of story structure is not just the result of reading comprehension skill, but a candidate cause of good comprehension, the less skilled comprehenders should produce poorer story structures than the younger comprehension-age match group in the topic prompt condition. Again, this difference should be significantly reduced with the structure provided by the picture sequence.

Results

The stories were transcribed and scored for the occurrence of four different story conventions and for the event structure of the story. The experimenter and another independent rater, both unaware of the subject group, agreed on over 90% of classifications. Disputes were resolved by discussion.

Story Conventions. The four story conventions were conventional openings, such as *"once upon a time," "one day"*; character-setting information, such as *"there was a mum, a dad, and a little girl"*; scene-setting information such as "*this boy went to the circus*"; endings, such as "*the end*," "*and they lived happily ever after.*" Analysis of these data revealed no significant differences between the groups in their use of any of these features. Furthermore, the only effect of prompt type was for endings: All of the groups included more conventional endings when the stories were elicited by means of a topic prompt.

Event Structure. The event sequence of each story was classified into one of three categories, designed to capture the extent to which the main story events were causally related. Examples can be seen in Table 8.2. The first category was nonstories, which were either totally incoherent or lacked any sequence of events. For example, some of these nonstories were simply comprised of an opening and character-setting and/or scene-setting information, but nothing else was given. The second was intermediate stories. These contained a sequence of events, but the main events were not causally related to each other. Finally, complete stories had an integrated sequence of events where the main events were causally related.

No points were awarded for a nonstory, 1 for an intermediate story, and 2 for a complete story. Thus, each subject could score between 0–6 points in each prompt condition.

These data were subjected to a 2-way (Skill Group × Prompt Type) analysis of variance. As the means in Table 8.3 show, there was a main effect for skill group: the less skilled comprehenders told poorer stories in general, $F(2, 40)$

TABLE 8.2
Examples of Stories Produced in Story Production Experiment

Example of "nonstory" category

Topic prompt: The Holiday
"Once upon a time there was a girl and she went on holiday."

Examples from "intermediate" category

Topic Prompt: The Seaside
"It was a lovely day. The family decided to go down to the seaside. They saw lots of people there. The baby was making a sandcastle, the older children were playing in the sea, the mum and dad had their last swim before they went home."

Examples from "complete story" category

Picture sequence: The Haircut
"There was once a girl who had scruffy hair. Her mum said she had to have her hair cut, but she didn't like to have her hair cut, she thought she might have the wrong haircut. So she went in mum's . . . her mum's room and got her hair scissors and she cut her hair short so . . . and she looked in the mirror and she didn't like the haircut she did, so her mum came in the room and gave her a hat, so it didn't show her fringe. The end."

TABLE 8.3
Sample Means for Story Event Structure

Prompt Condition	Less Skilled Comprehenders (n = 16)	Skilled Comprehenders (n = 12)	Comprehension- Age Match (n = 15)
Topic	2.94	4.92*	4.27*
Picture	4.31	5.33*	4.80
Difference	1.37	.41	.53

Note. Maximum score possible for each prompt type is 6. Difference score is difference between picture and topic prompt scores.
*Planned comparisons, significant at $p < .05$ level.

$= 8.15, p < .002$. There was also a significant main effect for story prompt, $F(1, 40) = 11.01, p < .002$, because all of the groups told better stories in the picture prompt condition. Although the interaction did not reach significance, planned comparisons using Bonferroni's t' were conducted to test the specific predictions made above. In the topic condition, the less skilled comprehenders produced stories with significantly poorer structures than both the skilled group and the comprehension age-match group (p's < .05). In the picture prompt condition, the less skilled comprehenders again produced inferior stories to the skilled group ($p < .05$). However, as predicted, there was no significant difference between the less skilled comprehenders and the comprehension-age match group in this condition.

Discussion

There was no evidence of a relationship between comprehension skill and the inclusion of conventional, formulaic features in the stories generated in this experiment. In addition, only one sort of feature, endings, was affected differentially by the type of prompt: The frequency of conventional endings was reduced, for all groups, by the picture prompt. However, group and prompt type affected the structure of the stories produced by the children. When the stories were elicited by a topic title prompt, both the skilled comprehenders and the comprehension-age match group produced stories with more integrated event sequences than did the less skilled comprehenders. When the stories were elicited by a sequence of pictures, the less skilled comprehenders were aided most by this prompt, producing more integrated stories than in the topic prompt condition. Consequently, the difference in performance between the same-age skilled and less skilled groups was reduced, and the difference between the comprehension-age match group and the less skilled comprehenders was eliminated.

The absence of group effects in the use of conventional story features and the frequent inclusion of them by all groups suggests that most children in this age group are aware that such features are commonly included in stories. These findings are supported by other story production studies. Story conventions are frequently included by children even younger than those who participated in this experiment (Applebee, 1978; Stein & Glenn, 1982). Indeed, such features are not only very salient, but feature heavily in the simple, straightforward style of storytelling common to the genre of fairy tales and young children's reading books. Furthermore, contrary to Spinillo and Pinto (1994), the children did not appear to simply describe the stories in the Picture Prompt condition; the use of three of the story conventions (beginnings, character- and scene-setting information) was unaffected by prompt type. However, conventional endings occurred far less frequently in stories in the picture prompt condition. There are (at least) two plausible explanations for this latter finding. First, the pictures clearly illustrated that the story had ended, making a formal marker less necessary. In addition, all groups tended to tell more complete stories in this condition, thus reducing the need to formally signal the end of the narrative. For these reasons, and in conjunction with lack of prompt effects for the other features, it is not feasible to conclude that the pictures caused the children to describe the individual pictures rather than to tell a story.

A different pattern of data emerged from the analysis of the story event structure. Complete stories were more likely to be told when the elicitor was a sequence of pictures, thus indicating that this prompt provided a clear and integrated event structure around which the children could base their stories. The differences between the two prompt conditions for each group demonstrated that the less skilled comprehenders were helped more by this prompt than the other two groups. These findings strongly suggest that the picture sequence was providing some of the information that the less skilled group required to produce an integrated narrative structure. In addition, the findings rule out the possibility that good story structure knowledge is simply the result of lots of reading comprehension practice, and instead promote the alternative explanation that such knowledge might be causally related to comprehension skill for two reasons. First, the less skilled comprehenders produced stories that were less well-structured than the comprehension-age match group (CAM group) in the topic prompt condition, that is, two groups of equivalent comprehension skill performed differently on this task. So we cannot say that poor story knowledge is the consequence of poor reading comprehension skill because these two groups were matched for comprehension level. In addition, the less skilled comprehenders produced stories of comparable level to the CAM group when a picture sequence was used as the prompt. This result suggests that it was precisely this structural framework that the less skilled comprehenders needed to be given in order to produce integrated stories, and that one of the reasons for poor story comprehension might be a lack of knowledge about how such texts are organized. The implications of these findings are discussed later.

INTERVIEWS TO INVESTIGATE METACOGNITIVE KNOWLEDGE ABOUT NARRATIVE

Another way to explore children's concept of stories is by asking questions to measure their consciously accessible story knowledge. In this section, I discuss interview work investigating such metaknowledge about stories, looking specifically at children's understanding of the fictional nature of stories, and the purpose of specific textual features, namely titles, beginnings, and endings. Three groups of children participated in this work; less skilled comprehenders, skilled comprehenders, and a comprehension-age match group. This research was conducted with several different cohorts of children over 2 years and the interview schedule altered during this period as the more interesting issues were investigated in greater detail and unfruitful lines of inquiry were dropped. The data reported here was collated across the cohorts, and consequently, the size of the sample that was asked particular questions varied. However, the children were all selected and matched according to the criteria outlined previously. Thus, the skilled and less skilled groups were 7–8 years old and were matched for reading accuracy and sight vocabulary but differed with respect to comprehension skill. The comprehension-age match group were 6–7 years old and were matched with the less skilled group for comprehension level. Each child was interviewed individually, and the interviews for the two types of knowledge, understanding of fiction and textual features, were conducted on separate occasions in that order. These results are reported, in turn, below.

Comprehension Skill and the Recognition of Fiction

As part of Applebee's (1978) investigation into children's "*sense of story*," he explored their understanding of the fictional nature of stories. He found that major changes in awareness about narrative occur during the first few years of schooling. Approximately 40% of 6-year-olds believed that a character from a fairy tale, such as Cinderella, was a real person. Furthermore, of the 60% who said that the character was not real, more than half thought that she was a puppet or a dolly rather than a fictional creation. By the age of 9, over 90% of children expressed a firm conviction that such characters were fictional. Applebee proposed that while children do not believe that stories are fictional, they can only be seen as representations of the true state of affairs in the world, so that children cannot use stories to see alternatives in the world (Applebee, 1978). In a similar manner, children may be less likely to talk about possibilities in stories if they regard their events as fixed certainties. This understanding and acknowledgment of fiction might, therefore, be an important factor in children's approach to stories in terms of the way they will work on a story and think about it. If children believe that stories are true depictions of events, they will be less likely to see that there is often a simple format underlying most stereotypical stories, knowledge of which can be used as a framework in which to place events and predict outcomes. For example, Applebee discussed how some young children do not allow the word order of simple stories and refrains to be altered; stories to them are fixed and immutable, rather than representations of events. Young children may also be less likely to bring outside knowledge to bear on their interpretation of story events if they hold such views. In short, they may less likely to see that comprehension is an active, constructive process, guided by strategies. For such reasons, I decided to investigate children's sense of fictionality in relation to comprehension ability, postulating that one of the reasons for poor story comprehension might be an immature understanding of fiction.

The children were asked a series of questions, based on some of Applebee's work, to ascertain how aware they were that (most) children's stories and fairy tales are fictional. The story around which I based the interview was the popular fairy story Little Red Riding Hood and all of the children said that they knew this story. The format of the interview and the specific questions asked differed according to an individual child's responses. However, all of the children were asked questions to determine whether they thought that the main character was a real person or not and whether the events described in the story had really happened.

Overall, the less skilled comprehenders had a less highly developed sense of fiction than the skilled comprehenders and their pattern of responding was similar to the comprehension-age match group. Table 8.4 shows the three groups' responses to specific questions. (Although the analysis was performed on the raw frequency data, these frequencies were converted into percentages to aid comparison between groups, because of the unequal sample sizes).

Very few of the skilled comprehenders held the belief that the main character, Little Red Riding Hood, had ever been real or alive; 85% recognized that she was a fictional creation. However, approximately 50% from the groups of less skilled comprehenders and comprehension-age match children suggested that the story was about a real person who had either once been alive, or was still alive. Those holding the latter belief were quite ready to explain what Red Riding Hood might be doing now. Fewer in these two groups believed that all of the events were true, suggesting that the majority of these children recognized that even "true" stories can undergo some embellishment. The pattern of responding suggested that, for some children, the concept of stories as fiction was still developing. It was not yet a concrete belief as some children believed that Red Riding Hood was real but that the events in the story did not really happen. Therefore, each child's responses to all questions were checked and the number of children who had always expressed a firm belief that the stories were definitely fictional was compared to those who either held

TABLE 8.4
Responses to Questions Assessing Understanding
of Fictional Nature of Fairy Stories

	Less Skilled Comprehenders (n = 29)	Skilled Comprehenders (n = 24)	Comprehension- Age Match (n = 27)	$\chi^2 = 80$ (df = 2)
Could we go and visit Little Red Riding Hood?				
Yes	31.0	.0	22.2	8.62, $p < .02$
No	69.0	100.0	77.8	
Is Little Red Riding Hood a real person, or was she ever real?				
Yes	55.2	15.4	48.1	10.07, $p < .007$[a]
No	44.8	84.6	51.9	
Did the things in the story really happen?				
Yes	27.6	4.2	11.1	6.13, $p < .05$[a]
No	72.4	95.8	88.9	
Percentage of children who demonstrated a firm understanding of fiction for every question				
Yes	37.9	75.0	44.4	7.98, $p < .02$
No	62.1	25.0	55.6	

Note. Due to unequal sample sizes, the data were converted into percentages in this table to aid comparison between groups. The analysis was conducted on the raw frequency data.

[a]These analyses are unreliable because more than 20% of cells were below expected frequency (Siegel & Castellan, 1988).

some aspects to be true or possibly true. These values are shown in the last row of Table 8.4. They demonstrate that the skilled comprehenders were significantly more likely to appreciate that stories are fictional than were the less skilled comprehenders and comprehension-age match group. Three fourths of skilled comprehenders demonstrated a firm understanding that stories are fictional whereas under 40% of the less skilled comprehenders and 44% of the CAM group did, that is, the majority of the latter two groups believed that some or all aspects of the story were true. The performance of the comprehension-age match group compares favorably with Applebee's finding that 50% of 6-year-olds responded similarly. So it seems that the less skilled comprehenders have an immature understanding of the nature of stories when compared to skilled comprehenders of the same age.

Comprehension Skill and Awareness of Textual Features

Titles. Titles can aid comprehension by providing a context or framework in which to interpret events and actions in texts and stories. Adults' comprehension and memory for obscure texts is improved by the presence of a title (Dooling & Mullet, 1973). Yuill and Joscelyne (1988) showed that children can also benefit from informative titles. They found that less skilled comprehenders understood abstract stories better when provided with a title describing the main consequence of the story, for example, "Billy's sandcastle gets broken by a wave," than when the title only gave information about the main participants, for example, "Billy and his mother." The sort of title did not significantly aid good comprehenders' understanding. They argued that the more informative sort of title provides a framework in which to interpret the text, which aids the less skilled comprehenders more than the good comprehenders because this latter group are already more skilled at selecting and organizing ideas in text.

Yuill and Joscelyne found a relation between comprehension skill and sensitivity to title information by using an indirect (or implicit) measure. In the interviews in the current study, questions were asked to investigate children's explicit awareness of the purpose of a story title. Forty-one less skilled comprehenders, 34 skilled comprehenders, and 27 comprehension-age match children were asked these questions. There was a highly significant relationship between comprehension skill and awareness of titles, $\chi^2(4, N = 102) = 25.38$, $p < .0001$. Over 80% of the skilled comprehenders and 56% of the comprehension-age match group were able to explain how the title of a story could inform the reader. Examples of such responses are "they tell you what it's about and who's in it" and "tells us what the story's about." Just under one fourth of the less skilled comprehenders were able to do so. Even when provided with a specific title as an example, nearly half of the less skilled comprehenders still gave incorrect responses such as "tells you whether you like the story or not" and "it doesn't tell us anything." And some of these children simply said that they didn't know.

I also found that less skilled comprehenders were poorer than skilled comprehenders at suggesting ways to make up a title for a story. A smaller sample participated in this work, 12 each of skilled and comprehension-age match children and 14 less skilled comprehenders. The children were presented with a hypothetical situation in which the experimenter was going to read them a story that did not have a title. The children were asked to suggest how they could make up a title for such a story. On this measure the less skilled comprehenders' performance was similar to that of the comprehension-age match group. The majority of these two groups responded that they didn't know how to go about making up a title, or could only suggest using external cues such as looking for the title at the top of the page of the book. Only 29% of the less skilled comprehenders and 25% of the CAM group said that they would listen out for the important bits in the story, the characters' names, and/or that they would think of what the story was about, whereas 83% of the skilled comprehenders responded that they would adopt such a strategy.

Beginnings and Endings. Another possible difference between the skilled and less skilled comprehenders is their awareness of the purpose of conventional story features such as beginnings and endings. In the production experiment reported earlier, children in all skill groups made great use of these features, and other work described earlier has shown that such features are the most likely ones to be included in recalls or story productions by young children (e.g., Applebee, 1978; Stein & Glenn, 1979, 1982). However, Paris and colleagues (e.g., Myers & Paris, 1978; Paris & Jacobs, 1984) found that explicit awareness of features such as these is related to age and reading comprehension skill. Poor knowledge about such structural features may account for some difficulties with story comprehension. Comprehension could be impaired by not knowing how to use introductory information as a context setter, which guides the reader or listener in relating the different episodes to one another and slotting events into structures and schema representations. Additionally, endings are often used as a summary device to reiterate the main point and/or present the moral of the tale, in general to wrap things up and relate the story events together.

The children were asked whether they thought the first few sentences in a story were special and if they agreed, they were asked to explain why they considered these sentences to be special. The same was asked about the last few sentences in a story. There were 41 less skilled comprehenders, 34 skilled comprehenders, and 27 comprehension-age match children.

I found that skilled comprehenders were more likely than the other two groups to say that the first few sentences in a story were special. Of the children who did think that this part of a story was special in some way, the skilled comprehenders were also more likely to be able to say how it was special, for example, "tells you about the characters and what's going to happen in the story." Fifty-four percent of the skilled comprehenders, but only 21% of the less skilled group and 26% of the comprehension-age match group responded in this manner. An analysis of these data demonstrated that comprehension level was significantly related to explicit understanding of this feature, with better performance by the skilled comprehenders to the other groups $\chi^2(2, N = 102)$, $p < .03$. The proportion of children in each group who thought that the last few sentences might be important was fairly similar, between 58–67% in each group. However, the pattern of awareness of what made story endings important was similar to the data on story beginnings. The group percentages indicated that the skilled comprehenders were better able to substantiate this belief than the other groups. Fifty-four percent of the skilled comprehenders gave acceptable explanations such as "tells you if the characters lived happily ever after, if anyone died or if it was a happy ending or not." Only 38% of the less skilled group and 37% of the comprehension-age match group could do so. Incorrect responses included "they have full stops." However, performance on this measure was not significantly related to comprehension skill.

Discussion of Work on Explicit Awareness of Story Knowledge

The work reported in this section reveals that the less skilled comprehenders behaved very similarly to the comprehension-age match group on a variety of measures used to assess their explicit awareness of stories. Their appreciation of the fictional nature of stories was immature for their age. Whereas the skilled comprehenders demonstrated a clear understanding that stories are generally made up, the less skilled comprehenders were confused on this issue and their beliefs were at a stage of development similar to a group of children of equivalent comprehension ability who were a year younger in chronological age. The work on specific textual features revealed that less skilled comprehenders were unaware of the purpose of story titles, that is, how they could provide useful information or a framework to guide comprehension. Although Yuill and Joscelyne (1988) found that less skilled comprehenders could use the information provided by a title to aid understanding, in this study many less skilled comprehenders could not say what information was provided by a title and they were poorer at this task than younger children of the equivalent comprehension ability. When asked to reveal strategies to work out a story title, the less skilled group were as poor as the CAM group. These two groups were significantly worse than the skilled comprehenders, and the less skilled and CAM children were also less aware than the skilled comprehenders of why the beginnings of stories might be important. It appears that less skilled comprehenders have a less stable understanding of the role of certain features common to stories, which might be affecting their story comprehension. In particular, their understanding of the use of titles might even be causally related to their comprehension deficit.

GENERAL DISCUSSION AND CONCLUSIONS

Comprehension Ability and Story Knowledge

Two important conclusions can be drawn from the work reported in this chapter. First, both the experimental and the interview work demonstrate a strong relationship between reading comprehension skill and different aspects of story knowledge. Furthermore, the design of the work has identified two specific types of story knowledge, story structure knowledge and understanding of titles, as possible causes of comprehension difficulties.

An experiment using a story production task as an indirect measure of story knowledge revealed that all of the groups included characteristic openings, settings, and endings of stories regularly, and with equal frequency, findings that are supported by other research studies. However, the less skilled comprehenders were less likely to generate stories that had an integrated sequence of events. There was evidence to suggest that this was more likely to be a cause rather than a consequence of the less skilled group's comprehension difficulties. Although they told poorer quality stories than a comprehension-age match group when the prompt was a topic title, there was no difference between these two groups when a picture sequence providing structural information was the prompt. The finding that a picture sequence facilitated structural integration is also supported by research investigating the role of illustrations on the recall and comprehension of written text. Rusted (1984) proposed that the reason for finding greater and more general facilitation by pictures for memory of expository, rather than narrative, texts, is because children's well-established knowledge and utilization of story schemata as a memory aid can override any additional strategic benefits that illustrations offer, such as a good knowledge about the structure and elements in a story makes picture aids redundant for narrative texts. This hypothesis supports the interpretation of the findings in this study. The less skilled comprehenders were aided by the picture sequence because they lacked the structural knowledge it provided, whereas there was little additional benefit to be gained by the skilled and comprehension-age match groups, who already had adequately developed story concepts.

An assessment of the children's metaknowledge about stories revealed that in other respects the less skilled comprehenders also had an immature sense of story. They were unsure about the fictional nature of stories, being more likely to believe, like the younger CAM group, that certain aspects of stories were based on fact. Similarly, both the less skilled comprehenders and the CAM group were equally poor at stating what sorts of information are contained in the beginnings of stories and at suggesting ways to make up titles for stories. As noted by Bryant and Goswami (1986) such data are ambiguous and difficult to interpret. Comparable performance by less skilled comprehenders and comprehension-age match children does not rule out the possibility that the less skilled comprehenders are deficient in the skill being assessed. Because the less skilled comprehenders are older, they may, therefore, have a higher mental age than the younger comparison group, which may enable them to adopt alternative strategies that could mask a genuine deficit. It is difficult to see how this explanation could account for these findings, although the older children have probably had greater experience at answering questions, which may benefit them to some degree. The alternative explanation is that the less skilled comprehenders are demonstrating a developmental lag with regard to their understanding about these aspects of stories.

One measure of metaknowledge where the less skilled comprehenders were poorer than both of the other groups was at stating what information story titles provided: They were less likely to show explicit awareness that a story title can provide information about, for example, the theme, characters, and main events in a story. The greater explicit awareness of skilled and CAM children of a title's meaning may, in part, account for the differences in the topic title condition of the production task. The skilled and CAM children may be better able to plan a story around the central theme of the given topic because they have a greater understanding of how story titles work, whereas the less skilled comprehenders do not see their relative worth and are therefore less likely to access relevant story schemata and background information. The finding that the less skilled comprehenders and the comprehension-age match group were less likely to know what sorts of information occur at the beginning of stories than the skilled comprehenders contrasts with the absence of group differences in the inclusion of such material in the production task. It suggests that the skilled comprehenders have a more stable, explicit awareness and understanding of such features and are therefore more likely to use and be guided by that information when reading.

One way in which such knowledge might affect comprehension skill is in the ability to build a representation of a story. Such ability could be affected by knowledge about stories and story schemata. If the less skilled comprehenders do not realize how stories are causally linked through elements such as desires, motives, goals, actions, and consequences, they will be less likely to produce a narrative that consists of related events. It therefore follows that they will be less likely to impose such a structure on a story during reading or listening, because they will not be linking up the individual events and actions through the use of these elements. Consequently they will construct inferior representations of text, lacking in linkage between sentences and episodes. Partial support for this hypothesis comes from a training study conducted by Fitzgerald and Spiegel (1983). These researchers designed an instruction program for developing knowledge about narrative structure. Children, selected for demonstrating a poor sense of story structure, told significantly better stories after this training. More interestingly, their reading comprehension also benefited from the training. Unfortunately Fitzgerald and Spiegel did not include a group of children who already had a good sense of story structure, so this study sheds no light on whether a causal link between reading comprehension and narrative structure exists. If such a training program was only effective for children with poor story structure skills but not for those with good skills in this area, we would have good evidence that deficits in the trained skills were affecting the poor knowledge groups' original production performance.

The work in this chapter focused on knowledge about narratives. Knowledge about expository text structure needs to be assessed as well, and work investigating expository text comprehension itself must be conducted. This type of text has been relatively ignored in children's reading comprehension research, yet it becomes increasingly more important as a source of information during a child's school career. It is feasible that, if comprehension problems are apparent for narrative text structure, they might also be found with expository text. There is no a priori reason to suspect that difficulties in establishing links between different parts of a text and the ability to construct an adequate representation of its meaning, will be limited to just one form of discourse.

Possible Sources of These Differences

These results indicate that less skilled comprehenders' poorer story concept might be a cause of their comprehension difficulties. It is therefore necessary to explore how this difference between skilled and less skilled comprehenders could have arisen.

One could argue that such differences might be due to the less skilled comprehenders having had less exposure to stories than the skilled comprehenders. However, it is unlikely that they have had less total story exposure than the comprehension-age match children who are a year younger than they are. In addition, a proxy measure of exposure to print, similar to that developed by Stanovich and colleagues (e.g., Stanovich, 1993), was given to groups of skilled, less skilled, and comprehension-age match children (Cain, 1994), selected in a manner identical to the children who participated in the work reported in this chapter. This print exposure measure employed a forced-choice task. There were two versions of the task, one in which subjects were presented with pairs of items each comprising a book title and a foil, and one in which author names and appropriate foils were the materials. The children's task was to choose the real title (or author) in each pair. This measure served as an indicator of the children's exposure to print while controlling for biased responding, such as "recognizing" every item. Performance on both versions of the task indicated that the comprehension-age match group had not had greater total print exposure than the less skilled comprehenders: The CAM group's scores were lower than both the other groups (although the main effect of skill group was not significant for either version of the task).

Other work, however, has indicated that story experience may be a source of the differences found for story knowledge. Interviews were conducted with a larger sample of skilled, less skilled, and comprehension-age match children and questionnaires were sent home to their parents, with a return rate of over 70% for each group (Cain, 1994).[1] Responses suggested that

---

[1]Although a CAM group was included in this investigation into reading habits, such a design did not permit identification of any particular types of reading experience as candidate causes of poor comprehension. This was because any differences in reading experience between the CAM group and the less skilled comprehenders may be an artifact of the former group's age and lower word reading ability. For instance, children are read to more when they are young and are still learning the principles of decoding. We cannot tell whether the less skilled comprehenders' reading experiences a year ago differed from the CAM group's behavior now.

less skilled comprehenders do currently have less involvement in literacy-related activities in the home. The children who were skilled comprehenders reported reading books at home more frequently than the less skilled children, and their parents reported that they were more likely to read story books. The skilled comprehenders also reported that they were read to more frequently at home by their parents than the less skilled group and this was confirmed by parents' responses. In addition to such quantitative differences in home-based literacy activities, there were indicators that there might be important qualitative differences in home-based literacy events. The skilled children were significantly more likely to read books with their parents than were the less skilled children and also tended to talk about books and stories more frequently with their parents than did the less skilled comprehenders. This type of interaction between children and their caregivers could be an important source of information for children to learn, for instance, about how stories work, what sorts of things happen in them, and how events are related. Certainly, children's preschool experiences of literacy can affect their subsequent progress in the way that they prepare children for school (e.g., Brown, Palincsar, & Armbruster, 1984; Heath, 1982) and facilitate comprehension development (e.g., Mason & Dunning, as cited in Mason, 1992; Wells, 1985). And there is some evidence that older children are also affected by such factors. Greaney and Hegarty (1987) found that children whose parents discussed books with them, encouraged them to read, and bought books for them, tended to spend more time reading, a factor which, in turn, was correlated with reading achievement. We cannot make any claims on the source of these effects; it might be from the parents, the children, or an interaction between the two. For instance, it is not known whether parents find that better readers are more interested in being read to than their less skilled peers. Indeed, good readers may solicit story reading or discussions about books more frequently than their less skilled peers. Additionally, good readers may be more rewarding to read to and, thus, their parents may read to them more frequently than parents of poor readers. Further work is necessary to establish the source of this relationship.

CONCLUSIONS

The findings reported in this chapter suggest that story knowledge is strongly related to reading comprehension knowledge and that deficient knowledge about story structure is more likely to be a cause of reading comprehension difficulties than the result of them. The design of this research does not permit the conclusion that deficits in such knowledge cause poor comprehension. However, it usefully identifies story structure knowledge as a likely candidate cause for comprehension difficulties, worthy of further investigation. Other sources of evidence from training programs and longitudinal assessments are necessary to establish the precise nature of relationship. For example, the study by Fitzgerald and Spiegel (1983) suggested that tuition on various aspects of a story and its structure may prove beneficial. Furthermore, longitudinal assessment of the role of story knowledge in comprehension skill development should address the role of reading experience, in the light of the above findings. Such studies, if successful, would not only confirm the proposed causal relationship between story knowledge and comprehension skill outlined in this chapter, but they would also offer useful insights into the best sorts of interventionist measures, to prevent and remedy this specific comprehension deficit.

ACKNOWLEDGMENTS

The work reported in this chapter was conducted while the author was in receipt of a studentship from the Economic and Social Research Council Studentship. I would like to thank the heads, staff, and pupils of all the schools who participated in this work. Thanks also to Jane Oakhill for discussion on this work, and to Cesare Cornoldi and an anonymous reviewer for their comments on an earlier draft of this chapter.

REFERENCES

Applebee, A. N. (1978). *The child's concept of story: Ages two to seventeen.* Chicago: University of Chicago Press.

Brewer, W. F., & Lichtenstein, E. H. (1982). Stories are to entertain: A structural-affect theory of stories. *Journal of Pragmatics, 6,* 473–486.

Brown, A. L., Palincsar, A. S., & Armbruster, B. B. (1984). Instructing comprehension-fostering activities in interactive learning situations. In H. Mandl, N. L. Stein, & T. Trabasso (Eds.), *Learning and comprehension of text* (pp. 255–286). Hillsdale, NJ: Lawrence Erlbaum Associates.

Bryant, P., & Goswami, U. (1986). Strengths and weaknesses of the reading level design: A comment on Backman, Mamen and Ferguson. *Psychological Bulletin, 100*(1), 101–103.

Cain, K. (1994). *An investigation into comprehension difficulties in young children.* Unpublished doctoral thesis, University of Sussex, England.

Cain, K., & Oakhill, J. (in press). The nature of the relationship between comprehension skill and the ability to tell a story. *British Journal of Developmental Psychology.*

Dooling, D. J., & Mullet, R. L. (1973). Locus of thematic effects in retention of prose. *Journal of Experimental Psychology, 88,* 216–222.

Fitzgerald, J. (1984). The relationship between reading ability and expectations for story structures. *Discourse Processes, 7,* 21–41.

Fitzgerald, J., & Spiegel, D. L. (1983). Enhancing children's reading comprehension through instruction in narrative structure. *Journal of Reading Behavior, 15*(2), 1–17.

Fitzgerald, J., Spiegel, D. L., & Webb, T. B. (1985). Development of children's knowledge of story structure and content. *Journal of Educational Research, 72*(2), 101–108.

Garnham, A. (1983). What's wrong with story grammars? *Cognition, 15,* 145–154.
Gates, A. I., & MacGinitie, W. H. (1965). *Gates-MacGinitie Reading Tests.* New York: Columbia University Teacher's College Press.
Goswami, U., & Bryant, P. (1990). *Phonological skills and learning to read.* Hove, England: Lawrence Erlbaum Associates.
Greaney, V., & Hegarty, M. (1987). Correlates of leisure-time reading. *Journal of Research in Reading, 10*(1), 3–20.
Guthrie, V., & Greaney, J. T. (1991). Literacy Acts. In K. Barr, M. L. Kamil, P. Mosenthal, & P. D. Pearson (Eds.), *Handbook of reading research* (vol. 2, pp. 68–96). New York: Longman.
Haslett, B. (1986). A developmental analysis of children's narrative. In D. G. Ellis & W. A. Donohue (Eds.), *Contemporary issues in language and discourse processes* (pp. 87–109). Hillsdale, NJ: Lawrence Erlbaum Associates.
Heath, S. B. (1982). What no bedtime story means: Narratives at home and school. *Language in Society, 11,* 49–76.
Hickmann, M. E. (1985). The implications of discourse skills in Vygotsky's development theory. In J. V. Wertsch (Ed.), *Culture, communication & cognition: Vygotskian perspectives* (pp. 236–257). Cambridge, England: Cambridge University Press.
Joyce, J. (1964). *Finnegans wake* (3rd ed.). London: Faber & Faber.
Mandler, J. M., & Johnson, N. S. (1977). Remembrance of things parsed: Story structure and recall. *Cognitive Psychology, 9,* 111–151.
Mason, J. M. (1992). Reading stories to preliterate children: A proposed connection to reading. In P. B. Gough, L. C. Ehri, R. Treiman (Eds.), *Reading acquisition* (pp. 215–241). Hillsdale, NJ: Lawrence Erlbaum Associates.
Maxwell, J. (1977). *Reading progress from 8 to 15.* Windsor, England: NFER.
Myers, M., & Paris, S. G. (1978). Children's metacognitive knowledge about their reading. *Journal of Educational Psychology, 70,* 680–690.
Neale, M. D. (1989). *The Neale Analysis of Reading Ability—Revised.* Windsor, England: NFER-Nelson.
Oakhill, J. V., Yuill, N. M., & Parkin, A. (1986). On the nature of the difference between skilled and less-skilled comprehenders. *Journal of Research in Reading, 9,* 80–91.
Paris, S. G., & Jacobs, J. E. (1984). The benefits of informed instruction for children's reading awareness and comprehension skills. *Child Development, 55,* 2083–2093.
Perfetti, C. A. (1985). *Reading ability.* Oxford, England: Oxford University Press.
Peterson, C., & McCabe, A. (1983). *Developmental psycholinguistics: Three ways of looking at a child's narrative.* New York: Plenum Press.
Pitcher, E. G., & Prelinger, E. (1963). *Children tell stories: An analysis of fantasy.* New York: International Universities Press.
Rusted, J. (1984). Differential facilitation by pictures of children's retention of written texts: A review. *Current Psychological Research & Reviews, 3,* 61–71.
Siegel, S., & Castellan, N. J. (1988). *Nonparametric statistics for the behavioral sciences* (2nd ed.). Singapore: McGraw-Hill.
Spinillo, A. G., & Pinto, G. (1994). Children's narrative under different conditions: A comparative study. *British Journal of Developmental Psychology, 12,* 177–194.
Stanovich, K. E. (1993). Does reading make you smarter? Literacy and the development of verbal intelligence. In H. W. Reese (Ed.), *Advances in child development and behavior* (vol. 24, pp. 133–180). San Diego: Academic Press.
Stein, N. L., & Glenn, C. G. (1979). An analysis of story comprehension in young children. In R. O. Freedle (Ed.), *New directions in discourse processing* (pp. 53–120). Norwood, NJ: Ablex.
Stein, N. L., & Glenn, C. G. (1982). Children's concept of time: The development of a story schema. In W. J. Friedman (Ed.), *The developmental psychology of time* (pp. 255–282). New York: Academic Press.

Stein, N. L., & Policastro, M. (1984). The concept of a story: A comparison between children's and teachers' viewpoints. In H. Mandl, N. L. Stein, & T. Trabasso (Eds.), *Learning and comprehension of text* (pp. 113–151). Hillsdale, NJ: Lawrence Erlbaum Associates.

Stein, N. L., & Trabasso, T. (1981). What's in a story: An approach to comprehension and instruction. In R. Glaser (Ed.), *Advances in the psychology of instruction* (vol. 2, pp. 213–267). Hillsdale, NJ: Lawrence Erlbaum Associates.

Stenning, K., & Michell, L. (1985). Learning how to tell a good story: The development of content and language in children's telling of one tale. *Discourse Processes, 8,* 261–279.

Trabasso, T., & Sperry, L. L. (1985). Causal relatedness and importance of story events. *Journal of Memory and Language, 24,* 595–611.

Trabasso, T., & van den Broek, P. (1985). Causal thinking and the representation of narrative events. *Journal of Memory and Language, 24,* 612–630.

Wells, G. (1985). Preschool literacy-related activities and success in school. In D. R. Olson, N. Torrance, & A. Hildyard (Eds.), *Literacy, language and learning: The nature and consequences of reading and writing* (pp. 229–255). New York: Cambridge University Press.

Yuill, N., & Joscelyne, T. (1988). Effect of organizational cues and strategies on good and poor comprehenders' story understanding. *Journal of Educational Psychology, 80*(2), 152–158.

Yuill, N., & Oakhill, J. (1991). *Children's problems in text comprehension: An experimental investigation.* Cambridge, England: Cambridge University Press.

CHAPTER NINE

A Funny Thing Happened on the Way to the Classroom: Jokes, Riddles, and Metalinguistic Awareness in Understanding and Improving Poor Comprehension in Children

Nicola Yuill
University of Sussex, Brighton

"It's a joke. You're not supposed to get it!"
(comment from 7-year-old poor comprehender asked to explain a riddle)

Children having problems specifically with comprehension have been relatively neglected in reading research, in comparison to so-called "garden variety" poor readers. Oakhill and Yuill's chapter describes some of our research with such children over the past 15 years, and a clearer picture of their problems is emerging. We term this group of children poor comprehenders: They have decoding skills that are perfectly adequate for their age, but their comprehension may be anything from 6 months to 2 years behind. Yuill and Oakhill (1991) described three broad areas in which such children show deficient performance; working memory, inference making, and metacognitive skills. Our primary focus was on children's ability to achieve a consistent interpretation of a text, as opposed to a confused, nonintegrated text model. However, there are some uses of language that rely for their effect on the construction of two internally consistent interpretations that conflict with each other. Nonliteral language such as puns, riddles, irony, and sarcasm are examples of such uses. Appreciating riddles has been seen as a metalinguistic skill (e.g., Hirsh-Pasek, Gleitman, & Gleitman, 1978). Are such metalinguistic skills important for good text comprehension? The present chapter addresses this issue by relating metalinguistic skill to reading ability and by assessing the pedagogical value of joking riddles in improving poor comprehension.

Joking riddles (henceforth just termed riddles) are a useful tool for study-ing children's ability to reflect on different aspects of language. For example, some riddles, such as puns, rest on the double meanings of single words— *Why was the crab arrested? Because he was always pinching things*— whereas others rely on multiple interpretations of the intention of an entire utterance (e.g., the notorious *Why did the chicken cross the road? To get to the other side*). The point of a riddle is that either the question sets up a particular linguistic interpretation that is different from that needed to un-derstand the answer, or the answer can be interpreted in two different ways. We get the riddle if we understand the two different interpretations. Some children, as my introductory quotation shows, apparently do not even see riddles as having a single consistent interpretation!

Because this use of riddles to tap different metalinguistic skills is rather novel, the description of the empirical work is preceded by a discussion of some issues of theory and method. First I discuss the meaning of metalinguistic awareness and in what way it is tapped by the appreciation of riddles. Then I review the possible relations between such awareness and different aspects of reading skill. This is followed by a description of how different types of riddle may be used as indicators of different aspects of reading skill. The empirical part of the chapter reports two correlational studies relating appre-ciation of various types of riddle to decoding and comprehension skills and a training study testing the possible educational benefits of riddles.

WHAT IS METALINGUISTIC AWARENESS?

Metalinguistic awareness is often considered as a subset of metacognition (e.g., see Tunmer & Bowey, 1984). Metacognition was succinctly defined by Kurtz (1991, p. 77) as "(1) knowledge about, and (2) regulation of cog-nitive states and processes." For example, metacognition about memory (metamemory) might include the knowledge that semantically related items are easier to remember than unrelated ones and the ability to rehearse a list consciously in order to recall it better. There has been broad support for the very general notion that metacognitive skill in a task is related to better performance of that task. In the case of reading, for example, Paris and his colleagues demonstrated that good readers have more accurate knowledge about effective reading strategies than poor readers (Paris & Myers, 1981), and that poor readers may improve given training in such strategies (Paris, Cross, & Lipson, 1984).

However, I believe that metalinguistic awareness cannot be considered as just another type of metacognition. It is a special case in that it involves knowledge of an external socially shared object, language, in addition to knowledge about one's own processing. There are some "brute facts" about language, such as that it is made up of phonemes and it has rules by which sentences are constructed. In contrast, our knowledge about cognitive functions is open to empirical refutation and can be more personal, for example, I may find it easiest to remember word lists by linking items to images. In many cognitive tasks, such as memorizing and problem solving, we often consciously monitor the efforts and strategies we are using. In using language, however, we tend to reflect on the message rather than on the process of its delivery. Thus, we can metacognize about language without using metalinguistic awareness: Comprehension monitoring is metacognitive but not necessarily, or even usually, metalinguistic.

Metalinguistic tasks tend to be those focusing on knowledge, whereas metacognitive tasks place a primary demand on monitoring one's own comprehension processes or products. For this reason, I would classify comprehension-monitoring tasks as primarily metacognitive, and riddle appreciation as primarily metalinguistic. In practice, knowledge of language facts cannot be entirely separated from the need to monitor our own language-producing apparatus in order to gain such knowledge. For example, given the metalinguistic task of separating a sentence into words, we need not only the knowledge of what a word is, but also the capacity to monitor a series of sounds in order to extract words.

Metalinguistic Awareness and Reading Skill

Work on metalinguistic awareness and reading development has focused almost entirely on the possible link between phonological awareness and learning to decode the written word (e.g., Goswami & Bryant, 1990; Rack, Hulme, & Snowling, 1993). There would seem to be an a priori argument for a link between decoding skill and phonological awareness. As Tunmer (1989, p. 103) put it, "On logical grounds alone it would appear that at least some minimal level of explicit phonological awareness is required to discover the systematic correspondences between graphemes and phonemes." A child has to make some application of grapheme–phoneme correspondence rules when reading new words out of context. Thus, awareness of sublexical features of language has been linked to decoding skill, although the precise causal relations between phonological awareness and decoding skill is a matter of great contention.

Tunmer and Bowey (1984) presented a more general theoretical account of metalinguistic awareness and reading. They pointed out that sentence comprehension can be viewed in simple terms as progressing from extracting phonemes, constructing words, accessing word meanings, and building up a model of text using inferential rules. By analogy, metalinguistic awareness can be seen to involve controlled processing of the outputs of each of these processes, resulting in four broad types of awareness; phonological, word, form (apparently covering both syntax and semantics), and pragmatic. These different types of awareness, they argue, change in importance at different stages of learning to read.

Tunmer and Bowey hypothesized that children's initial focus on meaning in using spoken language has to be set aside when they learn to read. In mastering the skills needed to decipher words, they have to ignore meaning and focus on phonemic and graphemic form. Once decoding skills, such as the ability to read words accurately and automatically, are secured, children have to "put humpty-dumpty back together again" (p. 163) by paying attention to the sentential context of words, rather than to the words in isolation. Tunmer and Bowey highlighted the importance of syntactic awareness at this stage, but other higher levels of awareness, such as pragmatic aspects, seem also to be involved.

Tunmer and Bowey's general account of the transition of attention from form to meaning seems on the face of it to be a plausible way of describing the problems of poor comprehenders of the type we have studied. Although these children have mastered decoding skills well, they seem slow in putting humpty-dumpty together again. Thus, poor comprehenders may have failed to make this smooth transition from text decoding to text comprehension because they are less aware of the semantic and pragmatic functions of language. Although they may show metalinguistic awareness at the level of phonemes, their awareness of the products of text comprehension may be comparatively poor. That is, they may show awareness of the earliest (lowest) levels identified by Tunmer and Bowey but not of the later or higher levels.

A quite different account of the development of metalinguistic awareness is given by Hirsh-Pasek et al. (1978). Their general argument was that "humans find it easiest to access high-level (or fully processed) linguistic representations, and much more difficult to process lower level (syntactic and phonological) representations" (p. 103). Thus, understanding riddles that turn on ambiguities at deep levels of language will be easier than those involving more superficial aspects of language.

These accounts differ in two main ways; in predictions about the relation between aspects of reading skill and appreciation of different riddle types, and in predictions about the relative difficulty of understanding different types of riddle. I am more concerned with the first question, but the data in this chapter also speak to the second issue. As regards the first issue, the predictions of these two theories differ in relation to reading skill. Tunmer and Bowey proposed that phonological awareness is important for decoding skills whereas awareness of higher levels of language is related to later developing reading skills. Hirsh-Pasek et al. suggested a relation between general verbal talent and the ability to access increasingly superficial aspects of language. Taking into account the relative difficulty of different riddle types, the two accounts have opposing assumptions about difficulty of accessing earlier processed/superficial aspects of language versus later processed/deep aspects of language. Tunmer and Bowey claimed that "higher is harder" whereas Hirsh-Pasek et al. claimed the opposite. In order to assess these claims, the different levels of language tapped by different types of riddle needs to be identified.

Classification of Riddle Types

Several different classifications of riddles have been used in research on age changes in riddle appreciation (see, e.g., Yalisove, 1978). The most linguistically sophisticated of these is probably that of Hirsh-Pasek et al. Because I am concerned specifically with riddles as indices of metalinguistic awareness, I have developed a related but slightly different classification system, which is assuredly not perfect but which captures some of the aspects of linguistic awareness that seem important in learning to read and comprehend text.

Riddles involve multiple meanings, but vary in the level at which the ambiguity occurs. The categories described here are presented in order of increasing size of the linguistic unit involved in the ambiguity. The lowest level rests on phonological manipulation within words, either by segmenting a word (*What do you give a hurt lemon?—Lemonade*) or by replacement with a similar sounding phoneme or morpheme (*Where do you take a hurt wasp?—To a waspital*). These are termed *morphophonological. Lexical* riddles rely on double meanings of single words (e.g., *Why was the crab arrested?—Because he kept pinching things*). The words may be spelled the same or differently. The next highest category (more usually given in joke form) has not been identified or examined in previous studies, although it is common in children's joke books, and I term it the *word compound* type. It rests on the multiple interpretations of word compounds such as "sausage roll" and "watch dog," where the relation between the two words in the compound has to be "unpacked" and reassembled in a different and often unusual way. The two main subtypes involve jokes, such as *Would you like to buy a pocket calculator, sir?—No thanks, I know how many pockets I've got*, and the "how do you make" format, such as *How do you make a sausage roll?—Push it down a hill.*

Syntactic riddles play on ambiguity in syntactic structures. For example, the riddle *How do you stop a fish from smelling?—Cut off its nose*, has two different underlying structures involving the grammatical role of smelling, which provide two different interpretations of the question. Other syntactic riddles, as Hirsh-Pasek et al. pointed out, involve ambiguities in surface structure, for example *Tell me how long cows should be milked.—The same as short ones, of course.*

Next are what I term *pragmatic* riddles, which violate expectations about the speaker's intent, for example, *Why do firemen wear red braces?—To keep their trousers up.* This riddle poses a question that gives too much specific information, violating Grice's (1975) maxim of quantity: The speaker must be as explicit as the situation demands but not more so. A sufficient question for the given answer would be "Why do people wear braces?" Other riddles in this category violate general presuppositions of an utterance: *Why do birds fly south?—Because it's too far to walk.* The final category of linguistic ambiguity riddle is somewhat different in that it requires metalinguistic awareness in the strict sense of involving terms for linguistic entities, such as "word." For example, *What word is loud, even when you say it softly?—Loud.* These riddles involve a contrast between the use and mention of a word, and are termed *metalinguistic* riddles. The riddles of this sort that I have used involve either word or "letter," for example, *Why is the letter E lazy?—Because it's always in bed.*

So far, I have discussed riddles as if they always involve linguistic ambiguity. However, this is not quite true. There are also riddles (or more usually, jokes) that do not involve any form of linguistic ambiguity. One common example is the type that Yalisove (1978) termed *absurd.* For example, *How do you get 6 elephants in a mini car?—Three in the front and three in the back.* Here, the question is nonsensical (i.e., it is not possible), but is answered as if it were sensible. The interest of these jokes is that they share some features with all riddles (e.g., the question–answer format) but they do not have the crucial element of linguistic ambiguity. However, they do seem to involve counterfactual reasoning.

The most important distinction, by my account, is between sublexical skills (primarily phonological awareness) and awareness of units at the level of words and above. Thus, the prediction is that appreciation of phonological riddles will be related to accuracy rather than comprehension, whereas riddles at levels from the lexical level will be more closely related to comprehension than to decoding skill. While this work was being carried out, this hypothesis was partly supported in a study by Mahony and Mann (1992). These authors showed that reading skill (pronouncing difficult words and nonsense words) in second graders correlated with the ability to pick the correct punchline for phoneme/morpheme riddles but not for a group of "control" riddles which did not involve morphophonological ambiguity. They also showed that the results were not due to differences in IQ, as measured by the Peabody Picture Vocabulary Test (Dunn, 1981). This study does not provide a full test of my hypothesis as it did not show whether appreciation of riddles in general is related to comprehension, and whether morphophonological riddle understanding is related to comprehension as much as to accuracy; however, this is plausible given the high intercorrelation between accuracy and comprehension skills.

Two earlier studies also related reading skill to riddle appreciation. Hirsh-Pasek et al. (1978) compared the ability to explain riddles in good and poor readers from grades 1 to 6. Reading skill was assessed by the school reading specialist, although the authors acknowledged that the range of skill was restricted, and that the poor readers were probably about average when compared to the normal population. Poor readers in all age groups were less able to explain riddles than were good readers. Riddle types included phonological, lexical, syntactic (deep and surface structure), and morphemic. As the authors expected, ambiguities turning on more superficial aspects of language were somewhat more difficult than those depending on underlying structure. However, contrary to their predictions, Hirsh-Pasek et al. did not find any relation between reading ability and riddle type.

Fowles and Glanz (1977) also found an age-independent relation between reading ability and riddle comprehension. They asked 14 children between ages 6 and 9 to retell and explain riddles read out by an experimenter. The riddles included lexical, syntactic (deep and surface structure), and metalinguistic types. Half the children were identified by teachers as above average readers, and half were below average. Although no statistical tests were reported, the good readers were better at explaining riddles than the poor ones, although there was apparently no difference between the two groups' ability to retell the riddles. Both of these studies suggested a relation between riddle comprehension and reading skill, but in both cases, the measure of reading skill was not specified and probably included aspects of decoding, comprehension, and general verbal ability.

As there seem to be no studies relating riddle appreciation to reading comprehension except for pilot studies of our own (Yuill & Oakhill, 1991, chapter 6), the experiments reported here looked first at whether there was a correlation between riddle appreciation and reading comprehension. All types of verbal riddle require some form of linguistic awareness, and I therefore expected overall correlations with comprehension. However, it was also possible that correlations would be stronger for some types of ambiguity than for others, for the reasons discussed previously.

STUDY 1: RIDDLE RECALL
AND READING COMPREHENSION

The first study was designed to see whether there were links between riddle appreciation and comprehension skill, independent of basic reading accuracy skills and chronological age. It also allowed an initial comparison of the strength of correlations for different types of riddle. Rather than comparing skilled and less skilled comprehenders, as in our earlier work, this study involved an unselected group of children of varying ability. The relation between appreciation of different kinds of riddle and reading comprehension was investigated by correlating comprehension skill and riddle appreciation and partialling out the effects of differences in reading accuracy and chronological age (the two main factors on which we have previously matched skilled and less skilled comprehenders).

Measures of Riddle Appreciation

Various different measures of riddle appreciation have been used in the previous literature, such as explanation, recall, punchline choice, and humor ratings. I did not expect humor ratings to be related to understanding a riddle because children can find a riddle amusing for many different reasons. For example, many children like the fireman riddle just mentioned because they are amused by the slapstick element of trousers falling down, but they do not understand how the listener is deceived into thinking that the color of the braces is relevant. The results of the pilot work reported by Yuill and Oakhill (1991) supported this assumption: Funniness ratings were not related to ability to explain the riddles, particularly for less skilled children. The comparative utility of recall and explanation scores seems to depend on the design of the study. In previous work, we found that reading comprehension was related to riddle explanations when the method involved children explaining the riddle to an uncomprehending peer, but that comprehension skill was more strongly related to recall when the children had to explain the riddle to an adult. Explaining the riddle to a sober-faced peer, who apparently did not understand, was presumably more motivating to the children than explaining to an adult who had told them the riddle, and who presumably understood it. However, the peer procedure is time consuming and requires long-term service from a cooperative child stooge, so the present study involved the adult-listener procedure. Thus, recall in this case was a better measure of riddle appreciation than comprehension.

Subjects

The sample consisted of twenty-nine 8–11-year-olds with 16 girls and 13 boys. The children's reading skills were assessed using the Neale Analysis of Reading Ability (Neale, 1966). This test requires children to read aloud short stories with any reading errors corrected by the tester, and then to answer comprehension questions from memory. The comprehension questions are a mix of literal and inferential items. The test gives separate measures of reading accuracy (number of words read correctly) and comprehension (questions correct). The range of reading ability was broad, with age-referenced scores varying from about 7 to 12 years. The characteristics of the sample are shown in Table 9.1.

Materials and Method

There were five different types of riddle used; lexical, word compound, pragmatic, and metalinguistic, all examples of linguistic ambiguity at increasingly higher stages of processing, and absurd riddles, which do not involve linguistic ambiguity. There were four examples of each of the five types of

TABLE 9.1
Means and Standard Deviations of Characteristics of Children From Study 1

N	Chronological Age	Neale Accuracy Age	Neale Comprehension Age
29	9.9 (9.01)	10.1 (16.75)	9.8 (16.79)

Note. Age is expressed as years.months. Standard deviations are expressed in months in parentheses.

riddle, except for the pragmatic and absurd categories, for which there were only two examples each. This was because these latter categories rely on tricks that seem not to bear much repetition. (In fact, such repetition did not seem to cause problems in further studies.) Examples of each type of riddle are shown in Table 9.2. The categorization of riddles was made by the author and checked by a blind coder, who agreed 100% on the classifications.

The riddles were read one at a time to each child (in a different random order for each child), who then rated its funniness (using the conventional thumbs-up, level, or down gesture to correspond to very funny, quite funny, and not funny, respectively). Then the child repeated the riddle and tried to explain why it was funny.

Scoring

The explanation task was, as suspected, rather too difficult, so I concentrate here on the recall scores. Each recall was scored as essentially correct (the ambiguity was maintained even if there were changes in wording) or incorrect. For example, for the paper shop riddle shown in Table 9.2, an example of an incorrect retelling could be "Did you hear about the man who bought

TABLE 9.2
Sample Riddles Used in Each Category of Linguistic Awareness in Study 1

Lexical:
What's black and white and red all over? A newspaper.

Word compound:
Have you heard the one about the man who bought a paper shop? It blew away.

Pragmatic:
What would you do if you swallowed a pen? Use a pencil.

Metalinguistic:
Why is there so little honey in Brighton? Because there's only one B in it.

Absurd:
How do you get an elephant into a matchbox? Take the matches out first.

a shop?—It blew away" whereas a correct recall could use different words but maintain the joke, for example, "What happened to the paper shop?—It blew over." This scoring was usually very simple, and two raters showed 100% agreement on a sample of 48 riddle retellings.

Results

The mean number and percentage correct for recall of each riddle type is shown in Table 9.3. Before assessing the relation between retellings and comprehension, it was necessary to see whether ease of recall was approximately the same for each riddle type. Unfortunately for present purposes, this was not the case. Inspection of the data showed that the absurd riddles were subject to a ceiling effect, so they were excluded from any further analysis. An ANOVA and post-hoc comparisons on the mean recall scores for the remaining four categories showed that the metalinguistic riddles were significantly harder to recall than any of the others, $F(1, 28) = 20.0$, $p < .001$, and the word compound riddles harder than the pragmatic ones, $F(1, 28) = 6.15$, $p < .01$. However, the standard deviations of each riddle type were similar, suggesting a roughly equal a priori probability of finding correlations with each type (see Table 9.3).

With these cautions in mind, we can then look at the intercorrelations of riddle recall with comprehension scores, and the partial correlations. In these analyses, converted reading scores rather than raw scores were used, but the overall pattern of results and significance was identical for raw scores. As Table 9.4 shows, riddle recall was not significantly correlated with reading accuracy for any of the riddle types. However, recall scores for word compound and metalinguistic riddles were significantly correlated with comprehension score, and these correlations were even stronger when accuracy score and chronological age were partialled out. Correlations with the other two categories were moderately positive but not significant.

TABLE 9.3
Mean Number and Percentage Correct Recalls
for Each Riddle Type From Study 1

Riddle Type	Number Correct (Max = 4)	SD	Percentage Correct
Lexical	3.24	0.83	81
Word compound	2.83	1.10	77
Pragmatic[a]	3.45	0.91	86
Metalinguistic	2.21	0.98	55
Absurd[a]	3.86	0.52	96

Note. $N = 29$. Absurd riddles were excluded from further analysis.
[a]Scores for pragmatic and absurd riddles were multiplied by 2.

TABLE 9.4
Correlations Between Recall for Each Riddle and Reading Scores for Study 1

Riddle Type	r Comprehension, Accuracy and Age Partialled Out	Simple r Comprehension	Simple r Accuracy
Lexical	.13	.16	.10
Word compound	.63**	.38*	−.18
Pragmatic	.26	.16	−.10
Metalinguistic	.40*	.34*	.02

Note. Pearson's r (27).
*$p < .05$. **$p < .01$.

As expected, funniness ratings did not correlate with comprehension skill (either alone or with age and accuracy partialled out), and all correlations were not significant. Also, funniness ratings showed no correlation with riddle recall.

Discussion

The results should be treated with some caution, because both sample size and number of riddles of each type were small, but they provide some initial support for a link between awareness of linguistic ambiguity and reading comprehension specifically, rather than with general reading skills. There were positive correlations between riddle appreciation and comprehension in particular, rather than with accuracy, providing some initial support to the contention that ambiguity at or above the word level is linked specifically to comprehension skill rather than to basic decoding skills. There was no clear difference in the correlations for riddles with ambiguity at high and low levels, nor was there a clear pattern of differences in difficulty between riddles according to the level of language ambiguity. Metalinguistic and word compound riddles were recalled less well than lexical, pragmatic, and absurd riddles. However, the number of riddles used was restricted. The second study addressed the same issues as the first, using an extended range of riddle types, a larger sample of children, and more examples of riddles of each type.

STUDY 2: RIDDLE COMPLETION
AND READING COMPREHENSION

Study 1 showed no clear difference in the relation of comprehension to different riddle types. The present study added sublexical riddles to the types used in Study 1. From Tunmer and Bowey's (1984) account, one would expect that such riddles (e.g., phonological riddles) would be more closely related to accuracy than to comprehension.

Measure of Riddle Appreciation

This study used a slightly different method of assessing riddle appreciation, with the aim of increasing the generality of the earlier findings. The correlations should be observed not only for recall, but for other methods tapping appreciation of the essential ambiguities in riddles. This method was the one adopted by Mahony and Mann (1992), of giving children two possible punchlines for each riddle and asking them to choose the one that made the riddle work best. The alternative (incorrect) answers were either realistic (taking the riddle question in its literal or focal meaning) or absurd. For example, the syntactic riddle, *How do you stop a fish from smelling?* was presented with the intended answer, *Cut off its nose*, and with a realistic alternative answer, *Wash it with soap*. An example of an absurd alternative answer is as follows: For the morphophonological riddle, *What kind of witch do you find in the desert?—A sand witch*, the alternative answer was *A cactus witch*. For each riddle type, half the alternative answers were realistic and half were absurd. It was not possible to vary the two types of alternative answer within each riddle because some riddles do not lend themselves easily to realistic answers. To keep the children interested, we also introduced a neighing-horse puppet who occasionally laughed when the child told a joke.

Riddle Types

Seven types of riddle were used, as shown in Table 9.5, with eight examples of each type, and balanced as closely as possible across types for length (number of words). The categorization of riddles was made by the author and checked by 4 blind coders, all with specialized linguistic knowledge (e.g., psycholinguists and lexicographers), who agreed 100% on the classifications. The materials included the five riddle types used in Study 1, and two additional types. One of these, morphophonological, was sublexical, and I expected that appreciation of this type would relate more closely to reading accuracy, as found by Mahony and Mann (1992), than to comprehension. The other new riddle type was syntactic, as in the fish riddle above. No prediction was made about the relations between this riddle type and reading skill. Evidence regarding poor comprehenders' syntactic skills has been mixed, though tending to suggest they do not have grammatical difficulties (see Yuill & Oakhill, 1991, chapter 3). The syntactic riddles were subdivided into two types of ambiguity, either deep- or surface-structure ambiguity. According to Hirsh-Pasek et al. (1978), the surface-structure ambiguities should be more difficult to appreciate.

Subjects

The sample for this study was composed of 41 children, ages 7.10 to 9.9 (*M* = 8.7), who were tested on the Neale analysis, as in the previous study. Two children from this original sample were excluded because of their very

TABLE 9.5
Sample Riddles Used in Each Category of Linguistic Awareness,
With Alternative Answers From Study 2

Morphophonological:
What kind of keys are furry?
*a) Monkeys   OR
b) Fluffy keys

Lexical:
Why do leopards never escape from the zoo?
*a) Because they're always spotted   OR
b) Because they run too slowly

Word compound:
Why did the girl tiptoe past the medicine cabinet?
a) She didn't want to wake the carpet   OR
*b) She didn't want to wake the sleeping pills

Syntactic:
What animal can jump higher than a house?
a) The biggest kangaroo in the world   OR
*b) All animals, houses can't jump

Pragmatic:
When is a black dog most likely to go into a house?
*a) When the door is open   OR
b) When there's some dog food in the house

Metalinguistic:
What word is long but only has four letters?
a) A word you say slowly   OR
*b) Long

Absurd:
How do you fit 6 elephants into a mini?
a) You couldn't, they would have to walk   OR
*b) Three in the front and three in the back

Note. Correct answers are indicated by *.

extreme reading scores, which caused the original reading skill variables to be skewed. The remaining data showed no evidence of skew on any of the variables. There was as before a broad range of reading skill, ranging between about 6 to 12 years. The sample characteristics are shown in Table 9.6.

Results

I first checked whether the different riddle types were roughly equal in difficulty, using an ANOVA on the number of correct punchline choices for each type. The means and standard deviations are shown in Table 9.7. As in

TABLE 9.6
Means and Standard Deviations of Characteristics of Children From Study 2

N	Chronological Age	Neale Accuracy Age	Neale Comprehension Age
39	8.8	8.10	8.7
	(6.75)	(14.24)	(11.21)

Note. Age is expressed as years.months. Standard deviations are expressed in months in parentheses.

the first study, metalinguistic riddles were significantly harder than all other types, $F(1, 40) = 10.10$, $p < .01$, and syntactic ones also proved to be harder than the other types (except metalinguistic), $F(1, 40) = 11.42$, $p < .01$, but there were no significant differences between the other types, and no apparent ceiling effects.

Within the syntactic category, surface-structure riddles were significantly harder than deep-structure ones ($Ms = 1.9$ and 2.83, respectively), $F(1, 40) = 24$, $p < .001$, supporting Hirsh-Pasek et al. in their original idea that superficial aspects of language are harder to access.

Mean performance for metalinguistic riddles was at chance (50%) but this category was kept in the analysis, because the mean concealed the fact that some children scored better than chance whereas others did not.

As in the first study, the main analysis consisted of partial correlations of reading comprehension in months with riddle appreciation (in this case, number of correct choices of punchline), with chronological age and accuracy age partialled out. The pattern of correlations is shown in Table 9.8. Choice of correct punchline for all riddle types showed positive correlations with comprehension. When accuracy and age were partialled out, the correlations remained significant for all except morphophonological and syntactic riddles. Furthermore, none of the riddle types showed a simple cor-

TABLE 9.7
Mean Number and Percentage Correct Recalls
for Each Riddle Type From Study 2

Riddle Type	Number Correct (Max = 8)	SD	Percentage Correct
Morphophonological	5.74	1.62	72
Lexical	5.61	1.73	70
Word compound	5.38	1.63	67
Syntactic	4.64	1.31	58
Pragmatic	5.41	1.77	68
Metalinguistic	3.97	1.37	50
Absurd	5.44	1.76	68

Note. N = 39.

TABLE 9.8
Correlations Between Punchline Choice and Comprehension
Score for Each Riddle Type From Study 2

Riddle Type	r Comprehension, Accuracy and Age Partialled Out	Simple r Comprehension	Simple r Accuracy
Morphophonological	.21	.33*	.34*
Lexical	.46**	.48**	.19
Word compound	.33*	.19	−.20
Syntactic	.29	.28	.05
Pragmatic	.34*	.33*	.08
Metalinguistic	.51**	.54**	.23
Absurd	.40**	.32*	−.08

Note. Pearson's r (37).
$*p < .05.$ $**p < .01.$

relation with accuracy score except morphophonological. This type of riddle also showed a significant simple correlation with comprehension, but the partial correlation with comprehension, removing accuracy and chronological age, was not significant, suggesting that the simple correlation of morphophonological riddles with comprehension was to some extent due to the intercorrelation between comprehension and accuracy.

Inspection of the two subtypes of syntactic riddles showed a difference in patterns of correlation: The correlation of surface-structure riddles with comprehension was $r(37) = .41$, $p < .01$, whereas the correlation for deep-structure syntactic riddles was not significant.

Discussion of Correlational Studies

As in Experiment 1, the results show a pattern of significant correlation with riddles turning on ambiguity at the level of words and above. The results are not entirely consistent between the two experiments. The correlations of comprehension with lexical and pragmatic riddles were significant in the second study but not in the first. However, both studies show significant relations between comprehension, and both word compound and metalinguistic riddles. Also, the second study suggests distinctive links between different reading skills and riddle types. Appreciation of phonological riddles appears more closely linked to accuracy skill whereas other riddle types focusing on higher level units of language appear to be related to comprehension rather than to accuracy.

These two studies thus provide some intriguing early evidence that appreciation of riddles of some types is related to reading comprehension skill but not to accuracy skills. There is some tentative support for the idea that lexical and superlexical riddles are related specifically to comprehension whereas sublexical (phonological) riddles are more closely related to accuracy. Further work is needed to establish these findings more firmly and to assess the effects of task factors such as the provision of realistic or absurd answers in punchline choices. Even so, the basic pattern of results seems to be supported across differences in methods (recall and punchline choice) and in the riddle items used.

Riddle appreciation thus promises to be a useful technique for further work in understanding the role of metalinguistic awareness of different levels and reading skill. Riddle appreciation has certain advantages over some other assessments of metalinguistic awareness. One of the problems commonly encountered in addressing the issue of different types of metalinguistic awareness is of establishing task equivalence. For example, a test of phoneme awareness may not be equivalent to one of word awareness, simply because the degree of awareness is confounded with the type of awareness. For example, recognizing phonemes will be harder than recognizing words, given that one can read, because normal reading involves explicit marking of words (i.e., they are separated by spaces). The use of riddles varying in level of ambiguity avoids this potential confounding by using a single type of task to assess different types of awareness. Thus, the task taps a common set of skills (e.g., picking one of two alternative punchlines or recalling a riddle), but the level of ambiguity involved in the riddle varies. Of course, as with all such tasks, there will be differences in difficulty between individual riddle items, because of variations in features such as vocabulary, syntactic complexity, length, and so forth. This difficulty can be combatted in various ways by roughly equating such factors across riddles, performing multiple experiments, and using a large number of different riddles in each category.

STUDY 3: TRAINING IN AMBIGUITY
AND COMPREHENSION IMPROVEMENT

What implications do these results have for children with a specific comprehension problem? From the outset of this research, I hoped that the research might be pedagogically useful in helping poor comprehenders. Can riddles and other word games be used to increase metalinguistic awareness, and if so, will this increase produce corresponding gains in comprehension skill? The final study reported here was designed to address this question. At the same time, if such increases were found for poor comprehenders specifically, this would boost the argument that metalinguistic skills contribute to the development of comprehension skills. First, I describe briefly some ideas about methods of remediating comprehension problems, and on the difficulties of poor comprehenders specifically, then I suggest some ways in which riddles and other forms of word game might help.

Using Riddles to Remediate Comprehension Problems

Fowles and Glanz (1977) speculated that riddles could be used as a technique for improving children's reading skills. Given that the studies just described showed appreciation of some types of riddle to be related specifically to reading comprehension, any remedial effect of using such riddles should influence comprehension rather than other aspects of reading. Comprehension skills are often taught using explicit metacognitive and study skills, such as the successful "informed strategies for learning" approach developed for fifth graders by Paris and colleagues (e.g., Paris et al., 1984; Paris & Jacobs, 1984). However, this approach may be less useful for younger children than the use of word games they engage in naturally at around this age. Word games can address awareness of linguistic features without requiring explicit discussion of study skills. A good example in relation to accuracy skills is the work of Bryant and Bradley (1985), who claimed that the everyday activity of rhyming games can play a part in learning to decode the written word because it increases children's awareness of sounds and corresponding letter patterns. In a similar way, it is possible that practice with word games involving linguistic ambiguity, such as riddles, is a way of fostering awareness of alternative meanings, and hence comprehension skills. Although there have been several studies of children's comprehension of riddles and ambiguity, there appears to be no work that has used ambiguity as a training technique.

Poor Comprehension and Sensitivity to Meaning

As we saw in the previously mentioned experiments, appreciation of verbal ambiguity in riddles is clearly linked to text comprehension skill. From previous research, we already have a general picture of poor comprehenders as relatively insensitive to the derivation of meaning from text (and indeed from the spoken word). Children with a specific comprehension deficit seem to have little or no explicit awareness of either language or comprehension activities. Not only are they poor at the actual process of making inferences, but they also tend to see reading purely in terms of decoding, are often unaware of textual inconsistencies, and are poor at understanding deductive inferences or how they know what they know (Oakhill, Yuill, & Donaldson, 1990; Yuill & Oakhill, 1991). A good example of this last difficulty is the following observation made when administering the Neale analysis. Part of one story reads, "A surprise parcel for Jane and Peter arrived on Saturday." Children are asked, "How do you know that Jane and Peter were not expecting the parcel?" Less skilled children, even if they knew that the parcel was unexpected, seemed to have particular difficulty with this question. It requires awareness of the source of one's knowledge in the text, that is, the relation between the text on the page and its meaning: The single word "surprise" is the only clue indicating the unexpected nature of the event.

A general lack of sensitivity to meaning is also suggested by the results of some training studies (Yuill & Joscelyne, 1988; Yuill & Oakhill, 1988) that were inspired partly by the above observation. One component of our training was to give children instruction in "lexical inference" by sensitizing them to the inferences that could be drawn from single words or combinations of words. We did this by presenting children with passages that were deliberately obscure, so as to make the effort after meaning more open to awareness than it might otherwise have been, and by asking them what they could work out about the story from particular words in the text. For example, one story in the training began, "Anna tried and tried to turn the key, but the castle had been empty for too long." Children were shown how the repetition of *tried* suggests difficulty, *key* is presumably the key to the door of the *castle*, and *empty for too long* implies that the key was hard to turn because the keyhole was rusty due to neglect. Thus, a whole series of inferences can be drawn from what might otherwise be a rather opaque sentence. This conscious reflection on deriving inferences from text is a metalevel skill, that is, it involves not just comprehending the text, but understanding about the way in which the text supports particular interpretations. It involves both metalinguistic and metacognitive skills, as defined earlier. The lexical inference activities we used were not part of the normal language activity in which children engage. Riddling is a more familiar activity that focuses on language. The aim of the present study was to assess the potential benefits of word games that focus on ambiguity, and on meaning in general, in addressing the relative insensitivity to meaning displayed by poor comprehenders.

Overview and Rationale of the Training Study

In this study, we used the type of contrasting groups design used by Yuill and Oakhill (1991), having two groups of children matched on decoding skills and age but differing in comprehension skill. Half of the children in each group were given training in understanding ambiguity and the other half were given a control treatment. If the poor comprehenders improved with the ambiguity training but not with the control treatment, such training would have a pedagogical benefit. If the trained poor comprehenders improved more than the trained good comprehenders, this would suggest that the training addressed a causal factor in poor comprehension.

Materials

Ambiguity Training. There are several ways of focusing children's attention on alternate interpretations of text. One method is to help children develop their skills in explaining ambiguity in riddles, and to make up their

TABLE 9.9
Summary of Activities in Ambiguity Training Sessions

---

1. Defining and finding words with double meanings (e.g., bank, fan)
   Introduction to explaining puns (e.g., What's black and white and red all over?)
2. Explaining sentences with double meanings (e.g., The mayor asked the police to stop stealing).
   Further work on explaining jokes beyond the word level.
3. Given word compounds, with double meanings, inventing meanings different from the usual meaning (e.g., sausage roll, watch dog)
4. Communication game: One child describes a picture in such a way that others can work out which picture in an array is referred to (e.g., "umbrella" would be an inadequate description for an array of a red and a yellow umbrella (e.g., see Pratt & Bates, 1982).
5. Given a word pair, such as "cow–horse," thinking of a clue so that a peer can pick out one of the words (e.g., "milk" would prompt cow). Word pairs were either similar in meaning (e.g., river–ocean) or dissimilar (wash–give) (see Asher & Parke, 1975). Evaluating good and poor clues.
6. Explaining metalinguistic jokes.
7. Finding key words to help understand abstract stories (see Yuill & Joscelyne, 1988, for examples).

---

own riddles and this was the main method used here. Other methods include the communication games used in research on children's understanding of linguistic ambiguity (e.g., Glucksberg, Krauss, & Weisberg, 1966). We used a combination of different types of word games in this treatment, as summarized in Table 9.9. Some sample quotes from training sessions are given in Table 9.10, to help give an impression of the sorts of interactions that occurred.

Control Treatment. There were two underlying factors involved in designing the control treatment. First we needed to control for features of the ambiguity training incidental to the main goal of increasing sensitivity to meaning. An appropriate control group for a training study needs to be given all the elements of the training except for the crucial ingredient of fostering linguistic awareness of alternative meanings. In addition to individual attention, familiarity with the experimenter and other such general features of training, a group given riddles are being exposed to humorous material. This in itself might have a motivating effect and hence help comprehension for reasons other than those of interest here. The control group in this study therefore read and made up funny stories, in the hope that their motivation would be similarly boosted. The second general rationale underlying the control treatment was to assess whether comprehension skills would be helped by training in metalinguistic awareness at a sublexical level. For this reason, the control groups were given tasks to foster awareness of sounds rather than of meanings. It seemed more likely that increasing such awareness would produce gains in decoding skills rather than in comprehension skills. A summary of activities is given in Table 9.11.

TABLE 9.10
Selected Quotes From Ambiguity Training Sessions

Some children learned very quickly how to clarify two possible meanings:

Kate (trainer): "Andy went lion hunting with a club." What could that mean?

Sabine: You use a club like that (*swings her arm to demonstrate*) and a club with people in.

Kate: "Sabine saw a man eating fish."

Kerry: ... and she wanted some
... and a fish eating a man.

(offering two alternative sentence completions)

and could produce a response that combined the two meanings creatively:

Kate: Tell me how long cows should be milked.

Sabine: Until they are their normal size.

Others did not ...

Kate: "This restaurant even serves lobsters."

Andy: A restaurant is like a big place.

Kate: And they serve ..?

Andy: Lobsters.

Cathy: It could mean that the lobsters are serving something.

and some found unintended double meanings ...

Sabine: Even, it's even like you give one to one person and the other half to another person.

Some children were resistant to the possibility of double meanings ...

Kate: Why did the teacher wear sunglasses? Because the children were so bright. Can you explain that?

Andy: Bright when it's light ... Bright clothes.

Sabine: Clever. Bright means clever as well.

Andy: No it doesn't.

In short, it was hypothesized that children in the ambiguity training group would improve their comprehension skills more than children in the control group, independently of any increase in decoding skills. In fact, decoding skills might even be fostered more in the control group, given the focus on awareness of sounds. I also expected less skilled comprehenders given training to improve more than skilled ones, because previous research by

TABLE 9.11
Summary of Activities in Control Treatment Sessions

---

1 Reading amusing stories (exaggerations, impossible events)
2 Reading amusing stories (disgusting events, playing tricks)
   Inventing absurd scenarios
3 Finding rhyming words, inventing limericks
4 Finding rhyming and nonrhyming words
5 Tapping out rhythms of sentences (Tunmer, Herriman, & Nesdale, 1988)
6 Matching middle sounds of words
7 Reading amusing stories (all involving slapstick and incongruity rather than specifically linguistic humor).

Yuill and Oakhill (1991) suggested that the first group is poorer in metalinguistic skills than the second.

Subjects

Over 100 children in three different schools were given the Neale analysis in order to provide a sample of 18 poor comprehenders, as defined by Yuill and Oakhill (1991). Their accuracy age was no less than 5 months below their chronological age, but their comprehension age was at least 6 months below their accuracy age. Eighteen good comprehenders from the same overall sample were matched with the poor comprehenders for Neale accuracy (regressed scores), chronological age, and word recognition using the Gates–MacGinitie (1965) Primary One Vocabulary Test. The resulting two groups differed significantly on the Neale comprehension score. Characteristics of the sample are shown in Table 9.12. The children in each skill group were divided into trained and control subjects. This was done randomly with the constraint that the resulting subgroups had to be equal in age and decoding skills, and had to fulfill the practical requirement of allowing us to construct treatment groups of similar size (3–4 children) in each school. This was no mean feat, but the resulting groups were appropriately matched, as shown in Table 9.12, with the sole exception of the control skilled comprehender group, who tended to be slightly younger than their trained counterparts, $t(17) = 2.07$, $p < .06$.

TABLE 9.12
Means and Standard Deviations of Characteristics of Children
in Each Skill and Training Group From Study 3

	n	Chronolog. Age	Vocab. Score	Neale Accuracy Age (Regressed)	Neale Comprehension Age
Less skilled comprehenders:					
Ambiguity	9	92.6	34.0	93.2	87.9
		(4.2)	(3.3)	(5.3)	(2.4)
Control	9	92.7	33.0	93.7	86.3
		(4.8)	(3.5)	(5.8)	(2.9)
Mean		92.7	33.5	93.5	87.1
Skilled comprehenders:					
Ambiguity	9	93.9	32.0	94.9	100.9
		(4.9)	(5.4)	(5.5)	(7.4)
Control	9	89.4	32.4	94.3	98.7
		(4.3)	(4.7)	(4.5)	(5.9)
Mean		91.7	32.2	94.6	99.8
Difference: skilled − less skilled (related t, 17 df)		0.4	0.6	0.4	5.2*

Note. Standard deviations appear in parentheses. All ages are expressed in months.
*$p < .005$.

Each group was given seven treatment sessions of about 30 minutes each over a period of 7 consecutive weeks, in sets of 2 to 5 children. Within two weeks of finishing the treatment, they received a parallel version of the Neale Analysis and specific posttests, described below.

Results

Comprehension. The main measure of interest was the difference between the pretest Neale comprehension score and the posttest. As Table 9.13 shows, all children improved quite substantially, but no great significance should be attached to this, as the differences could be due to several factors, including differences between the two forms of the test used, practice effects, time of year, and so on. An ANOVA on the pre and posttest differences showed a main effect of treatment group, $F(1, 32) = 4.18$, $p < .05$. As expected, children given ambiguity training showed greater increases in comprehension age than those in the control group. The same effect occurred when increases in raw comprehension scores were used. There was also a marginal effect of skill group, $F(1, 32) = 3.73$, $p < .06$, although this did not appear for the raw comprehension scores. The less skilled comprehenders tended to improve more than the skilled ones. There was no significant interaction between skill group and training.

There was clearly individual variation in the extent of the increase in comprehension scores, and it was therefore also useful to examine the comprehension outcomes for individual children. Children were classified on the basis of their posttest comprehension scores as "good" (comprehension age above both chronological and accuracy age), "poor" (comprehension age below both chronological and accuracy age), or "mixed" (comprehension age below either chronological or accuracy age). The resulting classification of each group is shown in Table 9.14. If children showing any

TABLE 9.13
Mean Improvements (in Months) and Standard Deviations
in Comprehension Age as a Function of Treatment
Group and Comprehension Skill for Study 3

| | Treatment Group | | | |
Skill Group	Ambiguity	Control	Mean	Difference
Less skilled	20.56	13.11	16.83	7.45
	(8.07)	(7.92)		
Skilled	13.44	8.89	11.16	4.55
	(6.73)	(10.13)		
Mean	17.00	11.00	14.00	

Note. Standard deviations appear in parentheses.

TABLE 9.14
Posttreatment Comprehension Status as a Function
of Treatment and Skill Group for Study 3

Skill and Treatment Group	Posttest Comprehension Status			Combined Data	
	Low	Mixed	High	Low	Mixed + High
Less skilled					
Ambiguity	0	4	5	0	9
Control	4	3	2	4	5
Skilled					
Ambiguity	0	1	8	0	9
Control	1	1	7	1	8

Note. Categorization of posttest comprehension status; low = Neale comprehension age below accuracy and chronological age, mixed = Neale comprehension age above either accuracy or chronological age, high = Neale comprehension age above accuracy and chronological age.

improvement (mixed or good comprehenders) were combined (as on the right side of Table 9.14), significantly more of the less skilled children improved in the trained than in the control group, Fisher's exact test $p < .05$. There was unsurprisingly no such relation for the skilled children, as all but one child continued to be classified as high or mixed.

Accuracy. Accuracy ages increased overall by about 8 months. The effects on comprehension did not seem to be moderated by changes in accuracy scores, as an ANOVA on the accuracy age differences pre and posttreatment showed no significant effects or interactions. Furthermore, there was no correlation between comprehension improvement and accuracy improvement.

Specific Posttests. Specific posttests were used to look at whether children had learned what was intended during the treatments. A riddle task tested the efficacy of the ambiguity training. Children had to retell a series of 10 riddles after rating their funniness, in a similar way to the method of the first riddle study mentioned here. The rhyming task, to test the utility of parts of the control training, was a list of 74 words, divided into 11 groups of 6–10 words each. The words in each group had a similar final sound although they varied in spelling, for example, snare, fair, lair, pear, share. In each group there were 1–3 exceptions, such as "mere" for the above group. Children had to find the nonrhyming words in each list as quickly and accurately as possible.

Children in both treatment groups were given both posttests, so that we could check whether those given training in a particular skill (riddles or rhyming) became better at that skill. Sample sizes were slightly reduced for these posttests as some children were absent due to illness. The riddles test scores were subjected to an ANOVA, with treatment condition and skill group as between-subjects factors. Although ambiguity-trained children did better than control children, with means of 5.19 and 3.78 out of 10 respectively, the main effect of treatment was not significant. There was no significant effect of skill group (Ms = 3.87 for less skilled, 4.94 for skilled children). An ANOVA of the rhymes posttest showed a marginal effect of treatment, $F(1, 32) = 3.81$, $p < .06$. Children in the control group tended to score higher on this task than ambiguity-trained children (Ms = 59.67 and 55.28 respectively, out of 74). The effect of skill group did not reach significance although skilled children tended to score higher than less skilled ones (Ms = 59.33 and 55.61 respectively). Scores on the specific posttests were not correlated with rates of improvement in comprehension or accuracy.

Discussion

This study provides preliminary evidence that riddles and ambiguity can indeed be useful in advancing children's text comprehension. However, there were two substantial aspects in which the results were unexpected; improvements were not confined to the less skilled group, and were not linked to improvement in the specific posttests. To take the first point, the effects of ambiguity training were not specific to less skilled comprehenders: Children in the trained groups improved regardless of their initial comprehension level. This is surprising, because the work by Yuill and Oakhill (1991) on such groups of children showed that less skilled comprehenders have poorer metalinguistic skills in general. They are less likely to pick out the main point of a story, less likely to notice inconsistencies in stories, and find it harder to resolve anomalies in text when processing demands are high. The present Studies 1 and 2 also show a link between comprehension skill and appreciation of riddles involving complex linguistic ambiguity. Furthermore, Yuill and Oakhill reported training studies showing a specific benefit for less skilled comprehenders.

Why did the training produce general, rather than specific effects? It seems that although skilled comprehenders are superior in linguistic awareness, they can show further gains given training of the sort used here. The children in this study were only 7–8 years of age, and the correlational studies above showed that even 9–10-year-olds had difficulty appreciating some riddles. Although the results tell us less about the differences between skilled and less skilled comprehenders than about comprehension skill in general, it means that the training technique could be useful to improve comprehension skills generally rather than for poor comprehenders in particular, as in the techniques used previously by Yuill and Oakhill.

The processes by which training produced improvement are unclear for another reason. There were no clear differences between treatment groups on the specific posttests of rhyming and riddles. The trained children's lack of improvement on the riddles task may be due to the fact that their training was rather general. It addressed more than just riddle appreciation, so may have helped children more generally in considering alternative meanings and in understanding relatively implicit aspects of text. The lack of a clear difference between treatment groups on the rhyming task is somewhat more straightforward: This treatment was not effective in improving accuracy skills, so there is no treatment effect to explain!

The results of this study are pedagogically interesting, suggesting that riddles and word games may be a useful general technique, but they throw little light on the processes underlying gains in comprehension. Furthermore, we should not expect these processes to be uniform across children. Rates of improvement were very variable in the present study, and more work is needed to try and specify the processes by which comprehension increases occur. This would lead to a better theoretical understanding of the link between linguistic awareness and normal comprehension processes, and would help in developing more effective training programs.

GENERAL DISCUSSION

The studies reported here provide convergent evidence, using different techniques, that linguistic awareness is implicated in the development of text comprehension skills. There are significant correlations between riddle appreciation (riddle recall and punchline choice) and comprehension skill, and training with riddles produces greater improvement in comprehension skills than a control treatment. More specifically, the results suggest that some types of linguistic awareness, but not others, are related to comprehension skill. This complements the study by Mahony and Mann (1992), which indicated that basic reading accuracy skills are related to the ability to choose appropriate punchlines for morphophonological riddles but not for control riddles. In their study, they called for evidence of the relation between riddle appreciation and comprehension skills. The present chapter provides that evidence, but further work will be needed to examine the degree to which accuracy and comprehension skills are independently related to riddle appreciation, and to investigate how the relations between reading skill and riddles change as reading skills develop.

The results of the correlational studies do not unambiguously support either of the two positions outlined by Hirsh-Pasek et al. (1978) or by Tunmer and Bowey (1984). Phonological riddles, according to the former position, should be harder to understand than riddles playing on less superficial aspects of language, but the results did not bear this out. However, within the syntactic category, surface-structure ambiguities were harder to understand than deep-structure ones, in accord with this account. Tunmer and Bowey's view is supported insofar as there are distinctive relations between different reading skills and appreciation of different kinds of ambiguity.

Authors such as Olson (1994) have argued that learning a written language makes us reflect on language in a more explicit way than we do when we just speak. The idea is that the introduction of written language can encourage us to view language disembedded from the here and now context. Riddles are particularly interesting, because they are a naturally occurring form of oral language in which attention is explicitly focused on a single surface form with two internally consistent meanings. The riddle question is generally designed to set up an interpretation different from that needed to understand the answer. The incongruity itself may generate a comprehension-monitoring signal to the hearer, who then has to determine the nature and resolution of the apparent incongruity. The pedagogical advantage of riddles is that they make this monitoring of double meanings salient. Our own initial misinterpretation is, I would argue, one of the reasons we find riddles funny.

It is interesting to speculate on how practice with riddles might help reading comprehension. Some recent work by Stanovich and colleagues (this volume; see also, Stanovich, 1993; Stanovich & Cunningham, 1992) could provide some indicators. Stanovich argued that print experience is important in developing reading skills; riddles, of course, involve primarily listening skills. Print experience is supposed to make its contribution to reading skill via increases in vocabulary, world knowledge, and metalinguistic knowledge, although most research supporting this claim has focused on only the first two of these factors. Riddles may provide a relatively rare occasion for oral language to contribute to the third factor, by helping the kind of decentered awareness of language sometimes thought to be exclusive to written text. This idea is in line with the thinking of Tunmer and his colleagues, who stressed the role of decentration in developing metalinguistic awareness. The reason riddles may have an interesting role to play here is that they require a focus on the superficial form of language, but they are an oral form. That is, they may fulfill some of the functions that are traditionally thought to be peculiar to written text. Furthermore, they may contribute a useful tool in the attempt to "unpack" the concept of print experience in order to see precisely how such experience influences reading development.

I have presented riddle appreciation here as a measure of metalinguistic awareness and more generally as involving metacognitive knowledge. It is worth noting that for many of the measures I used here, this knowledge need only be implicit (e.g., as reflected in accurate recall of a riddle). Much research on training metacognitive skills has focused primarily on highly explicit forms of learning (e.g., see Baker, this volume), but as the work by

Ruffman (this volume) demonstrates, there is a long developmental road to travel in acquiring metacognitive skills.

Riddle appreciation may be linked to text comprehension for reasons other than the metalinguistic demands on which I have focused. Another possible account of the relation between riddles and reading comprehension is in terms of processing demands. The verbatim recall and simultaneous reinterpretation that is needed to appreciate riddles presumably impose a considerable load on working memory. It may be that the relations found in the present studies are moderated by such memory demands. However, such an account would also need to explain why some types of riddles are more demanding of memory resources than others, and this brings us back to the issue of metalinguistic awareness.

One final point concerns individual differences between poor comprehenders. Cornoldi, De Beni, and Pazzaglia (this volume) suggest that poor comprehenders can show quite different patterns of performance deficit. In the present training study, and in previous work (e.g., Yuill & Oakhill, 1988), rates of improvement have been very variable. Investigations such as that by Cornoldi will be useful in helping to specify different underlying factors in poor comprehension and eventually, to target training at specific aspects of comprehension difficulty.

ACKNOWLEDGMENTS

I would like to thank Kate Easton (Studies 1 and 3) and Pat George and Horace (Study 2) for help with data collection, and the University of Sussex for financial support of the pilot project. Grateful thanks also to Jane Oakhill, Deborah Yuill, Elizabeth Manning, and anonymous lexicographers for help with categorization of riddles, and to Cesare Cornoldi, Jane Oakhill, Kate Cain, Alan Garnham, and anonymous reviewers for helpful suggestions.

REFERENCES

Asher, S. R., & Parke, R. D. (1975). Sampling and comparison processes. *Journal of Educational Psychology, 67,* 64–75.

Bryant, P. E., & Bradley, L. (1985). *Children's reading problems: Psychology and education.* Oxford, England: Basil Blackwell.

Dunn, L. M. (1981). *Peabody Picture Vocabulary Test–Revised.* Circle Pines, MN: American Guidance Service.

Fowles, B., & Glanz, M. E. (1977). Competence and talent in verbal riddle comprehension. *Journal of Child Language, 4,* 433–452.

Gates, A. I., & MacGinitie, W. H. (1965). *Gates–MacGinitie Reading Tests.* New York: Columbia University Teachers' College Press.

Glucksberg, S., Krauss, R. M., & Weisberg, R. (1966). Referential communication in nursery school children: Method and some preliminary findings. *Journal of Experimental Child Psychology, 3,* 333–342.

Goswami, U., & Bryant, P. E. (1990). *Phonological skills and learning to read.* Hove, England: Lawrence Erlbaum Associates.

Grice, H. P. (1975). Logic and conversation. In P. Cole & J. L. Morgan (Eds.), *Syntax and semantics: Vol. 7. Speech acts* (pp. 41–58). New York: Academic Press.

Hirsh-Pasek, K., Gleitman, L. R., & Gleitman, H. (1978). What did the brain say to the mind? A study of the detection and report of ambiguity by young children. In A. Sinclair, R. J. Jarvella, & W. J. M. Levelt (Eds.), *The child's conception of language* (pp. 97–132). New York: Springer.

Kurtz, B. E. (1991). Cognitive and metacognitive aspects of text processing. In G. Denhiere & J.-P. Rossi (Eds.), *Text and text processing* (pp. 77–103). North Holland: Elsevier.

Mahony, D. L., & Mann, V. A. (1992). Using children's humor to clarify the relationship between linguistic awareness and early reading ability. *Cognition, 45,* 163–186.

Neale, M. D. (1966). *The Neale Analysis of Reading Ability* (2nd ed.). London: Macmillan Education.

Oakhill, J., Yuill, N., & Donaldson, M. (1990). Understanding of 'because' in skilled and less-skilled text comprehenders. *British Journal of Developmental Psychology, 8,* 401–410.

Olson, D. R. (1994). *The world on paper: The conceptual and cognitive implications of writing and reading.* Cambridge, England: Cambridge University Press.

Paris, S. G., Cross, D. R., & Lipson, M. Y. (1984). Informed strategies for learning: A program to improve children's reading awareness and comprehension. *Journal of Educational Psychology, 76,* 1239–1252.

Paris, S. G., & Jacobs, J. E. (1984). The benefits of informed instruction for children's awareness and comprehension skills. *Child Development, 55,* 2083–2093.

Paris, S. G., & Myers, M. (1981). Comprehension monitoring, memory, and study strategies of good and poor readers. *Journal of Reading Behavior, 13,* 5–22.

Pratt, M. W., & Bates, K. R. (1982). Young editors: Preschoolers' evaluation and production of ambiguous messages. *Developmental Psychology, 18,* 30–42.

Rack, J. P., Hulme, C., & Snowling, M. J. (1993). Learning to read—a theoretical synthesis. *Advances in Child Development and Behavior, 24,* 99–132.

Stanovich, K. E. (1993). Does reading make you smarter? Literacy and the development of verbal intelligence. *Advances in Child Development and Behavior, 24,* 133–180.

Stanovich, K. E., & Cunningham, A. E. (1992). Studying the consequences of literacy within a literate society: The cognitive correlates of print exposure. *Memory and Cognition, 20,* 51–68.

Tunmer, W. E. (1989). The role of language-related factors in reading disability. In D. Shankweiler & I. Liberman (Eds.), *Phonology and reading disability: Solving the reading puzzle* (pp. 91–131). Ann Arbor: University of Michigan Press.

Tunmer, W. E., & Bowey, J. A. (1984). Metalinguistic awareness and reading acquisition. In W. E. Tunmer, C. Pratt, & M. L. Herriman (Eds.), *Metalinguistic awareness in children* (pp. 144–168). New York: Springer.

Tunmer, W. E., Herriman, M. L., & Nesdale, A. R. (1988). Metalinguistic ability and beginning reading. *Reading Research Quarterly, 23,* 134–158.

Yalisove, D. (1978). The effect of riddle structure on children's comprehension of riddles. *Developmental Psychology, 14,* 173–180.

Yuill, N., & Joscelyne, T. (1988). Effects of organizational cues and strategies on good and poor comprehenders' story understanding. *Journal of Educational Psychology, 80,* 152–158.

Yuill, N., & Oakhill, J. (1988). Effects of inference awareness training on poor reading comprehension. *Journal of Applied Cognitive Psychology, 2,* 33–45.

Yuill, N., & Oakhill, J. (1991). *Children's problems in text comprehension: An experimental investigation.* Cambridge, England: Cambridge University Press.

CHAPTER TEN

Metacognitive Monitoring in the Processing of Anaphoric Devices in Skilled and Less Skilled Comprehenders

Marie-France Ehrlich

EPHE, Université René Descartes, CNRS, Paris (France)

Following a cognitive approach, investigations of individual differences in reading comprehension show that less skilled readers are deficient in word processing and vocabulary knowledge, as well as in processing syntactic and textual structure (Carr, 1981; Perfetti, 1985). This group of less skilled readers, however, is heterogeneous. Some children, defined as less skilled comprehenders, show deficiencies in their comprehension of text but they are skilled decoders (Carr, Brown, Vavrus, & Evans, 1990; Pazzaglia, Cornoldi, & Tressoldi, 1993). These children have difficulties in processing anaphoric devices, in making inferences, in selecting main ideas, and in using story schemas. They also show a lower working-memory efficiency (see Yuill & Oakhill, 1991).

The main goal of this chapter is to examine the hypothesis that less skilled comprehenders suffer deficiencies in metacognitive monitoring. The historical roots of metacognition can be found in research on regulation mechanisms by Luria (1961) and Vygotsky (1962) and in the notion of "prise de conscience" developed by Piaget (1974). According to Flavell (1976), who coined the term,

> Metacognition refers to one's knowledge concerning one's own cognitive processes and products or anything related to them, e.g., the learning-relevant properties of information and data. For example, I am engaging in metacognition (metamemory, metalearning, metaattention, metalanguage, or whatever) if I notice that I am having more trouble learning *A* than *B*; If it strikes me

221

that I should double-check *C* before accepting it as a fact; . . . Such examples could be multiplied endlessly. In any kind of cognitive transaction with the human or nonhuman environment, a variety of information processing activities may go on. Metacognition refers, among other things, to the active monitoring and consequent regulation and orchestration of these processes in relation to the cognitive objects or data on which they bear, usually in the service of some concrete goal or objective. (p. 232)

Flavell (1981) proposed a model with four components; cognitive goals, cognitive actions, metacognitive knowledge, and metacognitive experiences. Metacognitive knowledge consists of long-term memory representations concerning cognitive functioning. This knowledge may be retrieved and used during a cognitive enterprise either automatically or deliberately. Metacognitive experiences are conscious experiences (ideas, thoughts, feelings) related to the progress of a cognitive enterprise. For example, to realize that you have not fully understood a passage of text that you just read is a metacognitive experience. It may lead to a revision of the cognitive action.

In the reading comprehension area, the metacognitive approach has been very popular because of its instructional implications (see Baker & Brown, 1984; Garner, 1987). Empirical studies have investigated two of the components of metacognition; metacognitive knowledge about reading comprehension processes and metacognitive monitoring of these processes. Concerning metacognitive knowledge, investigations have shown that younger and poorer readers have lower reading awareness than older and better readers. The former tend to consider reading as a decoding task whereas the latter view it as a meaning construction task (Cross & Paris, 1988; Myers & Paris, 1978; Paris & Myers, 1981). Reading awareness as well as word recognition skill emerge as significant predictors of reading comprehension in fifth-grade and seventh-grade children (Ehrlich, Kurtz-Costes, & Loridant, 1993; Ehrlich, Kurtz-Costes, Rémond, & Loridant, in press). These results should be interpreted cautiously. One problem concerns the reliability of what children assert that they know when questioned about their cognitive functioning. Because of limited language skills, a young child or even an adolescent or an adult may not always be able to express knowledge that he or she uses in natural conditions (Cavanaugh & Perlmutter, 1982).

As regards metacognitive monitoring of comprehension, many investigations have been published. Monitoring includes three steps; planning activities prior to reading, self-evaluation, and revision during reading. Self-evaluation of comprehension is viewed as playing an important role because it determines revision actions (Baker, 1989; Beal, 1990; Beal, Garrod, & Bonitatibus, 1990). Results have usually been interpreted as providing evidence that poor readers fail to successfully monitor their own understanding, in particular in the self-evaluation step (see Baker, 1989; Garner, 1987). However, these studies have raised some serious problems. At the theoretical level, the concept of metacognitive monitoring has not been firmly specified and the researchers have tended to report a wide variety of results under this term. Moreover, most studies have tended to ignore cognitive models of reading comprehension or have made only brief reference to them. The cognitive operations whereby monitoring might fail have not been clearly identified. At the methodological level, a frequently used paradigm to investigate self-evaluation has been error detection inspired by Markman's (1977, 1979) oral communication research. Detecting these errors is considered to indicate that the subject is evaluating his or her understanding in the course of reading. Performance on such a task has been shown to depend on age, reading ability, and the type of errors that are inserted in the text. In fact, researchers have used various kinds of errors that disrupt the meaning of the text to different degrees and in different ways. Baker (1984, 1985a) emphasized that evaluation is a multidimensional process requiring the use of a variety of standards or criteria against which to evaluate one's comprehension. Detecting nonsense words or difficult vocabulary items inserted in a text requires a lexical standard of evaluation; detecting information that violates prior knowledge requires a standard of external consistency, whereas detecting inconsistencies between several sentences in the text requires a standard of internal consistency. The use of these standards imposes different processing demands. Comparing fourth- and sixth-grade children differing in reading ability, Baker (1984) showed that the lexical standard was more likely to be adopted spontaneously than were the other two standards. It was the only standard used by a high proportion of both younger and poorer readers whereas older and better readers also used the other two standards. The age and reading ability variables interacted: The age-related improvement of the detection performance was observed only for the better readers. Moreover, specific instructions about the kinds of standards children should use led to a greater improvement for better readers. These data collected when children read brief expository texts showed that poor readers in elementary schools can evaluate their own comprehension to some extent, but tend to use different standards than better readers. Poor readers have marked difficulties in detecting errors that violate the internal consistency of the text.

Also using expository texts, similar main effects and interactions were observed in a further study dealing with the role of age, reading ability, type of errors and instructions in fourth, fifth, and sixth graders (Zabrucky & Moore, 1989). However reading ability did not interact with age or type of errors in Englert, Hiebert, and Stewart's (1988) study conducted with third and sixth graders. Some other data for older subjects, seventh to eighth graders (Garner, 1980) and college students (Baker, 1985b), corroborated the difference between good and poor readers in detecting errors in expository texts. These findings, and also results from elementary school children concerning the detection of errors violating text consistency in narrative texts, have tended to support the hypothesis that poor readers suffer deficiencies in comprehension monitoring (Reis & Spekman, 1983; Winograd & Johnston, 1982; Yuill & Oakhill, 1991).

However, most researchers have noted that error detection data require cautious interpretation. In a natural reading task, subjects follow Grice's (1975) maxim of relevance and assume that text is coherent. So searching and detecting errors is an unnatural task in which subjects have to forsake this maxim. In such a task, performance is very dependent on instructions, reading purpose, and the number of errors inserted in text. Even skilled, mature readers show low rates of error detection in particular conditions. Detection depends on the implicit standards the subject adopts for "what makes sense"; it also depends on inferences spontaneously constructed by the subject to establish text coherence. Additionally, young children can be hesitant to notice errors in a text coming from an adult. Another issue is the procedure used to measure error detection. In some investigations, children were asked to indicate any problem they detected by underlining words, clauses, or sentences in the text. Other times, children were asked to answer questions such as "did the passage make sense?" or to rate the comprehensibility of consistent or inconsistent passages in a text as easy or difficult to understand. Different ratings for consistent and inconsistent passages are interpreted as reflecting comprehension monitoring. These distinct methods may involve different metacognitive and metalinguistic demands, which tap different components of self-evaluation.

In some studies, several measures were collected in the error detection task (e.g., Zabrucky & Moore, 1989), sometimes in association with cognitive measures such as reading times or responses to comprehension questions collected after reading (Yuill & Oakhill, 1991). These studies showed that different measures are more or less sensitive and are not interrelated in a simple way. Nevertheless they provided interesting data that help to specify the characteristics of comprehension monitoring in good and poor readers.

Another method used to investigate the evaluation of one's own level of comprehension was developed by Glenberg and Epstein (1985, 1987) with adult readers. These authors were interested in the "calibration of comprehension," a notion coming from the feeling of knowing literature. Calibration of comprehension refers to the accuracy of self-evaluation in comparison with an objective test of comprehension. More specifically, subjects were asked to rate confidence in knowledge gained from reading an expository text and then they were asked to answer verification items. Texts were intact and did not incorporate any inconsistencies. For example, subjects read a 200-word text about "Viruses," then they rated with a 6-point scale their confidence in their ability to draw correct inferences from this text before they answered inference verification items. Calibration was measured by the correlation between the confidence ratings and performance on the verification test.

In the above mentioned studies, mean confidence ratings were rather high (e.g., $M = 4.45$ with a maximum value $= 6$) and did not correlate with objective performance (the mean of $r_{pb} = .07$). In other words, self-evaluation of one's own comprehension was inaccurate (i.e., calibration was poor). A surprising result concerned the role of domain knowledge on calibration of comprehension. Two groups of subjects with prior knowledge in physics or music read texts in both domains. Mean confidence ratings increased with domain knowledge but a negative relationship was observed between domain knowledge and calibration in this domain. In other words, subjects were more inaccurate when evaluating their own comprehension in their own domain. The authors suggested that subjects based their confidence ratings on their self-classification as expert or nonexpert in the domain of the text rather than on an assessment of the degree to which they had understood the text. Further experiments corroborated this interpretation: Domain familiarity ratings were correlated with confidence ratings suggesting that familiarity with the general domain of a text tended to control confidence ratings (Glenberg, Sanocki, Epstein, & Morris, 1987). Results showing poor calibration due to overconfidence in adult readers have been replicated under the same conditions as Glenberg et al.'s experiments. However, several factors can improve calibration such as presentation of examples and questions embedded in the text, encouraging self-testing (Walczyk & Hall, 1989), depth of text processing (Maki, Foley, Kajer, Thompson, & Willert, 1990), number of comprehension items per text (Weaver, 1990), and level of performance on the comprehension test, better subjects predicting their performance more accurately than poorer subjects (Maki & Berry, 1984). The question of domain familiarity as the basis of confidence ratings has been reexamined. Data from Morris (1990) using correlations and multiple regression analysis on confidence ratings, familiarity ratings, and recall test performance showed a weak influence of domain familiarity with an effect of availability of information in memory on both confidence ratings and test performance. Data from Maki and Serra (1992), analyzing several measures collected before and after reading, showed that subjects make accurate predictions about their performance. Before reading, test predictions were based on general domain familiarity rated by subjects themselves; after reading, the role of this variable declined and predictions were mainly based on specific information extracted from reading texts.

In the studies conducted along Glenberg's line, subjects were asked to rate confidence in knowledge gained from reading expository texts and actual performance was tested by means of various tests (verification items, multiple choice questions, recognition, or recall). Therefore, such studies were focused on learning from text more than on comprehension. On this point, Maki and her colleagues' studies provided interesting data. Two distinct measures were collected; subjects rated "how well they thought they would do" on the future test or "how easy the text was to comprehend." Actual performance was tested by multiple choice questions. Results showed that test predictions and judgments of text comprehensibility shared some common underlying basis, but test predictions were better predictors of test performance than were text comprehensibility ratings. The extent to which the multiple choice questions tested actual text comprehension remained unclear. In fact, this set of studies carried out on adult readers was developed within a framework that differed from research on metacognitive monitoring in reading comprehension. The role of reading ability has not been examined. In my view, confidence ratings and judgments of text comprehensibility (also used by Garner, 1980) are based on metacognitive experiences assumed in Flavell's (1981) model. Such ratings can be viewed as explicit indicators of the self-evaluation of comprehension (see Baker, 1989, for a similar position).

The goal of the two experiments reported below was to investigate the self-evaluation of comprehension in the course of reading in skilled and less skilled comprehenders matched on word recognition skill. Junior high-school children (ninth grade in Experiment 1 and seventh grade in Experiment 2) were selected, a population on which few data have been previously collected.[1] Given the methodological problems raised by the self-evaluation of comprehension, two different tasks were used. One task provided an indirect measure of self-evaluation based on the inconsistency detection paradigm. Another task provided a more direct measure of self-evaluation of a child's own comprehension inspired by Glenberg's paradigm. In order to link metacognitive monitoring to specific psycholinguistic processes involved in text comprehension, the present experiments focused on the processing of anaphoric devices.

Anaphoric devices are linguistic markers that maintain cohesion within and between sentences. Anaphoric markers refer to a part of the text that usually precedes them—the antecedent—and ensure the referential continuity of text (cf. Halliday & Hasan, 1976). It is clear that the processing of such anaphoric markers, which involves searching for and identifying their correct antecedents, is an important step in building a coherent representation of the text's content. Several classes of anaphoric markers can be distinguished. Among them, definite noun phrases and pronouns are frequently used. For example, in the sentences "*Mother saw the postman coming from a distance. The postman brought a letter from Uncle Charles who lives in Canada*", *the postman* is a repeated definite noun phrase, that is, an anaphor that merely requires matching two identical labels. The postman

---

[1] These experiments are part of a larger project that also included elementary school children from third grade to fifth grade (Ehrlich, 1993; Ehrlich, Rémond, & Tardieu, 1993).

can be replaced by "*The man*," a more general term or by "*He*," a personal pronoun (cf. Tyler, 1983).

Processing requires operations of differential complexity depending on either the relationship between the meanings of the anaphoric noun phrase and the antecedent, or on the syntactic matching (based on gender and number cues) between the pronoun and the potential antecedents. Other factors, such as the role of the antecedent with regard to the theme of the text and the distance between a marker and its antecedent, also contribute to the difficulty of processing. Indeed, the main factor to be considered in the processing of anaphoric devices is the relative accessibility of potential antecedents in the discourse representation built during the course of reading. Usually, this accessibility will lead to an automatic identification of a unique antecedent. In some other conditions, this automatic process will fail and the interpretation will remain incomplete if the subject does not use some strategic process (Dell, McKoon, & Ratcliff, 1983; Garrod & Sanford, 1982, 1983, 1985; Greene, McKoon, & Ratcliff, 1992).

In young children, investigations contrasting skilled and less skilled comprehenders (8- and 9-year-olds) have tended to show that less skilled children have difficulties in processing anaphoric devices, especially pronouns (Ehrlich, Rémond, & Tardieu, 1993; Oakhill & Yuill, 1986; Yuill & Oakhill, 1988). Moreover, less skilled children make inappropriate use of anaphoric ties in their written productions (Cox, Shanahan, & Sulzby, 1990). The interpretation given by the researchers suggests that deficiencies in metacognitive monitoring could contribute to the inadequate processing of anaphoric devices shown by less skilled comprehenders.

The two experiments reported below examine the extent to which processing of anaphoric devices involves self-evaluation of comprehension processes in skilled and less skilled comprehenders. Subjects read two series of expository texts about Canada and China containing three critical anaphoric devices. Monitoring was investigated using two tasks. The first one was derived from Glenberg's paradigm. In each text, the three critical anaphoric devices were either repeated noun phrases or pronouns. Subjects had to read and evaluate their own comprehension on a 6-point scale from (1) *I understood very poorly* to (6) *I understood very well*. After reading, subjects answered multiple-choice questions designed to test the processing of anaphoric devices. The second task was based on the inconsistency detection paradigm. The three critical anaphoric devices in each text were either consistent or inconsistent. Subjects had to read and detect inconsistencies. After reading, subjects answered three multiple-choice questions designed to test the resolution of the inconsistencies. The first experiment was conducted on ninth-grade children. The second experiment used seventh-grade children in order to investigate the role of the prereading level of domain-specific knowledge.

EXPERIMENT 1

Method

Subjects. Skilled and less skilled comprehenders were selected from a pool containing 100 ninth-grade children from a junior high school in the suburbs of Paris, France. In a first session, children were given three tests; reading comprehension, word recognition, and a questionnaire composed of 24 multiple-choice questions (M.C.Q.). Reading comprehension was assessed with the standardized French "Test de Lecture Silencieuse" (Aubret & Blanchard, 1991). This test includes three forms of increasing difficulty for children at each age level. Each form consists of a single page, with three texts printed on the page, and five questions immediately after each text. The questions are specific fill-in-the-blank questions. The texts remain available when subjects answer the questions. Time given to complete each form is limited to 12 minutes. Scoring gives one point for each correct response. Thus, the maximum possible score for each form was 15. Children completed form H, which was of intermediate difficulty for their age level.

Word recognition was assessed with a French reading measure, "La Pipe et le Rat" (Lefavrais, 1986). This test contains 486 nouns, 243 of which are the names of animals. The words are printed in rows of six across three pages. Children are given 3 minutes to read the words in sequence and underline all the animal names. The score for this measure is the total number of animal names underlined minus the number of words (i.e., nonanimal names) incorrectly underlined.

The third test aimed at assessing the prereading level of domain-specific knowledge when answering comprehension questions on experimental texts. This prereading test was a necessary control, given that the experimental texts were expository and contained domain-specific knowledge. Children completed 24 multiple-choice questions identical to the questions assessing comprehension after reading the experimental texts.

From the distribution of reading comprehension scores, the lowest 30% and the highest 30% of the children were selected. From these children, two groups were formed contrasting comprehension performance with the same average level in word recognition and prereading M.C.Q. performance. The less skilled comprehenders included 21 children (9 male and 12 female) with a mean age of 15 years (SD = 8 months); the skilled comprehenders included 19 children (8 male and 11 female) with a mean age of 14 years 8 months (SD = 5 months). The mean scores and standard deviations on the three tests for the two groups are displayed in Table 10.1. The two groups were significantly different on reading comprehension, $t(38) = 16.52$, $p < .001$, but they were equivalent on word recognition and prereading M.C.Q. (t values < 1).

TABLE 10.1
Mean Scores and Standard Deviations for Reading Comprehension,
Word Recognition, and Prereading M.C.Q. in Ninth-Grade Skilled
and Less Skilled Comprehenders

	Reading Comprehension (Max = 15)	Word Recognition	Prereading M.C.Q. (Max = 24)
Less skilled	7.57	69.48	11.33
$n = 21$	(1.32)	(15.65)	(2.29)
Skilled	13.16	74.16	11.79
$n = 19$	(0.69)	(16.54)	(2.42)

Materials. The materials consisted of eight expository texts, two series of four texts about Canada and China (agriculture, industry, transportation, etc.). The mean number of words per passage was 93 (range 85–111). Each text was composed of three sequences of two sentences. In each sequence, the second sentence began with a subject anaphor for which the antecedent was the noun phrase subject of the first sentence. For each of the eight texts, three versions were constructed with different subject anaphors. In the *nominal version*, the three anaphoric devices were the repetitions of the noun phrases preceded by demonstrative determinants. In the *pronominal version*, the three anaphoric devices were pronouns. On the basis of gender and number cues, each pronoun had two potential antecedents. In the *inconsistent nominal version*, the three anaphoric nouns were replaced by nouns whose meaning tended to be contrary (richness/poverty). These inconsistent nouns were preceded by demonstratives. Thus, the continuity of the two sentences of the sequence was disrupted, although the second sentence itself was consistent. By contrast with this inconsistent nominal version, the nominal version could be named a *consistent nominal version* when used in the detection task. An example of a text with its three versions is shown in Appendix 1.

For each text, three multiple-choice questions designed to test the processing of anaphoric devices were prepared with five possible responses; the correct antecedent, the incorrect antecedent with the same gender and number cues, the inconsistent noun, and two other plausible responses.

Procedure. The second session of the experiment took place 3 weeks after the first one. Children were tested in small groups and the same two experimenters tested all children. Each child received a booklet with which he or she could carry out the two tasks. First, subjects completed the direct self-evaluation task with two different consistent texts, one in a nominal version and the other in a pronominal version. Then they completed the inconsistency detection task with two other texts, one in a consistent nominal version and the other in an inconsistent nominal version. This procedure, applying the same order (self-evaluation before detection task) was repeated with different texts in order to get more observations. Therefore, a trial factor with 2 levels could be examined. In the course of experiment, each subject saw the eight texts; two in their consistent nominal versions and two in their pronominal versions under the self-evaluation task, two in their consistent nominal versions and two in their inconsistent versions under the detection task.

For the direct self-evaluation task, the booklet included three pages for each text. The first page displayed one whole text in a nominal or pronominal version, preceded by a title and double spaced without any paragraphs. The second page displayed the same text segmented into three sequences of two sentences. Below each sequence, a 6-point scale was printed from 1 (I understood very poorly) to 6 (I understood very well). The third page contained the three multiple-choice questions designed to test the processing of anaphoric devices in the previous text. Instructions were given orally by one of the experimenters. The instructions informed children about the three steps of the task. First, reading a text carefully in order to understand it, for a time limited to 60 seconds. Second, reading the same text again segmented into three parts and below each part indicating "the extent to which you think you understood the text" by circling one of the marks on a 6-point scale corresponding to increasing levels of understanding. Children were told not to be reticent in indicating a low level of understanding. For this second step, the time allowed was also 60 seconds. Instructions also described the third step, answering three questions concerning the preceding text by circling one of the five presented responses. Children could not reread the text and they had 60 seconds again. Subjects were also told that the questions were identical to those displayed in the first session several weeks earlier, but that they would be easier to answer after reading the text. The experimenter indicated orally the moment when the child had to turn the page of the booklet (every 60 seconds).

For the inconsistency detection task, the basic procedure was the same as the direct self-evaluation task. The booklet included three pages displaying one whole text in consistent nominal or inconsistent nominal version, the same text segmented into three sequences of two sentences, and the three corresponding multiple-choice questions. Subjects were told that they would be reading texts dealing with Canada or China as before, but some of the texts contained errors that made them incoherent. They were informed about the three steps of the task. First, they were told to read the text carefully in order to understand it. Second, they were asked to read the same text again, segmented into three parts, and attempt to detect errors. The instruction was as follows: "In each part, if you detect some errors, that is a word or a group of words that does not fit with the text, you underline it and you indicate the other word in the text with which it is inconsistent by the means of an arrow." An example of an inconsistent sequence was provided and the experimenter showed the way to give a correct detection. Instructions also described the third step concerning the three multiple-choice questions. The instructions specified that children should answer these questions by taking into account the corrections made by themselves in the case of error detection. The timing was the same as in the self-evaluation task, 60 seconds for each page.

Design. In each task, three factors were manipulated. The reading comprehension level (skilled vs. less skilled comprehenders) was a between-subjects factor. The text version (nominal vs. pronominal version in the self-evaluation task, consistent nominal vs. inconsistent nominal in the detection task) and the trial number (first vs. second) were within-subjects factors. For skilled and less skilled comprehenders, the eight experimental conditions obtained by crossing text version, trial number, and task were crossed with the eight different texts. Thus, each subject read one text in each of the eight experimental conditions and each text was presented in each of these conditions across subjects. Sixteen orders of presentation were prepared such that one trial was concerned either with texts on China or texts on Canada and for each trial, each task was carried out with the two versions in different orders, the self-evaluation task always coming before the detection task. Finally, the position of the correct response in the multiple-choice questions was randomized.

Results

Task 1: Reading and Self-Evaluation of Comprehension. The texts read in this task were all consistent texts, in nominal and pronominal versions. The mean ratings for the self-evaluation of comprehension, and the mean percentages of correct responses on M.C.Q. measuring actual comprehension are shown in Table 10.2. The data were analyzed in a 2 (comprehension skill)

TABLE 10.2
Mean Ratings for the Self-Evaluation of Comprehension and
Mean Percentages of Correct Responses on M.C.Q. as a
Function of Text Version for Skilled and Less Skilled Comprehenders

| | Self-eval. of Comp. | | Actual Comp. | |
	Nom. vs.	Pron. Vers.	Nom. vs.	Pron. Vers.
Less skilled gr. n = 21	5.27	5.28	79.4%	75.4%
Skilled gr. n = 19	5.42	5.38	88.6%	81.6%

× 2 (text version) × 2 (trial) × 3 (sequence of the text) ANOVA. For analyzing correct responses on M.C.Q., the number of correct responses on the prereading test was used as a covariate.

Self-evaluation of comprehension did not vary as a function of either comprehension skill or of text version. Most subjects asserted that they had understood well or very well. Self-evaluation did not vary as a function of trials, but it tended to decrease from the first to the third sequence of the text (Ms = 5.50, 5.30, 5.15 respectively), $F(2, 76) = 18$, $p < .0005$. Subjects asserted that they had understood the final sequence of the text less well than the first one. This decrease appeared for skilled and less skilled subjects and for nominal and pronominal versions. There were no significant interactions between the factors.

Actual comprehension, measured by the percentage of correct responses on M.C.Q. that tested the processing of anaphoric devices, was lower for less skilled than for skilled comprehenders, 77% versus 85%; $F(1, 38) = 3.99$, $p = .05$. For both groups, comprehension varied as a function of text version, $F(1, 38) = 4.15$, $p < .05$; it was lower in pronominal version than in nominal version, 78% versus 84%, revealing that the resolution of anaphoric pronouns was sometimes incomplete. The interaction between comprehension skill and text version was not significant showing that the difficulties in pronoun resolution appeared both in skilled and less skilled comprehenders. Neither the main effects nor the interactions concerning the trial and the sequence factors was significant.

Thus, the two factors that affected actual comprehension did not affect self-evaluation of comprehension. Skilled and less skilled comprehenders showed lower comprehension scores in pronominal versions although they evaluated their own understanding to be the same level in pronominal and nominal versions. Both groups seemed unaware of the difficulties of the pronouns and they did not process them in a complete way. Moreover, the less skilled comprehenders showed lower comprehension scores than the skilled comprehenders, although both groups provided similar evaluations. This result reveals that less skilled comprehenders were not aware of their deficiencies and they tended to overestimate their own understanding relative to the skilled group.

In calibration of comprehension studies, the relationship between subject predictions and actual performance has usually been examined by computing the Goodman-Kruskal Gamma correlation (Nelson, 1984). However, the prerequisite to compute Gamma was not fulfilled in the present experiment because many subjects never asserted that they understood the text poorly.

The relationship between self-evaluation and actual comprehension was thus examined by computing the percentage of correct responses in M.C.Q. associated with each level of the evaluation scale for each group. Data from the three sequences in pronominal and nominal versions and from all subjects were grouped together for this computation. Given the very low number of observations for the negative evaluations (1, 2, and 3 levels), the percentages were computed only for the positive evaluations of "I understood quite well" (4), "well" (5), and "very well" (6). For the less skilled comprehenders, the mean percentages of correct responses were 62.9%, 75.5%, and 84.2% for the fourth, fifth, and sixth levels respectively. For the skilled comprehenders, the mean percentages were 78.3%, 81.2%, and 90.1%. Thus, for both groups, the correct responses increased as a function of self-evaluation. These variations were stronger for the less skilled comprehenders. This result provides evidence that the feeling of understanding for the less skilled children was modulated in agreement with their actual comprehension. It also shows that, compared to skilled comprehenders, these children tended to overestimate their own understanding. For the same level of self-evaluation, their percentage of correct responses was lower than the percentage observed in the skilled.

Task 2: Reading and Detection of Inconsistencies. An inconsistent noun anaphor was considered as correctly detected when it was underlined and connected to the antecedent. The mean percentages of correct detections and the mean percentages of correct responses on M.C.Q. measuring actual comprehension are shown in Table 10.3. Detection data were analyzed in a 2 (comprehension skill) × 2 (trial) × 3 (sequence) ANOVA. For correct responses on M.C.Q., the text version factor was also considered and data were analyzed in the same way as for the first task.

Detection of inconsistencies was poor in both groups, in agreement with other studies. Detection tended to be lower for less skilled comprehenders than for skilled comprehenders, $F(1, 38) = 3.95$, $p < .06$. Detection did not vary as a function of trials, but it tended to decrease from the first to the third sequence of the text (34%, 26%, 15% respectively), $F(2, 76) = 6.07$, p

TABLE 10.3
Mean Percentages of Detection of Inconsistencies and
Mean Percentages of Correct Responses on M.C.Q. as a Function
of Text Version for Skilled and Less Skilled Comprehenders

	Detec. of Incon.		Actual Comp.	
	Consistent Nom. Vers.	Inconsistent Nom. Vers.	Consistent Nom. Vers.	Inconsistent Nom. Vers.
Less skilled gr. n = 21	[0%]	17.5%	80%	56.3%
Skilled gr. n = 19	[0%]	33.3%	87.7%	65.8%

< .005. Such variation from the beginning to the end of the text appeared in both skilled and less skilled comprehenders. There were no significant interactions between the factors.

Actual comprehension, measured by the percentage of correct responses on M.C.Q. that tested the processing of anaphors, was lower for less skilled than for skilled comprehenders (68% vs. 77%), $F(1, 38) = 4.37$, $p < .05$. It also was much lower for the inconsistent version than for the consistent version (61% vs. 84%), $F(1, 38) = 38.64$, $p < .0001$. The comparison between scores in consistent and inconsistent versions was not very interesting. The interesting points were the interaction between text version and comprehension skill, and the examination of the relationship between detection of inconsistencies and correct responses on M.C.Q. in inconsistent versions. The interaction between text version and comprehension skill was not significant, indicating that the negative effect due to inconsistencies was similar for both skilled and less skilled comprehenders. It is interesting to note that for both groups, comprehension performance on the consistent version that had been read with the purpose of detecting inconsistencies was very similar to the comprehension performance in the same version read for the self-evaluation of comprehension task. Also, performance on M.C.Q. did not vary as a function of trials, but decreased from the first to the third sequence of the text (80%, 71%, 66%), $F(2, 76) = 3.59$, $p < .05$. Such decrements appeared both in skilled and less skilled comprehenders. There were no significant interactions between the factors.

A close examination of the responses on M.C.Q. provided information about the actions subjects took when they detected problems. It also provided information about possible revisions made without any explicit detection. The responses were analyzed depending on whether or not the inconsistency had been previously detected. Three categories of responses were distinguished; correct responses corresponded to the correct antecedents, choices of inconsistent nouns, and other responses. In the case of correct detections, the percentage of correct responses was fairly high (77%) in less skilled comprehenders but lower than in skilled comprehenders (89%). The less skilled chose the inconsistent noun 9% and made other responses 14%. For the skilled subjects the corresponding percentages were 0% and 11%. Thus, the less skilled comprehenders had more difficulties detecting the inconsistencies in the texts. Moreover, they had more difficulties than skilled comprehenders in engaging in revision actions to solve inconsistencies even when they were correctly detected.

In the case of failures to detect the inconsistencies, the percentage of correct responses was 52% for less skilled comprehenders and 55% for skilled comprehenders. These scores were near the prereading score (48%). The percentages of inconsistent nouns and other responses were 26% and 22% for less skilled comprehenders, and 33% and 12% for skilled comprehenders.

Thus, neither the less skilled nor the skilled provided evidence of spontaneous revision in the absence of explicit detection of the inconsistency.

Discussion

Results from the two tasks were convergent. They clearly indicate that the processing of anaphoric devices was not submitted to efficient metacognitive monitoring. Such a conclusion can be made for both less skilled comprehenders and skilled comprehenders. Particularly noteworthy is the lack of interaction between comprehension skill and the factors that affected or did not affect the dependent variables concerning metacognitive monitoring. Thus, in the first task, the text version and the trial factors did not affect the self-evaluation of comprehension either in the skilled or the less skilled group; the sequence factor affected self-evaluation similarly in both groups. In the second task, the trial factor did not affect the detection of inconsistencies in either the skilled or the less skilled group whereas the sequence factor affected it similarly in both groups. This pattern of no interaction shows that the same underlying variables were involved in metacognitive monitoring for skilled and less skilled comprehenders. However, deficiencies in monitoring appeared to be more important for less skilled comprehenders. Their feeling of understanding was modulated in accordance with their actual comprehension, but it tended to be overestimated; less skilled comprehenders could detect only a few inconsistencies in the text and they had difficulties solving them.

How can we account for these results? One hypothesis is that an important factor in metacognitive monitoring is the difficulty of the task, as it is perceived by the subject. According to Flavell (1987), monitoring is not carried out if the task is too easy or too difficult. In reading comprehension, building a coherent mental representation of an expository text is dependent on domain-specific knowledge. For readers with high knowledge in a particular domain, the comprehension of a text dealing with information in this domain seems to be an easy task and, therefore, they do not engage efficient monitoring. Such an interpretation can account for Glenberg and Epstein's (1987) data which showed that subjects are inaccurate when they evaluate their own comprehension in their own domain. In the present experiment, subjects were ninth-grade children. The materials were rather short expository texts with sentences having a simple syntactic structure. They dealt with topics concerning Canada and China about which children already had prior information. This familiarity with the text domains was shown in the pre-reading level when answering comprehension questions: Children showed 48% correct responses although chance predicted only 20%. Subjects probably felt the texts were easy to understand and did not engage efficient metacognitive monitoring.

A second experiment, aimed at examining the role played by the pre-reading level of domain-specific knowledge, used the same materials and procedures as the first experiment; younger children (seventh graders) served as subjects. It was assumed that these children would have a lower level of knowledge than older ones and would tend to engage efficient control of their own comprehension.

EXPERIMENT 2

Method

Subjects. Subjects were selected on the same basis as in the first experiment, from a pool of 141 seventh-grade children, attending the same junior high school. In a first session, reading comprehension was assessed with form F of the "Test de Lecture Silencieuse," which was of intermediate difficulty for their age level. Word recognition was assessed with the same test as in the first experiment, but children were informed of the 3-minute time limit before testing. Children also answered the 24 M.C.Q. assessing their prereading level on comprehension questions. From the children within the lowest 33% and the highest 33% in the reading comprehension distribution, two groups were formed with the same average level in word recognition and prereading M.C.Q. performance. The two groups included 24 children each.[2] The mean age of the less skilled comprehenders was 13 years 1 month ($SD = 9$ months, 12 were male and 12 were female). The mean age of the skilled comprehenders was 12 years 8 months ($SD = 8$ months, 17 were male and 7 were female). The mean scores and standard deviations for the three tests in the two groups are displayed in Table 10.4. The two groups were very different on reading comprehension, $t(46) = 20.75$, $p < .0005$ but they were equivalent on word recognition and prereading domain-specific knowledge. This prereading score was about 35%, lower than in ninth graders (48%). Thus, the familiarity with the text domains was lower for the children participating in the second experiment.

Materials, Procedure, and Design. The second session of the experiment took place 3 weeks after the first one. The materials, procedure, and design were identical to those in the first experiment.

_____

[2]The whole sample in this second experiment was larger than the sample in the first one (141 vs. 100 subjects), but the number of subjects selected on the basis of word recognition test and prereading level of knowledge was only slightly higher (24 vs. 21 and 19 subjects). This circumstance was due to the large dispersion of prereading knowledge scores in the second experiment which led us to eliminate more subjects than in the first experiment in order to get two groups equivalent on prior knowledge.

TABLE 10.4
Mean Scores and Standard Deviations for Reading
Comprehension, Word Recognition, and Prereading M.C.Q.
in Seventh-Grade Skilled and Less Skilled Comprehenders

	Reading Comprehension (Max = 15)	Word Recognition	Prereading M.C.Q. (Max = 24)
Less skilled gr. n = 24	3.87 (0.68)	79.33 (10.73)	8.08 (1.32)
Skilled gr. n = 24	10.50 (1.41)	84.04 (10.73)	8.92 (1.69)

Results

Task 1: Reading and Self-Evaluation of Comprehension. The mean
ratings for self-evaluation of comprehension and the mean percentages of
correct responses on M.C.Q. are shown in Table 10.5. Self-evaluation tended
to be lower in this second experiment than in the first one, but the difference
was only marginally significant, $F(1, 84) = 3.22, p = .08$. Actual comprehension
was similar in both experiments when prereading score was considered as a
covariate. However, it is well known that comparisons across experiments are
problematic. What is interesting is to examine the pattern of main effects and
interactions in the two experiments.

Self-evaluation of comprehension varied as a function of comprehension
skill and as a function of text version. Less skilled comprehenders reported
understanding less well ($M = 4.87$) than skilled comprehenders ($M = 5.36$),
$F(1, 46) = 7.10, p < .01$. For both groups, children asserted that they had
understood the pronominal version better than the nominal version ($Ms = 5.23$,
5.00), $F(1, 46) = 5.91, p < .025$. The interaction between comprehension skill
and text version was not significant. The main effects of trial and sequence

TABLE 10.5
Mean Ratings for the Self-Evaluation of Comprehension and
Mean Percentages of Correct Responses on M.C.Q. as a
Function of Text Version for Skilled and Less Skilled Comprehenders

	Self-eval. of Comp.		Actual Comp.	
	Nom. vs.	Pron. Vers.	Nom. vs.	Pron. Vers.
Less skilled gr. n = 24	4.76	4.99	64.6%	66.7%
Skilled gr. n = 24	5.26	5.48	78.5%	79.2%

factors were also not significant. However, the interaction between comprehension skill and trial was significant, $F(1, 46) = 4.13$, $p < .05$: Self-evaluation was stable from the first to the second trial in less skilled comprehenders ($Ms = 4.93, 4.82$), whereas it tended to increase in skilled comprehenders ($Ms = 5.28, 5.45$). Also the three-way interaction between comprehension skill, trial, and text version was significant, $F(1, 46) = 6.74$, $p < .025$: In less skilled comprehenders, self-evaluation was higher in the pronominal version than in the nominal one only on the second trial ($Ms = 4.91$ vs. 4.94 in trial 1, 5.06 vs. 4.58 in trial 2) but in skilled comprehenders, self-evaluation was higher in the pronominal version on the first trial ($Ms = 5.46$ vs. 5.11) and reached a similar level on the second trial ($Ms = 5.49$ vs. 5.40). This result suggests that less skilled comprehenders modulated the evaluation of their own understanding as a function of text version later than the skilled comprehenders. The pronominal version was rated as better understood than the nominal one. Such a result indicates that the basis for this evaluation probably involves several variables in a complex way.

Actual comprehension was lower for less skilled than for skilled comprehenders, (66% vs. 79%) $F(1, 46) = 9.96$, $p < .005$, but no difference was observed between nominal and pronominal versions. The main effects of trial and sequence factors were not significant. There were no significant interactions between the factors.

Thus, it seems that all children, both skilled and less skilled comprehenders, devoted more effort to process the anaphoric pronouns. This enabled them to achieve similar comprehension performance in both nominal and pronominal versions. The self-evaluation would be based on both the amount of effort devoted to understanding and the final comprehension level. Moreover, the evaluations provided by the less skilled group were lower than those provided by the skilled group, in accordance with their actual comprehension. So, less skilled comprehenders were aware of their difficulties in understanding texts.

The relationship between self-evaluation and actual comprehension was analyzed in the same way as in the first experiment. For less skilled comprehenders, the percentages of correct responses increased as a function of self-evaluation; 54.5%, 61.6%, 67.4%, and 69.9% for the third, fourth, fifth, and sixth levels respectively. Skilled comprehenders used level 3 just a few times and the percentage of correct responses was not computed; the percentages for levels 4, 5, and 6 were 80.5%, 73.1%, and 81.6%. In less skilled comprehenders, self-evaluation was modulated in concordance with actual comprehension. However, compared to skilled comprehenders, they tended to overestimate their own understanding.

Task 2: Reading and Detection of Inconsistencies. The same rules as in the first experiment were used to compute correct detections. The mean percentages of correct detections and the mean percentages of correct responses on M.C.Q. are shown in Table 10.6. Detection of inconsistencies

TABLE 10.6

Mean Percentages of Detection of Inconsistencies and Mean Percentages
of Correct Responses on M.C.Q. as a Function of Text Version
for Skilled and Less Skilled Comprehenders

	Detec. of Incon.		Actual Comp.	
	Consistent Nom. Vers.	Inconsistent Nom. Vers.	Consistent Nom. Vers.	Inconsistent Nom. Vers.
Less skilled gr. $n = 24$	[9.1%]	24.3%	70.8%	47.9%
Skilled gr. $n = 24$	[8.3%]	40.3%	86.8%	66%

and actual comprehension reached the same values as in the first experiment.
Data were analyzed in the same way as in the first experiment.

Detection of inconsistencies was lower for less skilled comprehenders
than for skilled comprehenders, $F(1, 46) = 7.48$, $p < .01$. Detection did not
vary as a function of trials, but it decreased from the first to the third sequence
of the text ($Ms = 45\%$, 36%, 15% respectively), $F(2, 92) = 12.61$, $p < .0005$.
Such decrements appeared both in skilled and less skilled comprehenders.
No interaction between the factors was significant. These results concerned
the correct detections made in the inconsistent nominal version. However,
in these inconsistent texts, children sometimes underlined words that were
not inconsistent. These false detections appeared in less skilled (10%) and
skilled comprehenders (9%). Moreover, both groups made false detections
in the consistent version; 9% for less skilled and 8% for skilled comprehenders. Such false detections did not appear in the first experiment. They illustrate how difficult it is to specify an inconsistency.

Actual comprehension measured by the percentage of correct responses
on M.C.Q. was lower for less skilled (59%) than for skilled comprehenders
(76%), $F(1, 46) = 12.70$, $p < .001$. Comprehension was also lower for the
inconsistent version (57%) than for the consistent version (79%), $F(1, 46) =
11.95$, $p < .001$. The interaction between comprehension skill and text version
was not significant, showing that the negative effect due to inconsistencies
was similar for both skilled and less skilled comprehenders. The main effects
of and interactions with trial and sequence factors were not significant. In both
groups, comprehension performance in consistent versions read for the
purpose of detecting inconsistencies tended to be better than the comprehension performance when subjects read for the self-evaluation task.

To examine the relationship between detection of inconsistencies and
actual comprehension, the responses on the M.C.Q. were analyzed in the
same way as in the first experiment, depending on whether or not the
inconsistency had been previously detected. In the case of correct detections,

the percentage of correct responses was fairly high for less skilled comprehenders (71%) but lower than for skilled comprehenders (79%). The less
skilled subjects chose the inconsistent noun in 11% of the cases and other
responses in 17% of the cases. For the skilled subjects, the percentages were
7% for the inconsistent noun and 14% for the other responses. Thus, the
less skilled subjects had more difficulties detecting inconsistencies and solving the inconsistencies that they correctly detected.

In the case of no detection of the inconsistency, the percentage of correct
responses was 40% for less skilled subjects, which is only slightly higher
than the prereading score (35%). The percentage was much higher in the
skilled comprehenders (57%). The percentages of inconsistent responses
and other responses were 30% and 29% in less skilled comprehenders, and
26% and 17% in skilled comprehenders. These results show that some revision was conducted by the skilled children even in the absence of an
explicit detection of the inconsistency.

Discussion

This second experiment allowed the investigation of the role of the prereading level of domain-specific knowledge. In seventh-grade children, the
prereading score was 35%, which is lower than in ninth graders (48%).
Results were different as in the first experiment. Data from both skilled and
less skilled comprehenders tend to show that processing of anaphoric devices involved metacognitive monitoring.

In the first task, when asked to evaluate their own comprehension, both
skilled and less skilled comprehenders paid attention to pronouns, modulated
their evaluations as a function of anaphoric devices, and showed similar
comprehension performance for nominal and pronominal versions. Less
skilled comprehenders asserted that they understood less well than skilled
comprehenders, in agreement with their actual comprehension. Thus, less
skilled comprehenders seemed aware of their difficulties. However, the
examination of the relationship between self-evaluation and actual comprehension showed that compared to skilled comprehenders, less skilled subjects
tended to overestimate their own understanding. Additionally, the three-way
interaction between comprehension skill, trial, and text version showed that
less skilled comprehenders modulated their evaluation of their own understanding as a function of text version only in the second trial, whereas this
modulation appeared even on the first trial in skilled comprehenders.

In the second task, when subjects were asked to detect inconsistencies in
the texts, findings were similar to those observed in the first experiment: Less
skilled comprehenders showed lower detection performance than skilled
comprehenders and no interaction was observed between comprehension
skill and trial and sequence factors. Less skilled comprehenders again showed

more difficulties in solving the inconsistencies that were correctly detected. However, new findings emerged. Both groups tended to detect more inconsistencies than in the first experiment, although the difference was not significant. Both groups provided false detections for the inconsistent and consistent versions as well. These results reflect more active processing than in the first experiment. Moreover, skilled comprehenders seem to conduct revision actions in the absence of an explicit detection of the inconsistency. Their level of actual comprehension reached the same values as in older skilled comprehenders who participated in the first experiment.

GENERAL DISCUSSION

The purpose of the two experiments reported here was to examine the hypothesis that less skilled comprehenders suffer deficiencies in metacognitive monitoring. More specifically, the experiments investigated the extent to which the processing of anaphoric devices in expository texts involved self-evaluation in skilled and less skilled comprehenders. Two tasks were used; a classical inconsistency-detection task and a direct self-evaluation task. After reading, subjects answered multiple-choice questions designed to test the processing of anaphoric devices. Such questions are often used in comprehension research although they involve both comprehension and memory. In the present experiments, the questions tapped specific psycholinguistic operations made in the course of reading, that is, processing of anaphoric devices. The first experiment was conducted with ninth-grade children and the second one with seventh-grade children for whom the prereading level of domain-specific knowledge was lower.

Concerning the inconsistency-detection task, patterns of results were similar in the two experiments. In the first experiment, skilled and less skilled comprehenders showed rather poor detection performance and they were sensitive to the same factors. In particular, they showed decreasing scores from the first to the third sequence of the text. In the second experiment, when the subjects' level of domain knowledge was lower, the trial and the sequence factors affected detection in the same way as in the first experiment. However, both skilled and less skilled comprehenders detected more inconsistencies than in the first experiment and provided false detections for the inconsistent and consistent versions as well. These results suggest that subjects in both groups engage active processing and monitoring strategies when they read expository texts dealing with unfamiliar topics. All of these findings emphasize the similarities between skilled and less skilled comprehenders. However, some data revealed differences between the two groups: In both experiments, in agreement with previous findings in the literature (e.g., Baker, 1984; Garner, 1980; Yuill & Oakhill, 1991; Zabrucky & Moore, 1989), the less skilled comprehenders had more difficulties detecting inconsistencies and solving the inconsistencies that they correctly detected. In the second experiment, the examination of correct responses in the case of no explicit detection of inconsistency showed that only the skilled comprehenders made spontaneous inferences or conducted revision actions. Whether these differences were due to specific deficiencies in the metacognitive monitoring of less skilled comprehenders or to deficiencies of basic cognitive processes for building a mental representation of the text is an open question (cf. Perfetti, Marron, and Foltz's chapter in this book). Our results show that the role of domain-specific knowledge in the inconsistency-detection task using expository texts deserves further investigation. Previously, researchers have neglected this factor, and the influence of text difficulty as well. For example, Zabrucky and Moore (1989) used expository texts that were at a third-grade readability level for children in the fourth, fifth, and sixth grades. Garner (1980) selected a fifth-grade level expository text for seventh- and eighth-grade subjects. The level of prior domain knowledge was not controlled. Such texts may put the subject in a situation that minimizes the use of monitoring strategies.

Concerning the direct self-evaluation task, patterns of results were different in the two experiments. However, in both cases the results lead me to emphasize the similarities between skilled and less skilled comprehenders. In the first experiment, neither the skilled nor the less skilled comprehenders showed variation on their self-evaluation as a function of the type of anaphoric devices, whereas for both groups actual performance was lower in the pronominal version than in the nominal version. These results suggest that efficient control of the processing of anaphoric devices was not employed by either group of subjects. For both groups, some findings suggest that self-evaluation was modulated in agreement with actual comprehension. However, less skilled comprehenders seemed not to be aware of their comprehension difficulties because they provided similar evaluations although they had lower actual performance than skilled comprehenders.

In the second experiment, seventh-grade children gave only 35% correct responses on the prereading test showing a lower level of domain-specific knowledge. New findings emerged relative to the first experiment. Both skilled and less skilled comprehenders modulated the evaluation of their own understanding as a function of the type of anaphoric devices. Both skilled and less skilled comprehenders reached the same level of actual comprehension on nominal and pronominal versions. An interaction revealed that less skilled children modulated their self-evaluation only on the second trial, showing an adaptation to the demands of the comprehension task later than skilled children. Therefore, it appears that both skilled and less skilled comprehenders when reading expository texts dealing with unfamiliar topics engaged comprehension monitoring, taking the requirements of the processing of pronouns into consideration. Moreover, less skilled comprehenders were aware of their difficulties because they asserted that they understood less well than skilled comprehenders. Even if the level to which less skilled comprehenders evaluated their own understanding appeared to be too high, revealing a tendency towards overestimation (for example, when they asserted they had understood very well, they gave only 70% of correct responses), their evaluations were modulated in agreement with their actual comprehension. Such a relationship did not appear in skilled comprehenders probably because a ceiling effect occurred for self-evaluation. The main point that differentiates the two groups is that less skilled comprehenders were slower to exhibit efficient monitoring.

Thus, results from the two tasks are convergent. They clearly show that metacognitive monitoring is affected by the same variables in skilled and less skilled comprehenders. In particular, for both groups, metacognitive monitoring for understanding expository texts is dependent on the level of domain-specific knowledge. Our findings are similar to results from Glenberg and Epstein's (1987) study comparing experts and nonexperts in a specific domain. According to Flavell's (1987) suggestion, a high level of knowledge can lead children to view reading as an easy task that prevents the utilization of control mechanisms. A lower level of knowledge can lead children to view the texts as more difficult to understand and this engages more active processing and monitoring strategies. Overall, the hypothesis that less skilled comprehenders suffer deficiencies in metacognitive monitoring was not supported. In the two experiments, actual comprehension was lower for less skilled than for skilled comprehenders. However, deficiencies in metacognitive monitoring did not seem to be responsible for this difference. This conclusion, obviously, has to be limited to this population of 13- and 15-year-olds.

To my knowledge, the evaluation of one's own comprehension has not been investigated in a systematic way in children. However, the reported data show that this paradigm provides interesting evidence about metacognitive control. More recent experiments also have shown that this paradigm may be used reliably in elementary school children (see Ehrlich, 1993). On a theoretical level, self-evaluation may be considered a metacognitive experience, which is a component of metacognitive control according to Flavell (1981). The basis used by each subject to provide such self-evaluation of his or her own comprehension needs clarification. Our instructions were oriented toward the judgment of by-products of the comprehension processes, asking subjects to indicate "the extent to which you think you understood the text." Results from Experiment 2 showing that the level of self-evaluation was higher for the pronominal than nominal version of the texts suggest that subjects also took the amount of effort devoted to manage comprehension processes into consideration. This interpretation should be tested in further investigations attempting to specify the basis of self-evaluation of comprehension. Special attention should be given to the methodological characteristics ensuring the reliability of the test and cognitive variables such as reading times might be related to metacognitive variables (Maki & Serra, 1992; Papetti, Cornoldi, Pettavino, Mazzoni, & Borkowski, 1992; Weaver, 1990). These new investigations could increase knowledge of the factors that affect comprehension monitoring in skilled and less skilled comprehenders of different age levels.

AUTHOR NOTE

I would like to thank Catherine Loridant for her assistance in data collection and coding. I would also like to thank the principal, teachers, and students at the College G. Pompidou in Courbevoie (92) for their participation in this project.

REFERENCES

Aubret, J., & Blanchard, S. (1991). *L'évaluation des compétences d'un lecteur.* Issy-Les-Moulineaux, France: Etablissements d'Applications Psychotechniques.

Baker, L. (1984). Spontaneous versus instructed use of multiple standards for evaluating comprehension: Effects of age, reading proficiency and type of standard. *Journal of Experimental Child Psychology, 38,* 289–311.

Baker, L. (1985a). How do we know when we don't understand? Standards for evaluating text comprehension. In D. L. Forrest-Pressley, G. E. MacKinnon, & T. G. Waller (Eds.), *Metacognition, cognition and human performance* (Vol. 1, pp. 155–206). New York: Academic Press.

Baker, L. (1985b). Differences in the standards used by college students to evaluate their comprehension of expository prose. *Reading Research Quarterly, 20,* 297–313.

Baker, L. (1989). Metacognition, comprehension monitoring, and the adult reader. *Educational Psychology Review, 1,* 3–38.

Baker, L., & Brown, A. L. (1984). Metacognitive skills and reading. In P. D. Pearson, M. Kamil, R. Barr, & P. Mosenthal (Eds.), *Handbook of reading research* (pp. 353–394). New York: Longman.

Beal, C. R. (1990). The development of text evaluation and revision skills. *Child Development, 61,* 247–258.

Beal, C. R., Garrod, A. C., & Bonitatibus, G. J. (1990). Fostering children's revision skills through training in comprehension monitoring. *Journal of Educational Psychology, 82,* 275–280.

Carr, T. H. (1981). Building theories of reading ability: On the relation between individual differences in cognitive skills and reading comprehension. *Cognition, 9,* 73–114.

Carr, T. H., Brown, T. L., Vavrus, L. G., & Evans, M. A. (1990). Cognitive skill maps and cognitive skill profiles: Componental analysis of individual differences in children's reading efficiency. In T. H. Carr & B. A. Levy (Eds.), *Reading and its development: Component skills approaches* (pp. 1–55). New York: Academic Press.

Cavanaugh, J. C., & Perlmutter, M. (1982). Metamemory: A critical examination. *Child Development, 53,* 11–28.

Cox, B. E., Shanahan, T., & Sulzby, E. (1990). Good and poor elementary readers' use of cohesion in writing. *Reading Research Quarterly, 25,* 47–64.

Cross, D. R., & Paris, S. G. (1988). Developmental and instructional analyses of children's metacognition and reading comprehension. *Journal of Educational Psychology, 80*, 131–142.

Dell, G., McKoon, G., & Ratcliff, R. (1983). The activation of antecedent information during the processing of anaphoric reference in reading. *Journal of Verbal Learning and Verbal Behavior, 22*, 121–132.

Ehrlich, M.-F. (1993). Good and poor comprehenders: Metacognitive determinants of reading comprehension. *Abstracts of the twelfth biennial meetings of the International Society for the Study of Behavioral Development.* Recife (Brazil).

Ehrlich, M.-F., Kurtz-Costes, B., & Loridant, C. (1993). Cognitive and motivational determinants of reading comprehension in good and poor readers. *Journal of Reading Behavior, 25*, 365–381.

Ehrlich, M.-F., Kurtz-Costes, B., Rémond, M., & Loridant, C. (in press). Les différences individuelles dans la compréhension de l'écrit: Facteurs cognitivo-linguistiques et motivationnels [n° spécial] [Individual differences in reading comprehension: Cognitive–linguistic and motivational factors (n° special)]. *Cahiers d'Acquisition et de Pathologie du Langage (CaLaP), Aspects différentiels du langage* [Individual differences in language].

Ehrlich, M.-F., Rémond, M., & Tardieu, H. (1993). Composantes cognitives et métacognitives de la lecture: Le traitement des marques anaphoriques par des bons et mauvais compreneurs [Cognitive and metacognitive components of reading: The processing of anaphoric devices in skilled and less skilled comprehenders]. In J.-P. Jaffre, L. Sprenger-Charolles, & M. Fayol (Eds.), *Les actes de la Villette. Lecture-écriture: acquisition* [*Villette Proceedings. Reading and writing: Acquisition*] (pp. 279–298). Paris: Nathan.

Englert, C. S., Hiebert, E. H., & Stewart, S. R. (1988). Detecting and correcting inconsistencies in the monitoring of expository prose. *Journal of Educational Research, 81*, 221–227.

Flavell, J. H. (1976). Metacognitive aspects of problem solving. In L. B. Resnick (Ed.), *The nature of intelligence* (pp. 231–235). Hillsdale, NJ: Lawrence Erlbaum Associates.

Flavell, J. H. (1981). Cognitive monitoring. In P. Dickson (Ed.), *Children's oral communication skills* (pp. 35–60). New York: Academic Press.

Flavell, J. H. (1987). Speculations about the nature and development of metacognition. In F. E. Weinert & R. H. Kluwe (Eds.), *Metacognition, motivation and understanding* (pp. 21–29). Hillsdale, NJ: Lawrence Erlbaum Associates.

Garner, R. (1980). Monitoring of understanding: An investigation of good and poor readers' awareness of induced miscomprehension of text. *Journal of Reading Behavior, 12*, 55–63.

Garner, R. (1987). *Metacognition and reading comprehension.* Norwood, NJ: Ablex.

Garrod, S. C., & Sanford, A. J. (1982). The mental representation of discourse in a focussed memory system: Implications for the interpretation of anaphoric noun phrases. *Journal of Semantics, 1*, 21–41.

Garrod, S. C., & Sanford, A. J. (1983). Topic dependent effects in language processing. In G. B. Flores d'Arcais & R. J. Jarvella (Eds.), *The process of language understanding* (pp. 271–296). New York: Wiley.

Garrod, S. C., & Sanford, A. J. (1985). On the real-time character of interpretation during reading. *Language and Cognitive Processes, 1*, 43–59.

Glenberg, A. M., & Epstein, W. (1985). Calibration of comprehension. *Journal of Experimental Psychology: Learning, Memory and Cognition, 11*, 702–718.

Glenberg, A. M., & Epstein, W. (1987). Inexpert calibration of comprehension. *Memory and Cognition, 15*, 84–93.

Glenberg, A. M., Sanocki, T., Epstein, W., & Morris, C. (1987). Enhancing calibration of comprehension. *Journal of Experimental Psychology: General, 116*, 119–136.

Greene, S. B., McKoon, G., & Ratcliff, R. (1992). Pronoun resolution and discourse models. *Journal of Experimental Psychology: Learning, Memory and Cognition, 18*, 266–283.

Grice, H. P. (1975). Logic and conversation. In P. Cole & J. L. Morgan (Eds.), *Syntax and semantics: Vol. 7. Speech acts.* New York: Academic Press.

Halliday, M. A. K., & Hasan, R. (1976). *Cohesion in English*. London: Longman.

Lefavrais, P. (1986). *La pipe et le rat*. Issy-les-Moulineaux, France: Etablissements d'Applications Psychotechniques.

Luria, A. R. (1961). *The role of speech in the regulation of normal and abnormal behavior* (J. Tizard, Trans.). New York: Liveright.

Maki, R. H., & Berry, S. L. (1984). Metacomprehension of text material. *Journal of Experimental Psychology: Learning, Memory, and Cognition, 10*, 663–679.

Maki, R. H., Foley, J. M., Kajer, W. K., Thompson, R. C., & Willert, M. G. (1990). Increased processing enhances calibration of comprehension. *Journal of Experimental Psychology: Learning, Memory, and Cognition, 16*, 609–616.

Maki, R. H., & Serra, M. (1992). The basis of test predictions for text material. *Journal of Experimental Psychology: Learning, Memory, and Cognition, 18*, 116–126.

Markman, E. M. (1977). Realizing that you don't understand: A preliminary investigation. *Child Development, 48*, 986–992.

Markman, E. M. (1979). Realizing that you don't understand: Elementary school children's awareness of inconsistencies. *Child Development, 50*, 643–655.

Morris, C. C. (1990). Retrieval processes underlying confidence in comprehension judgments. *Journal of Experimental Psychology: Learning, Memory, and Cognition, 16*, 223–232.

Myers, M., & Paris, S. G. (1978). Children's metacognitive knowledge about reading. *Journal of Educational Psychology, 70*, 680–690.

Nelson, T. O. (1984). A comparison of current measures of the accuracy of feeling-of-knowing predictions. *Psychological Bulletin, 95*, 109–133.

Oakhill, J., & Yuill, N. (1986). Pronoun resolution in skilled and less-skilled comprehenders: Effects of memory load and inferential complexity. *Language and Speech, 29*, 25–37.

Paris, S. G., & Myers, M. (1981). Comprehension monitoring, memory and study strategies of good and poor readers. *Journal of Reading Behavior, 13*, 5–22.

Papetti, O., Cornoldi, C., Pettavino, A., Mazzoni, G., & Borkowski, J. (1992). Memory judgments and allocation of study times in good and poor comprehenders. *Advances in Learning and Behavioral Disabilities, 7*, 3–33.

Pazzaglia, F., Cornoldi, C., & Tressoldi, P. E. (1993). Learning to read: Evidence on the distinction between decoding and comprehension skills. *European Journal of Psychology of Education, 8*, 247–258.

Perfetti, C. A. (1985). *Reading ability*. Oxford, England: Oxford University Press.

Piaget, J. (1974). *La prise de conscience*. Paris: Presses Universitaires de France.

Reis, R., & Spekman, N. (1983). The detection of reader-based versus text-based inconsistencies and the effects of direct training of comprehension monitoring among upper-grade poor comprehenders. *Journal of Reading Behavior, 15*, 49–60.

Tyler, L. K. (1983). The development of discourse mapping processes: The on-line interpretation of anaphoric expressions. *Cognition, 13*, 309–341.

Vygotsky, L. S. (1962). *Thought and language*. Cambridge, MA: MIT Press.

Walczyk, J. J., & Hall, V. C. (1989). Effects of examples and embedded questions on the accuracy of comprehension self-assessments. *Journal of Educational Psychology, 81*, 435–437.

Weaver, C. A., III, (1990). Constraining factors in calibration of comprehension. *Journal of Experimental Psychology: Learning, Memory, and Cognition, 16*, 214–222.

Winograd, P., & Johnston, P. (1982). Comprehension monitoring and the error detection paradigm. *Journal of Reading Behavior, 14*, 61–74.

Yuill, N., & Oakhill, J. (1988). Understanding of anaphoric relations in skilled and less-skilled comprehenders. *British Journal of Psychology, 79*, 173–186.

Yuill, N., & Oakhill, J. (1991). *Children's problems in text comprehension*. Cambridge, England: Cambridge University Press.

Zabrucky, K., & Moore, D. (1989). Children's ability to use three standards to evaluate their comprehension of text. *Reading Research Quarterly, 24*, 336–352.

APPENDIX

Les Ressources Naturelles

Nominal version

La richesse du Canada en tant que nation aux ressources naturelles abondantes est connue. <u>Cette richesse</u> est menacée par les effets d'une exploitation intense et par ceux de la pollution./L'exploitation des ressources, au rythme actuel, conduit à prévoir leur disparition prochaine. <u>Cette exploitation</u> est pourtant plus facile à contrôler que les productions de déchets qui nuisent à l'environnement./La protection des réserves existantes doit être assurée par les entreprises qui profitent de la richesse du pays. <u>Cette protection</u> doit être accompagnée d'une augmentation du budget que les entreprises consacrent à combattre la pollution.

The three critical anaphoric devices are underlined in the text. The limits between the sequences are noted by a /.

Pronominal version

1. Elle est menacée . . . 2. Elle est pourtant . . . 3. Elle doit être accompagnée . . .

Inconsistent nominal version

1. Cette pauvreté est menacée . . . 2. Cette non utilisation est pourtant . . . 3. Cette dilapidation doit être accompagnée . . .

Questions:

La pollution et la surexploitation des ressources naturelles menacent . . .
- *la nation canadienne,*
- *la richesse du Canada,*
- *les monuments historiques,*
- *la pauvreté du Canada,*
- *les entreprises industrielles*

Il est plus difficile de contrôler les produits nocifs qui envahissent l'atmosphère que de contrôler . . .
- *les finances de la nation,*
- *l'exploitation des ressources,*
- *la disparition des ressources,*
- *l'environnement,*
- *la non-utilisation des ressources*

Les entreprises doivent dépenser beaucoup d'argent pour combattre la pollution et . . .

- *augmenter leurs frais d'assurances,*
- *utiliser les compétences de leurs ouvriers,*
- *dilapider les réserves existantes,*
- *défendre leurs biens,*
- *protéger les réserves existantes.*

Natural Resources

Nominal version

It is well known that the wealth of Canada is a nation with plentiful natural resources. This wealth is endangered by the effects of pollution and an intense exploitation of the resources./ The present rate of this exploitation will lead to extinction in the future. Nevertheless this exploitation is easier to control than the production of wastes which damages the environment./ The protection of the existing reserves have to be controlled by the firms which make a profit from the wealth of the country. This protection must be accompanied by an increase in the budget that firms devote to control pollution.

The three critical anaphoric devices are underlined in the text. The limits between the sequences are noted by a /.

Pronominal version

1. It is endangered . . . 2. Nevertheless it is . . . 3. It must be accompanied . . .

Inconsistent nominal version

1. This poverty is endangered . . . 2. Nevertheless this absence of use . . . 3. This wastage must be accompanied . . .

Questions:

Pollution and overexploitation of natural resources are endangering . . .
- *the nation of Canada,*
- *the Canadian wealth,*
- *the historical monuments,*
- *the poverty of Canada,*
- *the industrial firms*

It is more difficult to control the noxious products which invade the atmosphere than to control . . .
- *the finances of the nation,*
- *the exploitation of the resources,*
- *the extinction of resources,*

- *the environment,*
- *the absence of use of the resources*

The firms must spend a lot of money to control pollution and . . .
- *to increase their insurance expenses,*
- *to use the skills of their workers,*
- *to waste the existing reserves,*
- *to defend their goods,*
- *to protect the existing reserves.*

CHAPTER ELEVEN

Reading Comprehension Deficits Arise From Diverse Sources: Evidence From Readers With and Without Developmental Brain Pathology

Marcia A. Barnes
Maureen Dennis
The Hospital for Sick Children
and
University of Toronto

This chapter describes a recent series of investigations of comprehension deficits in children with early-onset hydrocephalus, a developmental pathology of the brain. How and why the study of individuals with developmental neuropathologies provides information relevant to theories of reading comprehension is considered first. The condition of early-onset hydrocephalus is described, as well as some of the reasons why this special population provides an interesting perspective on reading comprehension disabilities. A case study of hydrocephalus is presented in which deficits in reading comprehension appear related to difficulties in inferencing, followed by a more in-depth investigation of inferencing in children with hydrocephalus and a group of neurologically intact poor readers who also have inferencing difficulties. Finally, the results of our studies of comprehension in children with hydrocephalus are discussed with reference to other poor readers without known brain anomalies, the remediation of reading comprehension deficits, and the neurological bases of comprehension disabilities.

WHY ARE SKILL DISSOCIATIONS IN NEUROLOGICAL CONDITIONS OF INTEREST TO COGNITIVE THEORIES?

Adult clinical conditions with associated neurological impairment often alter the usual relationships among cognitive skills. Neurological conditions that produce aphasia or amnesia, for example, have long been used to test theories

251

of language and memory (Geschwind, 1970; Teuber, 1955), the assumption being that damage to a mature and previously normal brain will cause a system such as language to break down in a principled fashion. How language disassembles following brain injury is deemed to be interpretable within some model of how language normally works (Zurif, 1990).

Conditions in which brain damage occurs early in life bear on theories about brain development and skill acquisition, as opposed to the mature function of the brain. Developmental brain pathologies are relevant to models of skill acquisition because they often produce dissociations among cognitive skills that are normally acquired together, and such information may be used to test hypotheses about skill decomposition within a given domain. For example, children with Down Syndrome have been used to test hypotheses about the necessary and sufficient relationship between phonemic awareness and the acquisition of word recognition skills (see Cossu, Rossini, & Marshall, 1993 vs. Bertelson, 1993; Morton & Frith, 1993).

Dissociations among normally related cognitive skills may arise not only in conditions where there is documented brain injury, but also in some children without known brain anomalies. Some proportion of children with no known brain anomaly, for example, are proficient at reading words, but poor at understanding what they read (see Oakhill, 1993; Oakhill & Garnham, 1988; Yuill & Oakhill, 1991 for reviews), a departure from the characteristic finding of a strong relationship between word recognition and reading comprehension.

If a cognitive skill breaks down in the same way regardless of the intactness of the brain, then a model of that skill need only posit one common path causing individual skill variation. Were the pattern of deficits within a domain to differ depending on the presence or absence of brain anomaly, however, a model of that skill would need to be more complex. If an adequate model must explain how variations in a skill may be produced by one, as opposed to more than one, underlying cognitive process, then comparisons of cognitive skills in children with and without brain pathology can provide information important for specifying the parameters of cognitive models.

WHAT IS EARLY-ONSET HYDROCEPHALUS AND WHY IS THIS CONDITION OF INTEREST TO THE STUDY OF READING COMPREHENSION DISABILITIES?

Neuropathology of Hydrocephalus

Hydrocephalus is a disturbance of pressure in the brain that arises from an imbalance in the production and absorption of cerebrospinal fluid, leading to dilated ventricles and loss of brain volume, especially in the white matter (Harwood-Nash & Fitz, 1976; Hoffman, 1989). Early-onset hydrocephalus originates before birth, from the time of birth, or from the first months of life; in all cases, certainly before language has been acquired. It stems from abnormalities of neuroembryogenesis like neural tube defects, from periventricular leukomalacia where the periventricular white matter is destroyed as a result of ischemia or hemorrhage, from brain infections and adhesions, or from congenital and idiopathic causes.

Early-onset hydrocephalus has a variety of neuropathological effects (reviewed in Del Bigio, 1993). It alters the formation and maturation of the brain's white matter, and the concurrent anomalies of cerebral white matter tracts cause problems in myelination, as well as atrophy of midline commissural structures such as the corpus callosum (Fletcher et al., 1992). The ventricular dilation and cortical thinning of hydrocephalus appear more pronounced in the vertex and occipital lobes than in the frontal lobes (e.g., Emery & Svitok, 1968; Epstein et al., 1977). Typically, treatment for hydrocephalus consists of the insertion of a shunt to control intracranial pressure. Although this is an effective treatment for hydrocephalus that may help restore the cortical mantle (Del Bigio, 1993), shunting need not result in normal neuropsychological function (Prigatano, Zeiner, Pollay, & Kaplan, 1983). That is, children with treated hydrocephalus, while less at risk for mental retardation than in an earlier treatment era, may still experience academic difficulties in later childhood (Fletcher & Levin, 1987).

The Development of Language Skills in Hydrocephalus

Several decades ago, the term "Cocktail Party Syndrome" was used to describe a pattern of aberrant speech, language, and behavior thought to be characteristic of children with hydrocephalus; namely, fluent speech that was nonetheless characterized by verbal perseveration, excessive use of stereotyped social utterances, irrelevant verbosity, and overfamiliarity of manner (e.g., Hadenius, Hagberg, Hyttnas-Bensch, & Sjogren, 1962). Their language was described as being an effective vehicle for social contact, though not a particularly successful means of conveying semantic content (Taylor, 1961). However, with early treatment and a lower incidence of mental retardation, it is questionable whether the descriptive characteristics of the Cocktail Party Syndrome actually cohere to form a syndrome, and also whether the full-blown pattern of symptoms characterizes most individuals with early-onset hydrocephalus. Our studies focused not on the validity of the putative syndrome, but on the characteristics of the language of early treated hydrocephalic individuals who are not mentally retarded.

Children with hydrocephalus have many oral (Dennis, Hendrick, Hoffman, & Humphreys, 1987) and written (Barnes & Dennis, 1992) language skills that are developed to similar levels as those in children without brain anomalies, so it is clear that they have no generalized linguistic deficit.

Nevertheless, they do evidence some language impairments that are most obviously revealed in discourse contexts.

In nonclinically referred samples, we have found that many children with hydrocephalus have unimpaired access to the oral lexicon through visual (pictures) and phonological (rhyme) routes (Dennis et al., 1987); that they can quickly access names from memory for colors, pictures, and letters, in rapid automatized naming tasks (Dennis et al., 1987); and that they are fairly accurate in understanding various active and passive grammatical forms (Dennis et al., 1987).

In discourse tasks, however, content-poor language is apparent. Although children with hydrocephalus tell fluent, fairly well-structured narratives, their stories fail to capture important aspects of the discourse content. In comparison to neurologically intact children, their narrative productions are more verbose, less concise, and lacking in core semantic content (Dennis, Jacennik, & Barnes, 1994). Children with hydrocephalus also perform less well than their peers on tasks that require them to derive the full intended meaning of utterances within discourse contexts, that is, to infer what happened, given a particular situation; to understand ambiguous sentences; and to understand common figurative expressions such as idioms (Dennis & Barnes, 1993).

The evidence concerning reading skill in children with hydrocephalus has been less than consistent. Some studies have suggested that children with hydrocephalus have word decoding difficulties (e.g., Halliwell, Carr, & Pearson, 1980; Tew & Laurence, 1975; Wills, Holmbeck, Dillon, & McLone, 1990), whereas others have not reported such deficits (Anderson, 1973; Prigatano et al., 1983; Shaffer, Friedrich, Shurtleff, & Wolf, 1985). The contradictory findings may have arisen because of methodological and procedural differences between the studies. Some studies used small numbers of subjects, some contained children with a very wide range of general cognitive deficits, and others compared reading in children with hydrocephalus to test norms rather than to a control group drawn from the same educational system as the hydrocephalus group. In addition, the factors related to good or poor word-level skills were not studied, and reading comprehension was rarely considered separately from word recognition (but see Anderson, 1973; Halliwell et al., 1980). In a more recent study with a large group of children with hydrocephalus who were not referred for clinical service and in which no children were mentally retarded, word recognition and phonological analysis were found to be developed to similar levels in hydrocephalus and control groups (Barnes & Dennis, 1992). Of interest to theories of reading comprehension was the finding that, although children with hydrocephalus had appropriately developed word recognition and phonological abilities, these word-level skills did not translate into proficient comprehension of text (Barnes & Dennis, 1992). This type of reading disability has also been found in some children without known brain anomalies (for a review, see Oakhill, 1993).

Skill Dissociations in the Language and Reading
of Normally Intelligent Children with Hydrocephalus

Despite this dissociation of decoding and comprehension seemingly produced by hydrocephalus, the range of developmental outcomes in our groups was still fairly broad, as indexed by standard measures of intelligence. Although mentally retarded children were excluded from our studies, IQs ranged from plus to minus two standard deviations of the population mean. Although not a direct measure of either potential ability or current verbalizable knowledge, verbal IQ is a marker of vocabulary knowledge, verbal memory, factual knowledge, and the like (Stanovich, 1991).

Poorer reading and discourse comprehension may well occur in children with hydrocephalus with below average IQs; of more interest to models of reading comprehension would be the demonstration that the dissociation between word recognition and reading comprehension holds even for children with average to superior verbal intelligence. Excluding subjects with lower verbal IQ would be a useful method here because it would remove some of the variance due to fairly general aspects of verbal functioning which might otherwise contribute to problems in reading and language comprehension (see Stanovich, 1991 for a discussion of the use of IQ measures in reading study designs).

We adopted this method in our first reading study (Barnes & Dennis, 1992), and found that the children with hydrocephalus who had verbal IQs ranging from 90 to 131 were as good as controls in naming words and pseudowords, producing antonyms and synonyms, and solving verbal analogies, but they still had significantly lower reading comprehension scores. For the controls, word recognition and reading comprehension skills were very similar, consistent with the observed close relation in normally developing readers between word-level and text-level skills (see Carr & Levy, 1990). In contrast, the reading comprehension scores of the children with hydrocephalus were significantly lower than their word recognition scores. The difference between word recognition and reading comprehension here could not be explained by variations in either single word comprehension or verbal IQ (Barnes & Dennis, 1992). In a group of children with normal verbal intelligence and good written vocabulary knowledge, then, the dissociation between word recognition and text comprehension remained.

Why might reading comprehension be deficient even when word recognition is not? The working hypothesis here is that reading comprehension requires additional skills. The literature has identified several skills thought to be important for reading comprehension. They are broadly as follows; automatic word recognition processes (see Carr & Levy, 1990; Lovett, 1987; Perfetti, 1985, although not all slow readers are poor comprehenders, see Oakhill, 1993; Rankin, 1993), vocabulary knowledge (Singer & Crouse, 1981, although vocabulary growth in children of reading age relies greatly on deriving meaning from reading contexts, McKeown, Beck, Omanson, & Pople, 1985; Nagy, Anderson, & Herman, 1987), syntactic knowledge (Bentin, Deutsch, & Liberman, 1990), understanding figurative aspects of text (Cacciari & Tabossi, 1993), the suppression of context-irrelevant semantic information (Gernsbacher & Faust, 1991), and inferencing and text integration skills that may rely on working memory as well as general knowledge (Kintsch, 1994; Oakhill, 1993).

Our reading studies suggested that normally intelligent children with hydrocephalus, unlike some groups of poor comprehenders (see Stothard & Hulme, this volume), seem not to have difficulty in vocabulary knowledge (Barnes & Dennis, 1992) and more recently, we showed that these same children were similar to normally developing children in a number of other skills that are important for adequate comprehension of both oral discourse and text. Despite their various intact verbal skills, hydrocephalic children of average and above-average verbal intelligence had deficits in specific aspects of discourse production and comprehension. A summary of the findings from our studies with this group of children is presented below (and see Table 11.1).

In a narrative discourse study, children listened to familiar ("The Frog Prince") and unfamiliar ("The Practical Princess") fairy tales. They were then required to retell each story (the actual story texts and details of scoring may be found in Dennis et al., 1994). Narration tasks are considered to be sensitive measures of discourse production (and probably of comprehension, too) because narrating a story requires the successful coordination and deployment of several core language skills in a discourse context (McCabe, 1991).

TABLE 11.1
Reading and Discourse Skills in Hydrocephalic Children
With Average to Above-Average Verbal IQs

Skill	Same as Normally Developing Children?
Reading	
Word recognition accuracy	Yes
Phonological analysis	Yes
Written vocabulary knowledge	Yes
Reading comprehension	No
Narrative production	
Quantity produced	Yes
Syntactic complexity	Yes
Core semantic content	No
Oral discourse elements	
Idiomatic expressions	Yes
Novel figurative expressions	No
Inferences	No

A successful narrative must contain sufficient content. Children with hydrocephalus in the average IQ group produced as much story content as controls, that is, they produced as many clauses and propositions as other children their age. Their narratives were also as economic as those of their normally developing peers in the sense that they contained an appropriate degree of syntactic complexity, being neither excessively complex nor containing too many short and redundant syntactic units (also see Byrne, Abbeduto, & Brooks, 1990). Despite producing similar numbers of well-structured propositions as controls, average IQ children with hydrocephalus produced less of the core semantic content of both familiar and novel stories (Barnes & Dennis, in press). Like children with hydrocephalus, good decoders/poor comprehenders without frank brain injury also produce adequately long but qualitatively poor stories (see Cain, this volume).

The narrative discourse deficits of children with hydrocephalus seem to involve not just language production, but a more general deficit in language comprehension. That is to say, difficulties in producing the core semantic content of a story indicate that the narrative was not understood as well by children with hydrocephalus as by normally developing controls. Our reason for thinking this comes from direct measures of how children with hydrocephalus understand several elements of oral discourse. In these studies, normal IQ children with hydrocephalus and normally developing children of the same age differed not in their understanding of individual words, of the various syntactic forms, or of some types of figurative language such as idioms, but in the relative inability of the children with hydrocephalus to make inferences and interpret novel expressions from context. The data upon which these statements are based are presented below.

These hydrocephalic children with average to superior IQs understood idiomatic expressions as well as their normally developing peers (Barnes & Dennis, in press; Dennis & Barnes, 1993). For example, they performed similarly to controls when asked to explain what the expression *He is high man on the totem pole* meant when two players were talking about their coach, and they chose another figurative expression meaning the same thing (e.g., "He is top dog") from among several figurative and literal alternatives. However, they had more difficulty than their peers in interpreting novel figurative expressions such as similes where the meaning of the simile must be derived by considering information specific to the discourse context (Barnes & Dennis, in press).

The difficulties with inferencing shown by the larger group of children with hydrocephalus (Dennis & Barnes, 1993) were apparent even in the average IQ subset (Barnes & Dennis, in press). These average IQ children with hydrocephalus had more difficulty than controls in making script-like inferences. For example, given a situation such as "Bob and Ray rode on the crowded bus to the shopping mall," and an outcome such as "They told the story of Bob's bad luck to a policeman," they were required to choose two plausible statements such as "Bob's wallet was stolen on the bus" and "Bob lost his money sometime before they got to the mall" from two other ones such as "Bob didn't have enough money for the movie," and "They were unlucky to get on a crowded bus."

In short, children with hydrocephalus with average to above-average IQs show deficient reading and discourse comprehension which seems unaccounted for by difficulties in word recognition processes, vocabulary knowledge, syntactic ability, and interpreting common discourse segments such as idiomatic phrases. Skills that are spared in hydrocephalic children with average verbal IQs appear to be the ones that rely relatively little (or not at all) on particular discourse contexts for their computation; these include word recognition and phonological analysis, understanding of single words and idioms, and use of well-formed syntactic constructions. The comprehension skills that are impaired in hydrocephalus, regardless of intelligence level, involve capturing the core semantic content of stories, and more specifically, in making inferences and interpreting novel figurative expressions.

What these impaired skills appear to have in common is that meaning must be computed from a particular and not a generic discourse context (Barnes & Dennis, in press). That is, a precomputed or stored meaning cannot be accessed directly from memory, but rather, meaning must be constructed by using information from within and without the discourse text. The comprehension deficits of children with hydrocephalus seem characterized by problems in using various sources of intra and extratextual information to derive meaning. Inferencing difficulties would come under this general heading, as would other skills that rely on the integrative use of context and knowledge to derive textual meaning. Studies of good decoders/poor comprehenders without developmental neuropathologies have also noted associated deficiencies in inferencing and text integration (Oakhill, 1982, 1983, 1984, 1993; Oakhill, Yuill, & Parkin, 1986; Yuill & Oakhill, 1988; Yuill, Oakhill, & Parkin, 1989).

Deficiencies in the component skills that account for relatively poor reading comprehension within a particular developmental neuropathology such as hydrocephalus show variability, just as they do within a group of school-age children without known brain anomaly (see Cornoldi, De Beni, & Pazzaglia, this volume). Even in the higher IQ subset, some children with hydrocephalus have slow word recognition, a few have weak vocabulary knowledge, some have poor figurative language understanding, and so forth. Despite the variability in other reading-related skills, however, inferencing deficits emerge as a stable and consistent feature of hydrocephalus as a whole, regardless of variations in IQ. To pursue the origins of comprehension difficulties in hydrocephalus, we chose to more closely investigate the nature of inferencing deficits. We begin with a case study of a child with hydrocephalus of average intelligence whose difficulty in reading comprehension is accompanied by selectively impaired inferencing. We then describe some group studies of knowledge-based inferencing in both hydrocephalic children with average and above-average verbal IQs, and poor readers/poor comprehenders without known brain anomalies.

Case Study: Inferencing and Reading Comprehension Deficits in a Child with Hydrocephalus

Case 1 is a 10.8-year-old girl in grade 5, with hydrocephalus secondary to an intraventricular hemorrhage. She was treated with a shunt within the first few weeks of life. On the Wechsler Intelligence Scale for Children–Third Edition (WISC–III, Wechsler, 1991), her Verbal IQ (VIQ) was 101, and her Performance IQ (PIQ) was 102. This IQ pattern was consistent with the finding that children with intraventricular hemorrhage do not reliably show the selectively lower PIQ of spina bifida children (Dennis et al., 1981). Case 1's testing is described for age 10, but also includes some testing at age 7.8. Except where otherwise noted, the results are from testing at age 10.

Word Recognition Speed and Accuracy. Case 1 demonstrated excellent ability to read words accurately (90th percentile, Grade Equivalent 8.7 on Word Identification from the Woodcock Reading Mastery Test–Revised or WRMT–R, Woodcock, 1987), and she was faster than other children her age in naming words varying systematically in their spelling to sound regularity (Backman, Bruck, Hebert, & Seidenberg, 1984; Seidenberg, Waters, Barnes, & Tanenhaus, 1984). Her word recognition speed, in fact, was consistent with that expected for grade 7 or 8, the level of her reading accuracy. On a timed serial naming task (Denckla & Rudel, 1974), she could name pictures, letters, and color patches faster than expected for her age.

Phonological Skills. On tests of phonemic awareness (rhyme, odd-word-out, phoneme deletion, and blending tasks from Bradley & Bryant, 1983 and from the GFW Sound Symbol Tests, Goldman, Fristoe, & Woodcock, 1974), pseudoword decoding (Word Attack from the WRMT–R), and spelling (Spelling of Sounds from the GFW Sound Symbol Tests), Case 1's scores were all above average at age 7. At age 10, her ability to name pseudowords derived from real words (Backman et al., 1984) was faster than expected for her grade.

Reading Comprehension. Case 1's reading comprehension scores were variable, depending on the particular test used to measure comprehension. On a cloze task (Passage Comprehension, WRMT–R), her reading comprehension score was high and consistent with her word recognition skill (91st percentile, Grade Equivalent 8.4), but, on the other task requiring her to read paragraphs and answer questions about the theme and story details, and to make inferences (Paragraph Reading from the Test of Reading Comprehension, Brown, Hamill, & Wiederholt, 1986), her score was below average (16th percentile). These results were reliable in the sense that Case 1 showed a similar pattern of ability and deficits when she was tested 3 years earlier at age 7. Considering that she showed a deficit on one comprehension task but not another, it might be noted that, in a group of 90 normally developing children, the variance shared by these particular reading comprehension tasks was only 10% (Barnes & Dennis, 1995).

Vocabulary and Discourse Skills. Case 1 had good oral and written vocabulary knowledge. She could provide antonyms and synonyms for heard words (94th percentile on Oral Vocabulary from the Woodcock–Johnson Tests of Cognitive Abilities, Woodcock & Johnson, 1989) and provide antonyms and synonyms, and complete verbal analogies for printed words (87th percentile on Word Comprehension, WRMT–R).

Oral discourse (from the Test of Language Competence–Expanded Edition, Wiig & Secord, 1989) showed a striking dissociation. Although Case 1 could interpret ambiguous sentences (e.g., provide two interpretations for sentences with ambiguous vocabulary or syntax, such as "He wiped the glasses carefully," or "Mary wanted to run as well as me") and common figurative expressions (e.g., "He is high man on the totem pole," in the context of a player talking about his coach), she had marked difficulty making inferences (2nd percentile). The same pattern of oral discourse skills was also noted at age 7.

Comprehension Monitoring. At age 7, Case 1 demonstrated age-appropriate ability to detect errors (tense, capitalization, and so forth) in a proofreading task (Proofing, Woodcock–Johnson Test of Cognitive Abilities, 1989).

Summary. Case 1's language skills, in many areas, were very well developed. In terms of both speed and accuracy, her word recognition and phonological abilities were well above average, as were her understanding of single words and some of her oral discourse skills. Her reading comprehension was commensurate with her good word recognition skills when she had to complete texts with missing words, but it was much poorer when she had to make inferences or show an appreciation of story theme. In oral discourse too, she had difficulty making inferences. Problems in reading comprehension for Case 1 seemed most related to difficulties in inferencing. Children without developmental brain pathology who are good decoders but poor comprehenders also have difficulty making inferences (Oakhill, 1982, 1983, 1984). Although Case 1 showed a relatively isolated deficit in inferencing, she does provide some evidence for the hypothesis that, in the absence of difficulties at the word level, difficulties in reading comprehension are related to inferencing deficits (see Oakhill, 1993; Oakhill & Garnham, 1988).

But inferencing is not in itself a single entity. There are different types of inferences, and not all are equally related to text comprehension. In addition, the failure to integrate different sources of information within and without a text to make an inference may be due to all or one of several factors including a lack of world knowledge (Kintsch, 1994), problems in holding the information necessary to make an inference in working memory (Oakhill, 1993), or problems in the reasoning needed to make some types of inferences (Das Gupta & Bryant, 1989). To understand more about inferencing deficits in children with hydrocephalus, it is necessary to analyze some of these factors more specifically, as we do in the study presented below.

Using as a starting point that inferencing deficits in children with hydrocephalus occur regardless of intellectual level, and that inferencing is poor in good decoders/poor comprehenders without demonstrable brain anomaly, we investigated inferencing in children with hydrocephalus as well as in children with comprehension difficulties with no known developmental neuropathology. The focus was on a particular class of inference—knowledge-based inferences—that links elements in a text with general or world knowledge. A novel method was used to study knowledge-based inferencing: Creating a controlled knowledge base, we required children to make two types of inferences—coherence inferences and elaborative inferences, each of which has a different function in text comprehension (Barnes, Dennis, & Haefele-Kalvaitis, 1996; Casteel, 1993).

Knowledge-Based Inferencing: Comparisons of Children With Hydrocephalus and Poor Readers Without Developmental Brain Pathology

General world and domain-specific knowledge is important for successful inferencing. Logically, it is a precondition for some types of inferences in the sense that it forms part of the information needed to make the appropriate inference. The typical advantage in inferencing for children with higher versus lower IQs can be reversed when the domain knowledge of the lower IQ children is more comprehensive than that of the higher IQ children. For example, lower IQ children knowledgeable about soccer make more inferences when listening to soccer stories than do higher IQ children with less soccer knowledge (Yekovich, Walker, Ogle, & Thompson, 1990). Given the influence of the knowledge base in skilled performance (see Chi, 1978), including inferencing, a deficient or circumscribed knowledge base may contribute to poor inferencing in children with comprehension problems.

Children with hydrocephalus may lack the knowledge needed to make some inferences. For example, physical disabilities in some cases may restrict their experiences (and hence their knowledge base) of particular situations and event sequences that involve activities such as riding on a bus or hiking. It is therefore important to differentiate inferencing difficulties (in children with hydrocephalus and in other groups of poor comprehenders) due to processes related to inferencing itself from inferencing problems due to a deficient knowledge base from which inferences need to be made.

Different types of inferences serve different discourse functions. Some inferences, those we term *coherence inferences* (Barnes et al., 1996) maintain a coherent story line by adding unstated but important information to explicit text. They form a causal link between knowledge and text that helps infer why an event occurred. For example, on hearing that a family ate lunch at home after starting out for a picnic in their car, an inference about the car's implied condition or a sudden change in the weather is important to understanding the events in the story. Other inferences, those we term *elaborative inferences*, though they are not necessary for narrative coherence, serve to elaborate on story content and strengthen memory for stories. By also making concepts more concrete, elaborative inferences may facilitate the integration of subsequent propositions within a text even though they are not central to textual cohesion (Whitney, Ritchie, & Clark, 1991). Elaborative inferences specify a fuller description so that what an event is like may be inferred. For example, inferring that the sky was a bright blue color on hearing "It was a gorgeous sunny day" contributes to the building of a richer mental model of the situation (Johnson-Laird, 1993).

Inferences that maintain coherence are made more frequently by both children and adults than are those that elaborate story content (Barnes et al., 1996; Casteel, 1993; Duffy, 1986; Garrod, O'Brien, Morris, & Rayner, 1990; Keenan, Baillet, & Brown, 1984; McKoon & Ratcliff, 1990, 1992; review in Whitney, 1987). Elaborative inferences, however, are more frequent when the comprehender has a highly accessible and rich knowledge of the physical domain of the story (Morrow, Bower, & Greenspan, 1990; and see Singer, Graesser, & Trabasso, 1994 for a more general discussion of the factors guiding inference processes).

We investigated elaborative and coherence inferencing in children with hydrocephalus of average or higher intelligence and in a group of poor decoders/poor comprehenders. In these studies, a new knowledge base was taught to all children and the only inferences required were those that drew on this newly acquired knowledge base. By exploring how children with hydrocephalus access information from an available knowledge base to make different types of inferences, and contrasting this with inferencing in normally developing readers and poor readers without frank brain injury, we hoped to begin delineating the deficient underlying processes that cause inferencing failure in each group. Data of this kind also bear on the issue of whether the origins of inferencing deficits in children with hydrocephalus are the same as those characterizing children without known brain anomalies. The answer to this question is relevant to the issues raised at the beginning of the chapter; namely, that comparisons of cognitive skills in children with and without brain pathology can provide information important for specifying the parameters of cognitive models.

Description of Subjects in the Hydrocephalus and Normally Developing Control Groups

From our larger cohort of children with hydrocephalus, a subset with verbal IQs equal to or greater than 90 (> 25th percentile) was chosen for the inferencing study. This average IQ group (30 subjects) was matched to normally developing control children from the same educational system, on a pair-by-pair basis, for age, school grade, and word recognition ability. The mean age of the hydrocephalus group was 11.19 years; that of the control group, 11.12 years (range from 6–15 years). The hydrocephalus group did not differ from the control group on word recognition accuracy, phonological analysis, or written vocabulary knowledge, but they were significantly poorer than controls at understanding text (although still within the average range). In addition, their reading comprehension scores were significantly lower than their own word recognition scores. Descriptive variables for the two groups are presented in Table 11.2.

The mean VIQ of the hydrocephalus group was 103, with a range of 90–131. The mean PIQ was 92, with a range of 65 to 120. These differences between verbal and performance IQ in hydrocephalus were consistent with other reports in the literature (Dennis et al., 1981; Shaffer et al., 1985; Wills et al., 1990). Although the relationship between lower performance IQ and some medical features of hydrocephalus has been well documented (Dennis et al.,

TABLE 11.2
Descriptive Characteristics for Hydrocephalus and Control
Groups and for Poor and Average Reader Groups

	Hydrocephalus Group	Controls	Poor Readers	Average Readers
Mean age				
(Years/decimal years)	11.19	11.12	10.9	11.0
Word identification				
(mean percentile)	56.5	52.4	24.2	48.3
Word comprehension[a]				
(mean percentile)	56.4	62.5	36.0	63.0
Passage comprehension				
(mean percentile)	43.5	57.2	15.9	57.7

[a]A written vocabulary measure (generating antonyms, synonyms, and solving verbal analogies) was used for the hydrocephalus and control groups, and an oral vocabulary measure (generating antonyms and synonyms) was used for the poor and average reader groups.

1981), we have found thus far no relationship between PIQ and any of the reading and language measures, which is generally consistent with reading studies in children without known brain anomaly (e.g., Cunningham, Stanovich, & Wilson, 1990; Siegel & Ryan, 1989; Stanovich, Cunningham, & Feeman, 1984).

Description of Subjects in the Poor Reader and Average Reader Groups

Using the same paradigm, another study compared a group of 21 poor readers matched to a group of 21 average readers for age and grade (Barnes & Savard, 1993). Poor readers were chosen on the basis of reading comprehension scores below the 25th percentile for their grade; the average readers were chosen on the basis of reading comprehension scores above the 45th percentile. The poor readers also had poorer word recognition scores than did the average readers. None of the children in the poor reader group had been identified as having a reading disability and none was receiving remedial assistance in reading. Although not sharing the good word decoding skills of children with hydrocephalus, these poor readers had consistent difficulties in language comprehension (e.g., their oral vocabulary was significantly poorer than the average readers; see Table 11.2 for descriptive characteristics of these groups).

In sum, the method of the inferencing studies involved comparing hydrocephalic children whose decoding was better than their comprehension with children without brain anomalies whose decoding was commensurate with their comprehension; and comparing poor decoders/poor comprehenders (garden variety poor readers, Stanovich, 1988) with children who were average in both decoding and comprehension.

The Knowledge-Based Inferencing Task

The paradigm involved learning a new knowledge base and then listening to a story in which inferences were to be made using the newly learned knowledge base. In addition, memory for the knowledge base was also tested at the end of the story so that inferencing could be conditionalized on knowledge base items that were actually available or recallable over the period in which inferences were to be made. Fuller descriptions of the task and the materials can be found in an investigation of knowledge-based inferencing in normally developing children (Barnes et al., 1996).

Learning the Knowledge Base. Characters for an invented world, "Gan," were introduced, and 20 facts about Gan were created by giving new properties to familiar objects (e.g., "Turtles on Gan have ice skates attached to their feet," "Bears on Gan have blue fur," and so forth). Only the information from this newly created knowledge base was relevant to making the inferences. The 20 knowledge base items were read to the subjects in a block at a rate of one item every 5 seconds.

Acquisition of the knowledge base was then tested by asking the subject to choose the picture of an item from Gan (e.g., a pair of turtles with ice skates on their feet) from among three distractors (true state on Earth, for example, a normal pair of turtles; property other than the one ascribed to the object on Gan, for example, a pair of turtles with roller skates on their feet; and the Ganian property ascribed to another object, for example, a pair of lizards with ice skates on their feet). Subjects were provided with feedback on items that were failed (an incorrect picture choice) by presenting the correct fact again before moving on to the next picture test item. After the 20th item had been tested with the pictures, any items that the child failed the first time through were retested with the appropriate pictures. This procedure was repeated until all items had been identified correctly once.

Presenting the Story and Asking Questions. The Gan story was made up of 10 one-paragraph episodes, each with simple grammatical constructions and content vocabulary within the capabilities of an average 6-year-old (Carroll & White, 1973). One Gan episode can be found in Table 11.3. The story was read one episode at a time, and after a brief delay, questions for that episode were asked. Each episode contained information from which several questions were to be answered (Table 11.3), and a neutral probe ("Tell me more about that") obtained more information, where required.

For the coherence inference, an inference must be made in order to understand a proposition in the story and to maintain story coherence (e.g.,

TABLE 11.3
Sample Episode From Gan Story

Episode 8:

It was getting so cold that Dack and Tane took their coats out of their bags too. They put on their coats which were made of bear's fur. It did not take long for the path to become icy and slippery. Dack and Tane kept falling on the ice. They saw two turtles ahead of them on the path. "I sure wish that I was a turtle," sighed Dack. Tane took a step and fell on top of her knapsack, crushing all the strawberries she had picked earlier that day. When Dack tried to help her up he fell too. Dack was covered in scrapes and bruises. He was like a boxer who had lost a fight. "Poor Dack," said Tane as she stood up. "You'll feel better tomorrow." She helped Dack up and they walked very carefully along the path, holding each other by the hand.

Elaborative Inference Question: What did Dack and Tane take out of their bags? (their blue coats, or their blue bear fur coats)

Coherence Inference Question: What did Dack wish? (he had ice skates; or he was a turtle because turtles have ice skates; or he was a turtle so he could skate)

Literal Content Question: What happened when Tane fell? (she fell on her knapsack or she crushed the strawberries for 1 point, and 2 points if both are included)

Note. Acceptable answers are shown in parentheses. From Barnes, Dennis, and Haefele-Kalvaitis (1996). Reprinted with permission from the Academic Press.

in the story, the proposition "Dack wished he was a turtle" makes little sense unless it is integrated with a part of the knowledge base, that turtles on Gan have ice skates). For an elaborative inference, a subject who made the inference that the children's coats were blue (the coats were made of bear's fur and the bears on Gan are blue) would add information and create a richer mental content to the proposition "They put on their coats made of bear's fur," even though textual coherence does not require this inference.

Questions about literal content were used to track the subject's understanding of literal text propositions. An example is provided in Table 11.3. Answers to literal questions were scored strictly, with 1 point given for partial recall of the relevant proposition (either Tane fell on her knapsack or Tane crushed the strawberries) and 2 points given for complete recall of the proposition (Tane fell on her knapsack and crushed the strawberries). Memory for text could be viewed as a prerequisite for further operations on that text such as inferencing (see Surber & Surber, 1983), although literal recall of a text is not always related to other types of comprehension for the same text (Bransford, Barclay, & Franks, 1972).

The entire story was presented orally for the hydrocephalus group and their controls. For the poor and average reader groups, half of the episodes in the story were read to them, as in the hydrocephalus group, and they read aloud the other half. The data were collapsed over listening and reading as this manipulation made no difference on any of the measures (Barnes et al., 1996; Barnes & Savard, 1993). The comprehension deficits of poor comprehenders (whether they are good decoders or not) were found to occur in listening as well as in reading. It has commonly been assumed that the origins of comprehension deficits in reading versus listening overlap substantially though not completely (see Horowitz & Samuels, 1987).

Remembering the Knowledge Base Over the Course of the Story. After questions for the last episode had been answered, the subject was asked to remember the knowledge base ("What are the turtles on Gan like?"; "What are the bears on Gan like?"). This memory test was used to measure whether the knowledge base was equally available, that is, equally well recalled, at the end of the story in the different groups, and to provide a means of conditionalizing inferencing on available knowledge so that consideration was given only for inferences for which the relevant knowledge was known to be available.

Findings for Children With Hydrocephalus and Normally Developing Children

The gist of the results is presented here. Actual statistical data may be found in Barnes and Dennis (in press). Like normally developing readers as young as 6 years of age (see Barnes et al., 1996), the children with hydrocephalus made more coherence than elaborative inferences suggesting that they were sensitive to the causal constraints that operate within stories. Children with hydrocephalus were found to make fewer coherence inferences than controls and they showed a trend towards making fewer elaborative inferences, despite inferencing having been conditionalized on available or remembered knowledge. The children with hydrocephalus were also less accurate than controls in answering questions about literal aspects of the text.

Two sources of inferencing failure were considered; failures to integrate recalled premise and knowledge-base information (integration errors) and failures to recall the important premise information from the episode even when the pertinent knowledge-base item could be recalled (premise errors). An example of an integration error would be where the subject included the relevant proposition from the story (i.e., that Dack wished he was a turtle) in his answer to the inference question (i.e., What did Dack wish?) and where he recalled the relevant knowledge-base item at the end of the story (i.e., that turtles on Gan have ice skates attached to their feet), but did not integrate the two sources of information to make an inference (i.e., that Dack wished he was a turtle because then he could skate and not fall on the ice). An example of a premise error would be where the subject recalled the relevant knowledge-base item at the end of the story, but did not recall the pertinent proposition from the episode in response to the inference question.

For coherence inferencing, the children with hydrocephalus showed a similar pattern of errors to controls. Both groups sometimes failed to make inferences because they did not integrate premise and knowledge-base information, and, in equal measure, because they did not access premise information. The difference in the number of each type of error between the groups failed to reach significance. For elaborative inferencing, the hydrocephalus group made fewer inferences than controls primarily because they failed to retrieve pertinent premise information. The two groups made similar numbers of integration errors for elaborative inferences.

Although correct inferences were conditionalized on remembering the pertinent knowledge-base items, children with hydrocephalus made fewer coherence inferences in absolute terms because they could not recall the knowledge base as well as controls. That is, the hydrocephalus group could not recall the knowledge base by the end of the story with the same facility as their controls (they also took more trials to learn the knowledge base than did controls, similar to younger children; see Barnes et al., 1996).

In sum, the hydrocephalus group had more difficulty learning the new knowledge base (though they all learned it to criterion) and they had more difficulty remembering that knowledge over the course of the story. However, even when inferencing was conditionalized on available or recalled knowledge, the children with hydrocephalus made fewer coherence inferences and showed a trend towards making fewer elaborative inferences too. Children with hydrocephalus and normally developing children failed to make coherence inferences for the same reasons; they sometimes failed to integrate available premise and knowledge-base information and they sometimes failed to recall the premise information from the story. For children with hydrocephalus, elaborative inferences were not made because they more often failed to recall the relevant proposition from the text. Children with hydrocephalus also were less successful in recalling the literal aspects of the story.

Findings for Poor Readers and Average Readers

Poor readers, like average readers, made more coherence than elaborative inferences, again suggesting some knowledge of the importance of maintaining coherence in stories. Poor readers, however, made significantly fewer coherence inferences than average readers and they also made fewer elaborative inferences when inferencing was conditionalized on having recalled the pertinent knowledge-base information (Barnes & Savard, 1993). Unlike children with hydrocephalus, however, these poor readers remembered the knowledge base as well as average readers (although they did take more trials than average readers to learn it), and they were as accurate as average readers in answering questions pertaining to literal content. The inferencing failures of both poor and average readers were due to not integrating recalled premise information (the proposition from the text important for making the inference) and knowledge-base information; the poor readers simply made more of these errors than did the average readers (Barnes & Savard, 1993).

An additional piece of information about inferencing is available in this study (though not in the hydrocephalus study). At the end of the experiment, immediately after they had recalled the knowledge base for the last time, the poor and average readers were asked direct questions to elicit inferences (e.g., *Why* did Dack wish he was a turtle?; *What color* were the children's coats made of bear's fur?). This type of question results in a condition of minimal processing complexity (Ackerman, 1984) in the sense that the inference was directly cued by using why and what questions, the premise information from the text that Dack wished he was a turtle or that the children's coats were made of bear's fur, was included in the question and did not have to be recalled, and the relevant knowledge-base items had just been recalled 1 to 2 minutes earlier. Under these conditions, the poor and average readers did not differ in either coherence or elaborative inferencing, and, in contrast to inferencing during story comprehension, all the children made more elaborative than coherence inferences here. This has been interpreted elsewhere (Barnes et al., 1996) as evidence for the hypothesis that children make more coherence than elaborative inferences during story comprehension because they are sensitive to the causal constraints operating in stories, and that the causal nature of coherence inferences may involve a more difficult computation or a more difficult type of reasoning than that required for elaborative inferences.

How Do Poor Comprehenders With Hydrocephalus Differ in Their Inferencing From Poor Decoders/Poor Comprehenders and Good Decoders/Poor Comprehenders Without Developmental Neuropathology?

A gist summary of the findings from our studies on children with hydrocephalus and poor readers (decoding and comprehension), as well as comparisons with good decoders/poor comprehenders from other studies (i.e., those of Oakhill, Yuill, and their colleagues), can be found in Table 11.4.

Inferencing, a skill hypothesized to be of central importance for reading and discourse comprehension (Kintsch, 1994; Oakhill & Garnham, 1988; Singer et al., 1994), was deficient in children of normal intelligence with hydrocephalus as well as in poor readers, and the problems occurred even when the groups demonstrably had an available knowledge base from which to make inferences. For children with hydrocephalus, the inferencing difficulties coexisted with good word recognition and adequate vocabulary skills.

Good decoders/poor comprehenders without developmental brain pathologies also have problems in inferring information implicit in the text (Oakhill, 1984). Similar to good decoders/poor comprehenders (Oakhill, 1984), our poor readers were just as accurate as average readers in recalling literal story content, although this was not the case for the hydrocephalus group. Poor readers were more likely to miss an elaborative inference because they did not integrate text-based and knowledge-based information

TABLE 11.4
Comprehension in Poor Comprehenders
With and Without Known Brain Pathology

	Brain Pathology	No Known Brain Pathology	
	Average IQ Hydrocephalus	Poor Decoders/Poor Comprehenders	Good Decoders/Poor Comprehenders
Word recognition	Intact	Poor	Intact
Vocabulary knowledge	Intact	Poor	Intact
Reading comprehension	Poorer than word recognition	Poor	Poor
Literal recall of text	Poor	Intact	Intact
Inferencing	Poor	Poor	Poor
Primary source of inferencing failure	Accessing text- & knowledge-based information	Integrating text- & knowledge-based information	Integrating text- & knowledge-based information

Note. Table 11.4 is a composite of data from our studies (Barnes & Dennis, 1992, in press; Barnes & Savard, 1993), and from those of Oakhill, Yuill, and their colleagues (see review in Oakhill, 1993).

during story comprehension (even though they actually recalled both separately), whereas hydrocephalic children were more likely to have difficulty initially retrieving text- and knowledge-based information during comprehension. The nature of such retrieval deficits remains to be explored.

Unaided, our poor readers often failed to integrate two available sources of information, but they could do so if cued and if both sources of information were contiguous. Good decoders/poor comprehenders, too, could resolve textual inconsistencies when the inconsistency and the resolving information were in adjacent sentences, but not when separated by intervening text (Yuill, Oakhill, & Parkin, 1989). A working memory hypothesis has been put forth for these results (also see Oakhill, 1993), and such an explanation may also fit the present set of results on inferencing for our poor readers. That is, poor readers can integrate two sources of information, but they may not do so spontaneously because such integration processes, in the context of text comprehension, may exceed their working memory capabilities.

Both children with hydrocephalus and poor comprehenders without brain anomalies (whether good or poor at decoding) had difficulties making inferences. These groups also differed in several important ways. Children with hydrocephalus had difficulty making inferences primarily because they failed to access either pertinent text-based or knowledge-based information, in keeping with the finding that they also had more difficulty retrieving literal content from the text. For children with hydrocephalus, then, inferencing difficulties may sometimes arise from failures to integrate different sources of information (just as they do in normally developing children), but they additionally arise because these children have problems in accessing or retrieving that information to begin with during comprehension. Poor comprehenders without frank brain injury, on the other hand, seem to have difficulty not so much accessing or retrieving text- or knowledge-based information, but in integrating these different sources of information. As Oakhill (1993) suggested, these integration difficulties may reflect limits in working memory to the extent that such integration relies on concurrent storage and processing capabilities. For poor comprehenders with hydrocephalus, difficulties in accessing text-based and knowledge-based information might be viewed as input problems for working memory in the sense that their difficulty is with the initial and/or sustained activation of relevant semantic information.

GENERAL CONCLUSIONS AND IMPLICATIONS

Reading comprehension deficits occur both in the presence and in the absence of demonstrable brain injury. In this chapter, we attempted to decompose a constituent of comprehension, inferencing, and to compare groups with and without developmental brain pathology. We found that both children with hydrocephalus who are good decoders but poorer comprehenders and poor decoders/poor comprehenders without developmental neuropathology have difficulty making inferences during text comprehension. We found further that the sources of the inferencing difficulties differed in the two groups: Children with hydrocephalus had some problems integrating different sources of information to make inferences (like their normally developing controls), but they also evidenced a more basic difficulty accessing both text- and knowledge-based information. Poor decoders/poor comprehenders, on the other hand, had problems confined to integrating text- and knowledge-based information they had successfully accessed. The data suggest that the final outcome of poor comprehension is not effected in the same way: Inferencing appears to decompose differently in poor comprehenders depending on whether there is a history of early brain damage. This has three important implications that concern both cognitive remediation and models of comprehension disabilities. If the origins of comprehension failure differ across groups with and without brain pathology, then the methods used to treat such disabilities must also differ in some aspects. Evidence that there are differences in the underlying processes that contribute to poor inferencing in children with and without developmental brain pathology bears on hypotheses about the putative neurological underpinnings of comprehension disabilities. Superficially similar deficits in groups of poor comprehenders with and without brain anomalies may arise from different sources, implying that an adequate decomposition of reading comprehension may be multicomponential at the level of basic processes.

Remediating Reading Comprehension Deficits

The academic achievement of children with hydrocephalus is something of a paradox. Speech and language are fluent, and word recognition appears to be mastered well. In the early grades, the expectations of parents and educators of these children are often quite high in terms of language and literacy. Because word recognition and reading comprehension are so closely related in normally developing children, it seems reasonable to assume that mastery of word decoding will augur well for later successful comprehension in children with hydrocephalus. But as achievement increasingly comes to draw on comprehension, many children with hydrocephalus fail to achieve at grade level, even in language areas, despite acquiring spoken language at the appropriate age, and despite the development of solid word recognition skills in the early primary grades. Reading comprehension attainments in middle childhood and adolescence are lower than word recognition levels in these children (Barnes & Dennis, 1992), which suggests that they do not use reading successfully to acquire widely based literal and inferential knowledge across subject areas. Hypotheses about the relationship between deficits in reading comprehension and the later course of academic progress of children with hydrocephalus need to be formally investigated.

The general compensatory effect of comprehension training (Oakhill, 1993), might benefit all poor comprehenders. But the remedial strategies that are most useful for some groups of poor comprehenders may not be those that would most benefit children with hydrocephalus. It would be informative to make systematic comparisons of the effectiveness of different treatment programs for children with hydrocephalus and for poor comprehenders without frank brain injury (see Oakhill & Patel, 1991; Yuill & Oakhill, 1988; and Yuill, this volume).

Neuropsychological Hypotheses and Comprehension Disability

A central tenet of cognitive neuropsychology is that the way in which a skill decomposes under conditions of brain damage is revealing of the normal functional architecture for that skill. Given that a skill such as inferencing decomposes differently in poor comprehenders depending on whether or not there is a history of early brain pathology, early lesions may impose changes on neural development that alter the normal relationships among developing skills (also see Thal et al., 1991). In the context of development, this highlights the importance of comparing basic cognitive processes in populations who show the same defective cognitive outcome on measures of more global skills.

Based on findings from lesion studies with adults and children, hypotheses have been put forth about possible brain dysfunction in children with aberrant behavioral typologies who do not have demonstrable brain damage (Barkley, Grodinsky, & DuPaul, 1992; Rourke, Bakker, Fisk, & Strang, 1983). A closer look at the cognitive processes underlying superficially similar disabilities in children with and without frank brain damage may reveal that different core deficits underlie similar comprehension outcomes. The processes that produce good decoding coupled with poor comprehension in the child with hydrocephalus, then, may not be those that produce this pattern in children without demonstrable brain damage. This suggests that brain-behavior inferences need to be cognizant of similarities and differences in the core processing deficits of children with and without known neuropathology, and of data provided by brain imaging in well-defined groups of children with comprehension deficits (for similar models in dyslexia research, see review in Hynd & Semrud-Clikeman, 1989).

Decomposing Reading Comprehension

In the knowledge-based inferencing studies discussed earlier, children with hydrocephalus had difficulties in inferential comprehension as well as in accessing factual information from the text, despite experimental manipulations that controlled for knowledge, vocabulary level, and syntactic difficulty, and despite these children having written vocabulary knowledge, word recognition, phonological processing, and other verbal skills (tapped by VIQ) well within the normal range. Inferencing was found to be a consistent deficit for children with hydrocephalus: Inferencing deficits were evident even when a number of other verbal skills were intact. But inferencing deficits were found to have different features in poor comprehenders with and without hydrocephalus. Although inferencing was a specific difficulty experienced by all the groups of poor comprehenders, inferencing itself may not be a sufficient explanation for comprehension disabilities (also see Oakhill, 1993). Perhaps a core component of comprehension is not inferencing itself, but a small set of more basic underlying processes, difficulties in any of which may produce defective inferencing.

That deficits in a skill such as inferencing might arise from different sources depending on the presence or absence of brain anomaly suggests that an adequate decomposition of comprehension requires attention not only to component skills, but also to the underlying processes that produce variations in those skills. This principle guides our current studies of reading comprehension in children with hydrocephalus.

We have suggested that poor comprehenders with hydrocephalus have difficulty accessing or activating knowledge-base information as well as information that they have previously read in a text. Poor adult comprehenders without known brain anomaly have been noted to have difficulties, not in activating information from memory, but in suppressing contextually irrelevant information (Gernsbacher & Faust, 1991). Activation and suppression might be viewed as processes that shape the contents of working memory (Just & Carpenter, 1992). Activation of the knowledge base and of previously read text provides input to working memory, whereas suppression of irrelevant information and sustained activation of relevant information ensures that only contextually appropriate information remains in working memory. In our ongoing work on comprehension, we are exploring how different groups (children with hydrocephalus, and good decoders/poor comprehenders without developmental brain pathology) access or activate as well as suppress information from memory during reading. Comparisons of activation and suppression processes in children with hydrocephalus, in children with poor reading comprehension without known brain pathology, and in children who read well, may help to further specify the nature and range of comprehension deficits, and tell us more generally about what it means to understand a text.

ACKNOWLEDGMENTS

The research in this chapter was supported by project grants from the Research Grants Program sponsored by the Ontario Ministry of Community and Social Services, the Ontario Mental Health Foundation, and the Ontario

Ministry of Health. We thank Margaret Wilkinson and Angeline Sarabura for research assistance.

REFERENCES

Ackerman, B. P. (1984). Storage and processing constraints on integrating story information in children and adults. *Journal of Experimental Child Psychology, 38*, 64–92.

Anderson, E. M. (1973). *The disabled schoolchild: A study of integration in primary schools.* London: Methuen.

Backman, J., Bruck, M., Hebert, M., & Seidenberg, M. S. (1984). Acquisition and use of spelling sound correspondences in reading. *Journal of Experimental Child Psychology, 38*, 114–133.

Barkley, R. A., Grodzinsky, G., & DuPaul, G. J. (1992). Frontal lobe functions in attention deficit disorders with and without hyperactivity: A review and research report. *Journal of Abnormal Child Psychology, 20*, 163–188.

Barnes, M. A., & Dennis, M. (1992). Reading in children and adolescents after early onset hydrocephalus and in normally developing age peers: Phonological analysis, word recognition, word comprehension, and passage comprehension skills. *Journal of Pediatric Psychology, 17*, 445–465.

Barnes, M. A., & Dennis, M. (1995). [Control children in a study of component reading skills]. Unpublished raw data.

Barnes, M. A., Dennis, M., & Haefele-Kalvaitis, J. (1996). The effects of knowledge availability and knowledge accessibility on coherence and elaborative inferencing in children from 6 to 15 years of age. *Journal of Experimental Child Psychology, 61*.

Barnes, M. A., & Dennis, M. (in press). Discourse after early-onset hydrocephalus: Core deficits in children of average intelligence. *Brain and Language.*

Barnes, M. A., & Savard, A. (1993, March). *Coherence and elaborative inferencing from a controlled knowledge base in poor and average comprehenders.* 60th Anniversary Meeting of the Society for Research in Child Development, New Orleans, LA.

Bentin, S., Deutsch, A., & Liberman, I. Y. (1990). Syntactic competence and reading ability in children. *Journal of Experimental Child Psychology, 48*, 147–172.

Bertelson, P. (1993). Reading acquisition and phonemic awareness testing: How conclusive are data from Down Syndrome? Remarks on Cossu, Rossini, & Marshall. *Cognition, 48*, 281–283.

Bradley, L., & Bryant, P. E. (1983). Categorizing sounds and learning to read—A causal connection. *Nature, 301*, 419–421.

Bransford, J. D., Barclay, J., & Franks, J. J. (1972). Sentence memory: A constructive versus interpretive approach. *Cognitive Psychology, 3*, 193–209.

Brown, V. L., Hamill, D. D., & Wiederholt, J. L. (1986). *Test of Reading Comprehension.* Austin, TX: Pro-ed.

Byrne, K., Abbeduto, L., & Brooks, P. (1990). The language of children with spina bifida and hydrocephalus: Meeting task demands and mastering syntax. *Journal of Speech and Hearing Disorders, 55*, 118–123.

Cacciari, C., & Tabossi, P. (1993). *Idioms: Processing, structure, and interpretation.* Hillsdale, NJ: Lawrence Erlbaum Associates.

Carr, T. H., & Levy, B. A. (1990). *Reading and its development: Component skills approaches.* Toronto: Academic Press.

Carroll, J. B., & White, M. N. (1973). Age-of-acquisition norms for 220 picturable nouns. *Journal of Verbal Learning and Verbal Behavior, 12*, 563–576.

Casteel, M. A. (1993). Effects of inference necessity and reading goal in children's inferential generations. *Developmental Psychology, 29*, 346–357.

Chi, M. T. H. (1978). Knowledge structures and memory development. In R. Siegler (Ed.), *Children's thinking: What develops?* (pp. 73–96). Hillsdale, NJ: Lawrence Erlbaum Associates.

Cossu, G., Rossini, F., & Marshall, J. C. (1993). When reading is acquired but phonemic awareness is not: A study of literacy in Down Syndrome. *Cognition, 46*, 129–138.

Cunningham, A. E., Stanovich, K. E., & Wilson, M. R. (1990). Cognitive variation in adult college students differing in reading ability. In T. H. Carr & B. A. Levy (Eds.), *Reading and its development: Component skills approaches* (pp. 129–159). Toronto: Academic Press.

Das Gupta, P., & Bryant, P. E. (1989). Young children's causal inferences. *Child Development, 60*, 1138–1146.

Del Bigio, M. (1993). Neuropathological changes caused by hydrocephalus. *Acta Neuropathologica, 18*, 573–585.

Denckla, M. B., & Rudel, R. (1974). Rapid automatised naming of pictured objects, colors, letters and numbers by normal children. *Cortex, 10*, 186–202.

Dennis, M., & Barnes, M. A. (1993). Oral discourse after early-onset hydrocephalus: Linguistic ambiguity, figurative language, speech acts, and script-based inferences. *Journal of Pediatric Psychology, 18*, 639–652.

Dennis, M., Fitz, C. R., Netley, C. T., Sugar, J., Harwood-Nash, D. C. F., Hendrick, E. B., Hoffman, H. J., & Humphreys, R. P. (1981). The intelligence of hydrocephalic children. *Archives of Neurology, 38*, 607–615.

Dennis, M., Hendrick, E. B., Hoffman, H. J., & Humphreys, R. P. (1987). Language of hydrocephalic children and adolescents. *Journal of Clinical and Experimental Neuropsychology, 9*, 593–621.

Dennis, M., Jacennik, B., & Barnes, M. A. (1994). The content of narrative discourse in children and adolescents after early onset hydrocephalus and in normally developing age peers. *Brain and Language, 46*, 129–165.

Duffy, S. A. (1986). Role of expectations in sentence integration. *Journal of Experimental Psychology: Learning, Memory, and Cognition, 12*, 208–219.

Emery, J. L., & Svitok, I. (1968). I: Intra-hemispherical distances in congenital hydrocephalus associated with meningomyelocele. *Developmental Medicine and Child Neurology, 10*, 21–29.

Epstein, F., Naidich, T., Kricheff, I., Chase, N., Lin, J., & Ransohoff, J. (1977). Role of computerized axial tomography in diagnosis, treatment and follow-up of hydrocephalus. *Child's Brain, 3*, 91–100.

Fletcher, J. M., Bohan, T. P., Brandt, M. E., Brookshire, B. L., Beaver, S. R., Francis, D. J., Davidson, K. C., Thompson, N. M., & Miner, M. E. (1992). Cerebral white matter and cognition in hydrocephalic children. *Archives of Neurology, 49*, 818–824.

Fletcher, J. M., & Levin, H. S. (1987). Neurobehavioral effects of brain injury in children. In D. Routh (Ed.), *Handbook of pediatric psychology* (pp. 258–295). New York: Guilford.

Garrod, S., O'Brien, E. J., Morris, R. R., & Rayner, K. (1990). Elaborative inferencing as an active or passive process. *Journal of Experimental Psychology: Learning, Memory, and Cognition, 16*, 250–257.

Gernsbacher, M. A., & Faust, M. E. (1991). The mechanism of suppression: A component of general comprehension skill. *Journal of Experimental Psychology: Learning, Memory, and Cognition, 17*, 245–262.

Geschwind, N. (1970). The organization of language and the brain. *Science, 170*, 940–944.

Goldman, R., Fristoe, M., & Woodcock, R. W. (1974). *Auditory Skills Test Battery: Sound Symbol Tests.* Circle Pines, MN: American Guidance Service.

Graesser, A. C., & Kreuz, R. J. (1993). A theory of inference generation during text comprehension. *Discourse Processes, 16*, 145–160.

Hadenius, A-M., Hagberg, B., Hyttnas-Bensch, K., & Sjogren, I. (1962). The natural prognosis of infantile hydrocephalus. *Acta Paediatrica Scandinavica, 51*, 117–118.

Halliwell, M. D., Carr, J. G., & Pearson, A. M. (1980). The intellectual and educational functioning of children with neural tube defects. *Zeitschrift fur Kinderchirurgie, 31*, 375–381.

Harwood-Nash, D. C. F., & Fitz, C. R. (1976). *Neuroradiology in infants and children* (Vol. 2, pp. 609–667). St. Louis: Mosby.

Hoffman, H. J. (1989). Diagnosis and management of posthemorrhagic hydrocephalus in the premature infant. In K. E. Pape & J. S. Wiggleworth (Eds.), *Perinatal brain lesions* (pp. 219–229). Oxford, England: Basil Blackwell.

Horowitz, R., & Samuels, S. J. (1987). *Comprehending oral and written language.* San Diego: Academic Press.

Hynd, G. W., & Semrud-Clikeman, M. (1989). Dyslexia and brain morphology. *Psychological Bulletin, 106,* 447–482.

Johnson-Laird, P. N. (1993). Foreword. In C. Cacciari & P. Tabossi (Eds.), *Idioms: Processing, structure, and interpretation.* Hillsdale, NJ: Lawrence Erlbaum Associates.

Just, M. A., & Carpenter, P. A. (1992). A capacity theory of comprehension: Individual differences in working memory. *Psychological Review, 99,* 122–149.

Keenan, J. M., Baillet, S. D., & Brown, P. (1984). The effects of causal cohesion on comprehension and memory. *Journal of Verbal Learning and Verbal Behavior, 23,* 115–126.

Kintsch, W. (1994). Text comprehension, memory, and learning. *American Psychologist, 49,* 294–303.

Lovett, M. W. (1987). A developmental approach to reading disability: Accuracy and speed criteria of normal and deficient reading skill. *Child Development, 58,* 234–260.

McCabe, A. (1991). Preface: Structure as a way of understanding. In A. McCabe & C. Peterson (Eds.), *Developing narrative structure* (pp. ix–xvii). Hillsdale, NJ: Lawrence Erlbaum Associates.

McKeown, M. G., Beck, I., Omanson, R. C., & Pople, M. T. (1985). Some effects of the nature and frequency of vocabulary instruction on the knowledge and use of words. *Reading Research Quarterly, 20,* 522–535.

McKoon, G., & Ratcliff, R. (1990). Dimensions of inference. *The Psychology of Learning and Motivation, 25,* 313–328.

McKoon, G., & Ratcliff, G. (1992). Inference during reading. *Psychological Review, 99,* 440–466.

Morrow, D. G., Bower, G. H., & Greenspan, S. L. (1990). Situation-based inferences during narrative comprehension. In A. C. Graesser & G. H. Bower (Eds.), *Inferences and text comprehension* (pp. 123–135). San Diego: Academic Press.

Morton, J., & Frith, U. (1993). What lesson for dyslexia from Down's syndrome? Comments on Cossu, Rossini, and Marshall. *Cognition, 48,* 289–296.

Nagy, W. E., Anderson, R. C., & Herman, P. A. (1987). Learning word meanings from context during normal reading. *American Educational Research Journal, 24,* 237–270.

Oakhill, J. (1982). Constructive processes in skilled and less skilled comprehenders' memory for sentences. *British Journal of Psychology, 73,* 13–20.

Oakhill, J. (1983). Instantiation in skilled and less skilled comprehenders. *Quarterly Journal of Experimental Psychology, 35A,* 441–450.

Oakhill, J. (1984). Inferential and memory skills in children's comprehension of stories. *British Journal of Education and Psychology, 54,* 31–39.

Oakhill, J. (1993). Children's difficulties in reading comprehension. *Educational Psychology Review, 5,* 1–15.

Oakhill, J., & Garnham, A. (1988). *Becoming a skilled reader.* Oxford, England: Basil Blackwell.

Oakhill, J., & Patel, S. (1991). Can imagery training help children who have comprehension problems? *Journal of Research in Reading, 14,* 106–115.

Oakhill, J., Yuill, N. M., & Parkin, A. J. (1986). On the nature of the difference between skilled and less-skilled comprehenders. *Journal of Research in Reading, 9,* 80–91.

Perfetti, C. A. (1985). *Reading ability.* New York: Oxford University Press.

Prigatano, G. P., Zeiner, H. K., Pollay, M., & Kaplan, R. J. (1983). Neuropsychological functioning in children with shunted uncomplicated hydrocephalus. *Child's Brain, 10,* 112–120.

Rankin, J. L. (1993). Information-processing differences of college-age readers differing in reading comprehension and speed. *Journal of Reading Behavior, 25,* 261–278.

Rourke, B. P., Bakker, D. J., Fisk, J. L., & Strang, J. D. (1983). *Child neuropsychology: An introduction to theory, research, and clinical practice.* New York: Guilford.

Seidenberg, M. S., Waters, G. S., Barnes, M. A., & Tanenhaus, M. (1984). When does irregular spelling or pronunciation influence word recognition? *Journal of Verbal Learning and Verbal Behavior, 23,* 383–404.

Shaffer, J., Friedrich, W. N., Shurtleff, D. B., & Wolf, L. (1985). Cognitive and achievement status of children with myelomeningocele. *Journal of Pediatric Psychology, 10,* 325–336.

Siegel, L. S., & Ryan, E. B. (1989). The development of working memory in normally achieving and subtypes of learning disabled children. *Child Development, 60,* 973–980.

Singer, M. H., & Crouse, J. (1981). The relationship of context-use skills to reading: A case for an alternative experimental logic. *Child Development, 52,* 1326–1329.

Singer, M. H., Graesser, A. C., & Trabasso, T. (1994). Minimal or global inference during reading. *Journal of Memory and Language, 33,* 421–441.

Stanovich, K. E. (1988). Explaining the differences between the dyslexic and the garden-variety poor reader: The phonological-core variable-difference model. *Journal of Learning Disabilities, 21,* 590–604.

Stanovich, K. E. (1991). Discrepancy definitions of reading disability: Has intelligence led us astray? *Reading Research Quarterly, 26,* 7–29.

Stanovich, K. E., Cunningham, A. E., & Feeman, D. J. (1984). Intelligence, cognitive skills, and early reading progress. *Reading Research Quarterly, 19,* 278–303.

Surber, J. R., & Surber, C. F. (1983). Effects of inference on memory for prose. *Merrill-Palmer Quarterly, 29,* 197–207.

Taylor, E. M. (1961). *Psychological appraisal of children with cerebral defects.* Cambridge, MA: Harvard University Press.

Teuber, H. L. (1955). Physiological psychology. *Annual Review of Psychology, 6,* 267–296.

Tew, B. J., & Laurence, K. M. (1975). The effects of hydrocephalus on intelligence, visual perception and school attainment. *Developmental Medicine and Child Neurology, 17,* 129–134.

Thal, D. J., Marchman, V., Stiles, J., Aram, D., Trauner, D., Nass, R., & Bates, E. (1991). Early lexical development in children with focal brain injury. *Brain and Language, 40,* 491–527.

Wechsler, D. (1991). *Wechsler Intelligence Scale for Children–Third Edition.* New York: The Psychological Corporation.

Whitney, P. (1987). Psychological theories of elaborative inferences: Implications for schema-theoretic views of comprehension. *Reading Research Quarterly, 22,* 299–310.

Whitney, P., Ritchie, B. G., & Clark, M. B. (1991). Working memory capacity and the use of elaborative inferences in text comprehension. *Discourse Processes, 14,* 133–145.

Wiig, E. H., & Secord, W. (1989). *Test of Language Competence: Expanded Edition.* San Antonio, TX: Psychological Corporation.

Wills, K. E., Holmbeck, G. N., Dillon, K., & McLone, D. G. (1990). Intelligence and achievement in children with myelomeningocele. *Journal of Pediatric Psychology, 13,* 161–176.

Woodcock, R. W. (1987). *Woodcock Reading Mastery Tests–Revised.* Circle Pines, MN: American Guidance Service.

Woodcock, R. W., & Johnson, M. B. (1989). *Tests of Cognitive Ability.* Allen, TX: DLM Teaching Resources.

Yekovich, F. R., Walker, C. H., Ogle, L. T., & Thompson, M. A. (1990). The influence of domain knowledge on inferencing in low-aptitude individuals. In A. C. Graesser & G. H. Bower (Eds.), *Inferences and text comprehension* (pp. 259–278). San Diego: Academic Press.

Yuill, N. M., & Oakhill, J. V. (1988). Effects of inference awareness training on poor reading comprehension. *Applied Cognitive Psychology, 2*, 33–45.

Yuill, N. M., & Oakhill, J. V. (1991). *Children's problems in text comprehension: An experimental investigation.* Cambridge, England: Cambridge University Press.

Yuill, N. M., Oakhill, J. V., & Parkin, A. J. (1989). Working memory, comprehension ability and the resolution of text anomaly. *British Journal of Psychology, 80*, 351–361.

Zurif, E. B. (1990). Language and the brain. In D. N. Osherson & H. Lasnik (Eds.), *Language: An invitation to cognitive science* (Vol. 1, pp. 177–198). Cambridge, MA: MIT Press.

CHAPTER TWELVE

Success and Failure in Learning to Read: The Special Case (?) of Deaf Children

Marc Marschark
National Technical Institute for the Deaf
Rochester Institute of Technology

Margaret Harris
Royal Holloway—University of London

As the other chapters in this volume illustrate, there are many reasons why children might have difficulty learning to read. Reading is a complex and multileveled task, even if most children appear to learn it with relative ease. Among deaf children,[1] however, reading is the single most difficult academic hurdle, and most do not surmount it without faltering. As a result, the average deaf high-school graduate reads at about the same level as the average 8- to 9-year-old hearing child.

This chapter explores some of the reasons why deaf children have so much trouble learning to read and why many of them will continue to have reading comprehension difficulties into adulthood. In some domains, deaf children appear to experience the same kinds of reading difficulties as hearing children. In other domains, they may be handicapped by the fact that they are not fluent producers or receivers of a language that corresponds to the written vernacular. Further, most deaf children do not share an effective mode of communication with their parents, who should be their most important reading teachers. The implications of this unique language situation, together with possible interactions among the relevant variables,

---

[1]Throughout this chapter, references to "deaf children" pertain to children with relatively serious hearing losses, in the severe to profound range. Clearly, the degree of a child's hearing loss will affect the accessibility to spoken language and, concomitantly we argue, the development of reading skills. We do not address issues of reading in children with mild to moderate hearing losses primarily because of the lack of literature relevant to that group.

suggest that the fundamental problems of young deaf readers may not be "special," even if they are more numerous and more extreme. At issue, then, are the most effective ways to go about eliminating those common, if uncommonly prevalent, obstacles to attaining literacy.

READING DIFFICULTIES OF DEAF CHILDREN: A LONG-STANDING PROBLEM

Despite the fact that the reading abilities of deaf children have attracted so much attention from educators and researchers over the last two decades, the available evidence has indicated that the great majority of them continue to show relatively poor reading progress. DiFrancesca (1972), for example, found that across the school years, deaf children's reading scores increased only about 0.2 grade levels per year of schooling. Vernon (1972) found the reading skills of deaf students between 10 and 16 years of age to gain little more than 0.1 grade levels per year in reading achievement. Both of these statistics stand in marked contrast to the full year improvement in reading that is expected in hearing children.

Fourteen years later, Allen (1986) found that, as a group, the 18-year-old sample of deaf students involved in the 1983 norming of the Stanford Achievement Test (SAT) had not reached even the third-grade level of reading comprehension. Moreover, he demonstrated that lags in the reading comprehension of that American sample actually increased through the school years, as shown in Table 12.1. A similarly disturbing conclusion emerged from a study

TABLE 12.1
Approximate Reading Comprehension Scaled Scores and Reading Levels
for the 1983 Norming of the Stanford Achievement Test Reading
Comprehension Subtest and Median 1982 Performance for
Hearing Age-Mates (adapted from Allen, 1986)

	Deaf		Hearing	
Age	Score	Grade Level	Score	Grade Level
8	510	1.75	585	3.0
9	520	1.90	615	4.0
10	540	2.25	635	5.0
11	545	2.30	645	6.0
12	560	2.55	660	7.0
13	570	2.70	670	8.0
14	580	2.85	680	9.0
15	590	3.05	690	10.0
16	585	3.05		
17	585	3.00		
18	575	2.80		

by Gaines, Mandler, and Bryant (1981) in the United Kingdom, which found only 1.4% of deaf 16-year-olds reading at an age-appropriate level. Taken together, these findings suggest that deaf students in both the United States and the United Kingdom are at a relatively greater disadvantage when they leave than when they enter the educational system, because their gains are far outpaced by those of their hearing peers.

Traditionally, *functional literacy* has been defined as corresponding to a fourth- to fifth-grade level of reading and writing, although the demands of the "information age" may require a criterion closer to an 11th- or 12th-grade level (e.g., Waters & Doehring, 1990). In these terms, Allen's (1986) data suggested that over 30% of deaf students now leave school functionally illiterate, compared to less than 1% of hearing students. These global statistics, however, disguise the great heterogeneity in deaf children's reading attainment. Some deaf children read at an age-appropriate level or better all the way through their school years while others constantly struggle. Some areas of difficulty across deaf children resolve with age, while others remain more intractable. Any attempt to fit deaf children's reading problems into a simple or well-defined model, therefore, is doomed to failure. There are many potential barriers to deaf children's reading success, and, as we see in the next section, these factors are a challenge to disentangle.

Early Language Experience, Parental Involvement, and Reading

Several investigators have attributed the relatively poor reading abilities of deaf children to the fact that over 90% of them have hearing parents who do not share with them an effective mode of communication. Early intervention programs that focus solely on spoken language generally are unsuccessful for children with more severe hearing losses (see Marschark, 1997), and most hearing parents of deaf children either do not know sign language or have only rudimentary sign skills. Such skills are insufficient for the purposes of reading "aloud" to their children, let alone for the explicit teaching of literacy skills. Deaf children who are born to deaf parents, in contrast, are likely to be exposed to sign language from an early age, and they are also more likely to attend a school where signing is used in the classroom. Their parents often read to them and facilitate their acquisition of literacy skills in both sign and print. It therefore should not be surprising that deaf children of deaf parents generally read at about two grade levels above deaf children with hearing parents.

Although such findings have led several authors to conclude that early exposure to sign language is the main factor that determines whether deaf children will learn to read successfully or not, Marschark (1993a) argued that there are more differences between deaf children with deaf parents and those with hearing parents than just their early exposure to sign language. Deaf and hearing parents, for example, may have very different expectations for the education of their deaf children; and due to both communication and cultural differences, their children might have different academic and personal goals. More basically, the quality and content of early communication between deaf children and their hearing parents will have significant effects on their social and cognitive development, thereby creating significant developmental differences relative to children who share a common language with their parents, either spoken or signed (Vaccari & Marschark, 1996).

Another potential problem with the assumption that early exposure to sign language is sufficient to provide an advantage in reading development lies with the character of sign language itself. Natural sign languages such as American Sign Language (ASL) or British Sign Language (BSL) have their own vocabularies, morphologies, and syntaxes, which do not parallel those of spoken or printed English.[2] Deaf parents who are fluent in ASL or BSL use those languages in the home with their deaf (and hearing) children, where they are acquired as a first language. Learning to read, therefore, is a case of second-language learning for those children (see discussion below), and there is no more reason to believe that ASL or BSL as a first language will facilitate reading of English than reading of Chinese. Although we acknowledge that early exposure to a regular, conventionalized language is essential for normal reading development, it is important to be cognizant of the fact that the transition from signing to reading is different and more difficult than the transition from a spoken language to reading that same language in printed form.

There are other forms of signing to which deaf children may be exposed which attempt to overcome the transition problem while providing for early access to language. In fact, these artificial systems have been developed explicitly to facilitate the development of reading and, to a lesser extent, spoken language skills in deaf children. *Sign English* is one of several such systems, in which ASL (or BSL) signs are made in English word order and with the addition of English morphology. Sign English thus provides a parallel with written English in a way that ASL and BSL do not. Unfortunately, while such systems can provide both early exposure to language and English-relevant linguistic experience, they also can leave children caught between hearing and deaf worlds, and not fluent in the language of either (see Marschark, 1997, for discussion).

The above arguments notwithstanding, it is clear that the generally higher level of reading attainment by deaf children of deaf parents is at least partially influenced by their early linguistic interaction, even if the relation is not as

---

[2]For convenience, we refer to ASL, BSL, and English, because those are the languages we are most familiar with and the languages within which most of the relevant research has been conducted. *English* should be understood, however, as referring to any "host language" or vernacular.

direct as some might believe, and that the exposure to English-based sign systems should lead to better acquisition of reading skills than either no early language training or training in spoken language only (but see footnote 1). These two contributors to deaf children's reading success are potentially in conflict, of course, as parents who are better able to give their children early access to language (deaf parents) are probably less likely to use English-based sign systems, and those parents who could provide the most comprehensive access to English (hearing parents) are less likely to be able to communicate effectively with their deaf children for the purposes of direct and indirect teaching. Nevertheless, there appears to be support in the literature for the optimization of reading skill in those children who have access to both languages from an early age.

In what is perhaps the most frequently cited study in this area, Schlesinger and Meadow (1972) compared the reading abilities of residential school samples of deaf children with deaf parents and deaf children with hearing parents to a group of day-school deaf students who had hearing parents. Half of the day-school students attended an oral program and half attended a total communication program (which optimizes the sources of information available to deaf children through sign language, spoken language, and amplification). Schlesinger and Meadow found that the residential school students with hearing parents were, on average, one grade level behind those with deaf parents in reading comprehension, while the day students scored midway between them. However, due to the heterogeneity of the groups, these differences did not approach statistical reliability.

More interesting for the present purposes was the finding that students enrolled in the total communication curriculum significantly surpassed the other groups in reading skill, including the group with deaf parents. These results indicated that the use of signed communication in a day-school classroom had a larger effect on reading ability than did parental hearing status per se (Brasel & Quigley, 1977). Of course, it is likely that the two day school groups and the residential-school groups also differed in ways not evaluated by Schlesinger and Meadow. For example, hearing parents who send their children to programs that include sign communication training (especially back in 1972!), likely are more accepting of their children's deafness; and the exposure to deaf role models as well as hearing role models may have contributed substantially to their children's success (Marschark, 1997; Vaccari & Marschark, 1996).

Beyond the findings of Schlesinger and Meadow (1972), there has been further evidence suggesting that early exposure to signed communication alone is insufficient to explain or produce superior reading abilities in deaf children with deaf parents relative to those with hearing parents. Jensema and Trybus (1978), for example, studied families with one deaf and one hearing parent, where speech was the primary form of home communication, and families with two deaf parents, in which sign language was the primary form of home communication. Despite the fact that sign language was available to deaf children in both groups of families from birth, deaf children with one deaf parent were found to be superior readers relative to those with two deaf parents. The precise locus of this advantage, however, was not investigated and remains unclear.

When hearing parents do learn sign language, it almost always differs from the kind of signing used by deaf parents, being English-based and used simultaneously with spoken language as well as starting later. It therefore should not be surprising to find that the significance of early sign language exposure does not appear to be the same for deaf children with deaf parents as it is for those with hearing parents. Studies by both Kusché, Greenberg, and Garfield (1983) and Kampfe (1989), for example, found no significant relationship between reading comprehension and age of sign acquisition among deaf children who had hearing parents. Children in the Kusché et al. study who had deaf parents, in contrast, showed a strong relation between reading comprehension and the age at which they had started signing. Reasons for this difference may lie in several domains, in addition to the acknowledged advantage of learning language during the critical period of the first 3 years rather than upon entry into a preschool or elementary (primary) school program. One contributing influence derives from the fact that through sign language, deaf parents can consistently expose their deaf children to the kinds of general world knowledge that is important in many aspects of reading comprehension (e.g., vocabulary and grammar). Just as importantly, deaf children who arrive at school with age-appropriate competence in ASL or BSL are in an excellent position to learn Sign English or English as second languages.

The advantages of early sign exposure to learning English as a second language were illustrated in a study by Charrow and Fletcher (1974). Although they failed to find a difference in the reading comprehension scores of groups of 17- to 18-year-olds with either deaf or hearing parents, Charrow and Fletcher observed marked advantages for the native signing group on several other dimensions of English reading and writing ability, including measures of vocabulary, paragraph meaning, and English grammatical structure. A similar pattern of findings was evident in a study involving younger children, reported by Harris and Beech (1995). They found that over the first 2 years at school (i.e., ages 5 to 7 years), there was no correlation between knowledge of signing or fingerspelling and reading progress, where reading progress was defined in terms of print vocabulary (i.e., through multiple-choice picture selection in response to printed words). However, there was a positive relationship between language comprehension (using a specially adapted version of the language comprehension test of the British Ability scales) and both of these measures. Taken together, these results suggested that early exposure to sign language may provide a firmer basis for the development of language skills which become increasingly important as reading progresses toward the text level.

Although deaf children of deaf parents already have familiarity with sign language and age-appropriate language ability when they enter school, a significant number of deaf children of hearing parents begin formal schooling with little fluency in either a spoken or signed language. In many cases, that situation persists into adulthood because their school experience does not provide an adequate opportunity for acquiring either language competently. Citing this situation, Johnson, Liddell, and Erting (1989) attributed many of the scholastic difficulties of deaf students to their inability to understand the English-based materials used in school. They acknowledged that most deaf children already lag behind hearing peers in language skill when they enter school, but Johnson et al. claimed that language used in the classroom is also impoverished. In their view, most teachers of deaf children do not use Sign English competently or consistently; and even when they do, their students rarely gain genuine competence in English. ASL and BSL, meanwhile, are rarely used exclusively in classrooms due to frequent resistance of parents and the continuing lack of clarity in relevant research. Interestingly, Woodward and Allen (1987) reported that although 7% of the teachers in one study reported using ASL regularly in the classroom, only 0.3% of them actually did so. This finding suggested a generic communication problem in deaf students' classrooms, one not likely to be resolved by the rejection of Sign English in favor of sign language (cf. Johnson et al., 1989).

In summary, the available evidence has suggested that the early environment most facilitative for deaf children's future reading abilities is one that combines effective early language experience—usually in the form of sign language—with English experience. The latter might be obtained either through some form of manually coded English or through extensive spoken language training, depending on the characteristics and motivations of parents and children. Effective language experience, however, is only one of the factors that has a significant effect on the reading comprehension abilities of deaf children. Parental and child motivation, developmental "readiness," and the characteristics of the learning environment will also play central roles. To better understand deaf children's reading skills and reading problems, we now turn to components of reading skill itself; phonological processing, vocabulary, and syntactic processing.

HOW DO DEAF CHILDREN PROCESS PHONOLOGICAL INFORMATION?

Many studies of hearing children have shown that implicit phonological knowledge (e.g., speech segmentation skills or the ability to identify similarity of rhyme and initial sound in words) is a good predictor of reading success for alphabetic languages (see Goswami & Bryant, 1990; Morais, Bertelson,

Cary, & Alegria, 1986, for reviews). In a pioneering study in this area, for example, Bradley and Bryant (1983) demonstrated that children with good phonological awareness, as assessed on a sound-similarity judgment task at the age of 4, go on to become good readers. Children with poor phonological awareness were found to learn to read much more slowly. Shankweiler and his colleagues also showed that level of phonological awareness is a robust measure for distinguishing children with good reading comprehension from those with poor comprehension both in Italian (Cossu, Shankweiler, Liberman, & Katz, 1988) and English (Fletcher, Shaywitz, Shankweiler, & Katz, 1994).

Good phonological skills are important for reading an alphabetic language because in learning to read, most children progress from using a whole-word, *logographic* strategy in which they build up a limited sight vocabulary on the basis of purely visual differences among words, to a *phonic* strategy (or alphabetic strategy) in which letters are translated into phonemes via grapheme-to-phoneme or spelling-to-sound rules (see, for example, Frith, 1985). The transition to a phonic strategy allows children to attempt to read unfamiliar words, but these attempts will only be successful where the spelling of a word is regular. In an orthographically irregular language such as English, therefore, children develop intermediate, *orthographic* strategies, in which words are broken down into orthographic units (strings of letters), which are then converted to phonemes. The attainment of this strategy allows children to attempt the pronunciation of irregular as well as regular words.

Successful use of both alphabetic and orthographic strategies requires good phonological skills, and it is easy to see why poor phonological skills gives rise to significant problems in reading. Given the apparent role of sound in such strategies, it also seems easy to see why deaf children might have so much trouble reading: They should have deficient phonological skills. In fact, the situation is not quite so simple or clear.

There has been considerable debate about how deaf children, and especially those who are severely to profoundly deaf, could make use of phonological coding in the absence of hearing. One obvious possibility is that they might depend on perception of their own articulation patterns. That assumption is consistent with findings of Conrad (1970), involving British children trained primarily in spoken language, and Reynolds (1986), in a study involving U.S. college students who regularly use sign language. Harris and Beech (1995) also found a positive correlation (0.57) between deaf children's speech intelligibility and their reading progress over the first year at school. Leybaert, Content, and Alegria (1989), and Campbell (1992, in press), in contrast, argued that deaf children's apparent phonological proficiencies are derived through a combination of articulation, speechreading (or lipreading), fingerspelling, and exposure to writing, no one of which is sufficient in itself.

However it is that they acquire phonological knowledge, the preponderance of evidence has suggested that younger deaf children generally have poor phonological skills in comparison to their hearing peers. As will become evident, however, the situation is not as clear as it might seem. Dodd (1980), for example, examined spelling skills of deaf and hearing 14-year-olds in the United Kingdom for words varying in the regularity of their sound-to-spelling correspondence (e.g., *problem* vs. *scissors*). She found an interaction of regularity and hearing status such that the hearing children performed three times better on phonetically regular than irregular words, whereas the deaf children performed equally well on both types. Further, the pattern of spelling errors that she observed indicated that hearing children relied primarily on direct sound-to-grapheme correspondence (writing words like *sizzers*). Deaf children appeared somewhat less likely to employ phonological coding, but still showed better memory for regular than irregular nonsense words. Dodd concluded that deaf children (older than those in Harris & Beech, 1995) can make use of a phonological code when unambiguous graphemic information is not available.

Waters and Doehring (1990) examined phonological coding by deaf students who were in elementary and secondary school programs (aged 7 to 20 years) using spoken language curricula. They found no phonological effects in word versus nonword judgments (i.e., lexical decisions) with regular versus irregular spellings or with words that varied in their visual and phonological similarity. These and other findings led them to suggest that deaf readers might make use of whole-word, logographic codes rather than the phonological processing indicated by Dodd's findings.

The findings of Waters and Doehring (1990) were confirmed by Harris and Beech (1995), who argued that deaf and hearing children already have very different levels of phonemic awareness of when they begin formal reading instruction. They gave 5-year-old deaf and hearing children a picture version of the Bradley and Bryant (1983) test of phonological awareness. In their version of the task, hearing and deaf children matched for reading age (between 7.0 and 7.11) were given a picture (e.g., of a doll) and were then shown two other pictures (e.g., a crib and a dog) and asked to pick out the picture with the name that started with the same sound (or had the same middle or final sounds). The performance of the deaf children was considerably lower than that of the hearing children, and many did not perform above chance.

In a lexical decision task, Harris and Beech found that hearing children's performance was disrupted both by nonwords that sounded like real words (such as *werd*) and by spelling irregularity, thus suggesting that they were relying on phonological coding. Deaf children in both spoken language- and sign language-oriented schools, in contrast, correctly rejected homophonic nonwords and correctly accepted irregularly spelled words far more accurately than the hearing children, suggesting that neither group relied on phonological coding. Merrills, Underwood, and Wood (1994) reached a similar conclusion in a study involving the same children. As in the Harris and Beech study, deaf children were found to make much less use of phonological recoding than younger hearing children at the same reading level. In addition, deaf readers relied more on visual word features than hearing readers of either the same chronological or reading age.

In contrast to Dodd's (1980) finding of a greater reliance of phonological codes by hearing than deaf children up to age 20, Hanson, Shankweiler, and Fischer (1983) found no interaction of hearing status and phonological regularity, in groups of deaf and hearing college students. Both groups performed better with phonetically regular than irregular words, at least when the many deaf nonresponders were omitted from analyses. In analyzing the relationship of spelling and reading, Hanson et al. (1983) found that the hearing students were both more proficient readers and more proficient spellers, although there was no relation between either spelling ability or speech intelligibility and reading among the deaf students.

It is interesting to note that the pattern of spelling errors exhibited in the Hanson et al. (1983) study indicated that even at college age, deaf students may rely on a visual or logographic coding more often than hearing students. That finding was consistent with earlier results obtained by Chen (1976), who used a silent reading task in which students had to cross out occurrences of the letter *e* in a passage. The typical finding among hearing subjects has been that more letters are missed when they are silent than when they are voiced, indicating an acoustic or articulatory component to reading. Chen compared the performance on this task of four groups of college students—one composed of congenitally, profoundly deaf students; one composed of adventitiously, profoundly deaf students; one with less than profound impairments (losses < 80dB); and a hearing group. She found that only the hearing group and the deaf group with the lesser hearing losses missed more silent than pronounced *e*s, suggesting that the two profoundly deaf groups were more likely to rely on visual coding than acoustic or articulatory coding during reading.[3]

Hanson (1986) further examined the relationship between speech intelligibility and reading success by contrasting sensitivity to orthographic regularity with sensitivity to letter positions in a task in which students judged whether a target letter appeared in a briefly presented letter string. She found that the use of orthographic regularity depended on speech production ability, as hearing college students showed greater benefits from orthographic regularity than deaf college students. That difference, however, was

---

[3]Gibbs (1989), however, noted that Chen did not examine the relation between performance on the *e*-canceling task and reading performance, per se. He found that *e*-canceling performance was unrelated to reading scores in a group of profoundly deaf 16- to 19-year-olds, even though they missed significantly more silent than sounded *e*s.

entirely restricted to those deaf students who were relatively poor in their speech skills (cf. Waters & Doehring, 1990), whereas those deaf students with better speech skills also made frequent use of orthographic regularity in their reading.

Hanson, Goodell, and Perfetti (1991) used a semantic acceptability judgment task in another examination of phonological processes in deaf college students who, in this case, all had ASL as their first language. The expectation was that use of phonological codes in reading would be disrupted by the presence of tongue twisters, resulting in more errors and slower responses in acceptability judgments. When the judgments of deaf and hearing students on sentences with and without tongue twisters were compared, the deaf students performed significantly faster but less accurately. Both groups showed reliable tongue-twister (interference) effects in their accuracy scores, however, and the effects were influenced specifically by the phonetic content of the sentences. Hanson et al. therefore concluded that the deaf students must have used phonological coding during reading.

From the studies reviewed to this point, it appears that phonological coding is not a frequent reading tool of younger deaf children, even if it is used effectively by deaf college students. The obvious question of when the "shift" in skills occurs has been answered, at least in part, by a recent study by Leybaert and Alegria (1995). They compared the spelling strategies of deaf French children in two age groups, a younger group around 11 years old and an older group around 13 years old. Overall, the older children showed evidence of sensitivity to sound-to-spelling regularities whereas the younger group did not. Leybaert and Alegria also obtained an interaction with speech skill, however, as only the 13-year-olds with intelligible speech demonstrated reliable phonological effects.

In summary, it appears that most deaf children begin reading with little phonemic awareness and so, by the time they have attained a reading age of 7, they may still show little evidence of reliance upon phonological recoding in either reading or spelling. Over the next several years, deaf children become increasingly more likely to make use of phonological recoding and to show evidence of phonologically based "inner speech" of the sort described by Campbell (1992, in press). At this juncture, those children with better articulation skills appear to be better able to use phonological information, but it is not entirely clear whether this is related to the intelligibility of external speech or whether it is sufficient to understand their own inner speech, regardless of whether others could understand it.

When sufficient orthographic regularity is available, phonological coding appears most beneficial for both deaf and hearing students. Those deaf students with better spoken language abilities appear better able to take advantage of such coding or to have a "higher threshold" for regularity. Deaf students are more likely than hearing students, however, to depend on visual spelling regularities, and thus are more likely to omit letters and to make transposition errors. Whole-word codes appear especially useful for deaf readers, allowing them to draw on both phonological and visual word information. The linkage of reading development to increasing phonological proficiency also is evidenced by the production of more phonologically accurate misspellings in older than younger deaf students (Leybaert et al., 1989) and in good articulators than in poor articulators (Hanson, 1986; Reynolds, 1986). It thus appears that at least some portion of deaf children's observed reading deficiencies derive from sources other than the most obvious one: their inability to hear the sounds of spoken–written language.

Vocabulary and Reading

Although it has been well-documented that vocabulary knowledge is a primary component in reading, consideration of deaf children's skill in this regard raises questions about the effects of coming from an environment that is likely to be restricted in the diversity of linguistic models and "informal teaching" available. That is, we would expect that there would be an interaction of having less knowledge about things in the world, knowledge about fewer things, and less linguistic experience related to such knowledge.

Young deaf children of hearing parents have been shown to have fewer verbal labels for things around them than hearing children of hearing parents (Griswold & Commings, 1974); and deaf children of both deaf and hearing parents are less likely to gain such verbal knowledge from reading (Trybus & Karchmer, 1977). In this context, the finding of reciprocal causation in reading—that more reading makes for better readers as well as the other way around (see Stanovich, 1986)—suggests that it is imperative that we expand the breadth of vocabulary to which deaf children are exposed, away from the concrete and familiar. Otherwise, they may be caught up in a cycle of having smaller expressive vocabularies, smaller receptive vocabularies, and fewer opportunities to expand either (Marschark, 1993a). Further, Bertelson (1987) showed that the acquisition of reading vocabularies is delayed when orthographies do not transparently mirror the structure of correlated speech (e.g., in Mandarin). Deaf children learning to read face a similar situation, regardless of their level of sign skill, unless they are among the minority of deaf children who have developed good speech or speechreading skills. Unfortunately, there has not been sufficient research to know whether those children demonstrate vocabulary-related advantages in reading development (see Campbell, in press).

A variety of early studies involving word association and word sorting tasks have demonstrated that young deaf children evidence less extensive and less associatively organized vocabulary knowledge than hearing age-mates, as well as a lesser ability to organize words into semantic categories (see Marschark, 1993b, for a review). More recently, those lags in vocabulary development have been attributed to the qualitative and quantitative linguistic shortages encountered by young deaf children and, in turn, held to be responsible in large measure for low reading scores (Johnson et al., 1989; Quigley & Paul, 1984). Contrary to any simple version of this deprivation hypothesis, however, Brasel and Quigley (1977) found that deaf children whose deaf parents used manually coded English at home scored higher on the Word Meaning and Paragraph Meaning subtests of the Stanford Achievement Test than deaf children whose deaf parents used ASL at home. That is, both groups received early language experience in the home, but the group that had experience with English as well as sign language clearly showed superior performance on meaning-related reading tests (cf. Schlesinger & Meadow, 1972).

Aside from deaf children possibly having relatively less breadth in vocabulary knowledge as a function of exposure, it is unclear whether even familiar vocabulary is recognized as quickly by deaf children as by hearing students. Deaf children typically perform poorly in evaluations of vocabulary knowledge, even when reading comprehension abilities are equated (e.g., Charrow & Fletcher, 1974). Alternatively, lack of reading experience, among other consequences, may well reduce the automaticity of word finding even when words are relatively familiar (Fischler, 1985; Marschark, 1993b, chapter 11) (for another example of reciprocal causation in reading, see Stanovich, 1986). These alternatives can be considered in terms of the meaning derived from both individual words and the syntactic structuring of those words.

Moores (1967), and Quigley and Paul (1984), for example, argued that deaf children show their largest reading-related deficits in the area of vocabulary knowledge. Moores (1967) found that deaf children obtained significantly lower scores than hearing children on a vocabulary test involving the cloze technique ("fill in the blank") despite the fact that the two groups had been matched on SAT reading scores. Charrow and Fletcher (1974) similarly found that deaf 17- and 18-year-olds who had hearing parents showed their worst performance on the Test of English as a Foreign Language (TOEFL) Vocabulary subtest, relative to peers with deaf parents, despite a trend in TOEFL Reading Comprehension scores favoring students with hearing parents.

Given deaf children's relative lags in reading, in general, it should not be surprising that they tend to score lower than hearing peers on vocabulary tests involving words in isolation. The Word Meaning subtest of the SAT is a particularly good example in this regard, as it generally yields the lowest scores obtained by deaf children and adolescents on the SAT battery. Deaf children also reveal lags in their expressive vocabularies in signed and oral productions (e.g., Griswold & Commings, 1974) as well as in writing (e.g., Marschark, Mouradian, & Halas, 1994) indicating that vocabulary limitations go beyond difficulties with printed English. Not only do deaf children have smaller vocabularies than hearing peers, but the classes of words they do know are often different. Deaf children generally are more likely to understand and use concrete nouns and familiar action verbs rather than more abstract or general words with which they may have less experience, especially if they have hearing parents (King & Quigley, 1985).

Compared to their performance on vocabulary tests involving words taken out of context, deaf children typically perform somewhat better on meaning-related tests that include context, such as the Paragraph Meaning subtest of the SAT. They still lag behind hearing peers (e.g., Gaines et al., 1981), however, and Trybus and Karchmer (1977) found that their vocabulary abilities tended to lag a year behind their own reading abilities (a situation that would create difficulties in both domains). Deaf children also perform better on vocabulary items with only a single meaning. When words can have multiple meanings, and especially when those meanings may not all be literal, deaf children perform poorly even when context is supplied.

Fischler (1985), for example, examined deaf and hearing college students' abilities to make lexical decisions in a task in which words were preceded by either "the most likely" sentence context, an incongruent sentence context, an unlikely but congruent sentence context, or no context. He found that both groups made faster decisions when words followed likely contexts and slower decisions when they followed incongruent contexts, relative to following unlikely but congruent contexts. The effects of sentence context were larger for the deaf than the hearing students, suggesting that deaf students used context to help offset lesser automaticity in word-recognition skills. Findings like those of Moores (1967), however, have indicated that such higher level syntactic and semantic processes may not be able to compensate fully for limitations of vocabulary knowledge. Demonstrating that deaf children can understand simple, well-controlled materials in semantically restricted contexts tells us relatively little about their reading potential or the reading strategies employed in more naturalistic contexts.

One consequence of vocabulary lags in either deaf or hearing children is that they are likely to impede higher level reading processes both by focusing the reader on "bottom-up" information and by tying up available cognitive processing capacity (see Marschark, 1993b, chapter 7). Both Burden and Campbell (1994), and Harris (1994), demonstrated that children who have profound prelingual hearing losses not only have a lower level of vocabulary development but also experience difficulties at the text level which are not explained by limited vocabulary repertoires. Burden and Campbell, for example, found that a group of congenitally deaf English school leavers (with reading ages between 9 and 10 years) showed word reading and spelling skills better than predicted by their reading comprehension scores. Harris (1994) compared the reading comprehension scores of two groups of deaf and hearing children matched for single-word reading level. She found that text-level performance was significantly lower in the deaf children. The same group also performed worse than hearing controls on a test of instantiation in which they were given sentences such as "The fish attacked the swimmer" and were prompted for recall with either the word "fish" or its instantiation "shark." Hearing children recalled more in response to the instantiation cues than to the original words as cues, whereas the deaf children performed at a similar level with both cue types, just like the poor comprehenders described by Oakhill and Yuill (this volume).

At this point, we are poised to consider difficulties evidenced by deaf readers at the text level of reading. When we move to the level of syntactic structure, for example, many deaf children evidence significant difficulty with a variety syntactic structures. The question remains, however, of whether those difficulties are primarily due to grammatical skills per se, to the disruption of higher level processing by vocabulary demands, or to the ability to attend to grammatical markers as a function of short-term memory capacity (Hansen & Bowey, 1994; Perfetti & Goldman, 1976). In any case, the result would be reduced comprehension and a tendency to remember disconnected portions of texts without higher level conceptual schemes, particularly when the material is unfamiliar. Precisely such findings have been demonstrated by Gaines et al. (1981), Banks, Gray, and Fyfe (1990), Griffith, Dastoli, and Ripich (1990), and Marschark, De Beni, Polazzo, and Cornoldi (1993).

Parsing the Syntax Problem

Deaf children's difficulties in mastering English syntax have long been recognized, even if we have not made great strides in overcoming them. Part of the problem, for both those children and researchers, stems from the fact that syntax has often been viewed as separate from other variables affecting language learning—both linguistic (e.g., vocabulary) and nonlinguistic (e.g., cognitive)—rather than as part of an integrated whole.

Perhaps the best known findings concerning deaf children's syntactic abilities are those reported by Quigley, Wilbur, Power, Montanelli, and Steinkamp (1976) and Quigley, Power, and Steinkamp (1977). Those studies involved a large sample of deaf students, aged 10–19 years. Quigley and his colleagues found that, whereas hearing children's performance varied from 78% to 98% correct across the 21 syntactic structures they examined, deaf children's performance ranged from 36% to 79%. In terms of age-related norms, those findings indicated that the syntactic abilities of the average, deaf 18-year-old were at a level below that of the average, hearing 8-year-old. The biggest gaps between deaf and hearing scores occurred for structures like question formation, complementation, and pronominalization; whereas the most similar performance was observed in the relatively simple constructions of negation and conjunction. These results, together with the results of Perfetti and Goldman's (1976) comparison of good and poor hearing readers, suggest that the most difficult syntactic constructions for deaf children may be those that involve short-term retention of verbal information while awaiting subsequent (semantic or syntactic) resolution (Marschark, 1993b, chapter 11; see also, Hansen & Bowey, 1994, on the relation of verbal working memory and phonological skills).

This conclusion would help to explain findings indicating that deaf children are less likely than hearing age-mates to draw inferences from contextual information, regardless of whether that context is verbal or nonverbal (Marschark, 1993b, chapter 7). It also underscores the point made earlier that nonlinguistic, experiential, and cognitive factors may impact on reading at levels beyond those of phonological coding and vocabulary. Consideration of the roles of such global cognitive factors as concept knowledge, cognitive style, and memory in deaf children's reading also bears on the issue of whether deaf children of deaf parents are better readers than deaf children of hearing parents.

Brasel and Quigley (1977) explicitly examined the development of syntactic abilities in groups of 10- to 18-year-olds as a function of parental hearing status and early linguistic experience. All of the children in that study were deaf by age 2, and all were profoundly deaf. Their full study actually included four groups—one whose deaf parents had good English skills and communicated with them via manually coded English; one with deaf parents who primarily used ASL in the home; one who received training exclusively in spoken communication at home and at school and whose hearing parents had received training in using spoken language methodologies; and one who also received spoken language training at school, but whose hearing parents did not have any training and did not attempt to initiate spoken language education prior to enrolling them in school.

Brasel and Quigley found that, overall, the manually coded English group showed the best syntactic competence, and that the two signing groups surpassed the two spoken language groups. In fact, although children in the manually coded English group performed significantly better than those in the two spoken language groups on most of the syntactic structures tested, they performed better than the ASL group only on the most difficult structure, relativization. This study has been frequently cited as indicating that deaf children of deaf parents are better readers than those with hearing parents, but such an assertion misses an important component of the results: Brasel and Quigley's ASL group did not significantly exceed the intensive spoken language group on any of the component tests. Consistent with the Schlesinger and Meadow (1972) study described earlier, the Brasel and Quigley results thus most clearly indicated that a combination of sign language and

English training is the most beneficial language environment for deaf children learning to read, at least with regard to the acquisition of syntactic abilities and gist comprehension.

Looked at another way, although it is true that Brasel and Quigley's (1977) groups of children with deaf parents performed better than the two groups with hearing parents, those children who received spoken language training at both home and school showed syntactic skills comparable to their peers who had deaf parents and who were exposed to ASL from birth. This finding appears to cast doubt on the argument that deaf children with deaf parents are better readers than peers with hearing parents simply because of their exposure to language from birth. As argued earlier, there clearly are other factors involved here, including the attitudes of parents toward their children's deafness and their involvement in teaching their children to read. Perhaps most importantly, it seems likely that the benefits accruing to syntactic abilities in the context of early language training likely result not only from exposure to syntax, but also from exposure to and acquisition of an expanded vocabulary.

Unfortunately, Brasel and Quigley's (1977) study did not include a control group of hearing children with hearing parents or a group of deaf children whose hearing parents used sign language intensively, so we are unable to clarify the locus of their results. As an estimate of how the manual English group compared to a group of hearing children, however, Marschark (1993b) compared Brasel and Quigley's data from deaf children's performance on the Illinois Test of Syntactic Abilities with data from hearing children receiving the same test in the Quigley et al. (1976) study. That comparison revealed that the manually coded English group was within 1% of the hearing group on negation, pronominalization, and relativization; within 8% on question formation and conjunction; and actually surpassed their hearing age-mates by 3% on verb use.

In summary, then, the available evidence suggests that in addition to lags in phonological processing and vocabulary knowledge, deaf children, on average, demonstrate lags in English syntactic abilities compared to hearing peers. These lags can be reduced or eliminated when such children receive early language training either in sign language from their deaf parents or in spoken language from hearing parents who seek out early intervention programs and regularly use intensive training methods in the home. As was the case in early vocabulary development, however, it appears that the best situation for deaf children learning to read is to be exposed to both sign and English, regardless of whether their parents are deaf or hearing (Marschark, 1993a). Such findings clearly contradict the rationale behind the strong proposals of Johnson et al. (1989) concerning the undesirability of English-based artificial sign systems in the education of deaf children. There may be a variety of reasons for supporting the exclusive use of ASL and BSL among deaf children but learning to read is not one of them.

SUMMARY AND CONCLUSIONS

Learning to read is easily identified as the most difficult challenge for deaf children in school. Two decades of intensive effort on the part of educational researchers and educators have resulted in moderately improved reading comprehension scores for deaf children during the school years. The difference between the reading levels of deaf students and their hearing peers, however, is still more than double the difference of the improvements we have accomplished thus far. More importantly, reading skill among 18-year-old deaf students, at the point when they should be graduating from high school, has not increased at all (see Table 12.1). As a result, the average deaf adult in the United States reads at about a fourth-grade level, and the average deaf adult in England may be even lower.

If this picture appears pessimistic, it must be emphasized that deaf children are far more heterogeneous than hearing children (see Marschark, 1993b, for discussion), and some deaf students are excellent readers. Nonetheless, among deaf students with severe to profound hearing losses, reading comprehension problems are endemic. In our review of research on the phonological skills underlying reading, for example, we found that deaf children are considerably less proficient than hearing children, at least during the early school years. During that time, they appear to depend largely on visual decoding of printed words, based on either orthographic or logographic characteristics. By the time they reach secondary school, however, many deaf students are relying on phonological information for irregular words at least, and by the time they reach college age, reliance on visual codes appears to be greatly diminished.

Although there is little research available on vocabulary skills in older deaf students throughout the school years, they show lags in vocabulary development in terms of both comprehension and expression. In fact, a variety of investigators have identified vocabulary as the single greatest barrier to deaf children's reading comprehension. The combination of smaller vocabulary repertoires and less automatic access to familiar vocabulary appears to disrupt reading comprehension both at the level of individual words and at the level of syntactic structure. Inefficient word "look-up" skills will result in both slower disambiguation of meaning for words with multiple meanings and slower determination of referential constructions such as relative clauses and pronouns. At the same time, it will require a greater proportion of working memory capacity, thus limiting syntactic and discourse level processes.

Syntactic skills have long been recognized as problematic for deaf children, although there is a large amount of variability evident in available studies across both children and syntactic structures. Beyond the apparently greater difficulty of structures that depend on working memory for instantiation or resolution, there do not appear to be any specific indicators of aspects of grammatical skill that should be of any particular problem for deaf children. On the nonlinguistic side, however, it may be that the lesser linguistic experience and fewer linguistic models available to the 90% of deaf children with hearing parents may result in less mapping of syntactic structure onto real-world episodes, thus resulting in slower grammatical development. A marked reduction in recent research in the area leaves this possibility speculative.

One area which clearly impacts on deaf children's reading is their early language environments. Deaf children of deaf parents generally read better than deaf children of hearing parents. This advantage cannot be ascribed solely to the early availability of sign language for a variety of reasons, not the least of which is the lack of a formal relation between any signed language and its spoken counterpart. Nonetheless, the access to language and to effective communication with parents during the critical years of language learning appears to have significant impact on deaf children's reading as well as in other cognitive and social domains.

Still to be investigated is the extent to which deaf and hearing parents might have different goals and values for their deaf children with regard to literacy. Clearly, hearing parents of deaf children, who typically have little if any sign language skill, are less able than deaf parents to communicate such values to their children. They also are less able to be actively involved in their children's reading development, a factor that we know contributes to the reading comprehension success of hearing children. Until such factors are unraveled, it appears that the safest and most effective route to improving deaf children's reading skills is the providing of early access to language, via signing, with simultaneous exposure to written language. Whether or not artificial sign systems based on spoken language grammar or morphology are truly effective, remains to be determined. At present, however, they are clearly more effective than exposure only to spoken language training or to no language training at all.

REFERENCES

Allen, T. E. (1986). Patterns of academic achievement among hearing impaired students: 1974–1983. In A. N. Shildroth & M. A. Karchmer (Eds.), *Deaf children in America* (pp. 161–206). San Diego: College-Hill Press.

Banks, J., Gray, C., & Fyfe, R. (1990). The written recall of printed stories by severely deaf children. *British Journal of Educational Psychology, 60,* 192–206.

Bertelson, P. (1987). *The onset of literacy: Cognitive processes in reading acquisition.* Cambridge, MA: MIT Press.

Bradley, L., & Bryant, P. E. (1983). Categorising sounds and learning to read: A causal explanation. *Nature, 301,* 419–421.

Brasel, K., & Quigley, S. P. (1977). Influence of certain language and communicative environments in early childhood on the development of language in deaf individuals. *Journal of Speech and Hearing Research, 20,* 95–107.

Burden, V., & Campbell, R. (1994). The development of word-coding skills in the born deaf: An experimental study of deaf school leavers. *British Journal of Developmental Psychology, 24,* 331–350.

Campbell, R. (1992). Speech in the head? Rhyme skill, reading, and immediate memory in the deaf. In D. Reisberg (Ed.), *Auditory imagery* (pp. 73–94). Hillsdale, NJ: Lawrence Erlbaum Associates.

Campbell, R. (in press). Read the lips: Relations of lipreading to academic and cognitive development of deaf children. In M. Marschark, P. Siple, R. Campbell, & D. Lillo-Martin, & V. Everhart (Eds.), *Relations of language and cognition: The view from deaf children's development.* New York: Oxford University Press.

Charrow, V., & Fletcher, J. D. (1974). English as a second language of deaf children. *Developmental Psychology, 10,* 463–470.

Chen, K. (1976). Acoustic image in visual detection for deaf and hearing college students. *Journal of General Psychology, 94,* 243–246.

Conrad, R. (1970). Short-term memory processes in the deaf. *British Journal of Psychology, 61,* 179–195.

Cossu, G., Shankweiler, D., Liberman, I., & Katz, L. (1988). Awareness of phonological segments and reading ability in Italian children. *Applied Psycholinguistics, 9,* 1–16.

DiFrancesca, S. (1972). *Academic achievement test results of a national testing program for hearing-impaired students: United States, Spring 1971.* Washington, DC: Gallaudet College, Office for Demographic Studies.

Dodd, B. (1980). The spelling abilities of profoundly pre-lingually deaf children. In U. Frith (Ed.), *Cognitive processes in spelling* (pp. 423–440). New York: Academic Press.

Fischler, I. (1985). Word recognition, use of context, and reading skill among deaf college students. *Reading Research Quarterly, 20,* 203–218.

Fletcher, J. M., Shaywitz, S. E., Shankweiler, D. P., & Katz, L. (1994). Cognitive profiles of reading disability: Comparisons of discrepancy and low achievement definitions. *Journal of Educational Psychology, 86,* 6–23.

Frith, U. (1985). Beneath the surface of developmental dyslexia. In K. E. Patterson, J. C. Marshall, & M. Coltheart (Eds.), *Surface dyslexia* (pp. 301–330). Hillsdale, NJ: Lawrence Erlbaum Associates.

Gaines, R., Mandler, J., & Bryant, P. (1981). Immediate and delayed story recall by hearing and deaf children. *Journal of Speech and Hearing Research, 24,* 463–469.

Gibbs, K. W. (1989). Individual differences in cognitive skills related to reading ability in the deaf. *American Annals of the Deaf, 134,* 214–218.

Goswami, U., & Bryant, P. (1990). *Phonological skills and learning to read.* Hove, England: Lawrence Erlbaum Associates.

Griffith, P. L., Dastoli, S. L., & Ripich, D. N. (1990). Narrative abilities in hearing-impaired children: Propositions and cohesion. *American Annals of the Deaf, 135,* 14–19.

Griswold, L. E., & Commings, J. (1974). The expressive vocabulary of preschool deaf children. *American Annals of the Deaf, 119,* 16–28.

Hansen, J., & Bowey, J. A. (1994). Phonological analysis skills, verbal working memory, and reading ability in second grade. *Child Development, 65,* 938–950.

Hansen, V. L. (1986). Access to spoken language and the acquisition of orthographic structure: Evidence from deaf readers. *Quarterly Journal of Experimental Psychology, 38A,* 193–212.

Hanson, V. L., Goodell, E. W., & Perfetti, C. A. (1991). Tongue-twister effects in the silent reading of hearing and deaf college students. *Journal of Memory and Language, 30,* 319–330.

Hanson, V. L., Shankweiler, D., & Fischer, F. W. (1983). Determinants of spelling ability in deaf and hearing adults: Access to linguistic structure. *Cognition, 14,* 323–344.

Harris, M. (1994, May). *Reading comprehension difficulties in deaf children.* Paper presented at the Workshop on Comprehension Disabilities, Centro Diagnostico Italiano, Milan, Italy.

Harris, M., & Beech, J. (1995). Reading development in prelingually deaf children. In K. Belson & Z. Reger (Eds.), *Children's language* (vol. 8, pp. 181–202). Hillsdale, NJ: Lawrence Erlbaum Associates.

Jensema, C. J., & Trybus, R. J. (1978). *Communicating patterns and educational achievements of hearing impaired students.* Washington, DC: Gallaudet College Office of Demographic Studies.

Johnson, R. E., Liddell, S. K., & Erting, C. J. (1989). *Unlocking the curriculum: Principles for achieving access in deaf education* (Report No. 89-3). Washington, DC: Gallaudet Research Institute.

Kampfe, C. M. (1989). Reading comprehension of deaf adolescent residential school students and its relationship to hearing mothers' communication strategies and skills. *American Annals of the Deaf, 134,* 317–322.

King, C. M., & Quigley, S. P. (1985). *Reading and deafness.* San Diego: College-Hill Press.

Kusché, C. A., Greenberg, M. T., & Garfield, T. S. (1983). Nonverbal intelligence and verbal achievement in deaf adolescents: An examination of heredity and environment. *American Annals of the Deaf, 128,* 458–466.

Leybaert, J., & Alegria, J. (1995). Spelling development in deaf and hearing children: Evidence for use of morpho-phonological regularities in French. *Reading and Writing, 7,* 89–109.

Leybaert, J., Content, A., & Alegria, J. (1989). The development of written word processing: The case of deaf children. *Ilha do Desterro, 21,* 11–42.

Marschark, M. (1993a). Origins and interactions in language, cognitive, and social development of deaf children. In M. Marschark & D. Clark (Eds.), *Psychological perspectives on deafness* (pp. 7–26). Hillsdale, NJ: Lawrence Erlbaum Associates.

Marschark, M. (1993b). *Psychological development of deaf children.* New York: Oxford University Press.

Marschark, M. (1997). *Growing up deaf.* New York: Oxford University Press.

Marschark, M., De Beni, R., Polazzo, M. G., & Cornoldi, C. (1993). Deaf and hard of hearing adolescents' memory for concrete and abstract prose: Effects of relational and distinctive information. *American Annals of the Deaf, 138,* 31–39.

Marschark, M., Mouradian, V., & Halas, M. (1994). Discourse rules in the language productions of deaf and hearing children. *Journal of Experimental Child Psychology, 57,* 89–107.

Merrills, J. D., Underwood, G., & Wood, D. J. (1994). The word recognition skills of profoundly, prelingually deaf children. *British Journal of Psychology, 12,* 365–384.

Moores, D. (1967). *Applications of "cloze" procedures to the assessment of psycholinguistic abilities of the deaf.* Unpublished doctoral dissertation, University of Illinois at Urbana-Champaign.

Morais, J., Bertelson, P., Cary, L., & Alegria, J. (1986). Literacy training and speech segmentation. *Cognition, 24,* 45–64.

Perfetti, C. A., & Goldman, S. R. (1976). Discourse memory and reading comprehension skill. *Journal of Verbal Learning and Verbal Behavior, 15,* 33–42.

Quigley, S. P., & Paul, P. V. (1984). *Language and deafness.* San Diego: College-Hill Press.

Quigley, S. P., Power, D., & Steinkamp, M. (1977). The language structure of deaf children. *Volta Review, 79,* 73–84.

Quigley, S. P., Wilbur, R., Power, D., Montanelli, D., & Steinkamp, M. (1976). *Syntactic structure in the language of deaf children.* University of Illinois: Institute for Child Behavior and Development.

Reynolds, R. N. (1986). Performance of deaf college students on a criterion-referenced modified cloze test of reading comprehension. *American Annals of the Deaf, 131,* 361–364.

Schlesinger, H. S., & Meadow, K. P. (1972). *Sound and sign: Childhood deafness and mental health.* Berkeley, CA: University of California Press.

Stanovich, K. (1986). Matthew effects. *Reading Research Quarterly, 4,* 360–406.

Trybus, R., & Karchmer, M. (1977). School achievement scores of hearing impaired children: National data on achievement status and growth patterns. *American Annals of the Deaf Directory of Programs and Services, 122,* 62–69.

Vaccari, C., & Marschark, M. (1996). *Communication between parents and their deaf children: Implications for social-emotional development.* Manuscript submitted for publication.

Vernon, M. (1972). Mind over mouth: A rationale for total communication. *Volta Review, 74,* 529–540.

Waters, G. S., & Doehring, D. G. (1990). Reading acquisition in congenitally deaf children who communicate orally: Insights from an analysis of component reading, language, and memory skills. In T. H. Carr & B. A. Levy (Eds.), *Reading and its development* (pp. 323–373). San Diego: Academic Press.

Woodward, J., & Allen, T. E. (1987). Classroom use of ASL by teachers. *Sign Language Studies, 54,* 1–10.

CHAPTER THIRTEEN

Focusing on Text Comprehension as a Problem-Solving Task: A Fostering Project for Culturally Deprived Children

Lucia Lumbelli
University of Trieste

The instructional project described here was designed to deal with reading comprehension in the context of an educational problem which I summarize first. A lot of the pupils attending the final grades of compulsory schooling (10–14 years of age in the Italian school system) were underachievers in basic abilities such as reading and writing, although without any cognitive or emotional deficit. This kind of underachievement can be traced back chiefly to environmental deprivation, because these pupils came from families with insufficient means and little formal schooling. In the 1960s and 1970s this problem was studied using various approaches and various enrichment or compensatory projects, mainly concerning verbal deprivation. This kind of deprivation was considered to be the main effect of sociocultural disadvantage and, in turn, the main cause of school underachievement (Bernstein, 1971; Giglioli, 1972; Passow, Goldberg, & Tannenbaum, 1967; Riessman, 1962).

The problem is still topical and it is being handled by new enrichment projects (Feuerstein, 1980) mostly as far as the earlier grades of school are concerned. However, urgent solutions are needed at the later stage of compulsory schooling, where the problem is very serious. This is also due to the fact that at these stages it is too late to intervene with organic, lengthy projects.

Educational strategies effective in reaching a few, main goals within the little time available are therefore needed. Given these particular constraints, any instructional project targeting this specific category of pupils must systematically implement the educational principle that the learning situation should be a problem-solving one, with the pupils playing an active, autonomous role (Collins, Brown, & Newman, 1989; Meichenbaum & Goodman, 1979; Palincsar & Brown, 1984; Zimmerman & Schunk, 1989). This principle is particularly valid for disadvantaged learners aged 11–14, because the environment in which their language acquisition has taken place is very likely to have very severely reduced their readiness to learn and their intrinsic motivation.

Any project for fostering their reading comprehension will therefore be effective only if it can also foster pupils' readiness to become problem solvers and self-regulated learners.

The learning situation must be compensatory not only with respect to these pupils' deficit in reading comprehension ability but also with regard to their intrinsic motivation. It must present them with learning experiences that are so rewarding as to change their attitude toward the cognitive activity previously rejected due to frustrating experiences at school.

Our instructional project for fostering reading comprehension was committed to encouraging the target pupils to be as motivated and as actively involved in the learning tasks as possible.

Indeed, certain features of this project were based on this commitment.

First, the educational situation had to be rigorously individualized, because the cognitive needs of the target pupils were very different from those of their peers and therefore could only be ascertained in a situation completely centered on them alone. In the case of the late disadvantaged pupils, the individualized session was the only way to implement the principle (closely connected with the above-mentioned principle) that the fostering intervention must be adjusted to fit the precise cognitive needs of each individual:

> the teacher must somehow be sensitive to each student's needs at any stage of the process. She must engage in an *on-line diagnosis* that will guide her own level of participation, a level of participation that is finely tuned to the student's changing cognitive status. Diagnosis involves . . . continuous evaluation and revision in the teacher's theory of the student's competence. (Palincsar & Brown, 1984, p. 169)

A second feature derived from that commitment was the relatively high-ordered nature of the comprehension processes focused upon. The assumption has been that the higher and more complex the processes concerned, the easier it should be to stimulate them with instructional tasks that mean something to the readers. Only if the task is meaningful can the readers cope with it in a motivated, autonomous way. This was also why the decoding component of reading ability was not considered here; this did not imply that decoding is less important than reading comprehension.

We can stimulate reading comprehension ability alone on the basis of the evidence of the possible independence of this ability from decoding ability (Cornoldi, 1990; Cromer, 1970; Oakhill, 1994; Perfetti & Hogaboam, 1975; Stothard & Hulme, this volume).

Third, the goal of the fostering intervention had to involve the metacognitive level. This feature too was closely connected both to the emphasis on the active role of the learner in the instructional situation and to the category of target learners. In fact, on the one hand, a real problem-solving situation entails intentional, conscious monitoring on the part of the learners while posing the problem and searching for the solution; on the other hand, as far as late disadvantaged pupils are concerned, one of the most urgent instructional objectives seems to be the ability to be aware of a serious comprehension problem encountered while reading, and thus to ask for help effectively.

Obviously, the only definitions of metacognition relevant here were those that stress its close relationship with consciousness (Baker, 1994). This choice was not meant to exclude other definitions or to claim a complete overlapping of metacognition and awareness of cognitive processes. Conscious monitoring was selected here to define the instructional object just as a direct consequence of the educational principle of assuring the learners' active role in any late compensatory intervention.

In the first section of this chapter, I define the instructional goal that was chosen according to the above-mentioned criteria and briefly review the experimental evidence and the rationale used in my definition; in the second section, I describe the methodology of the comprehension-fostering project, which was constructed from Ericsson and Simon's (1980) suggestions for the use of verbal protocols in the study of cognitive processes and from C. Rogers' (1945) theory of the interview centered on the interviewee; I also discuss some instances of the verbal protocols elicited by applying that methodology to the exploratory implementation of the project and the experimental evidence on the project's effectiveness.

GOAL AND TASK OF THE FOSTERING APPROACH

There has been a lot of evidence that verbal comprehension very often involves cognitive integration of verbally expressed information obtained by drawing inferences from both the information and from prior knowledge (Bransford, Barclay, & Franks, 1972; Bransford & Franks, 1971; Just & Carpenter, 1980; Perfetti & Lesgold, 1977).

Every theory of text processing acknowledges that prior knowledge has a certain amount of influence, but there is no agreement about just how much influence is attributable to prior knowledge versus text information although there have been interesting theoretical attempts to specify their respective function in text comprehension processes (van Dijk & Kintsch, 1983).

The kind of inference that best lends itself to specifying how prior knowledge may interact with explicit text information has been named *bridging inference* (Clark, 1977) and is performed when two information items expressed in text are connected or *bridged* by means of a cognitive integration drawn either from prior knowledge alone or from other text information as well.

Here, only the latter kind of bridging inference was considered, that is, those that restore coherence between two adjacent pieces of information by using not only pieces of prior knowledge but also pieces of text information that may be rather distant. Drawing this kind of bridging inference requires the correct "exploitation" of explicit text information or *textbase* (van Dijk & Kintsch, 1983) as a basic condition for a correct use of prior knowledge. The distinguishing feature of this kind of inference is the high number of textual constraints that have to be respected to make the correct integration from prior knowledge and thus the particular adequacy to provide evidence of *how* prior knowledge interacts with text in comprehension.

This was not the only specification of the bridging inferences focused upon here. Other criteria were derived from the educational reasons mentioned earlier. Unlike other projects aimed at improving the ability to draw bridging inferences in general (Beal, Garrod, & Bonitatibus, 1990; Yuill & Oakhill, 1988), the only bridging inferences considered here were those which seem to be most suited to enhancing intrinsic motivation in the target learner.

The bridging inferences considered were those that involve a pattern of processes complex enough to be structurally similar to the paths necessary to solve a problem, and difficult enough to bring about "automatic pilot's block" (Brown, 1978), namely the interruption of the smoothly automatic performance of text processing, thereby making the reader's efforts to understand a matter of conscious monitoring. The occurrences of simpler bridging inferences were not taken into account because they are performed automatically and unconsciously.

The kind of bridging inference analyzed here consists of two main steps. First, readers must detect a gap or local incoherence between two information items and thus pose the problem of finding the bridging inference that provides the appropriate cognitive integration. Second, readers must have the chance to find the information from which to infer the integration within the text itself (and not just in their minds). The search for prior knowledge must be guided by an accurate exploitation of text information. This information consists of the two incoherent items (*problem posing*) in the first step, and of the items from which the bridging integration must be inferred (*problem solving*) in the second.

The instructional objective consisting of the correct performance of this kind of bridging inference can be attained by presenting the learners with comprehension tasks which are also problem-solving tasks.

Given the crucial role played by local coherence detection in defining our instructional goal, most of the evidence obtained by means of the "inconsistency paradigm" could be used to design the fostering project. It has been shown that the ability to detect inconsistencies inserted into a text makes it possible to discriminate between subjects who differ in age and comprehension ability (Garner, 1980, 1981; Markman, 1977, 1979), but that detection is difficult for all subjects, irrespective of their level of formal education and reading expertise (Baker, 1979; Baker & Anderson, 1982).

In comprehension monitoring, there is a general tendency for subjects to adopt any standard rather than the Internal Consistency Standard (I.C.S.), that is the criterion by which comprehension processes are monitored and evaluated with regard to the coherence between information items within a text. Preference is given not only to lexical and syntactic standards, but also to semantic standards such as the so-called External Consistency Standard (E.C.S.), or the criterion used in comprehension monitoring when each text information item is compared with prior knowledge and is evaluated independently of its relationship to other text information (Baker, 1979, 1984; Markman, 1979; Osherson & Markman, 1975). Regardless of differences in age and comprehension ability, everyone seems to have problems monitoring their own reading processes according to that criterion of coherence among information items which distinguishes the text itself from a set of juxtaposed sentences (Grice, 1975; van Dijk & Kintsch, 1983).

How can the general tendency to integrate the text (which also implies the ability to detect the gaps) be reconciled with the evidence that even adults with good comprehension ability (Baker, 1979; Baker & Anderson, 1982) have difficulty noticing the glaring coherence gaps that appear in the experimental material used to study comprehension monitoring?

A first hypothetical answer comes still from inconsistency paradigm research and, more precisely, from the comparison between the use of the I.C.S. versus the E.C.S. in comprehension monitoring. Subjects seem to prefer the latter and tend to evaluate each product of comprehension processes simply by asking themselves, "Is it true?" and answering this question by checking each item of text information against their own prior knowledge (Osherson & Markman, 1975). In the course of some experiments, Baker (1979, 1984) observed that a few good comprehenders failed to notice glaring inconsistencies and apply the I.C.S. to their text processing, because they had integrated the text too hastily with information inferred from prior knowledge. These subjects seemed to process the text in such a way that the inconsistency inserted by the experimenter no longer existed for them. Their good inferential ability was used not to detect the inconsistency but to cancel it. The readers failed to compare the two inconsistent items of information using the I.C.S. because they had already transformed at least one of them by means of an elaborative inference (Clark, 1977). They immediately used the E.C.S. to check the information item against their prior knowledge, thus preventing the use of the I.C.S.

This general tendency should be more marked in poor readers, as they are less likely to detect inconsistency in text. Other research findings could be used to corroborate this hypothesis. Experiments have shown that poor readers exhibit a greater loss of superficial information (Perfetti & Goldman, 1976; Perfetti & Lesgold, 1977) and these findings were explained by Gernsbacher (1985, 1988; Gernsbacher, Varner, & Faust, 1990). According to Gernsbacher, the poorer access to recently comprehended information shown by these comprehenders is due to the fact that they shift too frequently from one to another of the episode structures or substructures into which they divide the text they are reading. This oversegmentation of text information seems to derive from an inability to suppress the contextually irrelevant information in favor of the gist. It follows that, when deciding to shift from one episode to another, they are obliged to take into account this secondary information too. This characteristic of poor readers may explain both their inability to detect inconsistencies and their preference for the E.C.S., including the inability to notice the incoherence between immediately adjacent items.

All those research findings can be used to specify the category of bridging inference focused upon in this educational project. As to the first of the steps mentioned earlier, the local incoherence to be identified as a necessary condition for posing the problem must be glaring enough to likely be perceived "spontaneously" by the disadvantaged learners. This should help the learners pose the problem autonomously and thus be intrinsically motivated to search for the solution.

As to the second step, the bridging integration has to be identifiable by means of a search not only in the reader's mind, but also (and primarily) within the text, if that search has to be similar to the search for a solution in a problem-solving situation.

On the one hand, we have to consider the evidence of the relationship between rereading and the ability to make inferences. Oakhill (1984) compared the performance of good and poor comprehenders by asking comprehension questions in two different conditions; when children could not look back to the text, and when they could reread it. Some of the questions required pieces of information directly expressed in the text, whereas others required information that could only be inferred from it. On the first type of question, both groups of subjects benefited from the chance of rereading the text. On the second type, however, only the good comprehenders showed improvement; the poor comprehenders did not gain from repeated consultation of the text, thus demonstrating their disadvantage only in inferencing skill. It can therefore be predicted that, while searching through the text in the second step, disadvantaged readers will take some time to find the information item from which the bridging inference is to be drawn.

It follows that the subjects should find themselves in a situation very similar to a real problem-solving task.

On the other hand, investigations based on the "inconsistency paradigm" (Baker & Anderson, 1982; Baker, 1985) have shown that the inconsistency detection can be facilitated by giving poor readers the chance to reread the text. The fact that rereading enables readers to detect an inconsistency they failed to detect during the first reading implies that a chance to reread may make their exploitation of text information more accurate and exhaustive. Rereading may therefore improve any performance which depends on that accuracy and completeness.

Further suggestions for defining the training task can be drawn from research on the relationship between bridging inference and *textual distance* (Ackerman, Silver, & Glickman, 1990; Danner & Mathews, 1980; Rickheit, Schnotz, & Strohner, 1985; Walker & Meyer, 1980). These findings allow us to predict that by increasing the distance between the local incoherence (problem) and the information from which the bridging integration (solution) must be inferred, we can also increase the difficulty of the problem and hence the likelihood that the bridging inference needed to solve it will be performed consciously, by means of a number of trials autonomously monitored by the pupils themselves.

However, when applying suggestions concerning textual distance, we have to bear in mind that the available evidence is conflicting. In fact, Mandler and Goodman (1982) and Gernsbacher (1985) found that textual distance measured in terms of the quantity of intervening information does not significantly affect access to recently comprehended information. The above-mentioned theory of Gernsbacher on the loss of superficial information leads us to assume that the same textual distance, measured as the number of sentences, or propositions, may work in different ways depending on the kind of text segmentation operated and on the consequent rate of the loss of superficial information. If an accurate text analysis of the intervening paragraphs is made, it should be possible to identify every source of comprehension difficulty and predict the real textual distance between the comprehension problem and the text information relevant to its solution.

Further research has shown that the definition of textual distance in terms of the number of sentences or propositions is debatable and has produced a different criterion for determining the grade of difficulty of the problem-solving processes needed for drawing a bridging inference.

Trabasso and Suh (1993) compared the comprehension of subjects of average comprehension ability when presented with the same pieces of information placed in two textual versions differentiated according to whether inferences drawn from one hierarchically superordinate goal were permitted or not; this text quality was found to be much more important than the distance measured by counting the sentences between the items that needed to be linked to restore text coherence. The difficulty of a problem-solving path could thus be predicted not only by counting how many intervening items there are, but also (and mainly) by ascertaining how they are organized in a text.

Furthermore, the processes needed to draw the bridging inference may be predicted not only by text analysis, but also by testing subjects' working memory. This kind of memory has been shown to influence verbal comprehension in general and the ability to detect text inconsistency in particular (Daneman, 1987; Yuill, Oakhill, & Parkin, 1989).

It is well known that working memory is involved in how processing is monitored and connected to both prior knowledge and previous text paragraphs already processed and stored. The subjects' attention and the level of cognitive activation in online processing are more important here than memory as storage. It seems that subjects' attention, in turn, may be enhanced or reduced by objective communication features. This assumption is derived from the findings of an experimental investigation in which an inconsistency was inserted into a text in order to check hypotheses on different attitudes and sets in movie audiences versus written text readers (Lumbelli, 1967). Two groups of subjects were presented with the same inconsistency inserted into the same dialogue. For one group, the dialogue consisted of a piece of film and for the other it was a written story passage. All subjects were adults and had completed secondary schooling. The movie audience detected the inconsistency significantly less frequently [$\chi^2(1, 50) = 20.78$, $p = .001$] than the readers, showing that the kind of processing may vary according to the communication medium. The movie situation may prevent the audience from detecting an inconsistency by decreasing their cognitive activation and thus making the processes needed to detect the inconsistency less likely.

There is a final piece of evidence that readers' attention can be enhanced or reduced by choosing certain communication features: The frequency of inconsistency detections increases significantly when subjects are presented with a specific instruction about the standard to be used in their reading comprehension monitoring (Baker, 1984; Markman & Gorin, 1981). This instruction can be considered as one way to enhance readers' attention. In our case, enhancing pupils' attention might be one way of increasing the likelihood of detecting inconsistency and posing the problem themselves.

Another feature of our educational goal was the *metacognitive monitoring* (Brown, 1978; Flavell, 1976) of the processes needed to draw the kind of bridging inference focused on here. The concept of metacognition has been called "fuzzy" (Wellman, 1983) and has produced conflicting evidence as regards its influence on cognitive development and cognitive learning (Baker, 1994; Brown, 1987; Flavell, 1981). Bearing in mind the distinction between metacognition as knowledge and metacognition as monitoring (Brown, 1978;

Flavell, 1976), we took the latter into consideration. Furthermore, because there are no definite reasons for deciding whether metacognitive monitoring is both conscious and unconscious (Brown, 1987), or whether only conscious metacognitive monitoring is to be assumed (Baker, 1994), we specified conscious monitoring of cognitive integration processes as the goal of our comprehension-fostering intervention. In fact, in both steps (inconsistency detection and search for bridging information) the necessary monitoring of comprehension processes must be conscious in order to make the training task a problem-solving one. The preference for conscious metacognition followed mainly from the educational stance consisting of stressing motivated and active learning when dealing with disadvantaged pupils.

METHODOLOGY OF THE FOSTERING PROJECT

There were three different methodological problems, each of which was faced by the main stages of the project:

The first was to define a kind of text analysis that served to identify those pieces of text exhibiting the features mentioned above, that is a local incoherence that was glaringly apparent but which could be restored by means of inferences drawn from another piece of the same text.

The second was to define an online procedure for ascertaining each single reader's comprehension processes, by drawing on the discussion about the use of verbal protocols in the study of cognitive processes. That discussion seemed to be relevant to this fostering project because one of its main stages consisted of ascertaining the cognitive processes each single reader performs while reading a text.

The third was to define a communicational context suited to enhancing each learner's autonomous initiative in the search for the solution to the comprehension problem identified in the previous stage.

In this section, these three methodological problems are illustrated by providing examples of the solution suggested for each of them. The kind of text analysis defined is applied to a specific piece of text with a coherence problem and extracts are quoted from think-out-loud protocols obtained both in the course of the first reading of that piece of text and in the rereading of the whole text aimed at solving the coherence problem.

The Preliminary Text Analysis. The educational problem this project aimed at solving determined the nature of the text material used in its implementation. First of all, target pupils were assumed to be more easily motivated to read narrative versus informative or argumentative texts, and "natural" versus artificial texts. For this reason natural narrative texts were used.

The criteria defined in the previous section were not used to construct or manipulate the experimental material, but *analyze* those texts selected as the most interesting for the target readers. These criteria helped us identify those paragraphs that could be correctly understood through the kind of bridging inference focused upon here.

Several narrative texts have been used in the exploratory implementation of the fostering approach; however, the stories collected in *Marcovaldo* by Italo Calvino (1963) were preferred by both teacher–experimenters and target pupils. These stories have independent plots but always concern the same main character, Marcovaldo. He is a rather poor factory hand who lives in a big city with his family but shows a great attachment to the country life. Calvino provides readers with both a creative linguistic form and an amusing informational content. Furthermore, a deeper and easier reading are always possible and correct, and therefore readers can be adequate comprehenders without necessarily having to draw a moral.

The example analyzed here was taken from the story entitled "Father Christmas' Sons." It contains a paragraph with a local incoherence likely to become a real comprehension problem. It appears as a glaring inconsistency which requires an unambiguous solution that is likely to be lengthy and laborious.

Before analyzing this critical paragraph, I quote the part of the previous text that has to be used in its processing. The paragraph appears around the middle of the story with Marcovaldo dressed up as Father Christmas to deliver Christmas presents to the most important customers of the company he works for. Before starting his round of deliveries, he calls in at home, where he finds his children engrossed in a singular activity:

> They seemed to be particularly engrossed in the game they were playing. They were gathered together on one of the landings, sitting round in a circle. "What's the council of war in aid of?" asked Marcovaldo. "Leave us alone, Dad, we've got to get the presents ready." "Presents for who?" "For a poor child. We've got to find a poor child to give presents to." "Who told you, that?" "It's in our reading-book." Marcovaldo was about to say "You're the poor children!" but during that week he had convinced himself so much that he was living in the Land of Plenty, where everyone was buying things and enjoying themselves and giving presents, that it seemed rude to mention poverty, so instead he said "There are no poor children any more!"
>
> Michelino got up and said "Is that why you're not giving us presents, Dad?" (p. 133)

This paragraph contains various elements that make an elaboration problem likely, but the most significant is the anaphor at the beginning of Michelino's question: "Is *that* why you're not giving us presents, Dad?" This cannot be understood without using the following bridging inference: Marcovaldo has said that there are no poor children anymore; it follows that his own children are not poor either; his children, on the one hand, never get presents and, on the other, have learned from their schoolbook that poor children get presents at Christmas.

All this must be used to explain the coreference of the anaphor that: You don't bring us presents because we're not poor, because, on the one hand, nobody is poor anymore, and, on the other, only poor children get presents at Christmas. If readers manage to identify this coreference, they can also use the information that Michelino believes that only poor children get presents at Christmas, and are ready to correctly integrate the following critical paragraph.

This paragraph comes after one describing the round of Marcovaldo and Michelino's visits to deliver the parcels containing the presents.

> He rang the doorbell of a splendid house. A housekeeper opened the door.
> "Oh, another package, who's it from?"
> "SBAV wishes you . . ."
> "Well, bring it in," and she preceded Father Christmas down a corridor which was all tapestries, carpets and majolica vases. Michelino, all agog, followed his father.
> The housekeeper opened a glass door. They entered a room with an incredibly high ceiling, so high that there was enough space for an immense spruce tree. It was a Christmas tree lit up with balls of all different colours, and sweets and presents of every kind hung from its branches. Hanging from the ceiling were heavy crystal chandeliers, and the top branches of the spruce were entangled in the sparkling drops of glass. Laid out on a large table were glasses and silverware, boxes of crystallized fruit and cases full of bottles. The toys, scattered on a big rug, were as many as in a toy shop, mostly complicated electronic gadgets and models of spaceships. On the same rug, in an empty corner, there was a boy about nine years old, sprawled face downwards, with a bored, sulky expression. He was flicking through a picture-book, as though he had nothing to do with anything around him.
> "Gianfranco, come on, Gianfranco," said the housekeeper. "You see that Father Christmas is back again with another present?."
> "Three hundred and twelve," sighed the boy, without lifting his eyes from the book. "Put it over there."
> "It's the three hundredth and twelfth present that's arrived," said the housekeeper. "Gianfranco is so good, he keeps count. He doesn't miss a single one. He loves figures."
> On tiptoe, Marcovaldo and Michelino left the house.
> "Dad, is that child a poor child?" (p. 136)

The obvious local inconsistency here is between the showy wealth of the house and Michelino's idea that the child is poor.

This local inconsistency can be overcome by using the information given in previous paragraphs; that Christmas presents are given to poor children. Michelino's question can be made consistent by inferring from that paragraph that Michelino really believes that only poor children are given Christmas presents and therefore that a child who receives so many presents must be poor.

This reading path was reconstructed as the most correct one and involved the whole pattern of processes at the core of our educational project.

First, there was a local incoherence that must be detected but that may not be. This failure may arise from the automatic, overly hasty performance of an inference that only concerns one term of the inconsistency, that is an elaborative inference that calls into play a piece of prior knowledge before further text information has been decoded, and that removes the meaning which makes it inconsistent with the other term.

Second, if and when readers have detected this inconsistency, they must search the text for the information item from which the correct bridging inference can be drawn.

It is true that a piece of prior knowledge must be used here too: Children may have a mistaken or vague representation of what indicates poverty and wealth. This representation may explain why Michelino misjudges the social condition of the child in the house and why he interprets the schoolbook's suggestion not only as an invitation to give presents to poor children but as the statement that *only those children* get presents at Christmas.

We can consider the correct comprehension of the critical paragraph as an occurrence of *text-based* comprehension (Reis & Spekman, 1985). There the comprehender first examines text information accurately and exhaustively and then searches for prior knowledge suited to make that information coherent, instead of connecting it to one single piece of text information (*reader-based* comprehension). The better readers are at paying attention to every single item of explicit text information, the better they are at detecting the local incoherence and finding the required integration within the text.

Even if readers manage to detect the local incoherence between the luxury of the home and Michelino's question (first step), they may not manage to identify the text information to be used in inferring the integration (second step). That information is very distant in the text (about two pages) and is therefore very likely to have been forgotten. Obviously, this textual distance is irrelevant for those readers who have not even noticed the local incoherence and have thus simply failed to pose the problem.

This absence of the conditions needed to pose the problem is evident in the readers' verbal protocols. Most of them show the following transformation in the meaning of Michelino's question to his father: Michelino might not really be asking his father whether the boy is poor in a financial sense, but whether he is emotionally poor (because he is alone, both his parents are absent, etc.). This elaborative inference has often shown to be based on the text information that the boy has a "bored, sulky expression" and on pieces of prior knowledge about rich children being unhappy however many toys and amusements they have, about rich parents being very busy and not giving much time to their children, and so on.

These inferences are drawn so quickly and automatically that the readers no longer had a local incoherence to detect and a correct integration to make.

The Interview Centered on the Thinking Aloud Reader. After identifying one or more coherence problems in a text, the next procedural step was ascertaining the specific route each reader follows while reading. In particular, the experimenter had to ascertain whether the predicted difficulty had really been met or, instead, the coherence problem had been detected and correctly solved (only in the first case is the fostering intervention required), whether the incomprehension was caused by the failure to detect inconsistency (first step error) or, whether the reader posed the problem but did not solve it correctly (second step error), and whether in the latter case, the reader was uncertain or certain (Lumbelli, 1992) about the solution attempted and was thus ready or not to start looking for another one.

The interview technique by which all that was ascertained was not chosen to contrast the canonical methodology consisting of standardized, multiple-choice questions, but was considered as the most suited to pursue the specific goals listed above.

If we examine the points listed above, it is clear that defining how to answer them was an important part of the fostering project. The reasons for this were that if the educational treatment was to be tailored to the individual reader's cognitive needs, these needs must have been previously identified. Because the cognitive needs in reading comprehension may correspond to a great variety of mistakes in text processing, this prior identification must capture the very processes each single reader is performing while processing each single piece of text. This knowledge on the part of the teacher/experimenter was a necessary condition for making the subsequent treatment relevant to those processes. Because this knowledge could only be provided by subjects' verbal protocols, the debate on the use of verbal protocols in the study of cognitive processes (Ericsson & Simon, 1980, 1984; Nisbett & Wilson, 1977; White, 1988) became pertinent to the educational project methodology. The technique here described was a combination of the think-out-loud method, which has emerged as the most promising in that debate, and the interviewer's verbal behavior defined by Rogers (1945, 1951). Here is the rationale of this combination.

Piaget (1926) first noted the advantages of using the clinical method for studying the development of mental representations, arguing that, by using stimuli which are not prestructured, information that was not influenced by stimuli could be obtained from subjects. This requirement is of particular relevance when we need to know whether or not subjects have detected a local inconsistency. The data available regarding how the kind of instruction influences this performance (Baker, 1984; Markman & Gorin, 1981) has also demonstrated that direct questions are likely to make it impossible to distinguish between subjects who would have detected the inconsistency spontaneously and subjects who detected it only with the help of the questions. Thus, an effective tool for educational intervention becomes a confounding factor when the aim is to base the intervention on the specific cognitive needs of every single subject with regard to every specific comprehension problem.

Here I refer to the use of subjects' spontaneous verbal protocols in experimental research inasmuch as this use is relevant to information on each single reader's comprehension processes.

Ericsson and Simon (1980, 1984) provided suggestions about the conditions in which verbal protocols may be considered as accurate and reliable data about cognitive processes in general.

A clear distinction is to be made between *concurrent* and *retrospective* protocols. The former are produced when the cognitive processes are being performed or are still in short-term memory. Subjects do not therefore have to search long-term memory for them. Retrospective protocols, just because they concern information already stored in long-term memory, must be elicited with direct questions and there is always the risk that subjects are led by the questions instead of by the information stored in their long-term memory.

It follows that protocols on text comprehension should not be elicited offline (after the whole text has been read) but online, that is, just after subjects have read a piece of text. In this way, the information processed is much more likely to still be in short-term memory. This means that the best method for eliciting verbal protocols on verbal comprehension is to ask the subjects to think aloud. This method was originally proposed by Duncker (1935) and Claparède (1933) for observing the subjects' problem-solving paths. It was also applied later to research on problem solving by Newell and Simon (1972) and to the study of text comprehension by Olson, Duffy, and Mack (1984), Johnson and Afflerbach (1985), and Trabasso and Suh (1993).

Ericsson & Simon (1980, 1984) have also stated that subjects' verbal utterances concerning what they are thinking about can only be obtained when the cognitive processes are performed consciously and not automatically. This statement further supported my decision to concentrate on the pattern of processes described earlier.

Generally speaking, only those cognitive processes that can be performed in a nonautomatic way, and thus can access the subjects' consciousness, are likely to be found in their verbal protocols. This not only excludes the visual and motor processes referred to by Ericsson and Simon (1980, 1984), but also all those processes of verbal comprehension that are performed automatically in the course of both correct and incorrect performances, from the decoding processes to most of the inferences. Therefore, in order to study text processing by means of thinking aloud protocols, we must focus on sufficiently high-level cognitive processes usually performed in either a conscious way, or which are likely to become conscious in poor comprehenders because they are likely to be "blocked" when the cognitive task is too difficult (Brown, 1980). In other words, Miller, Galanter, and Pribram's (1960) suggestions about motor skills could also be applied to expertise in reading: The more expert the performer, the more unconsciously the operations are performed, whereas the novice is likely to operate in a conscious way.

But the consciousness of the processing to be expressed aloud cannot be considered a sufficient condition when the subjects are poor readers, and are therefore very likely to be poor speakers too. Even with subjects of high ability in verbal production, the verbal protocols may be incomplete; they may not conform to the actual speed and other features of thinking (Claparède, 1933). The problem is all the greater when we are trying to ascertain the cognitive processes of disadvantaged pupils, who present severe deficits in verbal production also and thus produce verbal protocols that may be incomplete and ambiguous. Further, we need protocols that enable us to check whether the gaps and fuzziness are due to real gaps and fuzziness in the subjects' mental representations, or whether they are just clues to failures in verbal planning, which can be easily overcome through further protocols. This is why I combined the thinking aloud protocols with undirected probing (Kahn & Cannel, 1957), an interview technique based on a kind of verbal behavior first described in psychotherapy and called *reflection-response* (Rogers, 1945, 1951; Rogers & Kinget, 1966). The interviewer responds with a hypothetical paraphrase of the interviewee's utterance which requires completion (beginning something like: If I have understood correctly, you mean that . . .). In this way the interviewer can ask the subjects for more information on topics already referred to in the previous utterance. This avoids both the risk of cueing the content of the subsequent utterance and of frustrating the subject. In fact, if the subjects cannot produce any more verbal protocols on their ongoing cognitive processes, they can simply answer, "Yes, I do." This interview centered on the thinking aloud reader (Lumbelli, 1992; Lumbelli & Cornoldi, 1994) was used to find out how each reader processes the local incoherence identified by the preliminary text analysis.

Before giving some examples of this technique, a few more procedural details should be mentioned.

The text was divided into pieces short enough to avoid an excessive memory load and long enough not to affect the *ecological validity* (Neisser,

1982) of the procedure. The subjects were requested to read piece by piece with the following instruction:

> We are now going to read a story together. We shall read it one short piece at a time and right afterwards you'll tell me what you remember about the passage you've just read. It's important that you say anything you have in mind, not only what you think you've understood clearly but also what seems difficult, what you feel you don't understand. This isn't a school examination where you have to try and say only things that are right and avoid the ones that might be wrong. What am I going to do? I'll listen to you and record what you say, and if necessary, I'll try to understand more.

The subjects read the text on their own or followed while the experimenter read it. They were encouraged to choose the approach that was more comfortable for them so as to ensure that possible decoding difficulties (of which the subject's decision could be seen as a clue) did not interfere with the high-level comprehension processes that were the target.

For the same reason, subjects were instructed to ask the meaning of unknown words online. Some of these words were explained by the experimenter anyway, again online. No other kind of explanation or help was given in the phase that prepared the fostering intervention.

Here are some of the spontaneous protocols produced by readers (around 13 years of age, low social status, and low school achievement) immediately after reading the paragraph ending with Michelino's question, "Dad, is that child a poor child?" They have in common the fact that they all show the reader's perplexity when confronted with the local incoherence, thus indicating that the incoherence was detected (the utterances that can be regarded as markers of perception of inconsistency are in italics), but they can also be considered as belonging to three separate categories explained below:

1. Here the son asks Marcovaldo whether that child is poor or not . . . *I can't understand* . . . that is . . . Marcovaldo answers him: no that's the son of the boss of a big firm . . . that is he is not poor . . . practically he says . . . he's astonished because the son cannot understand that the child is rich and asks this question . . . *it's really strange because after going into such a luxurious house and seeing all those presents* . . .

2. I don't know . . . *I didn't understand very well* . . . *maybe* as he had seen him bored he thought he had nothing to do . . . that he was a poor child left there alone . . . because normally poor children haven't got things to play with . . . they haven't got anything have they? Then Michelino . . . seeing this child lying on his belly on the floor and reading a book all bored . . . thought he was a poor child . . . in fact this child had nobody to play with . . . lots of poor children enjoy themselves more than rich children because they've got friends.

3. *Maybe* he says he was poor because he was so sad . . . *maybe* because his parents didn't seem to consider him a lot . . . *maybe* they didn't pay much attention to him and gave him all he wanted . . . then it might be that Michelino seeing him there so sad thought that he would be happy to receive the toys he received and then open them all and play with everything . . . whereas . . . seeing this child he must have thought he was poor.

The utterances of the first informant clearly show that the subject detected the inconsistency, but made no attempt to repair it.

The second subject briefly expressed incomprehension and then immediately proceeded to try to repair revealing the action of prior knowledge: Perhaps this subject interpreted the child's bored expression as a clue that the child had nothing to do and decided he was poor on the basis of the idea that poor children have no toys to play with. The same subject made recourse to prior knowledge again in a final objection to Michelino's reasoning; it is not that poor children are always so bored. On the contrary, they enjoy themselves more than rich children because they have friends, whereas this child is alone and has nobody to play with.

In the third case, the detection of the inconsistency was only implied, but was the premise for a whole sequence of hypotheses. The *maybe* which introduces three utterances indicated that the informant intended them as such. Furthermore, whereas the first two subjects expressed their representations clearly and completely, the final part of this last protocol contained gaps and ambiguities. The subject suggested that Michelino might have thought the child was poor because he compared the child's sad expression surrounded by all those presents with what his own reaction would have been (open them all immediately and play with them). But the protocol contained no sign of a logical connection between this premise and the conclusion drawn from it. Clearly, the link was not expressed, and it is highly unlikely that the reader found it. This third protocol can be taken as an example of that large group of poor readers' spontaneous protocols presenting methodological problems which can only be solved by going on presenting the subjects with reflection-responses.

This supplementary interview becomes even more necessary when the spontaneous protocols are of a fourth type:

4. Here's Michelino with his father . . . they go into a luxury house, where they've got all the trees really done up . . . with loads of presents . . . the table was all laid out . . . they had nice carpets . . . but then they see a child about nine years old lying on his tummy counting the Father Christmases coming to the house . . . and then he said he was the 113th . . . so he was counting them . . . then the housekeeper says that another Father Christmas has arrived bringing him another present . . . then Michelino

and his father go out on tiptoe and Michelino asks his father if that was a poor child but he says: Poor? Of course not! He's the son of a man who's got a big firm . . . I mean he doesn't understand that he was rich . . . I mean he didn't realize about all that richness . . . that he was rich . . . so his father explains that he's not poor at all and that he's the son of a big boss of a big firm . . .

The spontaneous report presented many details and seemed accurate but nonetheless there was no marker to indicate whether the subject found Michelino's question strange and thus whether the inconsistency was actually detected (there was only the statement, "he doesn't understand that he was rich"), or whether the explanation was automatic or deliberate. The interviewer then used the following reflection-responses in an attempt to elicit completions of the initial protocol that might provide answers to these questions:

1. *I:* So he's a rich child and Michelino doesn't even realize when he sees all that luxury.
2. *S:* Maybe because perhaps Michelino is young . . . I mean he thinks he's the same as other children . . . because his father has told him that there aren't any poor children anymore . . . or maybe because he was lying there with his face all sulky . . . so he thought . . . (she stops).
3. *I:* He sees he's sulking so he thinks he's poor.
4. *S:* Yes, yes . . . I mean he doesn't understand that he's rich because he's got all those things that the others haven't got . . . that's it.
5. *I:* You mean Michelino doesn't recognize those things as . . .
6. *S:* (interrupting) luxury things.
7. *I:* Luxury things . . . and you told me: because Michelino is young . . . and then you said something else: that perhaps Michelino remembered what his father had told him earlier, that there are no poor children any more.
8. *S:* Yes, I mean his father told him that before because they were giving presents . . . they wanted to give presents to poor children . . . his father told him that there were no poor children any more . . . so maybe from what I understood maybe he had . . . maybe he . . . seeing that boy looking so sulky . . . so he thought that he was poor.

The first reflection-response (1. I) recapitulated the content of the spontaneous report so as to get the gist of the two contrasting pieces of information and implicitly stress the incoherence. This interviewer's utterance added nothing to what the subject had already said but invited her to say something more about the two crucial information items already mentioned. The advantage of this method with respect to the corresponding direct questions (Why is it that Michelino asks that question when he has seen how luxurious the house is? Why hasn't he understood that the child is rich? Did you find Michelino's question strange? Why?) is twofold: The interviewer is not asking for an answer, but proposing a restatement, to which the subject may respond with a simple *yes*, and so the risk of creating frustration if the subject happens not to have understood and does not wish to admit it (a very likely eventuality) is kept to a minimum; and the method is very likely to obtain a completion, thus clarifying whether the subject failed to generate information about the two points mentioned above simply because of limits in verbal planning, or whether it was really a case of incomprehension, that is, a failure to detect the inconsistency and/or a failed attempt to resolve it. In this case, the outcome of assessment through reflection-response was that the subject had detected the incoherence and tried to resolve it, but the attempts failed.

The subject's first response (2. S) revealed a situation analogous to that of the third subject mentioned above, and presupposed the detection of an incoherence that needed explaining. In fact, the subject prefaced her various attempts at explanation with the usual *maybe*. The first hypothesis is another example of a statement so incomplete that it defies comprehension, and it is made even more ambiguous by the very fact that the subject mentioned the earlier dialogue between Marcovaldo and his children; again, the explanation was intended but not implemented. The statement of the second hypothesis is once more elliptic, but lends itself more easily to reformulation and thus to reinspection. For this reason, the interviewer decided to use it as the starting point to elicit a possible completion. Through this probing (in the sequence from 3. I to 6. S), information was collected about the subject's cognitive processes which may be paraphrased as follows: Michelino does not understand that the child is rich because he has all those luxuries which other children (Michelino included) do not get the chance to see, and so Michelino does not perceive the house as a rich person's house. Only after concluding the assessment regarding the first hypothesis did the interviewer probe (7. I) that part of the utterance referring to the coherence problem (and then you said something else . . . etc.). The subject's response (8. S) clearly showed that there was no logical connection in her mind between that reference and the incoherence to be explained. Perhaps it was recalled by association, given that the word *poor* is present in both sentences ("There are no poor children now" and "Dad, is that child a poor child?"). In any case, we might say that both of the references to Michelino's comment were clues to how it remained isolated in the text representation; it would seem that not only were the necessary links with the crucial inconsistency missing, but there was no solid link with the text paragraph of which it was part. On the other hand, because the information was recalled spontaneously, the subject's failure could not have been due to the textual distance involved, and thereby to memory deficit, but rather to the kind of segmentation into structure units taking place in the course of text processing.

These examples show that subjects' verbal protocols can tell us whether detection of a local incoherence has occurred and whether subjects have produced integrations in the course of reading. Sometimes these integrations are already expressed in the spontaneous protocols supplied by the subjects without any stimulation on the part of the interviewer. When the spontaneous protocols present ambiguities or gaps, reflection-responses may be used to elicit further utterances to complete the initial protocols, thus making it possible to ascertain whether the subjects had some more hypotheses in mind that they failed to express, or perhaps because they considered them to be secondary or dubious.

A more important function of the reflection-responses is checking whether the subjects have not mentioned the inconsistency in their spontaneous protocols but have actually detected it. They might have hesitated to tell it because they could not solve the problem it poses. The reassuring effect of the reflection-response may encourage them to express their puzzling mental representation. Ascertaining this latter condition allows the trainer–interviewers to establish whether readers are aware of the inconsistency, and, consequently, whether or not they are ready to cope with the problem they have posed themselves. If readers show they have not detected the local incoherence, and thus have not yet posed the problem, the trainers themselves will have to point out the incoherence before inviting subjects to reread the text. We can summarize all this by concluding that this interview phase is a necessary component of the educational intervention, because it guarantees the relevance of the subsequent phases. In fact, its function is to provide information about the specific cognitive needs of each single reader, thus enabling trainers to fit the whole intervention to the target.

Text Exploration as Problem Solving. In the instruction, trainers must clearly express the points that make the search in the text similar to the classical tasks of problem solving (Duncker, 1935; Wertheimer, 1945). They must clearly indicate both the *goal* (i.e., finding a piece of information that restores coherence in the critical paragraph) and the *field of the problem* (i.e., the part of the text to be explored in order to identify that piece of information). By producing an accurate instruction suited to the specific cognitive needs of every single reader, trainers provide a first kind of *scaffolding* (Wood, Bruner, & Ross, 1976).

A second kind of scaffolding consists, once again, of trainers' reflection-responses. They support learners in their search by preventing them from failing so miserably in their attempts that the frustration becomes unbearable.

The risk of excessive frustration is minimized by the reflection-responses with which the trainers encourage the trainees to keep searching, supporting them in any hypothesis they might attempt in the course of text exploration and express in their thinking aloud protocols.

In this stage of the project, the reflection-response was a form of precisely defined *feedback*, whereas most research about the effects of feedback on verbal comprehension (Baker, 1984; Garner & Taylor, 1982) has contained no precise description of the exact verbal behavior involved. For example, we have frequently not been told whether the feedback included direct or indirect probes, or whether, and to what extent, the direct probes may have been leading. During the text rereading, the trainers have also had to use the reflection-responses to reassure the subjects when they make hypotheses about pieces of information useful to solving the problem, and to encourage them to go on exploring the text and thinking about possible solutions.

This can be done without necessarily praising the subjects' performance. Praising is not a suitable tool for reassuring learners when the performance is incorrect, because it is very likely to conflict with the trainer's subsequent (and necessary) statements, such as correction or invitation to produce a better performance. Praising a disadvantaged pupil is thus very likely to become the first item of a *double bind* in the trainers communication (Sluzki & Ransom, 1976).

We might say that reflection-responses guarantee an effect which is almost diametrically opposed to the inevitable effect of direct questions: Whereas the latter lead the addressee's mind to some extent, reflection-responses (inasmuch as they only reformulate meanings already expressed by the addressee and never add anything new) encourage the addressee's own initiative in searching their mind and the text for information from which to draw inferences suitable for solving the coherence problem.

The following are excerpts from the initial interview and from the text exploration as problem solving, both with the same subject. As can be seen, N. does not understand the critical paragraph during the first stage, but easily manages to solve the coherence problem in the second stage:

N: Marcovaldo went to a very splendid house, he rang the bell and a housekeeper opened the door and said: One more Father Christmas . . . well, come in . . . they went in and there were very beautiful chandeliers and a Christmas tree so high that it touched the ceiling and there was a room full of presents and toys and in a corner there was a boy flicking through a picture book . . . and then they went out and Michelino asked: "Dad, is that child a poor child?" Marcovaldo didn't answer at once because he was busy sorting out the parcels in his van but after he said that the boy was not poor . . . he was very rich . . . Michelino wanted to find a poor child and so he asked if

that boy was a poor boy because if he had been poor he would have
given him a present.

I: He was looking for a poor child and so he asks his father if that boy
was poor . . .

N: Yes, because he didn't play with all those toys . . .

I: He was poor because he didn't play with his toys . . .

N: Perhaps he thought they weren't his and for that reason he didn't play
with them . . . if he is a small child he probably didn't know the
difference between poor and rich.

At this stage, N. did not seem to have noticed the contrast between
Michelino's idea and the reality facing him; he imagined that Michelino's
only concern was to find a poor child to give a present to, and therefore
that he would have asked his father that question regardless of what he had
seen. In this case, the influence of memory deficits can be excluded. In fact,
N. stressed the relevant piece of information in the previous part of the text.
However, Michelino's question was matched and linked to that recalled text
information but it was not matched to the adjacent inconsistent information,
and for this very reason local coherence did not emerge. N. provided other
hypotheses in reaction to just two reflection-responses: Michelino might
have thought the toys did not belong to the boy, because he was not playing
with them, and he did not know the difference between rich and poor
because he was still too small. These further elaborative inferences confirmed
the above-sketched evaluation based on the initial protocol.

The following excerpt from the phase based on text exploration is an
example of the effect of rereading on local incoherence detection:

1. *I:* Now I am going to give you a different task . . . last time we spoke
about Michelino's question and you told me that Michelino probably asked that question because he had no clear idea of who is
poor and who is rich . . . he had to make a present to a poor child
and he had no clear idea of who is poor and that's why he asked
his father that question . . . now let's see if it's possible to find a
different explanation of Michelino's question . . . read the story
again to look for a sentence or something said by someone which
might help you to understand why Michelino asked that question
. . . so start from the beginning . . . you can read it silently and
stop when you find a passage that you think might help you understand why Michelino asked that question . . . then you will tell
me as usual what you are thinking and we will talk about it . . .

2. *N:* (reads as far as the following sentences: "There are no more poor
children any more." Michelino got up and said "Is that why you're

not giving us presents. Dad?") Perhaps they thought that children who didn't get presents were not poor . . . that's why he wanted to take presents to that boy.

3. *I:* That's what Michelino thought . . .
4. *N:* Since his father didn't bring him any presents he thought that rich children didn't get presents . . . only poor ones did.

Immediately after rereading the text paragraph containing the information item crucial to solving the coherence problem, N. showed that he was able to identify all the elements needed for the solution. He also used the above-mentioned anaphor in a productive way. Here, the function of the reflection-responses (3. I) is only to help N. produce a more complete verbal protocol (4. N). In 2. N, Michelino's question to his father (Is that why you're not giving us presents, Dad?) seemed to have given rise to a dual inference from Marcovaldo's previous statement (there are no poor children any more). Marcovaldo's sons seem to have derived from that statement not only the idea that they themselves are not poor, but also the idea directly relevant to the comprehension problem to be solved: If Marcovaldo's sons are not poor and they do not receive presents either, it follows that "children who did not receive presents were not poor." This also implies that whoever receives presents must be poor and therefore the solution of the comprehension problem as well: Michelino "wanted to take presents to that boy," because he thinks that anyone receiving so many presents must be poor.

In 2. N, only the conclusion of this reasoning was explicity stated. This conclusion led us to hypothesize that N. actually performed each of the steps described above. This hypothesis was confirmed by means of the subsequent reflection-response 3. I which elicited 4. N. N. showed that he compared the explicit text information (Marcovaldo's statement) with the inferred information that Marcovaldo's sons are not receiving presents. The performance of this "bridge" was already clear in 2. N, but was made explicit, and thus even clearer in 4. N through the sentence, "since his father didn't bring them any presents."

Trainer's Modeling as Last Resort. But not every session of remedial treatment concludes with the trainee's autonomous attainment of the solution to the coherence problem. When the solution is not found, the trainer's help changes. Instead of providing reflection-responses only, he proposes some help-questions designed to direct the learner's attention toward the textual information to be used for the bridging inference. Obviously, this phase only takes place if learners have not already dwelled on those information items on their own initiative, without necessarily being able to make the correct inferences. Only when these help questions have failed to be effective does another phase begin which may be called *modeling*. The trainer thinks aloud while processing the crucial text paragraph, and provides the trainee with verbal protocols on those text paragraphs which are relevant to restoring text coherence.

The trainer's expertise consists of the ability to produce a verbal formulation of all the processes involved in the solution of the coherence problem, including processes that have obviously been performed automatically and can therefore only be reconstructed with the preliminary logical-linguistic analysis of the text itself. This inversion of the phases of *reciprocal teaching* (Palincsar & Brown, 1984) ensures that learners have had the chance to find the solution on their own to those comprehension problems that they had the *proximal capacity* to solve, and that learners without this proximal capacity to solve a specific problem are provided with the pattern of solution processes. In the latter case, too, the experience of an autonomous search should have the positive effect of making the outcome of the modeling less superficial and temporary. In fact, modeling is presented as the solution to a problem that has already been an object of efforts of autonomous reflection, even if the reflection had been without success.

What I have described is only a single session focused on a single, crucial paragraph. A text may contain more than one crucial paragraph, and so numerous sessions may be devoted to one single text.

Furthermore, the material of a whole educational treatment consists of several texts. An effective outcome can only be predicted if poor readers are given several different chances to perform the pattern of processes described earlier. The compensatory project should, therefore, be composed of a sequence of sessions focused upon different crucial paragraphs of different texts, all endowed with the same structure, that is, all requiring the same pattern of processes: Heeding the explicit text information carefully enough to detect any inconsistency, avoiding any overly hasty elaborative inference from prior knowledge, and searching the preceding part of the text for information items from which the bridge can be inferred, thus restoring text coherence.

Because the comprehension problems used as instructional tasks present a similar structure, it may be predicted that, in the course of the sequence of sessions, the learners will gradually form a concept of that structure and will use it in any subsequent text-reading task. The instances of the same structure which are repeatedly encountered may be considered as prototypes (Rosch, 1978) of the concept of a kind of comprehension problem and of its corresponding solution path, that is, as prototypes of a strategy to be consciously applied in order to solve that kind of problem. An effective transfer of this concept and of the corresponding solution strategy may also be predicted on the basis of the theory of "high-road transfer" defined by Salomon and Perkins (1989). According to this theory, stimulating metacognition improves the kind of transfer that implies intentional abstraction of cognitive elements and their application to contexts requiring the execution of nonautomatic, conscious processes. Because the performance focused upon involves cognitive processes of a high hierarchical level which are so difficult that the subjects are obliged to monitor them consciously, and because the treatment is designed to facilitate the abstraction of the concept of a kind of comprehension problem and of the corresponding cognitive strategy, the transfer of this concept can be considered a high-road one.

AN EXPERIMENTAL TEST
AND PROVISIONAL CONCLUSIONS

So far this project has been tested mostly by qualitative, exploratory research, and not by using experimental designs. The aim of this exploratory implementation was to evaluate the feasibility of the methodology described and to see whether it really does stimulate the intrinsic motivation of our target readers and thereby the problem-solving activity expected.

The methodology was first implemented by teachers who had already acquired expertise in interviewing with reflection-responses and then by teachers who were attending training courses in this interviewing technique.

I briefly present the findings of the only experiment made so far to check the effectiveness of this compensatory approach (Lumbelli, Paoletti, & Camagni, 1993). The main hypothesis was that the educational project described would also enhance conscious monitoring of cognitive integration of explicit text information in writing, and not only in reading, thereby improving both abilities. As they become aware of their coherence restoration as readers, the subjects should also become better at producing coherent texts as writers. In other words, by learning to pose and solve their own comprehension problems, they should also learn to avoid presenting their readers with them.

The experimental group was given the treatment described (three individual sessions of about 1 hour each) and was compared with a control group using pre and posttests that measured coherence in writing and verbal comprehension ability. Obviously, only the part of the investigation concerning the latter is mentioned here. Thirty-six subjects (about 11 years old and socioculturally disadvantaged) were divided into two groups of 18 matched on the standardized MT Reading Comprehension Test (Cornoldi et al., 1981) with mean scores of 7.17 (experimental group) and 7.28 (control group). After about 2 months, all subjects were reassessed with a parallel form of the MT test. There was a significant increase [$F(1, 34) = 12.40$, $p = .001$] in the comprehension ability scores in the experimental group (from mean scores 7.17 to 8.56), whereas the increase in the control group was not statistically significant (from mean scores 7.28 to 7.94).

These experimental findings obviously cannot be considered as definite confirmation of the effectiveness of our intervention. More extensive investigations with a greater number of subjects and sessions are needed. For the time being, one hypothesis we can draw from these findings is that this intervention might be effective not only in enhancing the specific form of comprehension ability to which it is directed, but also in enhancing the ability to perform lower level comprehension and decoding processes. The text exploration which is the core of the intervention might stimulate the disadvantaged readers to pay attention to every piece of explicit, superficial, text information. This increased attention might, in turn, increase their ability to exploit any information item. This intervention might therefore stimulate not only the high-level processes, but also the performance of the related low-level processes. The intensive enhancing of the readers' motivation and active attitude might thus also have a positive influence on those components of reading ability which we deliberately did not take into account.

The hypothesis of this kind of effectiveness obviously needs checking with investigations designed to compare the outcomes obtained by the *détour* of our fostering intervention with those obtained from other interventions aimed directly at improving decoding processes. Our *détour* may have some important advantages for the upper grade disadvantaged readers, because enhancing their intrinsic motivation is an important requirement for any educational project designed for them and projects designed to improve decoding ability tend, instead, to present pupils with drill tasks.

REFERENCES

Ackerman, B. P., Silver, D., & Glickman, I. (1990). Concept availability in the causal inferences of children and adults. *Child Development, 61*, 230–246.

Baker, L. (1979). Comprehension monitoring: Identifying and copying with text confusions. *Journal of Reading Behavior, 11*, 363–374.

Baker, L. (1984). Spontaneous versus instructed use of multiple standards for evaluating comprehension: Effects of age, reading proficiency and type of standard. *Journal of Experimental Child Psychology, 38*, 289–311.

Baker, L. (1985). How do we know when we don't understand? Standards for evaluating text comprehension. In D. L. Forrest-Pressley, G. E. MacKinnon, & T. G. Waller (Eds.), *Metacognition, cognition and human performance* (pp. 155–205). Orlando, FL: Academic Press.

Baker, L. (1994). Fostering metacognitive development. In H. W. Reese (Ed.), *Advances in child development and behavior* (Vol. 25, pp. 201–239). Orlando, FL: Academic Press.

Baker, L., & Anderson, R. I. (1982). Effects of inconsistent information on text processing: Evidence for comprehension monitoring. *Reading Research Quarterly, 17*, 281–294.

Beal, C. R., Garrod, A. C., & Bonitatibus, G. J. (1990). Fostering children's revision skills through training in comprehension monitoring. *Journal of Educational Psychology, 82*, 275–280.

Berstein, B. (1971). *Class, codes and control.* London: Routledge & Kegan Paul.

Bransford, J. D., Barclay, J. R., & Franks, J. J. (1972). Sentence memory: A constructive versus interpretative approach. *Cognitive Psychology, 3*, 193–209.

Bransford, J. D., & Franks, J. J. (1971). The abstraction of linguistic ideas. *Cognitive Psychology, 2,* 331–350.

Brown, A. L. (1978). Knowing when, where, and how to remember: A problem of metacognition. In R. Glaser (Ed.), *Advances in instructional psychology* (pp. 77–165). Hillsdale, NJ: Lawrence Erlbaum Associates.

Brown, A. L. (1980). Metacognitive development and reading. In R. J. Spiro, B. C. Bruce, & W. F. Brewer (Eds.), *Theoretical issues in reading comprehension* (pp. 453–481). Hillsdale, NJ: Lawrence Erlbaum Associates.

Brown, A. L. (1987). Metacognition, executive control, self-regulation, and other more mysterious mechanisms. In F. E. Weinert & R. H. Kluwe (Eds.), *Metacognition, motivation, and understanding* (pp. 65–116). Hillsdale, NJ: Lawrence Erlbaum Associates.

Brown, J. S., Collins, A., & Duguid, P. (1989). Situated cognition and the culture of learning. *Educational Research, 18,* 32–41.

Calvino, I. (1963). *Marcovaldo.* Torino: Einandi.

Claparède, E. (1933). La genèse de l'hypothèse [The origin of hypothesis]. *Archives de Psychologie, XXIV,* 93–94.

Clark, H. H. (1977). Bridging. In P. N. Johnson-Laird & P. C. Wason (Eds.), *Thinking: Readings in cognitive science* (pp. 243–263). Cambridge, England: Cambridge University Press.

Collins, A., Brown, J. S., & Newman, S. (1989). Cognitive apprenticeship: Teaching the crafts of reading, writing and mathematics. In L. B. Resnick (Ed.), *Knowing, learning and instruction* (pp. 453–494). Hillsdale, NJ: Lawrence Erlbaum Associates.

Cornoldi, C. (1990). Metacognitive control processes and memory deficits in poor comprehenders. *Learning Disabilities Quarterly, 13,* 245–256.

Cornoldi, C., Colpo, G., & MT Group (1981). *Prove oggettive di lettura MT* [MT Reading Test]. Firenze: Organizzazioni Speciali.

Cromer, W. (1970). The difference model: A new explanation for some reading difficulties. *Journal of Educational Psychology, 61,* 471–483.

Daneman, M. (1987). Reading and working memory. In J. R. Beech & A. M. Colley (Eds.), *Cognitive approaches to reading* (pp. 57–86). Chichester, England: Wiley.

Daneman, M., & Carpenter, P. A. (1980). Individual differences in working memory and reading. *Journal of Verbal Learning and Verbal Behavior, 19,* 450–466.

Daneman, M., & Carpenter, P. A. (1983). Individual differences in integrating information between and within sentences. *Journal of Experimental Psychology: Learning, Memory and Cognition, 9,* 561–585.

Danner, F., & Mathews, S. R. (1980). When do young children make inferences from prose? *Child Development, 51,* 906–908.

Duncker, K. (1935). *Zur psychologie des productiven denkens* [The psychology of productive thinking]. Berlin: Springer.

Ericsson, E. A., & Simon, H. A. (1980). Verbal protocols as data. *Psychological Review, 87,* 215–251.

Ericsson, E. A., & Simon, H. A. (1984). *Protocol analysis.* Cambridge, MA: MIT Press.

Feuerstein, R. (1980). *Instrumental enrichment: An intervention program for cognitive modifiability.* Baltimore: University Park Press.

Flavell, J. H. (1976). Metacognitive aspects of problem solving. In L. B. Resnick (Ed.), *The nature of intelligence* (pp. 231–235). Hillsdale, NJ: Lawrence Erlbaum Associates.

Flavell, J. H. (1981). Cognitive monitoring. In W. P. Dickson (Ed.), *Children's oral communication skills* (pp. 35–60). New York: Academic Press.

Garner, R. (1980). Monitoring of understanding: An investigation of good and poor readers' awareness of induced miscomprehension of text. *Journal of Reading Behavior, 12,* 55–64.

Garner, R. (1981). Monitoring of passage inconsistency among poor comprehenders: A preliminary test of the "Piecemeal Processing" explanation. *Journal of Educational Research, 74,* 159–162.

328

Garner, R., & Taylor, N. (1982). Monitoring of understanding: An investigation on the effects of attentional assistance needs at different grade and reading levels. *Reading Psychology, 3*, 1–6.

Gernsbacher, M. A. (1985). Surface information loss in comprehension. *Cognitive Psychology, 17*, 324–363.

Gernsbacher, M. A. (1988). Mechanisms that improve inferential access. *Cognition, 32*, 99–156.

Gernsbacher, M. A., Varner, K. R., & Faust, M. E. (1990). Investigating differences in general comprehension skill. *Journal of Experimental Psychology: Learning, Memory and Cognition, 16*, 430–445.

Giglioli, P. P. (1972). *Language and social context.* London: Penguin.

Grice, P. (1975). Logic and conversation. In P. Cole & J. Morgan (Eds.), *Syntax and semantics: Speech acts* (pp. 41–58). New York: Academic Press.

Johnson, P., & Afflerbach, P. (1985). The process of constructing main ideas from text. *Cognition and Instruction, 2*, 207–232.

Just, M. A., & Carpenter, P. A. (1980). A theory of reading: From eye fixations to comprehension. *Psychological Review, 4*, 329–354.

Kahn, R. L., & Cannel, C. F. (1957). *The dynamics of interviewing.* New York: Wiley.

Lumbelli, L. (1967). In che senso esiste una "passività" dello spettatore cinematografico? [In what sense is the film audience "passive"?]. *IKON, 63*, 37–52.

Lumbelli, L. (1992). Uncertainty in text comprehension: Cues and effects. In B. van Hout-Wolters & W. Schnotz (Eds.), *Text comprehension and learning from text* (pp. 153–168). Amsterdam: Swets & Zeitlinger.

Lumbelli, L., & Cornoldi, C. (1994). Interaction between verbal and visual information in audio-visual text comprehension. In F. P. C. M. De Jong & B. H. A. M. van Hout-Wolters (Eds.), *Process-oriented instruction and learning from text* (pp. 183–193). Amsterdam: VU University Press.

Lumbelli, L., Paoletti, G., & Camagni, C. (1993, September). *Can the ability to monitor local coherence in text comprehension be transferred to writing?* Paper presented at the 5th European Conference for Research on Learning and Instruction, Aix-en-Provence, France.

Mandler, J. M., & Goodman, M. G. (1982). On the psychological validity of story structures. *Journal of Verbal Learning and Verbal Behavior, 21*, 507–523.

Markman, E. M. (1977). Realizing that you don't understand: A preliminary investigation. *Child Development, 46*, 986–992.

Markman, E. M. (1979). Realizing that you don't understand: Elementary school children's awareness of inconsistencies. *Child Development, 50*, 643–655.

Markman, E. M., & Gorin, L. (1981). Children's ability to adjust their standards for evaluating comprehension. *Journal of Educational Psychology, 73*, 320–325.

Meichenbaum, D. H., & Goodman, S. (1979). Clinical use of private speech and critical questions about its study in natural settings. In G. Zivin (Ed.), *The development of self-regulation through private speech* (pp. 325–360). New York: Wiley.

Miller, G. A., Galanter, E., & Pribram, K. H. (1960). *Plans and structure of behavior.* New York: Holt, Rinehart & Winston.

Neisser, U. (1982). *Memory observed.* San Francisco: Freeman.

Newell, A., & Simon, H. A. (1972). *Human problem solving.* Englewood Cliffs, NJ: Prentice-Hall.

Nisbett, R. E., & Wilson De Camp, T. (1977). Telling more than we can know: Verbal reports on mental processes. *Psychological Review, 3*, 231–259.

Oakhill, J. V. (1984). Inferential and memory skills in children's comprehension of stories. *British Journal of Educational Psychology, 54*, 31–39.

Oakhill, J. V. (1994). Individual differences in children's text comprehension. In M. A. Gernsbacher (Ed.), *Handbook of psycholinguistics* (pp. 821–848). New York: Academic Press.

Oakhill, J. V., Yuill, N. M., & Parkin, A. J. (1986). On the nature of the difference between skilled and less-skilled comprehenders. *Journal of Research on Reading, 9*, 80–91.

Olson, G. M., Duffy, S. A., & Mack, R. L. (1984). Thinking-out-loud as a method for studying real-time comprehension processes. In D. E. Kieras & M. A. Just (Eds.), *New methods in reading comprehension* (pp. 253–286). Hillsdale, NJ: Lawrence Erlbaum Associates.

Osherson, D., & Markman, E. (1975). Language and the ability to evaluate contradictions and tautologies. *Cognition, 3*, 213–226.

Palincsar, A. S., & Brown, A. L. (1984). Reciprocal teaching of comprehension-fostering and comprehension-monitoring activities. *Cognition and Instruction, 1*, 117–175.

Paris, S. G., Cross, D. R., & Lipson, M. Y. (1984). Informed strategies for learning: An instructional program to improve children's reading awareness and comprehension. *Journal of Educational Psychology, 76*, 1239–1252.

Passow, A. H., Goldberg, M., & Tannenbaum, A. J. (1967). *Education of the disadvantaged.* New York: Holt, Rinehart & Winston.

Perfetti, C. A., & Goldman, S. R. (1976). Discourse memory and reading comprehension skill. *Journal of Verbal Learning and Verbal Behavior, 15*, 33–42.

Perfetti, C. A., & Hogaboam, T. (1975). Relationship between single word decoding and reading comprehension skill. *Journal of Educational Psychology, 67*, 461–469.

Perfetti, C. A., & Lesgold, A. M. (1977). Discourse comprehension and sources of individual differences. In M. A. Just & P. A. Carpenter (Eds.), *Cognitive processes in comprehension* (pp. 141–183). Hillsdale, NJ: Lawrence Erlbaum Associates.

Piaget, J. (1926). *La réprésentation du monde chez l'enfant* [Child's representation of the world]. Paris: PUF.

Reis, R., & Spekman, N. (1983). The detection of reader-based versus text-based inconsistencies and the effects of direct training of comprehension monitoring among upper-grade poor comprehenders. *Journal of Reading Behavior, 15*, 49–60.

Rickheit, G., Schnotz, W., & Strohner, H. (1985). The concept of inference in discourse comprehension. In G. Rickheit & H. Strohner (Eds.), *Inferences in text processing* (pp. 3–49). Amsterdam: North-Holland.

Riessman, F. (1962). *The culturally deprived child.* New York: Harper & Row.

Rogers, C. R. (1945). The non-directive method as a technique in social research. *American Journal of Sociology, 50*, 279–283.

Rogers, C. R. (1951). *Client-centered therapy.* Boston: Houghton Mifflin.

Rogers, C. R., & Kinget, M. (1966). *Psychothérapie et rélations humaines* [Psychotherapy and human relations]. Louvain, Belgium: Nauwelaerts.

Rosch, E. (1978). Principles of categorization. In E. Rosch & B. B. Lloyd (Eds.), *Cognition and categorization* (pp. 27–48). Hillsdale, NJ: Lawrence Erlbaum Associates.

Salomon, G., & Perkins, D. N. (1989). Rocky roads to transfer: Rethinking mechanisms of a neglected phenomenon. *Educational Psychologist, 24*, 113–142.

Sluzki, C. E., & Ransom, D. C. (Eds.). (1976). *Double bind: The foundation of the communicational approach to the family.* New York: Grune & Stratton.

Trabasso, T., & Suh, S. (1993). Understanding text: Achieving explanatory coherence through on-line inferences and mental operations in working memory. *Discourse Processes, 16*, 3–34.

Van Dijk, T. A., & Kintsch, W. (1983). *Strategies of discourse comprehension.* New York: Academic Press.

Walker, C. H., & Meyer, B. J. F. (1980). Integrating different types of information in text. *Journal of Verbal Learning and Verbal Behavior, 19*, 263–275.

Wellman, H. M. (1983). Metamemory revisited. In M. T. H. Chi (Ed.), *Contributions to human development: Trends in memory development research* (Vol. 9, pp. 31–51). Basel, Switzerland: Karger.

Wertheimer, M. (1945). *Productive thinking.* New York: Harper.

White, P. A. (1988). Knowing more about what we can tell: 'Introspective access' and causal report accuracy 10 years later. *British Journal of Psychology, 79,* 13–45.

Wood, D., Bruner, J. S., & Ross, G. (1976). The role of tutoring in problem solving. *Journal of Child Psychology and Psychiatry, 17,* 89–100.

Yuill, N. M., & Oakhill, J. V. (1988). Effects of inference awareness training on poor reading comprehenders. *Applied Cognitive Psychology, 2,* 33–45.

Yuill, N. M., Oakhill, J. V., & Parkin, A. J. (1989). Working memory, comprehension ability and the resolution of text anomaly. *British Journal of Psychology, 80,* 351–361.

Zimmermann, B. J., & Schunk, D. H. (1989). *Self-regulated learning and academic achievement.* New York: Springer.

CHAPTER FOURTEEN

Social Influences on Metacognitive Development in Reading

Linda Baker
University of Maryland, Baltimore County

It has been well established that there are substantial individual and developmental differences in the metacognitive skills of reading (Baker, 1989a; Baker & Brown, 1984; Garner, 1987). In fact, many researchers have suggested that limited metacognitive skills may be a cause of reading difficulty, given the consistent correlational evidence that more successful readers exhibit higher levels of metacognitive knowledge about reading and are more skilled at regulating their comprehension processes than are less successful readers (Baker, 1982; Wong, 1985). An understanding of the factors that contribute to metacognitive growth is obviously critical to the development of effective intervention programs. However, the popular appeal of metacognition has led to a widespread and somewhat uncritical acceptance of the construct among educators, and intervention programs have proliferated, often without solid empirical evidence of efficacy (Baker, 1994). This situation is scientifically and pedagogically problematic, and highlights the need for further research on how metacognition develops and how it may best be fostered. Although descriptions of developmental changes in metacognitive skills are widely available, less is known about factors influencing those changes.

The purpose of this chapter is to examine one source of influence on metacognitive development in reading, the role of social agents such as parents and teachers. Many researchers have suggested that metacognitive growth can be facilitated by the use of socialization practices and instructional strategies that encourage children to plan, to evaluate their progress, and to revise their efforts if unsuccessful (Brown, 1987; Short & Weissberg-Benchell, 1989). To what extent do children actually receive such guidance during the course of their daily lives? How successful is such guidance when it is provided? To address these questions, the chapter explores social influences on metacognition in both naturally occurring and deliberately engineered contexts, with a selective focus on my own recent research. It examines the role of parental beliefs and practices relevant to metacognitive development in reading. It also examines the role of teachers, considering findings from naturalistic observations of classroom practice, teachers' reports of their practices, and teachers' evaluations of parental practices. The chapter also discusses intervention efforts designed to promote comprehension monitoring and metacognitive knowledge about reading. Special consideration is given to the implications for improving the reading abilities of students with comprehension difficulties.

Because metacognition has been defined in different ways by different researchers, it is important to begin by clarifying my own definition. The term metacognition initially was used by Flavell (1976) and by Brown (1978) to refer to knowledge about cognition and regulation of cognition. This two-component conceptualization of metacognition has been widely used in the literature since that time, even though some researchers have called for restricting its definition to knowledge about cognition, excluding the regulatory processes (e.g., Cavanaugh & Perlmutter, 1982). My own definition of metacognition encompasses both knowledge and control components (see Baker, 1994; Baker & Cerro, in press, for further discussion of definitional issues). Specifically, the first component concerns the ability to reflect on our own cognitive processes and includes knowledge about when, how, and why to engage in various cognitive activities. The second component concerns the use of strategies that enable us to control our cognitive efforts. These strategies include planning our moves, checking the outcomes of our efforts, evaluating the effectiveness of our actions and remediating any difficulties, and testing and revising our learning techniques (Baker, 1991).

SOCIAL INFLUENCES ON METACOGNITION IN NATURALLY OCCURRING CONTEXTS

Social interaction has increasingly been recognized as an important mediator of cognitive development in general (Azmitia & Perlmutter, 1990; Rogoff, 1990) and metacognitive development in particular (Baker, 1994; Day, Cordon, & Kerwin, 1989). The theoretical underpinnings of this perspective are attributable to Vygotsky (1978), who argued that children develop the capacity for self-regulation through interaction with more knowledgeable others. These individuals initially assume responsibility for monitoring progress, setting goals, planning activities, allocating attention, and so on. Gradually, responsibility for these executive processes is given over to the child, who becomes increasingly capable of regulating his or her own cognitive activities. This view, articulated by Wertsch (1978), has stimulated a great deal of interest in the social origins of cognitive and metacognitive development.

In this section, I examine the available evidence regarding the extent to which social agents, specifically parents and teachers, provide information about metacognitive skills and strategies during interactions with children. The concern here is with observations and self-reports of behaviors in naturally occurring contexts where there is not an explicit focus on metacognition.

Observations of Parent–Child Interactions

Working within the Vygotskian tradition, several researchers have explored the origins of metacognition through observations of adult–child interaction. Baker (1994) reviewed this literature and concluded that the evidence is still ambiguous as to whether and how adults foster a transition from other regulation to self-regulation, a key mechanism of metacognitive development. However, under at least some circumstances, social interaction has been shown to facilitate independent performance, and parents have been found to tailor their level of assistance to the needs and capabilities of the child (Baker, Gilat, & Sonnenschein, 1990; Freund, 1990). Moreover, these observational studies have suggested that parental verbalization of cognitive and metacognitive processes affects children's performance. For example, Freund found that some of the mothers participating in her study interacted with their 3- and 5-year-old children by discussing the strategies they would use to solve the problem and engaging in planning, monitoring, and goal setting. The children of these mothers scored higher on an independent posttest than children whose mothers devoted more attention to specific demands of the task. Thus, children seemed to benefit more when mothers' instruction focused on metacognitive awareness and control rather than on task-specific skills and knowledge.

One limitation of these observational findings for our present purposes is that the tasks have involved problem solving rather than reading. Although many studies have been conducted of adult–child interaction during book reading, these studies did not focus on metacognitive aspects of the interaction. Thus, an important avenue for further research is the investigation of the extent to which adults foster young children's metacognitive knowledge and control of reading through their spontaneous behaviors during joint book reading. Cox (1994) reported that children as young as 4 years of age demonstrated some metacognitive awareness and control of their literacy processes as they dictated stories for other children, and she suggested that the origins of this awareness may well lie in the nature of adult–child interaction during encounters with print.

Also needed are studies that explore the possibility that parent–child interactions during reading differ for children who are good readers and those who are poor readers. Research has shown that parents of lower achievers tend to be less involved in their children's education (e.g., Snow, Barnes, Chandler, Goodman, & Hemphill, 1991), but these correlational findings have typically been based on reports of attending parent–teacher meetings and volunteering to help in the classroom rather than on detailed observations of actual practices. Pratt, Green, MacVicar, and Bountrogianni (1992) found that the quality of parental assistance in helping fifth-grade children with their math homework was related to children's math performance, but Snow et al. (1991) did not find a similar relation when they looked at parent–child interaction during homework and several different indices of reading achievement in second-, fourth- and sixth-grade children.

Parental Reports of Beliefs and Behaviors Relevant to Metacognitive Development

Parents' behaviors toward their children undoubtedly are mediated by their beliefs about development and their perceptions of their children's capabilities (Goodnow & Collins, 1990). For example, Sonnenschein, Baker, and Freund (1993) found that mothers emphasized different aspects of a problem in their instruction depending on their perceptions of the nature of the task and of their children's competencies. Given that metacognitive skills are acquired at least in part through social transmission, it is important to study parents' implicit beliefs as well as their overt behaviors. To this end, Baker, Sonnenschein, and their colleagues conducted a series of studies exploring parents' awareness of the importance of metacognitive skills and the extent to which they reported engaging in activities with their children that foster metacognitive development.

In two studies, Sonnenschein, Baker, and Cerro (1992) questioned 110 middle-class mothers of preschool children about their role in fostering learning-to-learn skills, defined as encompassing basic cognitive processes such as listening and paying attention as well as metacognitive processes such as planning and monitoring. Most of the mothers believed they taught their children these skills, but when asked to provide examples of relevant instructional situations, mothers tended to focus on basic cognitive skills such as memory rather than strategies for promoting those skills. The failure to report metacognitive instruction does not necessarily mean it does not occur, of course, but it suggests a limited awareness of the importance of metacognitive skills. Alternatively, it may be that parents provide metacognitive guidance during the course of an interaction but this guidance occurs at a level not amenable to deliberate introspection.

Sonnenschein, Baker, and Lasaga (1991) explored more directly parental beliefs concerning the development of metacognition. Participants in the

study were 110 mothers of children enrolled in prekindergarten, kindergarten, and first-grade classes (mean ages of 4, 5, and 6 years, respectively) in
several parochial schools in a lower middle-income metropolitan area. Mothers completed several different questionnaires, only one of which is discussed in detail here. The Beliefs About How Children Learn Questionnaire,
adapted from Johnson and Martin (1985), consisted of six items that assessed
parents' beliefs about how children learn specific skills in three domains;
metacognitive skills (planning, comprehension monitoring), academic skills
(reading, mathematics), and life skills (getting dressed, cleaning up). Mothers
ranked the relative importance of maturation, self-discovery, learning via
parents, and learning via teachers as explanations for how children learn
the skills within each domain. Of particular interest was whether they would
see different forces as more important for different types of skills. The following item for comprehension monitoring is representative of the content
and format:

How do children become able to know whether they understand something?
a. Teachers teach them how to determine whether they understand (learning
via teachers).
b. Parents emphasize making sure they understand (learning via parents).
c. Children discover through daily experiences whether or not they understand
(self-discovery).
d. When children are ready, they are able to determine whether they understand. (maturation).

Table 14.1 shows the proportion of mothers selecting each of the four types
of options as their first choice for each situation. The pattern of maternal

TABLE 14.1
Mothers' Responses on the Beliefs About How Children Learn Questionnaire

	Primary Source of Influence			
	Mat	Self-Dis	Lrn-P	Lrn-T
Metacognitive situations				
Planning	.03	.65	.31	.01
Monitoring	.05	.50	.43	.03
Cognitive/academic situations				
Reading	.18	.18	.43	.21
Arithmetic	.02	.35	.37	.26
Life skills situations				
Dressing	.10	.51	.33	.06
Cleaning	.03	.16	.68	.13

Note. Figures correspond to proportion of mothers choosing each response option as their
first choice. Mat = maturation; Self-Dis = self-discovery; Lrn-P = learning via parents; Lrn-T =
learning via teachers.

responses did not differ depending on the ages of the children. As can be seen, the proportions varied depending on whether the situation involved metacognitive skills, cognitive/academic skills, or life skills. The majority of mothers felt the metacognitive skills of planning and comprehension monitoring were acquired through the child's daily experiences, with parental emphasis on the skills also considered important, but less so. It was striking how few mothers thought teachers were primarily responsible for fostering these skills. Teachers were more likely to be accorded a role in the acquisition of reading and arithmetic skills, but self-discovery and parental emphasis were considered equally if not more important in the academic domain as well.

It was interesting and somewhat surprising that these mothers believed that children acquire the metacognitive skills of planning and comprehension monitoring through their daily experiences rather than through direct instruction. Nevertheless, this belief in the child's active role in his or her own learning appears to be characteristic of middle-income parents (Johnson & Martin, 1985). We are currently exploring whether similar patterns obtain among a sample of low-income inner-city parents responding to the same questionnaire (Baker, Sonnenschein, & Serpell, 1995). It is important that we not overgeneralize the results of this series of studies undertaken primarily with middle-income European–American families to those from other sociocultural backgrounds.

Our research has also shown that middle-income parents do not emphasize metacognition in interactions with older children either, as revealed in their responses to hypothetical situations involving homework. In a study by Baker, Sonnenschein, and Cerro (1992), 108 mothers of second- and fourth-grade students (mean ages of 7 and 9, respectively) completed a questionnaire in which they described how they would assist their child in completing four different types of typical homework assignments. Parents were requested to describe what, if any, assistance they would give their child in completing four types of homework assignments: a book report (the child must read a book and complete a book report; the assignment is due in 2 weeks), a spelling assignment (the unspecified spelling assignment is brought home on Monday; the spelling test is to be on Friday), a math assignment (20 unspecified problems, due the next day), and a current events assignment (the assignment is brought home on Monday and the child must present a current event to the class sometime during the week).

Responses were coded as to the nature of the assistance provided based on an analysis of the components of the tasks. There were seven coding categories:

1. No parental involvement: Parent provides no assistance on key components of the task or on the entire task.
2. Task completion: Parent ensures/checks that the task is done.

3. Task structure: Parent ensures that the child has supplies, materials, space, or time, verifies instructions from the teacher, and checks the child's understanding of the assignment.
4. Processing and production: Parent assists the child in processing the materials and producing the final product.
5. Checking correctness: Parent checks the final product and quizzes the child.
6. Checking conceptual understanding: Parent questions the child to be sure he/she understands what was read/written/solved/spelled; asks the child to revise the product after checking correctness.
7. Metacognitive instruction: parent *explicitly* informs the child of the value of checking, revising, monitoring comprehension, and so on.

I focus here on the responses parents provided for the book report assignment, given its particular relevance to the present chapter. The following two responses reflected extremes in the levels of assistance hypothetically offered by the parents, both of whom were mothers of fourth-grade children.

Parent 1: I would encourage her to start reading the book and make sure she spends time on the project so that it's completed on time.
Parent 2: I would make sure she has time to read by herself. During this time of reading, she would know that I'm available to answer any questions she may have understanding her book. After reading the book to be read, she knows to make a rough draft of her report. I would go over this with her, asking questions about the book and the report. If she couldn't answer the questions, we would look for the answers together. I would also proofread the final draft for her.

The left column of Table 14.2 shows the percentages of parents reporting each type of involvement on this homework assignment. These figures were collapsed across child's grade level because there were no grade-related differences. Parents were most likely to report involvement in activities designed to facilitate the child's ability to get started on the task (task structure). The specific behaviors most often mentioned were helping the child find a suitable book. The second most frequently mentioned type of involvement was in the process/product component in which the child read the book and wrote the book report. Of particular interest was the extent to which parents assisted in fostering higher level conceptual understanding (category 6) and the metacognitive knowledge and skills necessary for self-regulated learning (category 7). The figures corresponding to these types of parental involvement were disappointingly low on the book report, as well as on the other three types of assignment. Approximately one third of the parents expressed concern that their children understand the reading material for

TABLE 14.2
Types of Parental Involvement on Homework: A Comparison of Parents'
Self-Reports and Teachers' Ideals on a Book Report Assignment

	Parents	Teachers
No involvement	14.8	02.3
Task completion	13.9	25.6
Task structure	67.6	72.1
Process/product	63.0	41.9
Correctness	41.7	20.9
Understanding	38.9	23.3
Metacognition	00.0	00.0

Note. Figures correspond to the percentages of parents and teachers who included each category of involvement in their descriptions of assistance.

the book report and that their book report be conceptually well-developed. However, no parent reported providing explicit explanation of metacognitive processes and strategies.

Because the data in this study came from self-reports, social desirability could affect outcomes, as could willingness and inclination to provide detailed responses. Nevertheless, parents did not report engaging in behaviors that would foster metacognitive skills and promote self-regulated learning on the part of the child, behaviors that psychologists and educators would consider desirable. Of course, that the parents did not explicitly report such instruction does not necessarily mean that they did not provide it. Moreover, it is possible that as the parents assisted in monitoring children's understanding, they served as effective models of comprehension monitoring even without explicit articulation of when, why, and how it should be done.

Also of interest was whether teachers value the same kinds of parental involvement valued by psychologists. Baker, Sonnenschein, and Cerro (1993) conducted a follow-up study to address this question and to determine whether the nature of assistance teachers would like parents to provide was consistent with what parents say they do. Participants in the study were 43 second-grade and fourth-grade teachers working in the same school district serving the families in the prior study. Teachers were asked to describe what their "ideal" parent would do to assist their child with homework in two of the situations given to the parents, completing a book report and a math assignment. Teachers' responses regarding the ideal parent were coded using the same coding scheme as that used for parental responses. The teachers' data for the book report are shown in the right column of Table 14.2. Results revealed a similarity between the parents and teachers in the kinds of assistance mentioned, with a primary emphasis on structuring the task for the child and providing basic assistance with cognitive processing. Teachers were even less likely than parents to endorse assistance with checking correctness and conceptual understanding. And, like the parents, no teachers mentioned metacognitively oriented instruction.

In a second part of the study, teachers were asked to evaluate their satisfaction with three actual responses provided by different parents for each of these assignments. The responses had been selected to represent variations in the nature of parental assistance (as in the above examples). On the book report, teachers of fourth graders were most satisfied with the parent who provided high levels of sensitive assistance. However, there were individual differences among the teachers overall in their evaluations of the parental responses, with about one third expressing most satisfaction with parents who provided high-level assistance and one third expressing most satisfaction with parents who provided low-level assistance. Moreover, the same features that one teacher cited to justify a negative rating were often the same as those cited by another to justify a positive rating.

Although the results of these two studies revealed considerable variability from parent to parent and from teacher to teacher in their views about homework assistance, one conclusion is clear: The scaffolded assistance and metacognitively oriented instruction valued by cognitive developmental psychologists is not typically given high priority by either teachers or parents.

Observations and Self-Reports of Teachers' Spontaneous Practices

To what extent do teachers themselves provide metacognitively oriented instruction? A few researchers interested in this question have conducted naturalistic observations of teachers' spontaneous behaviors in the classroom and have interviewed teachers about their practices (e.g., Kurtz, Schneider, Carr, Borkowski, & Rellinger, 1990; Moely et al., 1992; Schmitt & Baumann, 1990; Winfield, 1984). Moely et al. (1992) observed teachers in kindergarten through grade 6 during language arts and mathematics instruction. Teachers gave strategy suggestions during only 2.3% of the lesson intervals in which they were observed. Moreover, the majority of these strategy suggestions (86%) focused on cognitive strategies, such as using simple repetition and activating prior knowledge, rather than metacognitive strategies. The metacognitive strategy suggestions that were observed were of two types; self-checking (i.e., the teacher suggested that children check their work or use self-testing), and metamemory (i.e., the teacher told children that some procedures would be more helpful than others and why, and otherwise provided children with information about their memory processes). Moely et al. also found that teachers seldom provided rationales for the strategies they suggested, although they were somewhat more likely to do so for older children than younger, and they rarely provided instruction in strategy generalization.

Winfield (1984) studied teachers' encouragement of metacognitive strategies during lessons conducted with fourth-grade good and poor reading groups. Strategies were coded into four categories; planning (e.g., declaring reading goals, generating hypotheses), online monitoring (e.g., looking back, stopping at miscomprehension), storing or retrieving information (e.g., summarizing, outlining), and evaluating (e.g., evaluating text comprehensibility, readiness for a test). Encouragement of metacognitive strategies was infrequent, and there were no differences in the number and type of strategies mentioned to children in the two ability groups. When specific strategies were recommended, they most often involved goal setting, predicting, checking understanding, locating information in the text to support or refute predictions, and evaluating performance. Schmitt and Baumann (1990) observed teachers during classroom basal reader instruction and they too concluded that teachers tended to do little spontaneously to promote children's metacognitive awareness and ability.

Self-reports from teachers about their practices also suggest limited metacognitive instruction. Kurtz et al. (1990) gave German and American teachers of Grades 1 through 4 a questionnaire regarding their use of strategy instruction, their fostering of reflective thinking, their beliefs about sources of children's learning problems, and their modeling of metacognitive skills such as monitoring. The German teachers reported more instruction of task-specific strategies, and the American teachers reported more metacognitive guidance of children with learning problems and more instruction of monitoring. However, almost one fourth of the American teachers reported either no instruction of task-specific strategies or instruction of only one strategy. Although German teachers were more likely to report task-specific instruction, they seldom reported metacognitive instruction about monitoring and strategy utility.

SOCIAL INFLUENCES ON METACOGNITION IN DIRECT INSTRUCTIONAL CONTEXTS

A natural outgrowth of the research that documented the metacognitive limitations of younger and poorer readers was research aimed at fostering metacognitive development through direct intervention. As Flavell (1985) wrote, "School and other life experiences do not advance the child's metacognitive development as fast or as far as might be desirable, and there is a growing feeling that we should try to find ways to teach it more directly and systematically" (p. 263). In this section, I first describe interventions focused on comprehension monitoring in reading, and then I briefly consider broader intervention programs focused on comprehension per se that include a metacognitive component.

Interventions Aimed at Fostering Comprehension Monitoring

Given the evidence that elementary school children have the ability to evaluate their comprehension but often do not do so spontaneously (Baker & Brown, 1984; Garner, 1987; Paris, Wasik, & Turner, 1991), instructional efforts to promote comprehension monitoring are clearly warranted. Several training studies have been implemented within the past decade, providing solid evidence that the comprehension-monitoring skills of good and poor readers alike can be enhanced through direct instruction (e.g., Elliot-Faust & Pressley, 1986; Miller, 1985, 1987; Palincsar & Brown, 1984; Paris, Cross, & Lipson, 1984; see also Oakhill & Yuill, this volume). Space limitations preclude an exhaustive review of this line of research. However, for illustrative purposes, I discuss some of my own studies that assessed the effects of providing students with explicit instruction in evaluating their comprehension.

Baker (1985a) proposed a framework for conceptualizing the standards that readers use to evaluate their understanding, each of which contributes to comprehension. Seven different standards were identified: (1) The *lexical* standard involves checking that the meaning of an individual word is understood; (2) The *syntactic* standard involves an evaluation of the grammaticality of a sentence or phrase; (3) The *internal consistency* standard involves checking that the ideas expressed in the text are logically consistent with one another; (4) The *external consistency* standard involves verifying that the facts presented in the text are true and consistent with respect to what one already knows; (5) The *propositional cohesiveness* standard involves checking that there is a cohesive relationship among propositions sharing a local context; (6) The *structural cohesiveness* standard involves evaluating the thematic compatibility of the ideas in a paragraph or text; and (7) The *informational completeness* standard involves checking that the text provides all of the information necessary for full understanding.

Research has revealed developmental and ability-related differences in the use of each of the seven standards (see Baker, 1985a, for a review), but most studies of comprehension monitoring have focused on the use of a single standard or at most, two or three. For example, I examined readers' use of the lexical, internal consistency, and external consistency standards and found that both children (Baker, 1984) and adults (Baker, 1985b) were able to use all three standards of evaluation to identify problems embedded in expository passages and were more likely to do so when explicitly instructed. To determine readers' facility in using all of the standards identified in my conceptual framework, I designed a study to compare the effects of instruction, developmental level, and reading ability on comprehension evaluation (Baker, 1986).

Participants in the study were third graders, fifth graders, and college students, identified as average and above-average readers on the basis of standardized test scores (California Achievement Test for the children, Scholastic Aptitude Test-Verbal for the adults). The materials consisted of two 800-word passages adapted from children's expository texts; one passage dealt with life and customs in Guatemala, the second dealt with elephants. Each passage was modified to contain two instances of each of seven different types of problems that could be detected if readers applied each of the corresponding standards of evaluation. Half the participants received general instructions; they were told that the passages contained different types of problems that would make them harder to understand, but they were not given any additional information about the nature of the problems. The purpose of this condition was to find out what kinds of standards readers adopt spontaneously when faced with an evaluation task. The second group received specific instructions; they were provided with a description of the seven types of problems they would find in the passages, along with an example of each type. They were given a written copy of this information to refer to as they worked. The purpose of this condition was to find out whether students would be able to apply the different criteria when explicitly instructed to do so. Students were instructed to read each passage carefully, underlining anything they thought made the passage harder to understand and to explain why they had done so.

Analyses of the number of problems identified showed that students receiving specific instructions identified more problems than those receiving general instructions, consistent with previous studies (e.g., Baker, 1984, 1985b). In addition, skilled readers identified more problems than less skilled readers; this was true even at the college level. Adults identified more problems than the children, but there was still plenty of room for improvement; detection proportions ranged from .51 for the lower ability students under general instructions to .82 for the higher ability students under specific instructions. The third and fifth graders performed at comparable levels, with detection scores ranging from .12 for the lower ability students under general instructions to .38 for the higher ability students under specific instructions.

There were large differences in the success with which the individual standards were applied, though adults were more successful than children with all seven types. There were particularly large differences in the use of the lexical standard as a function of instruction condition. Children receiving general instructions identified fewer lexical problems, probably because they were reluctant to acknowledge word comprehension failures (see Baker, 1989b, for discussion of this issue). Moreover, the less skilled adult readers seemed to show the same reluctance as the children to identify nonsense words as problematic.

Also of interest was the number of different standards used. For the children, the effects of grade, reading level, and instruction condition were all significant in the expected directions. Even with specific instructions, the less skilled third-grade readers used a mean of only 2.55 different standards, whereas the higher ability fifth graders used a mean of 5.31 standards. Most of the college students used each of the seven standards on at least one occasion; all but 3% used five or more.

The study revealed that readers used a variety of different standards of evaluation, with most of the mature readers using all seven. It was encouraging to find that all students, both children and adults, used more different standards and used them more effectively when given specific instructions to do so. Moreover, skilled and less skilled readers benefited equally from the instruction. The data did not indicate that there are particular evaluation criteria which strongly differentiate older children from younger or better readers from poorer. Even younger and less skilled readers were able to use a variety of standards that differed in the complexity of the processing demands they imposed.

The positive effects of the simple instructional manipulation in the Baker (1986) study prompted me to devise a more elaborate training study (Baker & Zimlin, 1989). Of interest was whether providing children with instruction in the use of certain standards would generalize to their use of other standards and whether the instructional effects would be maintained over time. Also of interest was whether children would benefit more from training in "macrostructure" standards, which require more global text integration, than "microstructure" standards, which involve more local attention to words and sentences. Participants in the Baker and Zimlin study were 80 fourth graders, identified as average and above-average readers on the basis of their scores on the reading subtest of the California Achievement Test (mean stanine scores of 5.03 for the average readers, 7.70 for the above-average readers). Students were randomly assigned to one of three groups. One group was provided with instruction and practice in the use of three microstructure standards (lexical, external consistency, and propositional cohesiveness); a second group was provided with instruction and practice in the use of three macrostructure standards (internal consistency, informational completeness, and structural cohesiveness); the third group served as a control condition and received no instruction. After the training sessions, which lasted about 30 minutes, students were given two 250-word narrative passages containing problems corresponding to each of the six evaluation standards, and they were asked to identify parts of the passages that were hard to understand. They were explicitly told that the passages contained other types of problems besides those they had just learned about. Children in the control condition were instructed to find the problems intentionally embedded in the stories, but they were not told what the problems were. Two to 3 weeks later, all children were tested again with two different passages in order to assess the durability of the instruction.

It was expected that students in the two training conditions would identify more problems than those in the control group, in line with previous studies that have shown better performance when students are provided with information regarding the standards to be used than when no information is provided. Of particular interest was whether training in the use of standards at one level of evaluation would generalize to the use of standards at the other level. Although Markman and Gorin (1981) did not find generalization when children were set to expect problems of either internal consistency or external consistency, participants in their study were simply given two examples of the problem; they were not given practice applying the relevant standard on their own nor were they told that the test passages might contain other types of problems. Thus, there was still reason to believe that generalization might occur with more intensive training, a desirable outcome given the many ways that comprehension can fail and the difficulty of providing students with instruction in all of them.

Results revealed that children were more likely to identify problems of the types about which they received instruction, but both trained groups identified more noninstructed problems than the control group, indicating generalization of training. Moreover, the training advantage was maintained over time. In addition, the macrostructure group performed better than the microstructure group on the delayed test, indicating a longer-term benefit of global evaluation training. Although better readers outperformed average readers, the benefits of instruction were equivalent. The finding that above-average readers identified more problems overall than average readers is consistent with virtually all comprehension-monitoring studies that have included comparisons of skilled and less skilled readers. What was encouraging, however, was that skill level did not interact with training condition, level of standard, or test time. In other words, all readers benefited from training in both macrostructure and microstructure evaluation, all showed comparable levels of generalization, and all showed comparable maintenance over time. It is not clear whether similar findings would have resulted had we included a sample of truly poor readers. Nevertheless, the sample of average readers included many who were considered by their teachers to be low achievers, and so the results do have implications for the improvement of comprehension-monitoring skills among lower achieving students.

Several recent interventions have incorporated self-instructional training to help children control and regulate their own behavior during reading. Interest in such training was stimulated by Vygotsky's (1978) theory that private speech plays a vital role in fostering the transition from other regulation to self-regulation. Typical training proceeds as follows: First, an adult model performs a task while talking aloud; then the child performs the task under the direction of the model; next the child whispers the instructions while performing the task; and finally the child performs the task while guiding his or her performance through private speech. Self-instructional training and related think-aloud approaches have been successful in promoting metacognitive strategy use, including comprehension monitoring in reading (Baumann, Seifert-Kessell, & Jones, 1992; Miller, 1987; Pressley, Goodchild, Fleet, Zajchowski, & Evans, 1989).

Classroom-Based Intervention Efforts

The general conclusion emerging from these laboratory studies is that metacognitive knowledge and control of reading can be fostered through carefully designed training procedures. In view of such findings, many classroom reading interventions have been implemented that incorporate metacognitively oriented instruction. Most of these efforts have been based on the notion that the best way to promote metacognition is to discuss, model, and practice it explicitly (Duffy & Roehler, 1989). Many also incorporate the neo-Vygotskian notion of "cognitive apprenticeship" (Rogoff, 1990), which involves a gradual transfer of responsibility for regulating performance from the adult to the child.

The classroom-based intervention efforts have tended not to focus on metacognitive aspects of reading per se; rather, their goal has been to promote children's reading comprehension by increasing children's metacognitive skills. It has generally been acknowledged that metacognition should not be promoted as a goal in itself, but rather as a means to an end (Baker, 1994; Baker & Cerro, in press; Paris & Winograd, 1990). Two instructional programs that have become well-known in the past decade are reciprocal teaching (Palincsar & Brown, 1984) and Informed Strategies for Learning (ISL) (Paris, Cross, & Lipson, 1984). Another recent approach was described by Pressley et al. (1991, 1994) as transactional strategies instruction, exemplified by work at Benchmark, a school for children with learning problems, and by the Montgomery County, Maryland SAIL program (Students Achieving Independent Learning) for children with reading difficulties. All of these programs involve explicit instruction of metacognitive strategies of reading and provide students with opportunities to learn declarative, procedural, and conditional knowledge related to strategy use (Paris et al., 1991). Moreover, all of these approaches have been used with children with reading problems. Rotman and Cross (1990), for example, reported a successful extension of the ISL program to students attending a school for learning disabled children.

Although outcome data are not as clear-cut as one might like, the programs clearly affect children's metacognitive knowledge and control of reading. And they do seem to offer promise for enhancing the comprehension skills of children with reading problems. Support for this suggestion was provided by Haller, Child, and Walberg (1988), who conducted a meta-analysis to determine the effects of metacognitive instruction on reading comprehension. The 20 studies included in their analysis yielded a mean effect size of .71. This effect size, which represents the performance advantage of the experimental groups over the control groups, is considered substantial. The most effective metacognitive strategies were monitoring for textual consistency and self-questioning. Moreover, Rosenshine and Meister (1994) recently argued for the efficacy of reciprocal teaching in particular, which promotes the comprehension-fostering and comprehension-monitoring strategies of predicting, clarifying, summarizing, and questioning. Their analysis of 10 studies revealed a large median effect size of .88 on experimenter-developed comprehension assessments. In short, the recommendations that have been prevalent over the past 10 years in articles written for teachers, that teachers should provide explicit metacognitive instruction in conjunction with comprehension instruction, are finally coming to be backed by solid empirical evidence.

CONCLUSIONS

A growing body of evidence suggests that children acquire metacognitive skills through social interaction (Baker, 1994). For example, Borkowski and his colleagues found that children whose mothers and teachers provide more metacognitive instruction seem to be better able to regulate their own learning than children who receive less such instruction (Carr, Kurtz, Schneider, Turner, & Borkowski, 1989; Kurtz et al., 1990; see also Moely et al., 1992). Borkowski et al. (1992) proposed a model of metacognition that "invites analyses of the social contexts in home and school that give rise to the various components of metacognition and specifies how interchanges between children and their parents and teachers affect the development of linkages between cognition, metacognition, and motivation" (p. 4).

Although social agents may not routinely promote metacognitive knowledge and strategies, ample opportunities are available for doing so in everyday interactions. Short and Weissberg-Buchell (1989) discussed the value of increasing adults' awareness of such opportunities using the specific example of metamemory:

> Providing children with the opportunity both to produce and regulate the strategic activity should enhance the likelihood of systematic strategic performance in everyday contexts. In the home, opportunities present themselves for observable strategic behavior and parents need to be explicit about their use of lists (e.g., grocery, jobs around the house), their check-out system for monitoring whether tasks have been completed. In the school, numerous opportunities present themselves for observable strategic behavior. Teachers use lists consistently in the classroom (e.g., children who didn't complete assignments, classroom jobs) and could easily develop a lesson around the function of lists (e.g., discuss the fallibility of memory and the assistance gained from lists). (pp. 56–57)

Some people have argued that direct instruction in metacognitive skills related to literacy may be inappropriate during the early years of schooling (e.g., Chall & Squire, 1991), and there is special concern about formal instruction during the preschool years. Cox (1994) suggested instead "a model in which the child is actively involved in the learning activity and a more knowledgeable other (parent, teacher, or peer) may externalize his or her more expert thinking and reasoning through informal social/verbal interactions while assisting the child in completing the activity" (p. 255). It remains an empirical question whether metacognition may best be fostered through observational learning and apprenticeship in everyday experiences or through direct instruction. Indeed, there may be cultural differences in the optimal modes of providing guidance, as suggested by Rogoff, Mistry, Goncu, and Mosier (1993). Regardless, children are likely to benefit if adults play a more active role in facilitating metacognitive development.

Many instructional recommendations for promoting metacognition in reading are specifically directed towards children with learning disabilities (e.g., Billingsley & Ferro-Almeida, 1993; Billingsley & Wildman, 1990). Such children are frequently characterized as inactive learners, failing to use cognitive resources efficiently and effectively (Baker, 1982; Scruggs & Brigham, 1990). Many studies have shown that they benefit from explicit instruction in metacognitive strategies (e.g., Rottman & Cross, 1990; Wong, 1994). Indeed, cognitive strategy training has proven so promising that Orlando and Bartel (1989) suggested that parents of children with learning problems implement such training themselves to enhance their child's metacognitive and self-regulatory skills.

Information about metacognition has also begun to appear much more frequently in reading methods books and training for teachers at the preservice level. Although Moely et al. (1986) surveyed reading education textbooks and found very little attention to metacognitive issues, my own informal survey revealed that more recent textbooks do in fact address the importance of metacognitive skills and the need to promote them through direct instruction. Similar conclusions were reached by Baumann et al. (1992). Moreover, strategies are being given increased attention in teacher's manuals that accompany current basal reading series, as noted by Baumann et al. and Pressley et al. (1994), but Pressley et al. observed that there is still little metacognitive information included in the manuals that deals with where and when to apply the particular strategies that are taught. Nevertheless, attention to metacognition in teacher education is beginning to have an effect in the field. Kurtz et al. (1990) found that novice teachers were somewhat more likely to report that they would engage in metacognitive instruction than experienced teachers. And Pressley et al. (1991) found that novice teachers were more likely than experienced teachers to mention that college was helpful in providing them with information about strategy instruction. The emphasis on metacognition in literature for teachers, and indeed for parents as well, suggests that the great potential for fostering metacognitive development in reading through social guidance is increasingly likely to be realized.

REFERENCES

Azmitia, M., & Perlmutter, M. (1990). Social influences on children's cognition: State of the art and future directions. In H. W. Reese (Ed.), *Advances in child development and behavior* (Vol. 22, pp. 89–144). San Diego, CA: Academic Press.

Baker, L. (1982). An evaluation of the role of metacognitive deficits in learning disabilities. *Topics in Learning and Learning Disabilities, 2,* 27–35.

Baker, L. (1984). Spontaneous versus instructed use of multiple standards for evaluating comprehension: Effects of age, reading proficiency and type of standard. *Journal of Experimental Child Psychology, 38,* 289–311.

Baker, L. (1985a). How do we know when we don't understand? Standards for evaluating text comprehension. In D. L. Forrest-Pressley, G. E. MacKinnon, & T. G. Waller (Eds.), *Metacognition, cognition, and human performance* (Vol. 1, pp. 155–206). New York: Academic Press.

Baker, L. (1985b). Differences in the standards used by college students to evaluate their comprehension of expository prose. *Reading Research Quarterly, 20,* 297–313.

Baker, L. (1986, August). Standards for evaluating comprehension: Are some more critical than others? In S. Yussen (Chair), *Recent trends in research in cognitive monitoring.* Symposium presented at the meeting of the American Psychological Association, Washington, DC.

Baker, L. (1989a). Metacognition, comprehension monitoring and the adult reader. *Educational Psychology Review, 1,* 3–38.

Baker, L. (1989b). Developmental change in readers' responses to unknown words. *Journal of Reading Behavior, 21,* 241–260.

Baker, L. (1991). Metacognition, reading, and science education. In C. M. Santa & D. E. Alvermann (Eds.), *Science learning: Processes and applications* (pp. 2–13). Newark, DE: International Reading Association.

Baker, L. (1994). Fostering metacognitive development. In H. Reese (Ed.), *Advances in child development and behavior* (Vol. 25, pp. 201–239). San Diego: Academic Press.

Baker, L., & Brown, A. L. (1984). Metacognitive skills and reading. In P. D. Pearson (Ed.), *Handbook of reading research* (pp. 353–395). New York: Longman.

Baker, L., & Cerro, L. C. (in press). Assessing metcognition in children and adults. In G. Schraw (Ed.), *Issues in the measurement of metacognition.* Lincoln, NE: University of Nebraska Press.

Baker, L., Gilat, M., & Sonnenschein, S. (1990, April). *Mothers' sensitivity to the competencies of their preschoolers on a matching task.* Poster/symposium presented at the meeting of the American Educational Research Association, Boston, MA.

Baker, L., Sonnenschein, S., & Cerro, L. (1992, April). *Mothers' reports of their homework practices with their elementary school children.* Paper presented at the meeting of the American Educational Research Association, San Francisco, CA.

Baker, L., Sonnenschein, S., & Cerro, L. C. (1993, March). *How should parents help their children with homework? A comparison of teachers' and parents' views.* Paper presented at the meeting of the Society for Research in Child Development, New Orleans, LA.

Baker, L., Sonnenschein, S., & Serpell, R. (1995). [Parents' beliefs about children's learning]. Unpublished raw data.

Baker, L., & Zimlin, L. (1989). Instructional effects on children's use of two levels of standards for evaluating their comprehension. *Journal of Educational Psychology, 81,* 340–346.

Baumann, J. F., Seifert-Kessell, N., & Jones, L. A. (1992). Effect of think-aloud instruction on elementary students' comprehension monitoring ability. *Journal of Reading Behavior, 24,* 143–172.

Billingsley, B. S., & Ferro-Almeida, S. C. (1993). Strategies to facilitate reading comprehension in students with learning disabilities. *Reading & Writing Quarterly: Overcoming Learning Difficulties, 9,* 263–278.

Billingsley, B. S., & Wildman, T. M. (1990). Facilitating reading comprehension in learning disabled students: Metacognitive goals and instructional strategies. *Remedial and Special Education, 11,* 18–31.

Borkowski, J. G., Day, J. D., Saenz, D., Dietmeyer, D., Estrada, T. M., & Groteluschen, A. (1992). Expanding the boundaries of cognitive interventions. In B. Wong (Ed.), *Intervention research with students with learning disabilities* (pp. 1–21). New York: Springer-Verlag.

Brown, A. L. (1978). Knowing when, where, and how to remember: A problem of metacognition. In R. Glaser (Ed.), *Advances in instructional psychology.* Hillsdale, NJ: Lawrence Erlbaum Associates.

Brown, A. (1987). Metacognition, executive control, self-regulation, and other more mysterious mechanisms. In F. E. Weinert & R. H. Kluwe (Eds.), *Metacognition, motivation, and understanding* (pp. 65–116). Hillsdale, NJ: Lawrence Erlbaum Associates.

Carr, M., Kurtz, B. E., Schneider, W., Turner, L. A., & Borkowski, J. G. (1989). Strategy acquisition and transfer among American and German children: Environmental influences on metacognitive development. *Developmental Psychology, 25,* 765–771.

Cavanaugh, J. C., & Perlmutter, M. (1982). Metamemory: A critical examination. *Child Development, 53,* 11–28.

Chall, J. S., & Squire, J. R. (1991). The publishing industry and textbooks. In R. Barr, M. L. Kamil, P. Mosenthal, & P. D. Pearson (Eds.), *Handbook of reading research* (Vol. 2, pp. 120–146). White Plains, NY: Longman.

Cox, B. E. (1994). At-risk preschoolers' emerging control over literacy: Issues of observation, evaluation, and instruction. *Reading & Writing Quarterly: Overcoming Learning Difficulties, 10,* 259–275.

Day, J., Cordon, L. A., & Kerwin, M. L. (1989). Informal instruction and the development of cognitive skills. In C. B. McCormick, G. E. Miller, & M. Pressley (Eds.), *Cognitive strategy research: From basic research to educational applications* (pp. 83–103). New York: Springer-Verlag.

Duffy, G. G., & Roehler, L. R. (1989). Why strategy instruction is so difficult and what we need to do about it. In C. B. McCormick, G. E. Miller, & M. Pressley (Eds.), *Cognitive strategy research: From basic research to educational applications* (pp. 133–154). New York: Springer-Verlag.

Elliott-Faust, D. J., & Pressley, M. (1986). How to teach comparison processing to increase children's short- and long-term listening comprehension monitoring. *Journal of Educational Psychology, 78,* 27–33.

Flavell, J. H. (1976). Metacognitive aspects of problem solving. In L. B. Resnick (Ed.), *The nature of intelligence* (pp. 231–235). Hillsdale, NJ: Lawrence Erlbaum Associates.

Flavell, J. H. (1985). *Cognitive development* (2nd ed.). Englewood Cliffs, NJ: Prentice-Hall.

Freund, L. S. (1990). Maternal regulation of children's problem-solving behavior and its impact on children's performance. *Child Development, 61,* 113–126.

Garner, R. (1987). *Metacognition and reading comprehension.* Norwood, NJ: Ablex.

Goodnow, J. J., & Collins, W. A. (1990). *Development according to parents: The nature, sources, and consequences of parents' ideas.* Hillsdale, NJ: Lawrence Erlbaum Associates.

Haller, E. P., Child, D. A., & Walberg, H. J. (1988). Can comprehension be taught? A quantitative synthesis of "metacognitive" studies. *Educational Researcher, 17*(9), 5–8.

Johnson, J. E., & Martin, C. (1985). Parents' beliefs and home learning environments: Effects on cognitive development. In I. E. Sigel (Ed.), *Parental belief systems: The psychological consequences for children* (pp. 25–50). Hillsdale, NJ: Lawrence Erlbaum Associates.

Kurtz, B. E., Schneider, W., Carr, M., Borkowski, J. G., & Rellinger, E. (1990). Strategy instruction and attributional beliefs in West Germany and the United States: Do teachers foster metacognitive development? *Contemporary Educational Psychology, 15,* 268–283.

Markman, E. M., & Gorin, L. (1981). Children's ability to adjust their standards for evaluating comprehension. *Journal of Educational Psychology, 73,* 320–325.

Miller, G. E. (1985). The effects of general and specific self-instruction training on children's comprehension monitoring performance during reading. *Reading Research Quarterly, 20,* 616–628.

Miller, G. E. (1987). The influence of self-instruction on the comprehension monitoring performance of average and above average readers. *Journal of Reading Behavior, 19,* 303–317.

Moely, B. E., Hart, S. S., Leal, L., Santulli, K., Rao, N., Johnson, T., & Hamilton, L. B. (1992). The teacher's role in facilitating memory and study strategy development in the elementary school classroom. *Child Development, 63,* 653–672.

Moely, B. E., Hart, S. S., Santulli, K., Leal, L., Johnson, T., Rao, N., & Burney, L. (1986). How do teachers teach memory skills? *Educational Psychologist, 21,* 55–71.

Orlando, J. E., & Bartel, N. R. (1989). Cognitive strategy training: An intervention model for parents of children with learning disabilities. *Reading, Writing, and Learning Disabilities, 5,* 327–344.

Palincsar, A. S., & Brown, A. L. (1984). Reciprocal teaching of comprehension-fostering and comprehension-monitoring activities. *Cognition and Instruction, 1,* 117–175.

Paris, S. G., Cross, D. R., & Lipson, M. Y. (1984). Informed strategies for learning: A program to improve children's reading awareness and comprehension. *Journal of Educational Psychology, 76,* 1239–1252.

Paris, S. G., Wasik, B. A., & Turner, J. C. (1991). The development of strategic readers. In R. Barr, M. Kamil, P. Mosenthal, & P. D. Pearson (Eds.), *Handbook of reading research* (Vol. 2, pp. 609–640). White Plains, NY: Longman.

Paris, S. G., & Winograd, P. (1990). How metacognition can promote academic learning and instruction. In B. F. Jones & L. Idol (Eds.), *Dimensions of thinking and cognitive instruction* (pp. 15–51). Hillsdale, NJ: Lawrence Erlbaum Associates.

Pratt, M., Green, D., MacVicar, J., & Bountrogianni, M. (1992). The mathematical parent: Parental scaffolding, parenting style, and learning outcome in long-division mathematics homework. *Journal of Applied Developmental Psychology, 13,* 17–34.

Pressley, M., Almasi, J., Schuder, T., Bergman, J., Hite, S., El-Dinary, P. B., & Brown, R. (1994). Transactional instruction of comprehension strategies: The Montgomery County, Maryland, SAIL program. *Reading & Writing Quarterly: Overcoming learning difficulties, 10,* 5–19.

Pressley, M., Gaskins, I. W., Cunicelli, E. A., Burdick, N. J., Schaub-Matt, M., Lee, D. S., & Powell, N. (1991). Strategy instruction at Benchmark School: A faculty interview study. *Learning Disability Quarterly, 14,* 19–48.

Pressley, M., Goodchild, F., Fleet, J., Zajchowski, R., & Evans, E. D. (1989). The challenges of classroom strategy instruction. *The Elementary School Journal, 89,* 301–342.

Rogoff, B. (1990). *Apprenticeship in thinking.* New York: Oxford University Press.

Rogoff, B., Mistry, J., Goncu, A., & Mosier, C. (1993). Guided participation in cultural activity by toddlers and caregivers. *Monographs of the Society for Research in Child Development, 58* (8, Serial No. 236).

Rosenshine, B., & Meister, C. (1994). Reciprocal teaching: A review of the research. *Review of Educational Research, 64,* 479–530.

Rottman, T. R., & Cross, D. R. (1990). Using informed strategies for learning to enhance the reading and thinking skills of children with learning disabilities. *Journal of Learning Disabilities, 23,* 270–278.

Schmitt, M. C., & Baumann, J. F. (1990). Metacomprehension during basal reading instruction: Do teachers promote it? *Reading Research and Instruction, 29*(3), 1–13.

Scruggs, T. E., & Brigham, F. J. (1990). The challenges of metacognitive instruction. *Remedial and Special Education, 11,* 16–18, 31.

Short, E. J. & Weissberg-Benchell, J. A. (1989). The triple alliance for learning: Cognition, metacognition, and motivation. In C. B. McCormick, G. E. Miller, & M. Pressley (Eds.), *Cognitive strategy research: From basic research to educational applications* (pp. 33–63). New York: Springer-Verlag.

Snow, C. E., Barnes, W. S., Chandler, J., Goodman, I. F., & Hemphill, L. (1991). *Unfulfilled expectations: Home and school influences on literacy.* Cambridge, MA: Harvard University Press.

Sonnenschein, S., Baker, L., & Cerro, L. (1992). Mothers' views on teaching their preschoolers in everyday situations. *Early Education and Development, 3,* 1–22.

Sonnenschein, S., Baker, L., & Freund, L. (1993). Mother-child interaction on a spatial concept task as mediated by maternal notions about the task and the child. *Early Education and Development, 4,* 32–44.

Sonnenschein, S., Baker, L., & Lasaga, M. (1991, April). *Mothers' views on their role in fostering metacognition.* Paper presented at the meeting of the Society for Research in Child Development, Seattle, WA.

Vygotsky, L. (1978). *Mind in society.* Cambridge, MA: MIT Press.

Wertsch, J. V. (1978). Adult–child interaction and the roots of metacognition. *Quarterly Newsletter of the Institute for Comparative Human Development, 2,* 15–18.

Winfield, E. T. (1984). *Fourth grade teachers' encouragement of comprehension monitoring strategies among good and poor readers.* Unpublished doctoral dissertation, University of Maryland, College Park.

Wong, B. Y. L. (1985). Metacognition and learning disabilities. In D. L. Forrest-Pressley, G. E. MacKinnon, & T. G. Waller (Eds.), *Metacognition, cognition, and human performance* (Vol. 2, pp. 137–180). NY: Academic Press.

Wong, B. Y. L. (1994). Where we go from here. *Reading & Writing Quarterly: Overcoming Learning Difficulties, 10,* 91–101.

Author Index

Subject Index

A

Ambiguity, 1–2, 41, 197–208
Anaphora, 229, 247–249
  and comprehension skill, 144, 221,
    226–243

C

Causality in reading problems, direction of,
    89–91, 96, 171
Comprehension
  and decoding, 1–14, 71, 93–110
  tests, *see* Subject selection
  and intelligence, 23–24, 98–100
  and knowledge, 9–10, 16–17, 19–28, 142,
    146–147, 187
  and motivation, 159–160
  and vocabulary, *see also* Vocabulary,
    16–17, 143–146
Comprehension age match, 90, 96, 168–172,
    179
Comprehension monitoring, *see also* Meta-
    cognitive skills, 33–64, 70, 76–80,
    141, 156–158, 222–244, 305–326
  tasks to assess, 34–36

and metacognitive skills, 37–38
and memory, 38–39, 47–50, 79–80
and constructive processing, 42–44, 57–61
Connectives, 167–168

D

Deaf children, 279–297
Decoding, 1, 103–107
  accuracy, 104–105, 146, 150–151
  automaticity, 16, 71, 105
  speed, 71, 98, 105, 146

E

Early language experience, 281–285
Exposure to print, 15–29
  and vocabulary, 19–25
  and knowledge, 19
Eye movements, 1

H

Hydrocephalus, 252–273